SIBELIUS® 7 MUSIC NOTATION ESSENTIALS

James Humberstone

Course Technology PTR

A part of Cengage Learning

COURSE TECHNOLOGY
CENGAGE Learning·

Australia • Brazil • Japan • Korea • Mexico • Singapore • Spain • United Kingdom • United States

COURSE TECHNOLOGY
CENGAGE Learning

Sibelius® 7 Music Notation Essentials
James Humberstone

Publisher and General Manager,
 Course Technology PTR: Stacy L. Hiquet

Associate Director of Marketing: Sarah Panella

Manager of Editorial Services: Heather Talbot

Senior Marketing Manager: Mark Hughes

Acquisitions Editor: Orren Merton

Project Editor: Kate Shoup

Technical Reviewer: Neil Sands

Copy Editor: Kate Shoup

Interior Layout Tech: Bill Hartman

Back Cover Designer: Mike Tanamachi

CD-ROM Producer: Brandon Penticuff

Indexer: Valerie Haynes Perry

Proofreader: Caroline Roop

For product information and technology assistance, contact us at
Cengage Learning Customer & Sales Support, 1-800-354-9706.

For permission to use material from this text or product,
submit all requests online at **www.cengage.com/permissions**
Further permissions questions can be emailed to
permissionrequest@cengage.com.

Sibelius is a registered trademark of Avid Technology, Inc. All other trademarks are the property of their respective owners.

All images © Cengage Learning unless otherwise noted.

Library of Congress Control Number: 2011942188

ISBN-13: 978-1-133-78882-9

ISBN-10: 1-133-78882-3

Course Technology
20 Channel Center Street
Boston, MA 02210
USA

Cengage Learning is a leading provider of customized learning solutions with office locations around the globe, including Singapore, the United Kingdom, Australia, Mexico, Brazil, and Japan. Locate your local office at **www.cengage.com/global**

Cengage Learning products are represented in Canada by Nelson Education, Ltd.

To learn more about Course Technology, visit
www.cengage.com/coursetechnology

Purchase any of our products at your local bookstore or at our preferred online store **www.cengagebrain.com**

Printed in China
2 3 4 5 6 7 17 16 15 14 13

I would like to dedicate this book to my father in gratitude for investing in me a love of both musical and literary language, and a healthy level of pedantry. Pa, your wit and love remain an inspiration to me.

Acknowledgments

To all I have dealt with at Course Technology PTR/Cengage Learning for their professionalism, enthusiasm, and efficiency.

To Kate Shoup, who takes what I write and makes it much better (she'll be working hard on this copy), and to Neil Sands who became the first person to teach me lots about Sibelius.

To Avid, for inviting me to write this course and trusting me to do a good job of it, and especially to my friends at Sibelius including Daniel Spreadbury, Tom Clarke, and Sam Butler who provided advice and ideas from start to finish.

To the publishers of the virtual instruments shown in Lesson 5 (Garritan Personal Orchestra, Synful Orchestra, and Vienna Symphonic Library), who provided complementary copies for me to learn and write about.

To John Hinchey, Richard Payne, Robert Puff, Neil Sands, and Katie Wardrobe, who provided excellent expert tips throughout the book.

To Anthony Silvestrini and The Trobes for generously sharing their fabulous music.

To my colleagues at MLC School, Sydney, who are the most inspiring and gifted music educators anyone could ever work with. Special thanks to the inimitable Karen Carey for ongoing support of everything I do and principal Denice Scala for granting me leave on short notice to get this book finished on time!

To wonderful composers and supervisors John Peterson and Andrew Schultz at the University of New South Wales, who will be receiving the first draft of my Ph.D. a few months later than originally planned.

Finally to my wife Anna and children Jeremy, Zoë, and Finley, thanks for putting up with an absent husband/father the last few months. Aren't you glad there's much more time to play cricket now?

About the Author

James Humberstone is a composer and educator who specializes in composing for children and the use of music technology in education. Many of his instrumental and choral works for both children and adults are available from his Web site, www.composerhome.com, where he also shares resources for teaching music using technology.

James has been composer-in-residence at Sydney's MLC School since 2002 and is in high demand with additional commissions, residencies, and guest lectures all over the world.

James' experience with music notation is extensive. He was Director of Applications and Education at Sibelius in Australia, and trained hundreds if not thousands of Sibelius users himself. In addition to using Sibelius as a compositional tool, James was music typesetter for a great number of Australian publishers and composers including Warner Chappell Music and Symphony Australia. James developed this new course working closely with the Sibelius team.

Contents

Exercise 1 Rearranging a Score

Lesson 2
Beethoven's 3rd String Quartet, First
Movement, Opus 18, Number 3

Exercise 2 Practicing Entry Methods   177

Lesson 3
Purple   179

Exercise 3 Rearranging a MusicXML File   293

Lesson 4
Worksheets   295

Appendix A
Elementary Music Theory   415

Appendix B
Scores Required in This Course   427

Appendix C
Answers to Review/Discussion Questions   441

Index   445

Introduction

Welcome to *Sibelius 7 Music Notation Essentials* and the Avid Learning Series. Whether you are interested in self study or would like to pursue formal certification through an Avid Learning Partner, this book provides what you need to develop your core skills and introduces you to the power of Sibelius 7. This is the first-ever official, international course in Sibelius based on the most recent version, Sibelius 7.

The material in this book covers everything you need to know to begin creating your own scores, parts, and worksheets. Whether you write film scores, contemporary art music, rock-band arrangements, or excerpts for theses, *Sibelius 7 Music Notation Essentials* will teach all the fundamental skills you need.

About This Book

The curriculum in this book is taught over five lessons. Rather than starting at A and working through to Z, the book teaches the features of Sibelius in the order you need them to begin putting in your own music as soon as possible. The book gets you going with each lesson and then leaves you to complete it and extension tasks with the skills you've learned. At the end of each lesson, you should have completed a score, which, if you are using this book in conjunction with a course offered by an Avid Learning Partner, you can submit for ongoing assessment and feedback.

Using the CD

This book comes with a CD, which contains files you need to complete the projects contained in this course. Some files can be opened in Sibelius and printed out in order to copy them as you learn, which is easier than flipping to Appendix B, "Scores Required in This Course," where you'll also find them. To help you, at the start of each section of the book is a "catch-up file," which is a Sibelius score completed to that point. While you should try to complete each stage on your own, these files are useful if you miss a lesson, or if you're teaching yourself and want to start at a specific point in the process.

If you purchased an ebook version of this book, you may download the contents of the companion CD from www.courseptr.com/downloads. Please note that you will be redirected to the Cengage Learning site.

Accessing the Video Files

In addition to the resource files, found on the CD, there is also a series of videos to help you grasp the concepts covered in this book. These videos have been placed online. (For complete information on how to access these videos, please visit http://courseptr.com/avid/sibeilus.aspx.) You can watch the videos the whole way through, or you can pause them at the end of each step and then try practicing the skills covered in Sibelius. Particularly if you have purchased this book to teach yourself, I suggest you start each section by watching the corresponding video online (most are no more than 10 minutes long) before attempting to practice the skills taught, using the book to remind you of each step, to flesh out information, or to revise key points. If you find the videos go too fast, it is possible to learn directly from the book without watching them, but give them a go first. This course was *not* designed as a book with some videos tacked on; it's designed to be taught by *either* a teacher or the videos.

Prerequisites

This book is ideal for people who have never used Sibelius at all. You are not expected to have any knowledge of the program whatsoever. That being said, Sibelius is first and foremost *notation* software, so you need at least an elementary understanding of music theory (note values; how many beats are in a bar in 3/4 and 4/4 time signatures; reading pitches in treble, alto, and bass clef; dynamics; slurs/phrasing; and articulation marks). An ability to read music (however slowly) and some basic keyboard skills would assist in the sections on Flexi-time recording and step-time input, but are not essential. Without basic knowledge of music notation, you will struggle to understand this course. To help you, Appendix A, "Elementary Music Theory," provides a very short summary of this topic, which you should read before you begin.

System Requirements

This course assumes you have successfully installed and registered Sibelius 7 (if you have an earlier version of Sibelius, download and install the trial version of Sibelius 7 from www.sibelius.com to complete this course, because it is so different most menu shortcuts are now changed and all files are provided in Sibelius 7 format only). Ample documentation is provided with your copy of Sibelius, and the support team can assist you with any technical difficulties at this early point. This book does cover connecting a MIDI keyboard and setting up playback, so don't worry if you don't have that humming along quite yet.

Becoming Avid Certified

Avid certification is a tangible, industry-recognized credential that can help you advance your career and provide measurable benefits to your employer. When you're Avid certified, you not only help to accelerate and validate your professional development, but you can also improve your productivity and project success.

Avid offers programs supporting certification in dedicated focus areas, including Sibelius, Media Composer, Pro Tools, Worksurface Operation, and Live Sound.

In order to become certified in Sibelius, you must enroll in a program at an Avid Learning Partner and take your certification exam. For information about how to locate an Avid Learning Partner please visit: www.avid.com/training.

Sibelius Certification

Avid offers one level of Sibelius certification:

- Sibelius User

User Certification

Taking the Sibelius Certified User Exam allows you to become Avid Certified. This certification offers an established and recognized goal for both academic users and industry professionals. The Sibelius User Certification requires that you display a firm grasp of the core skills, workflows, and concepts of music notation in Sibelius.

One Course/book is associated with *User* certification:

- Sibelius 7 Music Notation Essentials (SB101)

For more information about Avid's certification program please visit: www.avid.com/US/support/training/certification.

Amazing Grace

You're going to begin learning Sibelius with a nice, simple task that should be quite satisfying. It will be a chance for you to get a feel for the program without learning any in-depth features.

Media Used: Amazing1.sib, Amazing2.sib

Duration: Between one and two hours

GOALS

- Open an existing score
- Learn how to move around a score
- Perform some simple edits
- Play back the score

Before You Begin:
Copying Course Files to Your Computer

Because you'll need to open a score soon, this would be a good time to copy the resources provided on the CD to your computer. To do so, use one of the following methods. Note that you *can* run them from your CD drive, but if you do that, you won't be able to save your changes until you save a copy on your hard drive, which may cause error messages to appear in Sibelius. If you are reading the eBook version of this book, you can download the resources from the Cengage Web site as advised in the online store where you bought the eBook.

Copying Files in Windows

To copy files from the CD to your Windows PC:

1. Insert the CD into your computer's CD drive. If the CD automatically starts playing in Windows Media Player or a similar program, stop playback and close the program. If Windows displays a dialog box that offers various options for accessing the contents of the CD, click the dialog box's CANCEL button.

2. Click the START button and choose DOCUMENTS.

3. Double-click the SCORES folder (see Figure 1.1) to open it. If you have many files in your Documents folder, you may need to scroll down to find it. (Alternatively, you can search for it using the Documents window's Search box.) Inside the Scores folder are two subfolders: Backup Scores and Sibelius Example Scores. Leave this window open, as it's where you'll copy the files for this course.

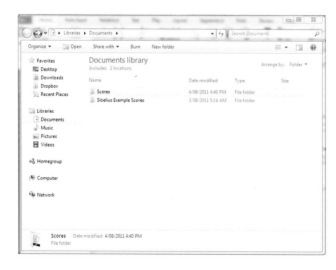

Figure 1.1

The Documents folder in Windows 7.

4. Click the START button again and choose COMPUTER.

5. Double-click the CD DRIVE icon (see Figure 1.2) to open the drive. You'll see a number of folders, including one called Core Resources.

Figure 1.2
The Computer window clearly showing the CD/DVD drive.

6. Arrange the two open windows so that the contents of both are visible. Then drag the CORE RESOURCES folder from the CD window to the Scores window. The files may take some minutes to copy. When they are finished, close those open windows.

Note: These instructions assume you're running Windows Vista or Windows 7. Sibelius 7 does not run on Windows XP.

Copying Files on a Mac

As you might expect, the process for copying files from the CD to your computer is very similar on a Mac.

To copy files on a Mac:

1. Right-click (or, if you don't have a mouse with a right-click button, Control-click) the FINDER icon on the left side of the dock and choose NEW FINDER WINDOW from the menu that appears, as shown in Figure 1.3. A Finder window opens.

2. Click the DOCUMENTS link in the sidebar on the left side of the Finder window. The Finder window displays the contents of your Documents folder.

Figure 1.3

Opening a new Finder window in Mac OSX 10.7 (Lion). Older versions of the OSX operating system work the same way, but may appear different, graphically speaking.

3. Double-click the **Scores** folder to open it. Its contents appear in Figure 1.4. (If you have many files in your Documents folder, scroll until you see the Scores folder.)

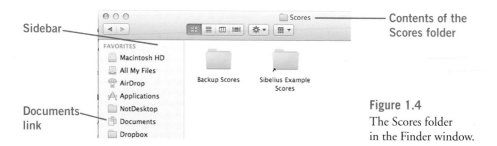

Figure 1.4

The Scores folder in the Finder window.

4. Insert the CD into your computer's CD drive. If the CD automatically starts playing, stop playback and quit the program.

5. Repeat step 1 to open another Finder window.

6. Click the **CD** link in the sidebar on the left side of the Finder window. The Finder window displays the contents of your CD, including a Core Resources folder.

7. Arrange the two open Finder windows so that the contents of both are visible. Then drag the **Core Resources** folder from the CD Finder window to the Scores Finder window. The files may take some minutes to copy. When they are finished, close those open windows.

Moving Around the Score

 If you're studying this lesson without a teacher, this is the perfect moment to watch the first video, **1.1 Moving Around the Score**. See the section "Accessing the Video Files" in this book's introduction for help finding and viewing the video content. You may be able to complete many of the following steps just by viewing the video.

You're going to start by opening a score. When you run Sibelius, you'll be greeted by the Quick Start dialog box, shown in Figure 1.5. If the Quick Start dialog box doesn't appear, it means the user before you has disabled it by default. (This is more likely if you share your home computer or are using a computer at a school or university.) In that case, you'll see a blank score. To manually open the Quick Start dialog box, choose File > New in Windows or File > Quick Start on a Mac (that's the File menu, not the File tab). You can also change your program preferences to open the Quick Start dialog box by default every time Sibelius launches; you will learn about the Preferences dialog box soon.

Figure 1.5
The Quick Start
dialog box.

Note: As mentioned, this course assumes you have installed and registered Sibelius. If you haven't yet registered it, you have 30 days to do so. If you're just trialing Sibelius, then you have 30 days to complete this course!

Exploring the Quick Start Dialog Box

As shown in Figure 1.6, there are five tabs along the top of the Quick Start dialog box: Learn, New Score, Recent, Import, and Latest News. Each tab is colored gray except the selected one, which is purple.

Learn	New Score	Recent	Import	Latest News

Figure 1.6
Clicking the tabs along the top of the Quick Start dialog box gives you a number of options for getting started in Sibelius.

At the bottom of the Quick Start dialog box are a number of buttons and options, which remain present regardless of which tab you click at the top (see Figure 1.7). These include the following:

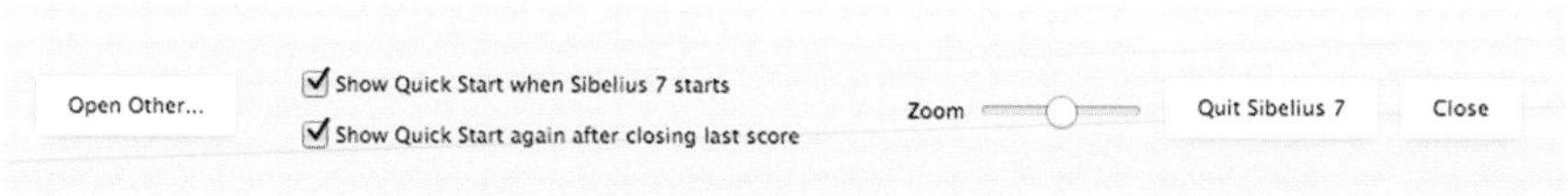

Open Other...   ☑ Show Quick Start when Sibelius 7 starts   Zoom ═══○═══   Quit Sibelius 7   Close
☑ Show Quick Start again after closing last score

Figure 1.7
Options at the bottom of the Quick Start dialog box.

- **The Open Other button.** Clicking this button opens an Open dialog box, which you can use to open any Sibelius file.

- **The Show Quick Start When Sibelius 7 Starts check box.** Select this check box if you want the Quick Start dialog box to appear whenever you open Sibelius.

- **The Show Quick Start Again After Closing Last Score check box.** Select this check box if you want the Quick Start dialog box to appear when you close the last open score in Sibelius.

- **A Zoom slider.** You will notice the effect of sliding the Zoom slider only when the New Score or Recent tabs are selected. Its use is explained in detail later in this lesson.

- **The Quit Sibelius 7/Exit Sibelius 7 button.** The wording of this button is slightly different in Windows and Mac computers, but it does the same thing: Click this button to shut down Sibelius.

- **The Close button.** Click this button to close the Quick Start dialog box.

Exploring the Learn Tab

If it's not already selected, click the Learn tab. You will see the options shown in Figure 1.5. The three links on the left direct you to the Sibelius Web site (an Internet connection is required), which offers a great introduction to Sibelius from its senior product manager, the inimitable Daniel Spreadbury. The links on the right direct you to the documentation that comes with Sibelius, including *Sibelius 7 Tutorials*, *Sibelius 7 Reference Guide* (a big PDF software manual that covers every feature of Sibelius in minute detail), and the *What's New* guide. Another link to the Sibelius Web site is provided in the Learn tab, this one to options for support.

Exploring the New Score Tab

Click the New Score tab at the top of the Quick Start dialog box (see Figure 1.8). You won't set up a score from scratch until Lesson 2, "Beethoven's 3rd String Quartet, First Movement, Opus 18, Number 3," but you might be interested to see that Sibelius ships with dozens of manuscript papers ready to go. (Just scroll down the list to see what's available.) In addition, you can add your own custom ones for ensembles for which you write regularly. As shown in Figure 1.8, the New Score tab contains a search field to help you find the manuscript paper you're looking for. To zoom in on these to get a closer look, drag the Zoom slider at the bottom of the Quick Start dialog box. If you were using one of these manuscript papers now, you would double-click it to get started (unless it was the blank manuscript)— but more about that later.

Figure 1.8
The New Score tab of the Quick Start dialog box.

Exploring the Recent Tab

Click the Recent tab. If you have only just installed Sibelius, you may not yet have many scores in the Recent tab. By default, you should be able to see the lessons from the tutorials and some of the sample files that were installed along with Sibelius. After you've been using Sibelius a while, it will organize the files you've been using by day, week, and month (see Figure 1.9). As with the New Score tab, you can use the Zoom slider to zoom in on any particular score to make sure it's just the one you need before you open it by double-clicking it or by selecting it with a single click and then clicking the Open button.

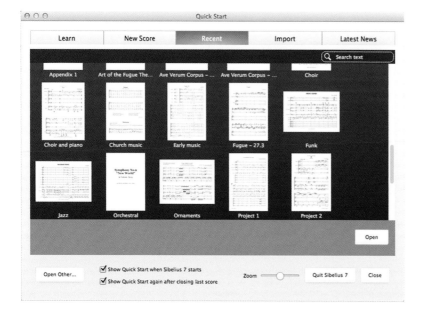

Figure 1.9
The Quick Start dialog box's Recent tab.

Exploring the Import Tab

Click the Import tab. On this tab are options to import music in various formats into Sibelius. On the left are links to two programs from Neuratron:

- **PhotoScore.** This program enables you to import music by scanning original copies of printed and handwritten scores. If you have scores in graphical formats such as PDF, these can also be imported. PhotoScore enables you to proofread its "read" version against the original, and then import it seamlessly into Sibelius. You'll learn to use PhotoScore Lite in Lesson 5, "Agent Zero."

- **AudioScore.** This program does what university researchers thought was impossible: It "listens" to a recording and notates the music within. Alternatively, you can hook it up to Sibelius and play a non-MIDI instrument straight into the score. You'll look at AudioScore Lite in Lesson 5.

If these buttons appear grayed out, as shown in Figure 1.10, you need to install these programs. Lite versions of each are found on your Sibelius installation DVDs. If you enjoy using the software, you can upgrade to the Ultimate versions, which are shown in Figure 1.11.

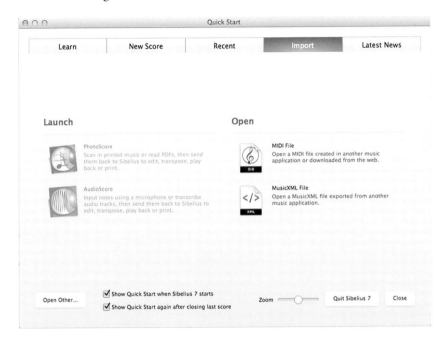

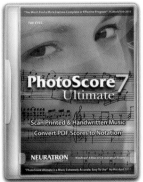

Figure 1.10
The Import page of the Quick Start dialog box.

Figure 1.11
Neuratron products PhotoScore and AudioScore, which work extremely well with Sibelius.

On the right side of the Import tab are options to open MIDI files or MusicXML files. These files can be exported from most other computer music programs, including sequencers and digital audio workstations (DAWs) like Pro Tools, Logic, Cubase, and Cakewalk Sonar, and notation programs like Finale. Using these files, you can collaborate with other musicians even if they don't have Sibelius. You'll learn more about this in Lesson 3, "Purple."

In the Avid Learning Series

Pro Tools is used in more recording studios than any other DAW. If you not only work in notation but also sequence audio and MIDI, there's a good chance you either use Pro Tools or have considered becoming a Pro Tools user. Because both Sibelius and Pro Tools are made by Avid, Pro Tools integrates beautifully with Sibelius. If you'd like to know more about how to export MIDI from Pro Tools or export a score in Pro Tools as a Sibelius file, books similar to this one are available in the same Avid Learning Series. See the following sections in *Pro Tools 101 Official Courseware, Version 10.0*:

- "Send to Sibelius in Pro Tools" in Lesson 2
- "Export MIDI in Pro Tools" in Lesson 2

Exploring the Latest News Tab

Click the final tab in the Quick Start dialog box, Latest News. Using this tab requires an Internet connection. The tab receives a live feed with all the latest news about Sibelius from (the aforementioned) Daniel Spreadbury's blog at www.sibeliusblog.com. Clicking the Read More link after any of the stories takes you to the corresponding page on the Web site.

On the Web

Opening a File

Having tantalized you with all the options for creating and importing files, it's time to open an existing one so you can get straight into using Sibelius.

To open a file:

1. Click the **OPEN OTHER** button in the bottom-left corner of the Quick Start dialog box (refer to Figure 1.7). By default, Sibelius opens your Scores folder, which is why you copied the Core Resources folder there.

2. Open the **CORE RESOURCES FOLDER**, open the **LESSON 1** folder, and locate the **AMAZING1.SIB** file. The file extension (.sib) may not appear on some computers, but the Sibelius file icon, shown in Figure 1.12, indicates that the file is a Sibelius file.

3. Double-click the **AMAZING1.SIB** file to open it. The score of a simple arrangement of "Amazing Grace" opens.

Figure 1.12
The Sibelius file icon. If you receive a Sibelius file via email, or you have saved one in an easy-to-access location on your computer, you can launch Sibelius and open the file just by double-clicking.

Navigating with the Mouse

You will start by learning to navigate the score using the mouse. The easiest way to move around the score is to simply drag the pages of manuscript paper as if they were pages on your desk. To do so, click and hold on a *blank* part of the page—that is, not on a staff, a note, text, or other markings, but on blank "paper" —and then move your mouse around. If the page doesn't move, or something unexpected happens, press the Esc (short for Escape) key on your keyboard. Typing Esc cancels any mode you may have inadvertently entered in Sibelius; you'll quickly learn it's your best friend. Try moving from page 1 to page 2, and back again.

On the right side and along the bottom of the score are scroll bars. You're probably used to using scroll bars in just about every program you've ever used, including word-processing programs and Web browsers. You can drag Sibelius' scroll bars to move around the score. If you don't like how much screen space the scroll bars consume, choose File > Preferences, and click Display in the list on the left. You'll see a Show Scroll Bars check box on the right side of the dialog box; uncheck it to turn them off. (See Figure 1.13.)

Figure 1.13
Turning off the scroll bars in Sibelius's Preferences dialog box.

You can also use the scroll wheel on your mouse (if you have one) to scroll up and down the page. Hold down the Shift key as you scroll the wheel to move left and right. If you have a new Apple "mighty" mouse, it has a ball instead of a wheel; this will enable you to scroll in any direction.

Tip: If you don't have a two- or three-button mouse, this might be a good time to get yourself to your local computer store, where a no-frills, three-button scroll-wheel mouse can be had for no more than $25.

You can work in any zoom setting in Sibelius—right up close to the notes or looking at the whole page at once (useful if you're watching a big score play back). In the bottom-right part of the screen is a Zoom slider (see Figure 1.14). Drag it to the left to zoom out of your score (as if you were farther away), and drag it to the right to zoom in to your score (as if you were resting your nose on the page). Try zooming in and out of the score, and moving about the pages at different zooms by dragging the pages or using the scroll bars.

Figure 1.14
The Zoom slider.

The ribbon offers additional zoom options. For example, choose View > Zoom to see four buttons in this ribbon group for zooming quickly to set percentages. As shown in Figure 1.15, the three buttons on the right are for quickly snapping to 100% zoom, zooming to fit a whole page on the screen, or zooming to fit the page width. On the left of the View > Zoom ribbon group is a split button. Click the bottom of the split button, where the down arrow is, to choose from a long list of preset zooms. Alternatively, click the top half of the split button to turn the mouse pointer into a magnifying glass; then click anywhere on the score to zoom in or right-click (Option-click) anywhere in the score to zoom out. You can also click and drag a box (try clicking at the top left of the screen and dragging to about three inches lower and to the right) and you'll zoom to that exact area. Press Esc to get out of the zoom mode.

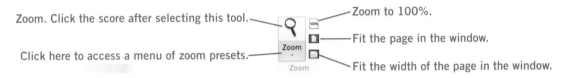

Zoom. Click the score after selecting this tool. — Zoom to 100%.

Click here to access a menu of zoom presets. — Fit the page in the window.

Fit the width of the page in the window.

Figure 1.15
The zoom buttons on the ribbon.

Another way to move around a score quickly—especially a big score—is with the Navigator panel. If you don't see the Navigator panel (look ahead to Figure 1.17 to see what it looks like), you can open it by choosing View > Panels > Navigator (see Figure 1.16) or, if you're ready to start learning shortcuts, pressing Ctrl+Alt+N (Command+Option+N).

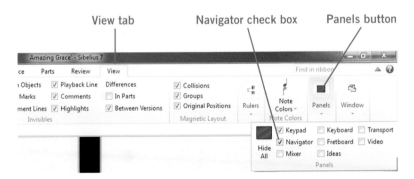

View tab   Navigator check box   Panels button

Figure 1.16
Displaying the Navigator panel.

The Navigator panel, shown in Figure 1.17, works like a mini-map of your score. If you've ever played a role-playing computer game, where you control various characters over a large landscape, you are probably used to having a mini-map of the terrain to quickly get about. In the Navigator panel, the white square shows you the exact part of the page or pages you're looking at. (Notice how the square changes size as you zoom in and out.) Behind it, you can see the page numbers and the positions of staves.

Figure 1.17
The Navigator panel.

To use the Navigator panel to move about your score, simply click and hold on the white square, and then move your mouse. If you move your mouse pointer to the edge of the Navigator panel, it keeps scrolling in that direction (sometimes quite quickly, so beware!). In this case, the "Amazing Grace" score doesn't have many pages in it, so you're unlikely to be able to scroll far. You can also click any point of the Navigator panel (i.e., outside the white square) to jump to that part of the page.

To close the Navigator panel, click the × button in its top-right corner (Windows) or the red button in its top-left corner (Mac).

Navigating with Keyboard Shortcuts

You already know everything you need to get about the score. As you become more proficient in Sibelius, however, you will use the mouse less often, and keyboard shortcuts more. Using keyboard shortcuts makes your use of the program faster. If you don't believe me, imagine typing a document with many italic and bold characters as well as normal ones. If you clicked the Italic and Bold buttons on your word processor at the start and end of every word, it would probably take you at least twice as long to type the document than if you used the shortcuts Ctrl+I (Command+I) for italic and Ctrl+B (Command+B) for bold. Musical notation is a much, much more complicated system than written text, so the more shortcuts you learn, the faster you'll use Sibelius!

Many shortcuts require you to select something (a note, a passage of music, some text) before using the shortcut to carry out the action. That is, you need to tell Sibelius "where" or "what" first. For example, when entering lyrics you should select the note at the start of the passage and then press Ctrl+L (Command+L). A cursor/caret will appear under the note and you can start typing the lyrics.

—Katie Wardrobe, teacher, arranger, and copyist with
extensive experience in Sibelius training

If you enjoyed this expert tip from Katie, check out her Web site at www.midnightmusic.com.au. You'll find dozens of free resources to
On the Web **download.**

Here are the simplest keyboard shortcuts for moving around your score. There are more, and you'll learn some of them in Lesson 2.

- **Home.** Move toward the start of your score, one page or screen at a time (depending on the current zoom setting).

- **End.** Move toward the end of your score.

- **Ctrl+Home (Command+Home).** Move to the first page in your score.

- **Ctrl+End (Command+End).** Move to the last page in your score.

- **Page Up.** Move toward the top of the pages that are showing.

- **Page Down.** Move toward the bottom of the pages that are showing.

- **Ctrl+= (Command+=).** Zoom in. (Associate the equal sign with the plus sign, which is above it on the same key, to make it easy to remember for zooming in.)

- **Ctrl+− (Command+−).** Zoom out.

The location of the Home, End, Page Up, and Page Down keys on a Mac keyboard is shown in Figure 1.18; they are in the same position on a Windows PC keyboard. If you use a laptop, these keys may have been repositioned to fit into the smaller space available, or they may be entirely absent. On all new Apple laptops, holding down the fn key and pressing the Left Arrow or Right Arrow key is the same as pressing Home and End, respectively. Holding down the fn key and pressing the Up Arrow or Down Arrow key is the same as Page Up or Page Down, respectively. Some new Macs also come with a narrower keyboard, which does not include these keys or the numerical keypad. For reasons that will become obvious in the second lesson, you are strongly recommended to buy a full-size keyboard if you plan to use Sibelius a lot.

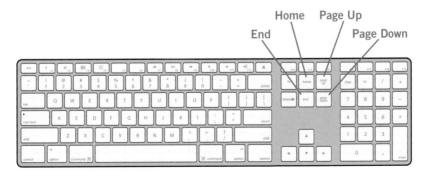

Figure 1.18
Shortcut keys for quickly moving around a score in Sibelius 7.

Try each of these shortcuts out now. Note that Sibelius doesn't require any special mode to use the mouse or the keyboard, so you can use the keys to get quickly to the right page, and then the mouse to nudge it into just the right position to begin working. You may also notice that when you zoom—whether you use the keyboard shortcuts or the Zoom slider—Sibelius automatically zooms toward any selected object, be it a note, a bit of text, or a whole bar.

Using Panorama and Other Document Views

If you zoom out of the "Amazing Grace" score, you will see two pieces of "paper" side by side. Some people prefer these pages to be displayed in different ways; a series of buttons on the right side of the status bar next to the Zoom slider enable you to do this (see Figure 1.19):

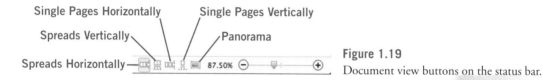

Figure 1.19
Document view buttons on the status bar.

- **Spreads Horizontally.** This button, selected by default, shows page spreads (a left and a right page together) arranged horizontally, as they would be in a book. As you add more music to the score, more pages appear to the right.

- **Spreads Vertically.** Clicking this button also displays pages as spreads, but it arranges them vertically—meaning you would scroll down to see the next spread if there were one. With only two pages, they appear diagonally opposite. (If this view doesn't make much sense to you, open one of Sibelius's sample scores with more pages and compare.)

- **Single Pages Horizontally.** Clicking this button is like clicking the Spreads Horizontally button, except the pages appear as single pages rather than bound like a book with left and right pages together.

- **Single Pages Vertically.** Clicking this button is like clicking the Spreads Vertically button, except the pages appear as single pages rather than bound like a book.

- **Panorama.** The view associated with this button, Panorama view, is quite different from the other views, and is one in which many Sibelius users prefer to work. Clicking this button makes your score infinitely long from left to right, as shown in Figure 1.20. Because Panorama view is not bound to the dimensions of a page, you won't be distracted when adding music across a page turn. In addition, finding exact points in a score is extremely quick.

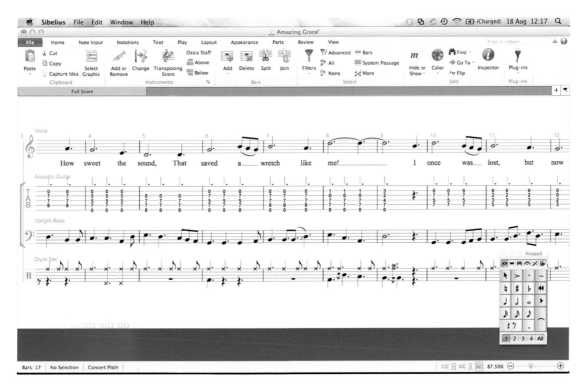

Figure 1.20
The same score in Panorama view.

These options are also available on much bigger buttons in the ribbon under View > Document View, as shown in Figure 1.21.

Figure 1.21
Document View buttons on the ribbon.

Click the Panorama button to switch to Panorama view; it's time to learn a little more about it. In Panorama view, when you scroll the score so far to the right that you can't see the instrument names, clefs, and key signatures, Sibelius does something very clever. It displays the *magic margin*—a blue clef, staff, and key signature (if you have one—"Amazing Grace" doesn't, because it's in C major) in the left margin of the screen. In addition to this, each instrument name is displayed in blue just above the start of each staff, and the bar numbers are shown in blue above every barline. Try scrolling up, down, left or right, and everything is updated instantly.

If you've used other notation software before, such as Finale, it may have had a view similar to Panorama. The magic margin, however, is unique to Sibelius. In addition, Sibelius tries to keep the note spacing as similar as possible to how it will be when you return to one of the other views (spreads or single pages). That means you can immerse yourself in Panorama view and not get too out of touch with what your score is actually going to look like in the end. That said, before you print your score, you need to carefully check it in another view for issues such as page turns, text that hangs off a page, or the general spacing of staves, which you'll look at later on. If you try to print when in Panorama, Sibelius warns you that what you're seeing now is not what you'll get—at least not unless you're printing onto a roll of toilet paper, which might have about the right dimensions!

Exploring the Ribbon and the Status Bar

 If you're studying this lesson without a teacher, this is the perfect moment to watch the second video, **1.2 Exploring the Ribbon and the Status Bar**. In less than 10 minutes, it will show you much of the information in this section.

Before you begin exploring the ribbon, note the very few visual differences between Sibelius on Windows and on a Mac. On a Mac, despite most of the commands having moved to the ribbon in Sibelius 7, a few menus (File, Edit, Window, and Help) remain at the top—at least until you put Sibelius in full-screen mode. (You'll learn more about that later.) In Windows, Sibelius doesn't have these menus. It does, however, have a few extra buttons in the Quick Access toolbar. As shown in Figure 1.22, this toolbar includes Save, Undo, and Redo buttons. You'll learn more about these functions later, too.

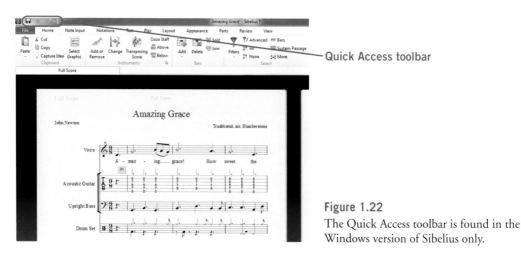

Figure 1.22
The Quick Access toolbar is found in the Windows version of Sibelius only.

You've already used the ribbon a few times while getting used to moving about the score. In this book, instructions for where to click the ribbon are written in the order Tab > Group > Button, Check Box, Combo Box, or Gallery. The tabs, shown in Figure 1.23, reveal new controls (buttons, etc.) when you click them. On the ribbon, groups are labeled in gray text and separated with gray lines to make them easily distinguishable. Groups are highlighted in Figure 1.24.

Tabs

Figure 1.23
Tabs on the ribbon, with the View tab selected.

Group names are shown in gray.

Figure 1.24
Group names become visible when you click a tab.

The ribbon can cleverly resize itself to fit the size of the window. This is particularly useful for laptop users. If there isn't enough room to show every control available in every group on the ribbon, Sibelius gathers the available controls into a drop-down menu, accessible from a single button. For example, if you were attempting to display the Navigator panel on a laptop with a small screen (by choosing View > Panels > Navigator), you would have seen the Panels group shrunk down to a single button, as shown in Figure 1.25. Had you been working on a nice big computer monitor, however, you would have seen not only all controls of the Panels group available, but all controls in the Rulers and Window groups as well (see Figure 1.26). Even if you have reason to make a window half its normal width—for instance, if you're comparing one score with another—you'll see that Sibelius can fit all the controls on the ribbon, as shown in Figure 1.27.

Figure 1.25

The Panels group in the ribbon, shrunk down to a single button.

Figure 1.26

The Panels group in the ribbon, fully expanded (as are the surrounding groups).

Figure 1.27

The View tab of the ribbon with every group shrunk to fit in a very small window.

Understanding Your Workflow and the Ribbon Layout

The tabs in the ribbon are organized approximately in the order you're likely to work on a score if you begin it from scratch. You can click through each tab as you read about it. Although there are some controls that this book won't cover, there's nothing wrong with just clicking anything that interests you to see what it does. You can always close Sibelius and start again without saving your work if you get confused. By the way, if you hover your mouse pointer over any control on the ribbon, you'll see a *screen tip*—an explanation of what the control does, as well as its keyboard shortcut (if there is one), as shown in Figure 1.28.

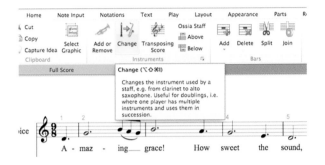

Figure 1.28
A screen tip appears if you hover your mouse pointer over any control in the ribbon.

The tabs are as follows:

- **The Home tab.** Your starting point on the ribbon is the Home tab (see Figure 1.29). (Yes, the File tab is first, but more on that one later.) As you might expect, the tools in the Home tab relate to setting up a score—adding, removing, and changing instruments or bars of music; selecting different objects in your score; and essential functions such as copy and paste. There is also a Plug-ins group on the Home tab. (If you've upgraded from a prior version of Sibelius, don't expect to find everything that was in the old Plug-ins menu here; many of these features have been integrated into the ribbon, making them easier to find and more seamless to use.)

Figure 1.29
Controls in the ribbon's Home tab.

- **The Note Input tab.** Just as it sounds, this tab, shown in Figure 1.30, has to do with getting your music into your score. You'll spend a lot of time looking at this tab in Lesson 2. There are options for inputting with the mouse, with a MIDI keyboard (or other MIDI device such as a MIDI guitar), or a combination of the two. There are also controls for quickly arranging scores and for helping you develop musical ideas when you're composing.

Figure 1.30
Controls in the ribbon's Note Input tab.

■ **The Notations tab.** Notations are what you need to add with notes after you've put them in or while you're inputting them. These notations might pertain to phrasing, dynamics, key and time signatures, repeats, and much more. Along with the Note Input tab, you'll probably use the Notations tab, shown in Figure 1.31, the most (at least until you've learned all the shortcuts).

Figure 1.31
Controls in the ribbon's Notations tab.

■ **The Text tab.** To round off all the basic elements that you need in your score, there is the Text tab (see Figure 1.32). Written dynamics, lyrics, titles for your scores, and musical playing techniques (such as *pizz.* or *arco*) can be added here. There are also controls for simple and complex guitar chord text and symbols.

Figure 1.32
Controls in the ribbon's Text tab.

Those first four tabs take care of all the core elements of your score. You are most likely to begin by putting in notes, articulations, phrasing, dynamics, and other performance instructions such as tempi, and all these elements are found there. Each of the next tabs has a very specific use. Again, they are organized in the order you are most likely to need them.

■ **The Play tab.** The Play tab, shown in Figure 1.33, contains not only controls to play back your score, but also options for how Sibelius should interpret the music you've written and options for composing to video.

Figure 1.33
Controls in the ribbon's Play tab.

- **The Layout tab.** The Layout tab, shown in Figure 1.34, is the most complicated-looking of all the ribbon collections, and is the one you'll learn least about in this book. The controls here are for completely changing the way your score is set out, for when you want to override Sibelius's default settings in note and staff spacing. As a rule, you'll find that Sibelius makes your scores look neat and clear with very little assistance. That means you'll only visit this tab for the occasional tweak or when you need to do something quite unusual. Lesson 4, "Worksheets," will teach you about creating scores with unusual layouts.

Figure 1.34
Controls in the ribbon's Layout tab.

- **The Appearance tab.** *Appearance* sounds similar to *layout*, but the Appearance tab is instead concerned with the default position of notes and other objects such as text and lines in the score. (See Figure 1.35.) As with the Layout tab, you won't have to worry very much about controls in the Appearance tab in this book; Sibelius automatically fixes things like note spacing so it looks just like it does in published music. Indeed, many of the world's biggest publishers use Sibelius, and they rely on it to save them time by getting the spacing right without constant adjustment.

Figure 1.35
Controls in the ribbon's Appearance tab.

- **The Parts tab.** The Parts tab is one of the most important tabs; it contains controls that will save you hours. If you need to quickly print a set of parts, or create a new part that combines the tubular bells and vibraphone parts, you can do it in a moment here. Because creating parts for your players is one of the things you do after your score is complete (or at least at first-draft status), the Parts tab, shown in Figure 1.36, is one of the last ones on the ribbon.

Figure 1.36
Controls in the ribbon's Parts tab.

- **The Review tab.** Another final process for a score is review. The controls in the Review tab, shown in Figure 1.37, enable you to mark up the score, highlight parts to be worked on, and even archive different versions so you never lose a note of the music you've written—even when you scrap a section. This tab is exceptionally useful both for professionals collaborating on big projects such as film scores and for students receiving advice and feedback from teachers.

Figure 1.37
Controls in the ribbon's Review tab.

- **The View tab.** The final tab is the View tab, shown in Figure 1.38. Changing how you see Sibelius isn't really part of the everyday process of using the program, which is why this tab appears last. From time to time, however, you will want to open a panel, such as the Navigator panel, or hide comments while you read a score. Note that the more common View controls, such as the zoom and page view options, are easily accessible in the status bar, as you have seen. For this reason, you won't need to use the View tab very often.

Figure 1.38
Controls in the ribbon's View tab.

The one remaining tab is the File tab. This tab is different from all the others, which is why discussion here has been left until last. Clicking the File tab hides the score, but reveals many options you can select that affect the score in its entirety. The options here, by the way, are known as "Backstage"; perhaps you can feel honored to be invited back here, and perhaps you'll find the odd compositional superstar hanging out.

As shown in Figure 1.39, a list of functions appears along the left side of the Backstage screen; choosing one of these functions displays further options on the right side of the screen. As you might expect, this is where you can open and save files, create new files, and close opened files. You can also append one score onto the end of another (useful if you're joining movements of a single work), print your score, export it in a number of useful formats, open hundreds of ready-made worksheets, and find help with the program. You will learn how to use many of these options in detail in this book.

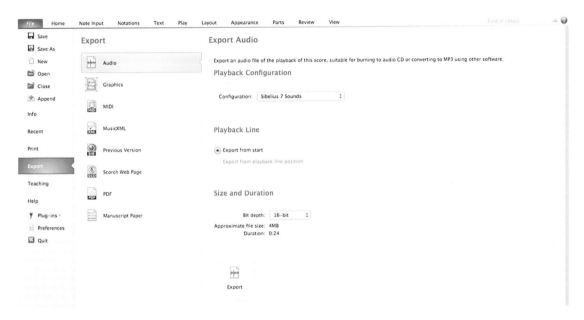

Figure 1.39
Controls in the ribbon's File tab, also called "Backstage."

A lot of careful thinking has gone into what is where in the ribbon. Getting around can be difficult if you're upgrading from a prior version of Sibelius, but if you're new to the program, the ribbon should make it much, much easier to find the functions you're after. Many existing users will probably notice features as they dig around the ribbon that they might think are new, but were just too hidden or obscure in previous versions of Sibelius. Do embrace the ribbon. It will make your workflow so much smoother. If you're finding the conversion hard, read on….

Finding What You Need in the Ribbon

You should be able to find everything you need in the ribbon by observing the grouping covered in the preceding section (see Figure 1.40):

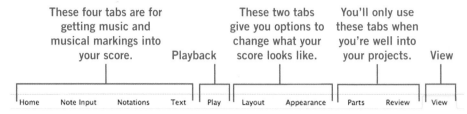

Figure 1.40
Conceptually grouping tabs in the ribbon makes it easier to remember where to find what.

- Think of the Home, Note Input, Notations, and Text tabs as the group of four that is all about getting everything into Sibelius.

- The Play tab is for playback—not just getting Sibelius to play back, but changing how it performs your score.

- You can group the Layout and Appearance tabs together in your mind, because both relate to changing how your score looks.

- Last in the process of score preparation are the Parts and Review tabs, which, again, can be grouped in your imagination—this time as the two tabs you don't need until you're nearing the end of your project.

- The Parts and Review tabs contrast with the View tab, which is about *how you look at Sibelius.*

- As mentioned, the File tab is a very different kind of tab; the lovely folks at Sibelius have reminded us of that by coloring it purple so that it even *looks* different.

Tip: If you've upgraded to Sibelius 7 from a previous version, you may find navigating the ribbon to be a little frustrating, especially because you knew where most of its features were back in the days when you had the trusty Create menu. You'll be relieved to know, then, that right-clicking (Control-clicking) an empty part the score displays the old Create menu, just as it has since version 1 of Sibelius.

Still can't find the control you need? Fear not. At the top right of the ribbon is a small text box that, by default, reads "Find in ribbon" (see Figure 1.41). Suppose, for example, you can't work out how to add expression text for a written dynamic in Sibelius 7. Simply type **expression** in the Find in Ribbon text box; before you've even finished typing, you should see a list of options related to expression. Clicking one of them highlights its associated control in the ribbon; from there, you can get on with your work.

Find in Ribbon text box

Figure 1.41
The Find in Ribbon text box.

There's one little problem with the Find in Ribbon text box—especially if you're a new user. If you don't know the name of a feature in Sibelius, you might not be able to use the Find in Ribbon text box to search for it. Sure, for some features, it works fine; if you type **transpose**, you'll see two controls listed. One is for trans-posing music you have selected, and one is to toggle your score between concert pitch and transposed pitches—just as you probably want. But what if you're after dynamics? Type **dynamics** in the Find in Ribbon text box, and you'll see four options: a filter for dynamics, two plug-ins to do with dynamics, and an option about playback. None of them, however, tell you how to put a dynamic into your score. That's because Sibelius places controls related to dynamics in two different places in the ribbon. If you want to put written dynamics like *p* and *mf* into your score, you need expression text from Text > Styles > Expression. If you want a nice crescendo line, you need Notations > Lines > Crescendo. Use Table 1.1 to help you find the feature you need via the Find in Ribbon text box.

Table 1.1 Terms to Search For in the Ribbon

Looking for	Search for
Dynamics	Expression text, crescendo, diminuendo
Phrasing	Slur
Instrument names	Instruments (not piano, violin, etc.)
Stave	Staff
Text	Technique text
Pizz. or *arco*	Technique text
Allegro, piu mosso, etc.	Tempo text
Poco a poco	Expression text
Quarter note or other note lengths	Look in the Keypad panel (View > Panels > Keypad)
Accidentals	Look in the Keypad panel (View > Panels > Keypad)
Articulations	Look in the Keypad panel (View > Panels > Keypad)
Pause (fermata)	Look in the Keypad panel (View > Panels > Keypad)

Discovering Ribbon Shortcuts

As you begin to learn Sibelius, you'll likely use the mouse. Although it's slower, it is much more intuitive. Want to select another note? Click it. Want to transpose it higher? Drag it up. Want to delete bars? Choose Home > Bars > Delete. Sure, all these things can be done with a keystroke or two, but the great thing about the ribbon is that it's all there in front of you.

As you progress through this book and the subsequent courses, however, you'll learn many shortcuts, which will speed your work significantly. Many of Sibelius's shortcuts are very easy to remember, being single keystrokes with no modifiers— that is, shortcuts where you don't have to hold down Shift or Ctrl (Command) keys. Examples of these are T for Time Signature and K for Key Signature. Yes, a four year old could remember those!

If you're really keen to become an expert Sibelius user as quickly as possible, there are a few ways to learn keyboard shortcuts as you go. One has already been mentioned: Hover your mouse over any control in the ribbon to reveal a *screen tip*, which includes the shortcut for the control (if there is one). You can also learn *key tips*, which are shortcuts just for the ribbon. To reveal key tips, first press the Esc key to make sure you don't have anything selected. Next, press the Alt (Control) key one time. In the ribbon, little letters in boxes pop up (see Figure 1.42). These are key tips for the tabs in the ribbon.

Figure 1.42
Key tips, the letters in boxes floating over the tabs and Find in Ribbon text box, appear when you press the Alt (Control) key.

Notice that each key tip in Figure 1.42 appears directly below the name of each tab in the ribbon. This is to help you avoid confusing them with the key tips for the various commands in each tab. As you can see, the key tip for each tab is typically the first letter of tab's name: F for the File tab, H for the Home tab, N for the Notations tab, T for the Text tab, L for the Layout tab, A for the Appearance tab, R for the Review tab, and V for the View tab. When the first letter has already been used, another initial (or initials) is employed—for example, I for Note Input, PL for Play, and PA for Parts. As you've probably guessed, pressing any of the corresponding keys for those key tips has the same effect as clicking that tab in the ribbon.

To use keyboard shortcuts to navigate the ribbon, try the following:

1. Press the **ALT (CONTROL) KEY** to invoke key tips; then press **V** to open the View tab. Notice that the key tips now appear over every control in the ribbon.

2. Because there are many controls, most have two-letter key tips; you can invoke these in turn by typing the two letters one immediately after the other (see Figure 1.43). To try doing this, type **PA** to toggle Panorama view on or off. The view of the score should change.

3. Now try invoking another key tip. Press the **ALT (CONTROL)** key as you type **PL**, then **PY**, and then **P**. Your score should start playing back; press **ESC** to stop it.

Figure 1.43
Key tips on the ribbon's View tab.

Key tips aren't always the quickest way to invoke a command. For instance, you could play your score just by pressing the space bar. Key tips do, however, provide a way to use the keyboard more than the mouse in Sibelius without completing the whole of this book. It's probably still not in your best interest to stop reading at this point, though. In case you're keen to use key tips a lot as you learn Sibelius, Figure 1.44 shows all the key tips of each ribbon tab, so you can review each one as needed.

File (Alt+7/Control+7)

Figure 1.44
Key tips on each tab of the ribbon.

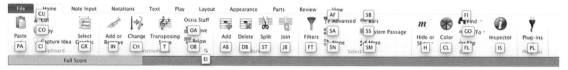

Home (Alt+H/Control+H)

Note Input (Alt+I/Control+I)

Notations (Alt+N/Control+N)

Text (Alt+T/Control+T)

Play (Alt+PL/ Control+PL)

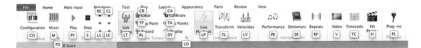

Layout (Alt+L/Control+L)

Appearance (Alt+A/Control+A)

Parts (Alt+PA/Control+PA)

Review (Alt+R/Control+R)

View (Alt+V/Control+V)

Tip: If you are looking for a control in the ribbon that you haven't been able to find with the Find in Ribbon feature, you can press Alt+ (Control+) *Key tip of any tab* to see what is in that tab, and then press Esc to return to the first set of key tips, showing each tab again. For example, press Alt+H (Control+H) to look at the Home tab, press Esc+T to look at the Text tab, and so on.

Exploring the Status Bar

The status bar is the strip along the bottom of the main Sibelius window (see Figure 1.45). You've already learned about everything on the right side of the status bar, including buttons for changing the way pages are viewed and a Zoom slider.

On the right, Page View buttons and the Zoom slider. On the left,
a range of information about your score and your position in it.

Figure 1.45
The status bar.

If you've installed Sibelius 7 Sounds, you'll sometimes see a percent symbol (%) to the left of the Page View buttons. Sibelius 7 Sounds came with your copy of Sibelius 7 and can be installed from the DVDs (or from the downloaded files, if you downloaded Sibelius). Sibelius Sounds includes high-quality samples—real recorded sounds—of dozens of instruments. When you open a big score, the % readout on the status bar shows you the progress of the sounds being loaded for playback.

If you try to play back the score before it reaches 100%, you'll have to wait for the loading to complete. (There is much more about playback in the next section, and in Lesson 5.)

On the left side of the status bar is a whole array of information about the score and about your current selection within it. As you click different things in your score, this readout changes. Some information, such as the position (bar and beat number) of the currently selected note, is obvious. Some, such as the ML status or transposing score status, may not be. Rather than get bogged down now in what each of these bits of information may be (some are barely touched in this book, so there isn't much point learning what they are yet), you'll learn them as you come to them. Most important is the note input status readout, which you'll use to make sure you always know *why* Sibelius is doing what it's doing.

To locate the note input status readout:

1. Press **Esc** twice to make sure nothing in the score is selected. You should see the words "No Selection" in the status bar, as shown in Figure 1.46.

Figure 1.46
The status bar, showing No Selection.

2. Click any note in the score. The status changes to Edit Note, as shown in Figure 1.47. Lots of other information pops up about the note you selected, too. This can cause the position of the status readout to change on the status bar, as shown in each figure.

Figure 1.47
The status bar, showing Edit Note.

3. Click one of the lyrics in the vocal part. The status changes to Edit Lyric, as shown in Figure 1.48.

Figure 1.48
The status bar, showing Edit Lyric.

It may be difficult to see how this is useful. After all, you just clicked on a lyric, so it makes sense it would say "Edit Lyric." But when you get into more complex operations, it will be very useful to be able to flick your eyes to the status and check exactly what you're doing to your score.

Exploring Playback

Tip: If you're studying this course without an instructor, begin this section by watching the third video, called **1.3 Exploring Playback**. The video gives an overview of everything covered in this section. You can then refer to the following pages to step you through the process if need be or to simply review.

The great thing about playback in Sibelius is that it reads nearly anything you write on your score. In fact, when you create your own score in Lesson 2, you'll discover that Sibelius plays back each instrument with the right sound from scratch. As you add dynamics, tempi, and articulation marks, those play back, too.

Playing Back from the Ribbon

There are a number of ways to play back your score. Because you already know how to access the Play tab on the ribbon, let's start there.

To play back from the ribbon:

1. Click the **PLAY** tab.

2. Look at the **TRANSPORT** group. You'll see a Play button and a Stop button, as shown in Figure 1.49.

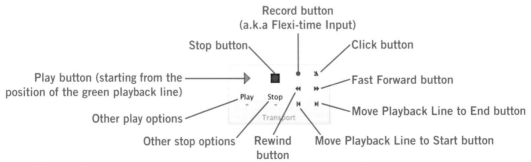

Figure 1.49
The Play tab's Transport group.

3. Click the **PLAY** button to play back the score. While the score is playing back, notice the green playback line moving along the score.

4. Click the **STOP** button to stop playing back the score. When you stop playback, the playback line stops moving; it remains where it was when you clicked the Stop button.

5. Click the **PLAY** button again. Sibelius continues playing from point at which you stopped (unless it had reached the end of the score, in which case Sibelius will start from the beginning).

The Play and Stop buttons are split buttons. If you click the top half of a split button, the default action associated with that button occurs. If you click the bottom half of a split button, you are presented with a number of other options. For example, clicking the bottom half of the Play button reveals various options, including Play from Selection, which enables you to play back from the note you have selected instead of wherever the green playback line happens to be.

Other buttons in the ribbon's Transport group are labeled in Figure 1.49.

■ **Record (a.k.a. Flexi-time Input).** This red button resembles the Record button that (if you're old enough) you may remember seeing on cassette players. In this case, however, the button is for recording with a MIDI keyboard directly into Sibelius. More on that in Lesson 2.

■ **Rewind and Fast Forward.** These buttons do exactly as you might expect and can be used whether Sibelius is already playing back or not. If it's not already playing back, you might use these buttons to move the green playback line to an appropriate position for your next playback.

■ **Move Playback Line to Start and Move Playback Line to End.** There probably isn't really a need to explain these eponymous buttons; their names say it all. (Note that unlike with some sequencers, clicking the Stop button twice in Sibelius does not move the playback line to the start. You'll need to use the button to do that—or learn the shortcut as described later in this lesson.)

■ **Click.** This button, which looks like a metronome, turns a metronome click off and on during playback. By default, Sibelius doesn't click while playing back your score, but *does* click if you choose to record into it.

I urge you to experiment to your heart's content with these buttons (although you might prefer to leave the Record button until the next lesson, where you'll be stepped through its use).

Exploring the Transport Panel

All the buttons in the Play tab's Transport group (plus a few more, along with extended playback information) can be made to permanently float in their own panel (see Figure 1.50). In earlier versions of Sibelius, this was known as the Playback window; in Sibelius 7, it has been renamed the Transport panel to align it with terminology used in sequencers and digital audio workstations (DAWs) such as Pro Tools. To display the Transport panel, choose View > Panels > Transport.

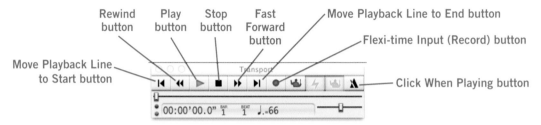

Figure 1.50
The Transport panel, showing the buttons in common with the Play tab's Transport group.

Figure 1.51 shows the features in the Transport panel that are not available in the Play tab's Transport group (although some of these features are available in other groups in the ribbon, or in the status bar):

- **Timeline.** This slider, which goes the full length of the Transport panel, enables you to quickly change the position of the playback line. The far left of the slider represents the beginning of the score, at the far right the end. Using this slider to move the playback line is much faster than clicking the Rewind and Fast Forward buttons. You don't even need to click and drag the handle; clicking anywhere on the line will make the playback line jump to that point.

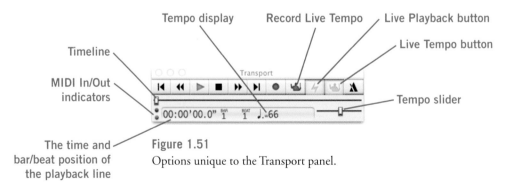

Figure 1.51
Options unique to the Transport panel.

■ **MIDI In/MIDI Out indicators.** These green and red indicators are useful if you're using a MIDI keyboard; they can help you confirm that signals are being sent. (More about this in Lesson 2.)

■ **The time and bar/beat position of the playback line.** These readouts contain much the same information as the status bar, but in relation to the green playback line (its time and bar/beat position) and the current tempo.

■ **Tempo display.** Sibelius reads any metronome mark written on your score, and also interprets words such as *Allegro* or *Faster* or lines such as *Rit.* or *Accel.* The Tempo display shows the tempo Sibelius will play back at the current position of the green playback line.

■ **Tempo slider.** By default, this is set in the middle, and the tempo is the prevailing metronome mark or an interpretation of any other tempo marking (such as *adagio*, moderately, or *plus vite*). Drag the slider to the right to increase the playback tempo (speed up the playback) or to the left to decrease it. Like the Timeline, you can also click at any point to make the tempo jump to that relative speed. There is a "sticky" point in the middle of the slider when dragging that enables you to easily revert to the written tempo. If there is no tempo indicated for your score, Sibelius plays back at 100 quarter note beats per minute.

Note: If you want to permanently change the tempo of your score, you should add it as a metronome mark or other tempo direction on the actual score. (You'll learn how to do this in Lesson 2.) The Tempo slider does not make permanent changes to the tempo, and this slider's settings cannot be interpreted by actual performers.

■ **Record Live Tempo, Live Playback, and Live Tempo buttons.** These buttons enable you to record live tempo, toggle live playback on and off, and toggle live tempo data on and off, respectively. (Don't worry if this doesn't make sense right now. It shouldn't yet. You'll find out about it in Lesson 5.)

To experiment with the Transport panel:

1. Click the **PLAY** button on the Transport panel to play back a score. The score will start to play back from the position of the green playback line.

2. Drag the **TEMPO** slider to change the tempo of playback. Drag it to the right to make playback faster and to the left to make it slower.

3. Drag the handle on the Timeline to change the position of the playback line. Alternatively, simply click any point in the Timeline.

4. Click **STOP** to stop playback.

As you can see, you can quite easily audition the tempo of different sections in real time!

Discovering Playback Shortcuts

Earlier, you learned how to play back the score using key tips and the controls in the ribbon's Play tab. There are, however, simpler shortcuts for nearly all the mouse commands you've learned so far. These are worth learning now.

Just about every sequencing program since the beginning of time has used the space bar to start and stop playback. Sibelius is no exception—although, as you might expect, if you are entering text into your score, pressing the space bar will add spaces in the text rather than starting and stopping playback each time you press it. The same is true if you have a dialog box open or are using galleries in the ribbon that you can select with the space bar. If you ever wonder why the space bar isn't working to start and stop play, check your status in the status bar or simply press Esc twice quickly to cancel all selections, close open dialog boxes, and so on. (Note that the Esc key can also be used to stop playback.)

You can view other shortcuts by hovering your mouse over the various buttons in the ribbon (the Transport panel does not show shortcuts). These are summarized in Table 1.2.

Table 1.2   Basic Playback Shortcuts

Shortcut	Function
Space bar	Start playback from the green playback line. Also stops playback.
P	Play back from the selection (e.g., from a selected note, barline, or dynamic).
Esc	Stop playback or recording.
[	Rewind.
]	Fast forward.
Ctrl+[(Command+[)	Move playback line to start.
Ctrl+] (Command+])	Move playback line to end.
Ctrl+Shift+F (Command+Shift+F)	Record (Flexi-time Input).

If you're lucky enough to own an M-Audio keyboard with HyperControl, you will also find that the playback controls on the keyboard work. Figure 1.52 shows an Axiom Pro 49, with buttons for Loop, Play, Stop, Fast Forward, Rewind, and Record.

If nothing is selected in the score when you click the Record button, press it on your M-Audio Axiom or press the Ctrl+Shift+F (Command+Shift+F) shortcut, Sibelius will begin recording from the beginning, in the top part in the score. (You will learn much more about Flexi-time recording in Lesson 2, and about using HyperControl and advanced playback settings in Lesson 5.)

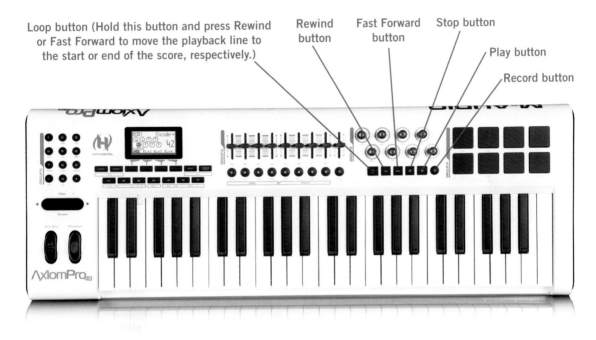

Figure 1.52
The playback buttons on an M-Audio Axiom Pro 49, connected to Sibelius by HyperControl.

Introducing Sibelius 7 Sounds

Perhaps you're a little disappointed in the quality of the instrumental sounds the first time you play back in Sibelius. If so, it could be that you haven't installed Sibelius 7 Sounds or, if you have, you haven't set up Sibelius to play back from it yet. With Sibelius 7 Sounds, samples used for playback are very high quality. (You will learn more about how to get the best out of Sibelius 7 Sounds in Lesson 5.)

Sibelius 7 Sounds does consume 40 GB of hard drive space, and requires a good deal of RAM (at least 4 GB is recommended, although it will run with fewer). By default, it is *not* installed when you install Sibelius.

Even so, if you plan to play back your scores often, it is highly recommended that you install Sibelius 7 Sounds from your Sibelius 7 DVDs. The sounds in the program are much better than your default computer sounds!

To find out whether Sibelius 7 Sounds is working:

1. Choose PLAY > SETUP > CONFIGURATION.

2. Make sure the SIBELIUS 7 SOUNDS check box is checked. If that option doesn't appear, it means you haven't installed Sibelius 7 Sounds correctly. Refer to the installation guide that came with your copy of Sibelius 7.

Troubleshooting Sibelius 7 Sounds

If you're using Sibelius 7 Sounds for playback and you notice it stutters or pops, it's most likely because the program can't access enough RAM (memory). To resolve this, try restarting your computer. Then, make sure no other applications (apart from Sibelius) are running.

If you're still having problems and you use Windows, check the system tray (next to the clock in the bottom-right corner of the screen) to see how many background programs are running. If you can identify ones you don't need, shut them down or, better yet, uninstall the software if you don't use it. If necessary, temporarily disable your antivirus software (you should disconnect your computer from the Internet first). Cheap sound cards can also create problems in Windows computers.

Both Windows and Mac users can also improve performance by defragmenting your hard drive, installing more RAM (an extra 2 GB is quite cheap nowadays), or, if you're really serious, installing a solid-state hard drive (the more expensive solution).

If you don't have enough hard drive space to install Sibelius 7 Sounds, you *can* install it on an external drive. However, not all external drives are equal. Ones with a disk speed of 7,200 rpm can load samples much more quickly than the standard 5,400 rpm. (If you look at a disk and it doesn't say, it's almost definitely 5,400 rpm).

In addition, while USB 2.0 and USB 3.0 speeds are theoretically as fast as FireWire 400 and 800 (also called IEEE 1394 and i.Link), most users find FireWire drives more consistently fast than USB. If you don't have a FireWire port on your computer, check with your computer manufacturer whether you have USB 2.0 or USB 3.0 ports and buy a compatible drive.

External hard drives are relatively inexpensive nowadays; you can expect to get a 500 GB hard drive easily under $100. Drives with 7,200 rpm speed should only be $30 to $60 more expensive than their 5,400 rpm counterparts.

Simple Editing

Tip: As usual, if you're using this book to teach yourself, it is recommended that you begin this section by watching the corresponding video, **1.4 Simple Editing**. This isn't necessary if you're being led through the course by a teacher, but may be useful later for review.

You'll start to discover the real power of Sibelius in Lesson 2, when you create a score from scratch. This first lesson is to acquaint you with the look and feel of the program so you won't wonder where things are or what is going on when you get to the more challenging stuff.

For now, don't worry about possibly "breaking" this score. This section gives you an opportunity to move notes and other objects around, make a few changes to the score, and generally make a bit of a musical mess.

If you're nervous about using a computer, rest assured that this stage is purely experiential. You just have to try. If the score becomes unrecognizable and you need to start again, that's no problem! Just close it and re-open it again from the project folder. If you've already saved over the original, don't worry; you can make another copy by dragging it from the CD as you did at the start of this lesson. Just have fun!

Note: This piece starts with an *anacrusis*, also known as a pickup or upbeat bar. It is shorter than a full bar because it contains just enough beats for the lead-in in the vocal part. Anacrusis bars *do not* count in bar numbering, so bar 1 is the first full bar, not the anacrusis bar. When bar numbers are given here (for example, "Click the note on the first beat of bar 1"), remember to ignore the anacrusis bar. To help you count bars, Sibelius shows the bar number at the start of each system or, if you're working in Panorama view, above the top staff in every bar.

Editing Pitch and Rhythm

In Sibelius, you can edit the pitch of notes simply by dragging them. To try this, press Esc twice to make sure you have nothing selected; then click the first note in the bass part and drag it up and down. You should hear the pitch changing as you drag the note and as it moves diatonically within the key. (Notes do not move chromatically as you drag them.)

If you drag the note below the E below the bass staff, it turns red (see Figure 1.53). The shade of red depends on how low you drag it. (If it doesn't appear red, just deselect the note by clicking a blank part of the page.) Sibelius turns notes a deep red color when they are out of comfortable range. If a note is considered completely impossible on a particular instrument, Sibelius turns it a lighter shade of red. Try dragging notes a little out of range, and then way out of range, to see the color change. These colors are clearest when the notes are not selected, so after dragging, press Esc or click a blank part of the page.

Figure 1.53
The low C is out of the range of the upright bass (whose lowest note is usually E) unless it has an extension C string, so Sibelius colors it deep red.

Drag the first note back to the G where it started. Then, drag the note on the second beat to G and the note on the third beat to A, as shown in Figure 1.54. Play back the changes to see how they sound. If you want, change the pitch of further notes.

Figure 1.54
Edit the pitches of the first bar of the bass part so it reads like this.

You can also change the pitches of notes with the arrow keys on the keyboard. After selecting a note, press the Up Arrow key to move the note up one step at a time. Press the Down Arrow key to move the note down one step at a time. You can also make notes jump by an octave by holding down Ctrl (Command) as you press the Up Arrow and Down Arrow keys.

To change the rhythm of notes, you can use the Keypad panel. This floating panel is positioned at the bottom-right corner of the window by default. If you can't see the Keypad panel, choose View > Panels > Keypad. By default, its layout should appear just as it does in Figure 1.55. If it doesn't, click the First Keypad Layout button shown to return it to the default layout.

Click again on the first note in the bass part. Instead of repeating the G, change it so that it is a dotted half note, as shown in Figure 1.56. To do this, click the Half Note button on the Keypad panel, and then the Dotted Rhythm button (the one with a dot on it) at the *bottom* of the Keypad panel. As you do this, you should see the dotted quarter note you selected turn first into a half note and then change to include the rhythmic dot that causes it to take up two beats in the 9/8 time signature.

Click the First Keypad Layout button to reset the layout.

Figure 1.55
The Keypad panel on a Mac (left) and in Windows (right).

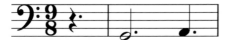

Figure 1.56
Edit the length of the first note of the bass part so it reads like this.

When using the Keypad panel's default layout, be careful to note that the dot at the bottom of the panel is for rhythm dots. In contrast, the one at the *top* of the panel is to add a staccato articulation to a note (see Figure 1.57).

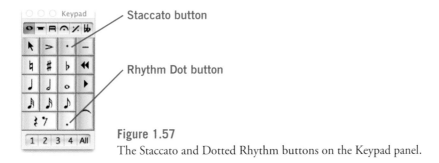

Staccato button

Rhythm Dot button

Figure 1.57
The Staccato and Dotted Rhythm buttons on the Keypad panel.

To revise what you just did, edit the first note in the drum part in bar 5 as shown in Figure 1.58:

1. Drag the FIRST NOTE in the drum part in bar 5 up so it is on the first leger line above the staff. (Note that in drum notation, each line and space is a different percussion instrument, and the cross-shaped notehead also changes the sound.) In this case, you're changing the note to a splash cymbal on the first beat of the bar.

Figure 1.58
Edit the drum part in bar 5 so it looks like this.

2. Click the **HALF NOTE** button on the Keypad panel to change the rhythmic value of the note to be a dotted half note, just as you did with the note in the bass part.

3. Click the **RHYTHM DOT** button on the Keypad panel.

4. **PLAY BACK** the **SCORE** and notice the edits you've made.

Feel free to practice these skills further. You won't learn how to input more notes until Lesson 2, but you can edit the ones that are there to your heart's content.

Note: Don't worry if you find drum notation confusing right now. You'll learn a lot more about drum notation in Sibelius (and drum notation in general) in Lesson 3.

Undoing and Redoing

As you've learned to move around your score, play it back, and make your first edits, you've been instructed to "press Esc twice" a few times already. In Sibelius, the Esc key is often described as your best friend. It will get you out of just about any confusing situation you could imagine. In short, Esc's role in Sibelius is to cancel things—anything, in fact.

You already know that pressing the Esc key stops Sibelius playing back. In addition, you've learned that Esc can be used to navigate back a step when using ribbon screen tips. And you know that by pressing it twice, you can be sure you have nothing selected on the score.

Try this now: Click any object in the score, and the status bar at the bottom of the window changes to Edit *Object*, with *Object* changing depending the type of object you've selected. Now press Esc; the status bar changes to No Selection.

Did you know, however, that pressing the Esc key also stops Sibelius recording, can be used to cancel dialog boxes, and can be used to stop editing text while leaving the text highlighted? As you work in Sibelius more, you'll get a feel for how to use Esc to change how you interact with Sibelius and how the program works. For now, all you need to know is that it will get you out of trouble!

If Esc is your best friend, Undo is a close second—perhaps your favorite work colleague. While Esc can cancel what is going on, Undo can actually take you back to before you made a mistake. Try this: Click any note in any part and drag it up until it is well out of range. Do this with two more notes, so you have three pitches in the wrong place.

If you use a Windows computer, follow these steps to see how Undo works:

1. In the Windows Quick Access toolbar, click the **Undo** button repeatedly and watch the notes you dragged hop back into their original positions. Figure 1.59 shows the position of the Undo button.

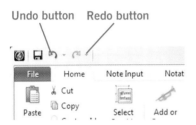

Figure 1.59
The Windows Quick Access toolbar, with the Undo and Redo buttons.

2. To redo the edit (that is, to undo the Undo), click the **Redo** button. Click it repeatedly to see the notes hop back to the ridiculous pitches you put them on.

3. To the right of both the Undo and the Redo button is a down arrow. Clicking this down arrow opens the Undo History and Redo History, respectively. Click the **Undo** down arrow, and the Undo History displays the three note-drags, indicated as a pair of events called Select and Drag (see Figure 1.60). Click the third **Select** in the list to undo all three moves at once.

Figure 1.60
The Undo History.

Mac OS users are sadly bereft of these lovely buttons. Instead, they must open the Edit menu (which Windows users miss out on, just to even things up) and choose Undo. The Edit menu also houses the Undo History command; selecting it launches the dialog box shown in Figure 1.61. Use this dialog box to undo the three note-moves mentioned earlier by clicking the third Select entry in the list then clicking OK.

Figure 1.61
The Undo History dialog box in Mac OS.

Although the Mac method of undoing seems a little clunkier than the Windows method, it's worth pointing out that most users never use the mouse to Undo anyway. If you've ever used a word-processing package like Microsoft Word, a graphics-editing program like Adobe Photoshop, or even a simple Web browser like Internet Explorer or Firefox, you probably know that the universal shortcut for Undo is Ctrl+Z (Command+Z)—and it's the same in Sibelius. If you don't believe me, do some more crazy dragging, and then try the shortcut out. The Sibelius shortcut for Redo is Ctrl+Y (Command+Y). In recent Mac OS applications, however, the standard shortcut for Redo has become Command+Shift+Z. If you press Command+Shift+Z in Sibelius, though, you'll open the Undo History.

Copying and Pasting

One great mantra when using any kind of software is that you shouldn't have to do the same thing twice. Because an awful lot of music is made up of repeated patterns (*ostinati*, chord patterns, structural repetition, motivic development—the list goes on), the next most important commands are Copy and Paste.

Sibelius provides a number of ways to copy and paste material around your score. By the time you finish reading this book, you will know every one of them. You can probably guess the simple keyboard shortcuts for copying and pasting objects from one part of your score to another without being told, just as you likely knew the Undo shortcut: In Sibelius, you copy an object to the clipboard with the shortcut Ctrl+C (Command+C), and paste the copied object into a different part of your score with the shortcut Ctrl+V (Command+V). (If this *is* a new idea to you, don't worry—you'll learn by doing it in a few seconds.) Of course, you can also copy and paste via the ribbon (choose Home > Clipboard > Copy and Home > Clipboard > Paste, respectively, as shown in Figure 1.62).

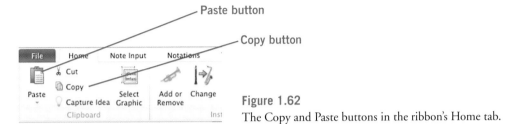

Figure 1.62
The Copy and Paste buttons in the ribbon's Home tab.

The arranger of this piece seems to have forgotten to give the bass player a beginning dynamic. Rather than adding a dynamic from scratch, you can copy a dynamic from one of the other parts.

To copy a dynamic:

1. Click a dynamic—in this case, the *mf* in the drum part at the start of bar 5. (Don't choose the one above the vocal part; it's on the wrong side of the staff, and Sibelius will remember its position.) The dynamic turns blue to show it's selected.

2. To copy the dynamic, press **CTRL+C** (**COMMAND+C**).

3. Click the first note in the bass part (the same note you just turned into a dotted half note).

4. Press **CTRL+V** (**COMMAND+V**). The *mf* appears below the staff, perfectly positioned relative to the note.

Try practicing this again:

1. Click one of the tablature numbers in the guitar part on the first beat of bar 5.

2. Press **CTRL+V** (**COMMAND+V**). The *mf* appears once more, now below the guitar part in bar 5.

Now, if you play back the score from the start, you will notice that the guitar plays discernibly louder at bar 5. If you click the *mf* again and press the Delete or Backspace key, the guitar reverts to its original dynamic. Sibelius really does play what you write on the score, including dynamics!

As you've seen, copying and pasting involves four basic steps:

1. Select the item you want to copy.

2. Copy it.

3. Click the spot where you want to paste.

4. Paste it.

Sibelius, however, has a Quick-Copy feature. With a single click, you can copy whatever you have selected—text, notes, barlines, piano pedaling, you name it.

To use Quick-Copy:

1. Suppose you want the band to play the final chord a little more softly. To start, click the **mp** in the guitar in the first bar.

2. While holding down the **ALT** (**OPTION**) key, click just below the bass player's final note in the final bar. (Be careful to leave the **mp** selected; you may need to zoom out or move the score so you can see the final bar.) The **mp** is copied where you clicked.

Incredibly, you can make Sibelius's Quick-Copy *with no keystrokes at all*, to make it even quicker to use. While the dynamic is still highlighted in the bass part, click the bottom of the guitar staff with either the middle mouse button (if you have one—remember, on most wheel mice, the scroll wheel is also a button) or the right and left buttons at the same time. (Sibelius calls this a *chord click*.) Sibelius copies the dynamic where you clicked.

You may notice that the dynamic is copied exactly where you clicked. This is great for giving you control, but you may prefer Sibelius to place the dynamic in its default position instead (as it did when you used the Copy and Paste functions). If so, hold down the Shift key in addition to the Alt (Option) key while you click. If you like, undo the last copy, and try it again with Shift to snap to default position.

Making Multiple and Passage Selections

To copy more than one object at once (for instance, all the notes in a drum pattern, a range of dynamics, a line of lyrics, and so on), you must first learn how to make multiple and passage selections in Sibelius. Suppose, for example, you want to create a crescendo for the guitarist in bar 4, just like the one the drummer has. To achieve this, you want to copy the beginning **mp**, the crescendo line (also known as a *hairpin*), and the **mf**.

To select all those items:

1. Click the first dynamic.

2. While holding down the **CTRL** (**COMMAND**) key, click the subsequent dynamic(s). The first dynamic remains selected, even as the next dynamics become selected (see Figure 1.63). That's a multiple selection, and you'll see the status bar readout reflects this.

Figure 1.63
The three dynamics turn blue as they are selected.

You can now copy and paste these dynamics into the guitar part using any of the copy methods mentioned earlier—Copy and Paste or one of the Quick-Copy methods. Note that you'll need to select a tablature number on the second beat of the bar in the guitar part to ensure the dynamics are pasted at the right position if you use the Copy and Paste method.

At the moment, the drum part doesn't play in the first three bars. It enters with a fill in bar 4. Although this adds to the drama and textural interest of the piece, suppose the rest of the band is having a hard time staying in time without the drum. To rectify this, you can copy the drum pattern from bars 9 to 12 into bars 1 to 4; this is much faster than writing new material. This technique involves making a *passage* selection.

To select a whole passage rather than just a single note inside it, you click inside the staff, but *not* on a note, stem, beam, or any other musical marking. Simply click within the five lines of the staff itself. Try it at bar 9 in the drum part. If you've done it correctly, the whole of bar 9 in the drum part will be highlighted in blue (see Figure 1.64), and the status (in the status bar at the bottom of the window) will have changed to Edit Passage. Notice, too, that the notes at the top of the staff with their stems pointing up are blue, while the notes at the bottom of the staff with their stems pointing down are green. (You'll learn more about this later.)

Tip: If you're finding it difficult to keep track of bars when you copy from one part of the score to the other, try changing to Panorama view. This view shows the bar number above every bar, and prevents you from having to navigate page turns.

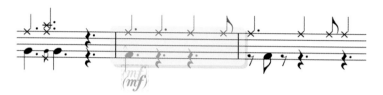

Figure 1.64
Selected bars are highlighted in blue, and the notes inside the bar change color.

Now that you've selected everything in bar 9, you could use the traditional Copy and Paste commands or Sibelius's Quick-Copy feature to copy that bar into bar 1 of the drum part. The only thing is, you want to copy the contents of bars 9, 10, 11, and 12 into bars 1 through 4, not just bar 9. Fortunately, you can extend your selection to bar 12. Simply hold down the Shift key and click anywhere inside bar 12 that isn't on a note or rest. All four bars, including the two in between bars 9 and 12, will be selected, as shown in Figure 1.65.

Figure 1.65
Shift-click bar 12 to extend the selection to include all four bars.

You can now copy all four bars using any of the aforementioned Copy methods:

1. With the passage selected, press **CTRL+C** (**COMMAND+C**) to copy it.

2. Click inside bar 1. (Be sure not to click the anacrusis/pickup bar, which appears right at the start.)

3. Press **CTRL+V** (**COMMAND+V**) to paste the selected passage into bars 1 through 4.

Alternatively, while the passage is selected, use Sibelius's Quick-Copy feature by using the middle mouse button (or both the right and left buttons together) to click the first bar of the drum part or holding down the Alt (Option) key as you click with the standard left button.

This writes over the fill that was already in bar 4, but don't worry about that. Play back your score, and you should find it sounds just fine.

On the subject of passage selections, you can make a selection of one part from start to finish by triple-clicking (three quick clicks with the left button of the mouse) in any bar (but not on a note) of any part. You'll have an opportunity to put this into practice soon.

Adding Instruments and Guitar Notation for Beginners

If you don't play guitar, you might have been wondering about the strange staff shown in Figure 1.66, with six wide-spaced lines, the word "TAB" instead of a traditional clef, numbers instead of noteheads, and rhythms written above. This is guitar tablature, a popular notation for guitarists who may not have learned to read traditional notation or who just need to be able to quickly read chords. Tablature is not just for crazy rock-and-roll guitars. In fact, it has been around since the first attempts at music notation, being used for lute notation often in early music.

Acoustic Guitar

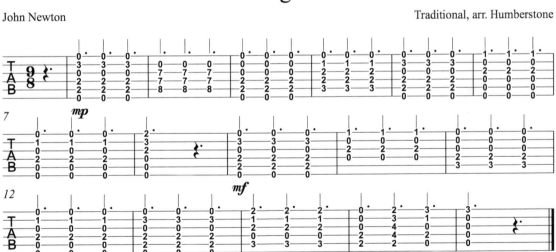

Figure 1.66
Guitar tablature.

Tablature is not the same as guitar chord symbols, which often appear above the guitar, vocal, or piano staff in pop music scores. (You'll learn how to input both types of notation from scratch in Lesson 3, and the easy way further on in this lesson.) In guitar tablature, the six lines of the staff relate to the six strings of the guitar. (Bass players also read tablature, although because most bass guitars have four strings, bass tablature has only four lines in the staff.) The numbers on each line tell the guitarist on which frets to place their fingers.

Although tablature can be set up to support other tuning, the bottom line typically corresponds to the lowest E string on a guitar in standard tuning, with the top line corresponding to the top string (also tuned to E in standard tuning). When an O appears on a line, it means to strum the string but leave it open; when nothing is written, the string should not be sounded at all. The rhythms written over the top of the staff show the guitarist what rhythm to use when playing the chords or notes. Note, however, that many tablature parts don't show rhythms at all, instead relying on the guitarist's memory of the piece to play it.

If you create a tablature part but find a guitarist who prefers traditional notation (or vice-versa), it's simple to switch in Sibelius.

To add a second guitar part in traditional notation:

1. Choose HOME > INSTRUMENTS > ADD OR REMOVE (the shortcut for which is I for instruments—another easy one to remember). The Add or Remove Instruments dialog box shown in Figure 1.67 appears.

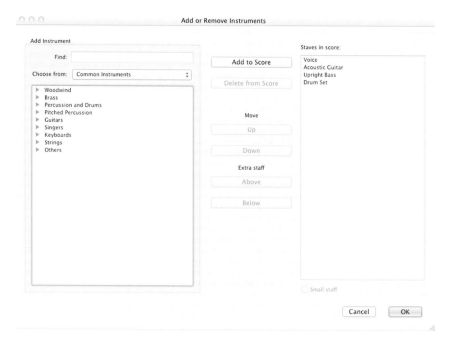

Figure 1.67
The Add or Remove Instruments dialog box.

2. If your version of this dialog box looks different from the one shown here, click the **CHOOSE FROM** drop-down list and choose **COMMON INSTRUMENTS**.

3. In the pane on the left, next to each family of instruments (e.g., Woodwind, Brass, Percussion and Drums, and so on), is a small triangle. Clicking this triangle expands or collapses the list of available instruments in that family. Click the triangle to the left of the Guitars family to expand the list of available guitars. You will notice a number of different kinds of guitars, each with [notation] or [tab] written after it, as shown in Figure 1.68.

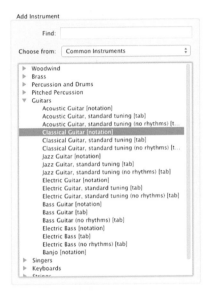

Figure 1.68
The list of available guitars.

4. Under the Guitars family, click **CLASSICAL GUITAR [NOTATION]**.

5. To add this notation to the score, click the **ADD TO SCORE** button. A Guitar entry appears at the top of the Staves in Score list on the right side of the Add or Remove Instruments dialog box.

Tip: Alternatively, you could simply double-click Classical Guitar [notation] in the list on the left to add it to the list on the right.

6. Although Sibelius usually gets score ordering correct, in a small combo like this one, it is standard to have the vocalist at the top. To reorder the score, moving the Classical Guitar [notation] entry farther down the list, first click the **GUITAR** entry in the **STAVES IN SCORE** list.

7. Click the **DOWN** button (see Figure 1.69) one time to move the Guitar
    entry below the Vocal entry.

Caution: Make sure you don't confuse the Down and Below buttons. The former is
           for changing the order of instruments in a score, while the latter actually
           adds a second staff for an instrument—something you'd only do if, for
           example, you had complex divisi violin 1 parts that couldn't be written
           on a single staff.

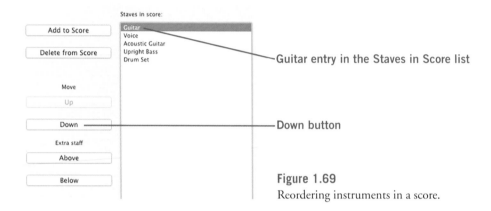

Guitar entry in the Staves in Score list

Down button

Figure 1.69
Reordering instruments in a score.

8. Click the **OK** button. The guitar part is added to the score.

Next, copy the whole guitar tablature part into the new guitar part:

1. To make a passage selection in the guitar tablature part, click the first bar
    and then Shift-click the final bar in that part. The entire part is selected, as
    shown in Figure 1.70.

Tip: As mentioned, an even quicker way to do it is to triple-click the staff. That
       is, move your mouse pointer to any bar in the guitar tablature part and, being
       careful to click an empty part of the staff, click rapidly three times. (You may
       need to try this a few times to get it right.)

2. Because the *whole* part is selected, you need to copy it into the anacrusis
    bar right at the start of the piece. Quick-Copy or use the Copy and Paste
    method to move the selected part from the guitar tablature staff to the
    new guitar staff. The music is pasted as traditional notation, even though
    you copied it from a tablature part. Sibelius makes the conversion for you,
    on the fly.

Figure 1.70
The entire guitar tablature part is selected.

If you're currently working in Panorama view, switch back to one of the page views now. You can toggle Panorama on and off with the shortcut Shift+P. In page view, it's likely that the new guitar part clashes somewhat with the original one. That's because although Sibelius left space between the staves, there are many notes on low ledger lines, and dynamics to squeeze in there too. In fact, Sibelius may have colored some dynamics in red to indicate that it can't find space for them, as shown in Figure 1.71. (This is called *magnetic layout*; you'll learn a lot more about it in the next lesson.)

Figure 1.71
With so many low notes on ledger lines, and dynamics to fit in too, some clashes are created.

The number-one rule of good music notation is to avoid clashes; clashes makes music very difficult to read. Fortunately, Sibelius can fix this problem for you: optimizing staff spacing.

To optimize staff spacing:

1. Press the **Esc key** twice to make sure nothing is selected.

2. Choose **Layout** > **Staff Spacing** > **Optimize** (see Figure 1.72).

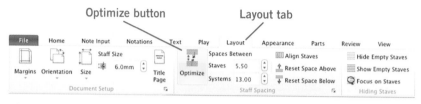

Figure 1.72
Optimize staff spacing.

3. A dialog box appears, asking whether you want the operation to apply to the whole score. Click **Yes**, and watch Sibelius fix all the spacing problems for you!

If you are working with a guitarist who reads neither tablature nor notation, the remaining option is chord symbols. Alone, chord symbols read simply as the names of chords—for instance, G7 for a G major 7 chord, or Dm for a D minor chord. Inversions (when the root note of the chord isn't in the bass) are usually shown with a slash—for example, Em/G means an E minor chord in first inversion, with G as the bottom-sounding note. An example of a series of chord symbols is shown in Figure 1.73. When guitarists read these symbols, they interpret the chord as they see fit. There are always a number of ways to play any chord; guitarists usually choose chord positions that are close, so they don't have to move their left hand on the fretboard too much.

Em⁷   F⁶⁽ᵇ⁵⁾   Cmaj⁷/E   C⁶   **Figure 1.73**
                                        Chord symbols, to be interpreted by a guitarist.

More detailed guitar chord symbols include chord diagrams. These show the position of the fingers plotted as dots on a grid, as in Figure 1.74. Chord diagrams are interpreted as follows:

■ The vertical lines indicate the six strings of the guitar, with the low E string on the left and the high E string on the right.

■ The horizontal lines indicate frets, with a thicker line at the top when the first fret is visible or a code such as 3fr when the diagram begins farther down the fretboard.

■ If an O appears above a vertical line representing a string, it means to sound that string but leave it open.

■ If an × is shown above a vertical line representing a string, it means the guitarist should not sound that string in the chord.

Figure 1.74
Guitar chord diagrams of Em7 chords in two different positions.

To add guitar chord diagrams to the new guitar part:

1. Press the ESC KEY twice to make sure nothing is selected.

2. Triple-click the new GUITAR STAFF (with traditional notation) to select it all.

3. Choose TEXT > CHORD SYMBOLS > ADD FROM NOTES, as shown in Figure 1.75. The Add Chord Symbols dialog box appears. This is a plug-in for Sibelius that analyzes the notes in each chord in the selection and writes the chord symbols (and diagrams, when the staff in question is a guitar staff) for you.

Figure 1.75
Clicking the Add from Notes button in the ribbon's Text tab.

4. Under Add Chord Symbols, click the EVERY X FROM THE START OF THE BAR option button to select it.

5. Click the EVERY X FROM THE START OF THE BAR drop-down list and choose DOTTED QUARTER NOTE (DOTTED CROTCHET), as shown in Figure 1.76. This is because, in the compound time of 9/8, each beat is a dotted quarter note, not a quarter note (which is the dialog box's default setting).

Every x from the Start of the Bar drop-down list

Add Chord Symbols		
This plug-in inserts chord symbols by analyzing notes across the staves you have selected.		

Add chord symbols:

○ at the start of every bar
● every [dotted quarter note (dotted crotchet) ⇕] . from the start of the bar

Notation options:

○ Insert chord symbols at every specified position
○ Only insert chord symbol if the root note has changed
● Only insert chord symbol if the chord name has changed

Put chord symbols on the following staff: [2 - Guitar ⇕]

☑ Only write chords with at least 3 distinct notes
☑ Use 'slash' inversion marks (e.g. G/D)

03.05.00   [Restore defaults]   [Cancel]   [OK]

Figure 1.76
The Add Chord Symbols dialog box.

6. Leave the other settings as is and click the **OK** button.

Note: The standard instruction to tell a guitarist who is reading a part with chord symbols only to *not* play is N.C., short for "no chords." (You could have worked that out, right?)

Sibelius adds the chord diagrams to the guitar part (pretty cool, right?), but again, there isn't space for them. To re-space the staves, make sure you have no selection and then choose Layout > Staff Spacing > Optimize. Your score should now look similar to the one shown in Figure 1.77. When you play it back, it might sound a bit funny with two guitars playing exactly the same thing, but don't worry about that.

Figure 1.77
The score with guitar notation part and chord symbol diagrams added.

Something that I say over and over again about Sibelius is, if you think to yourself, "There must be an easier way to do this," there probably is. Often, the "easier way" is found in the form of a plug-in. A plug-in is a small program that works within a larger program—in this case, Sibelius. Plug-ins are great at grouping tasks. You need to get from A to B. The customary steps to accomplish this may include two menu pulls and four keystrokes. A properly designed plug-in can group these tasks so all you need to do is run the plug-in and the same A-to-B procedure is done in one keystroke or menu pull.

There are 10 or 12 plug-ins I use every day and they really speed up my workflow. There are other plug-ins that I don't use for every project but when I do need them they save a lot of time. Many plug-ins are included with Sibelius when it installs. Many more are available for download (at no charge) from the Sibelius Web site on the Extra Plug-ins for Sibelius page. And still more are available for a reasonable charge from independent programmers. One of my favorites is The Music Transcriber, by Roman Milano Dunn (www.themusictranscriber.com/). He's got some very useful plug-ins and bundles of plug-ins.

—John Hinchey, composer, arranger, and notation software expert

On the Web

Expert John Hinchey writes regular tutorials for Sibelius at his Web sites, www.johnhinchey.com and www.hincheymusic.com.

Repeating

When music is made of repeated patterns (*ostinati*), Sibelius can help you repeat the material in your score very quickly. For instance, if the drum pattern is identical in each bar, you could repeat the pattern in the first bar for each subsequent bar.

To repeat a pattern:

1. Select the first bar in the drum part. It is highlighted in blue.

2. Press the **R** KEY (for repeat) three times. Alternatively, choose **NOTE INPUT** > **NOTE INPUT** > **REPEAT**, as shown in Figure 1.78. The drum part is repeated in the second, third, and fourth bars.

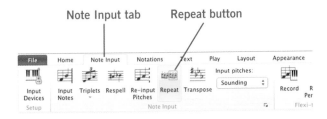

Figure 1.78
Repeating a selection.

Although you can't repeat selections that aren't notes—for example, you can't select text and repeat it—you can repeat as short (even just one note) or as long a selection as you like. You could even repeat this whole song for a second verse.

To repeat the whole song for a second verse:

1. Click the first note of the anacrusis bar in the vocal part (over the letter A in the word "Amazing"). It becomes blue, indicating it has been selected.

2. Zoom out, press **CTRL+END** (**COMMAND+END**), or switch to Panorama view to bring the last bar of the piece into view.

3. Shift-click the last note in the drum part. You choose the last *note* of the drum part, not the rest at the end of the bar, because when you repeat it, the anacrusis will fill up the last beat of the bar. (If you get this wrong, just undo the operation and try again.) Figure 1.79 shows what this selection should look like.

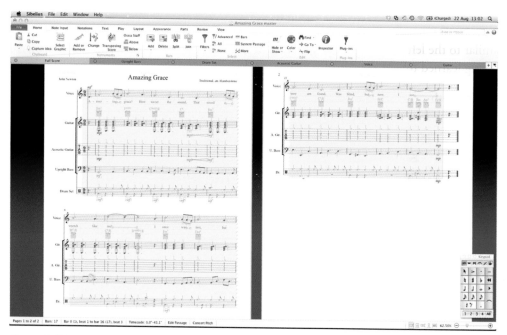

Figure 1.79
Selecting all of the song, but not the final rest, for repeating.

4. Press **R** to repeat the whole song.

5. The staff spacing is most likely too close for the chord symbols, lyrics, and notes on ledger lines. To fix this, make sure you have no selection, then choose **LAYOUT** > **STAFF SPACING** > **OPTIMIZE**.

If you compose minimalist music, or write ostinato-based educational music in the style of Carl Orff's famous *Schulwerk*, you might use the Repeat feature quite a lot!

Changing Instruments

Suppose your solo singer can play another instrument and wants to perform an instrumental solo in the second verse. In Sibelius, you can use the Instrument Change feature to write for more than one instrument on the same staff. (Obviously, the practical use for this will usually be common orchestral doubling combinations, such a flute and piccolo or clarinet in A and clarinet in B flat.)

To use Instrument Change:

1. Press **ESC** twice to make sure nothing is selected.

2. Move the score so you can see the start of the second verse in the vocal part (the second time it sings "Amazing").

3. Choose **HOME** > **INSTRUMENTS** > **CHANGE**, as shown in Figure 1.80. The Instrument Change dialog box opens (see Figure 1.81). Notice that it is similar to the left half of the Add or Remove Instruments dialog box; having learned to use that dialog box, you'll find this one intuitive to use.

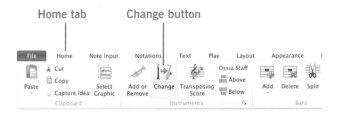

Figure 1.80
Launch the Instrument Change dialog box.

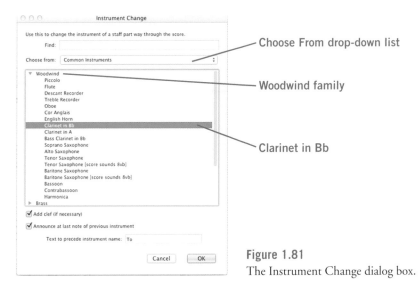

Figure 1.81
The Instrument Change dialog box.

4. If your version of this dialog box looks different from the one shown here, click the **Choose From** drop-down list and choose **Common Instruments**.

5. Click the triangle to the left of the **Woodwind** entry to expand the list of available woodwinds.

6. Under the **Woodwind** entry, click **Clarinet in B**♭.

7. Click the **OK** button. The mouse pointer becomes blue.

Note: If you had selected an item in your score before attempting to change the instrument or add something to the score (such as a time signature or text style), that item would have appeared next to the selection. Because you had nothing selected in this case, the mouse pointer turns blue to let you know it is "loaded" with the instrument change or the object you've chosen to add; next time you click, it will be placed in the score. If you ever notice that your mouse pointer is blue, or "loaded," but you're not sure why, you can cancel the function by pressing Esc before you click. Alternatively, click to find out what happens, and undo the operation if it is not what you were hoping for!

8. To make a change from singing to clarinet playing for the vocalist, click just to the left of the first note (corresponding to the "A" of "Amazing"). The result is the addition of text to the score, telling the vocalist to switch to the clarinet (see Figure 1.82).

Figure 1.82
The instrument change from voice to clarinet, shown in the clarinet part.

Sibelius is actually doing a lot more here than adding some text to tell the player to play clarinet. If you play the score back from just before the change (remember, you can click a note and play from that point with the shortcut P, for Play from Selection), you will notice that the sound has changed to a clarinet, too.

More notably, if you view the score in transposing pitch (by default, Sibelius begins all new scores in concert pitch unless they are for a band) you will notice that the new clarinet section correctly transposes up a tone. This score should already be shown in transposing pitch, but if it isn't you can change to a transposing score by choosing Home > Instruments > Transposing Score, as shown in Figure 1.83. A key signature with two sharps (because the piece is modal, it won't be suggested that it's D major or B minor) appears at the new clarinet section, and all music from that point is transposed up a tone.

Home tab   Transposing Score button

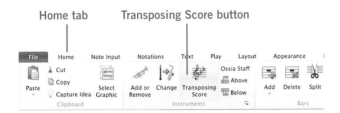

Figure 1.83
The Transposing Score button.

Transposing

You don't need to have a detailed understanding of what a transposing score is to complete the lessons in this book. You should, however, understand the two uses of the word *transpose* within different contexts and have a basic grasp of what a transposing instrument is.

First, there is a difference between a transposing instrument or score and the act of transposing itself. Any music in Sibelius can be transposed—that is, each pitch can be moved up or down by the same interval. You might do this to create a repeat of a section in a different key (which you'll try in the next section) or to develop an idea by beginning it on a different pitch.

A transposing instrument, on the other hand, must have its part transposed into a key that's different from the one the piece is in. The reason for this is physical—the timbre of an instrument is affected by its size and shape. As clarinets, trumpets, saxophones, and other transposing instruments evolved, their shape naturally fitted fundamental notes in one key.

Clarinets in B flat could theoretically read untransposed parts, but the natural tuning of their instrument leans toward playing music in flat keys—or at least keys with not too many sharps. Therefore, their music is written a tone higher, making it more likely to feature not too many sharps and not too many flats. As a composer or an arranger, you will need to keep this in mind if you write in concert pitch E major, because the four sharps that your string players will enjoy will result in the key of F sharp major (six sharps) for your poor clarinetist. Even those problems have solutions, though: Clarinets come in different shapes and sizes (each with its own particular timbre), so if you need to write in E major, you could consider writing for the second most popular clarinet which is in A. It would then read its part for an E major concert pitch score in G major (one sharp). Similarly, there are trumpets in different keys (or sometimes trumpets that can attach different *crooks*—different-sized tubing extensions —to change the key of the instrument).

In contrast to a transposing instrument, a transposing *score* is simply a score that shows all transposing instruments in the keys they're reading rather than the key the piece is actually in. Most classical and romantic scores are published as transposing scores, but contemporary scores are usually published in concert pitch. This is because contemporary scores are often atonal (without key or tonal centre) or change tonality extremely often; therefore, it's easier to summarize the harmony without what could be confusing key signatures or accidentals caused by transposing parts.

It doesn't make much sense for the clarinet part to have lyrics; these should be deleted. You could do this one by one, clicking each word or syllable and pressing Delete or Backspace, but there is a much quicker way to do it: by filtering the lyrics.

To filter the lyrics:

1. Select the first note of the second verse in the clarinet part.

2. Jump to the end of the score and Shift-click anywhere in the last bar in the vocal and clarinet part. This creates a passage selection for the second verse.

3. To filter out the lyrics within your passage selection, choose **HOME** > **SELECT** > **FILTERS** > **LYRICS**, as shown in Figure 1.84. Every lyric becomes blue, to show it's selected. (This selection replaces the passage selection.)

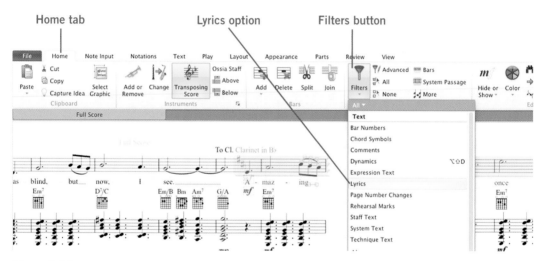

Figure 1.84
Filtering lyrics from a selection.

4. Press **DELETE** or **BACKSPACE** to delete the selected lyrics from your score.

The last bit of fun you can have is creating some melodic harmony:

1. Make a passage selection of the clarinet part in bars 17 and 18. (You can do it without explicit direction this time!) Both bars are highlighted blue.

2. To add a parallel harmony line a 6th below the melody, choose **NOTE INPUT** > **INTERVALS** > **BELOW** > **6TH**, as shown in Figure 1.85. (You don't specify major or minor because the note will be added diatonically within the key.) The notes are added below as specified.

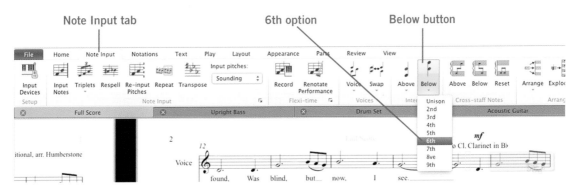

Figure 1.85
Adding an interval below the selection.

Your clarinet part should look the same as Figure 1.86, which shows a transposing score. Click any note before the instrument change and press P for Play from Selection to hear the change and the new harmony line. (Obviously, two clarinetists will be required; asking your vocalist to play a clarinet solo is probably already making enough demands on her without also asking her to work out some impossible multiphonics.)

Note: The mention of multiphonics here is flippant. *Multiphonics* are the only way some instruments (mostly woodwind or brass, such as the flute, clarinet, or trumpet) can play more than one note at once. They usually involve strange fingering combinations, embouchure changes, or even singing through the instrument.

Clarinet in B♭

Figure 1.86
The clarinet part with intervals added a 6th below to create harmony.

You can add more intervals above or below the melody line by using Note Input > Intervals > Above and Note Input > Intervals > Below, respectively. (In Lesson 2 you'll learn to do it an even quicker way.) In the example you just completed, parallel 6ths don't sound very good into bar 19, so you'll have to work out what intervals do if you'd like to continue adding harmony. (Hint: Try a 3rd below next.) Notes can be added above or below any selection, whether you select one note at a time or several instruments at once. For instance, if you select the clarinet part, extend your selection to the guitar part below by Shift-clicking it; then choose Note Input > Intervals > Above > 6th to add a note a 6th above the highest note in *both* staves. (In this case pointless, but useful to know nonetheless.)

Editing Text

Editing existing text is the final and easiest thing you'll have to do in this section. (You'll learn how to create many different types of text in the next lesson.)

Editing text goes like this:

1. Double-click any text item. A cursor starts flashing at the end of the text.

2. Edit the text just as you would in a word processor—select it, delete it, copy and paste, add more text by typing, and so on.

3. When you're finished, press **Esc** once to stop editing the text, and a second time to deselect the text.

Note: While the preceding is true, some kinds of text behave differently than others. For example, if you double-click a lyric to edit it, pressing the space bar or hyphen key will advance to the next note. (This makes it much faster to add lyrics.) Similarly, if you double-click a chord to edit it, pressing the space bar will move you onto the next beat of the bar. You'll learn much more about using text in the next three lessons.

Try this now: Double-click the name of the arranger on page 1 of the score. You've done most of the hard work now, so change the name to your own, then press Esc. Try it on a dynamic too. If you're finding those two guitars too loud together, double-click their *mf* dynamics and change them to *mp*, or even *p*. Of course, you'll hear the change in Sibelius's playback, too.

If you need to change the text even further—for instance, to make it bigger or change the font—you can. Choose Text > Format and consider the controls in this group. If you don't have any text selected, all the Format group controls will be grayed out. As soon as you click a piece of text, they become available, as shown in Figure 1.87.

Figure 1.87
The Format group in the ribbon's Text tab.

You don't actually need to double-click text to make these kind of changes. If you're editing text already, press Esc twice to clear it; then click once on the title of the piece ("Amazing Grace"). Try clicking the Size up arrow to make the text bigger. Then try clicking the Font drop-down list and choose another font; the font changes instantly. Note, too, that the standard text-editing shortcuts Ctrl+I (Command+I), Ctrl+B (Command+B), and Ctrl+U (Command+U) work in Sibelius for italic, bold, and underline, respectively.

There is much more to learn about editing text, but it requires more understanding of how Sibelius works. You'll come to that in Lesson 2.

Exploring the Ideas Panel

 As usual, if you're studying this course alone, begin this section by watching the video **1.5 Exploring the Ideas Panel** first.

It's time to finish Lesson 1 with a bit of fun. If you've ever used a program like Acid or GarageBand, you know what a loop browser is. In one way, the Ideas panel (see Figure 1.88) is like a loops browser for Sibelius. You can also use the Ideas panel to help in the composition process as a place to store your ideas. You'll use it like that in Lesson 3.

Tip: If you're dipping in and out of this book and want to begin this lesson from this point, you can open a catch-up file from the Core Resources > Lesson 1 folder you copied from your CD called **Amazing2.sib**.

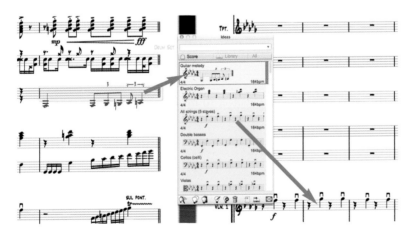

Figure 1.88
The Ideas panel in action.

Note: If you're a schoolteacher, you'll have lots of fun introducing your students to notation through the hundreds of loops in popular music styles provided in the Ideas panel. These can be copied and pasted together to get you started on a new composition.

In this score, to keep everything completely simple, there are only two ideas in the Ideas panel. Both have been created especially to help you complete this lesson. To open the Ideas panel, choose View > Panels > Ideas, as shown in Figure 1.89.

Figure 1.89

Opening the Ideas panel.

By default, the Ideas panel opens as a docked panel on the left of the window. If you'd prefer it to be floating over another part of the score, you can simply drag it away from its position. This is very useful if you're lucky enough to work on dual displays, so you can keep it completely out of the way of the score. When it is un-docked, you can resize it by dragging its top or bottom edge up or down (its width is fixed), as shown in Figure 1.90. To dock it again, just drag it near the left or right edge of the Sibelius window.

Figure 1.90

The Ideas panel.

As mentioned, the Ideas panel should currently contain just two ideas. The first is a part ideal for a rock organ or synthesizer.

Start by adding a rock organ to the score:

1. Press **I** to open the Add or Remove Instruments dialog box.

2. The instrument you want to add—a rock organ—will not appear in the Keyboards list if the Choose From drop-down list is set to Common Instruments. A quick way to locate the rock organ is to type **ROCK ORGAN** in the **FIND** field and press **ENTER** (**RETURN**). Sibelius locates and selects the rock organ for you. (Had you done this manually, you would have had to click the **CHOOSE FROM** drop-down menu, choose **ALL INSTRUMENTS**, expand the **KEYBOARDS** family, and choose **ROCK ORGAN**, as shown in Figure 1.91.)

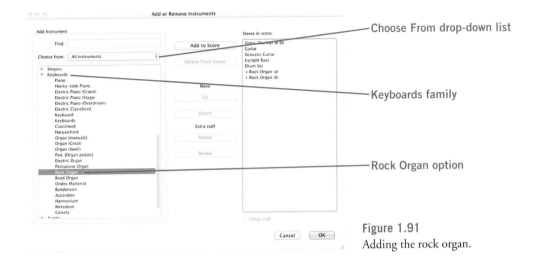

Figure 1.91
Adding the rock organ.

3. With the **Rock Organ** entry still selected in the list on the left, click the **Add to Score** button. An entry for the rock organ appears on the right.

4. Click the **OK** button.

After you've added the instrument for the idea, getting the idea from the Ideas panel to the score couldn't be easier. There are a number of ways to do it. The quickest is to select the bar in which you'd like to use the idea and then, with the idea selected in the Ideas panel, click the Paste button at the bottom of the panel, as shown in Figure 1.92.

In this example, select the right hand of the organ part in bar 17; then make sure the Organ Amazing Grace idea is selected and click the Paste button in the Ideas panel. You don't need to extend the selection to the left hand; Sibelius automatically includes the whole idea in subsequent staves. If there isn't room for all of the music from the idea, just optimize the staff spacing. Play back the score to see if you approve. If you want to change the balance, simply edit the dynamics.

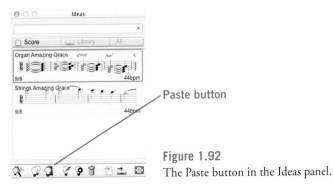

Figure 1.92
The Paste button in the Ideas panel.

Earlier in this lesson, there was some discussion about transposing a section into a new key. To explore another feature of the Ideas panel, create a cheesy modulation up a semitone for the second verse.

To create a modulation up a semitone:

1. Make a passage selection of the entire second verse by selecting the first note of the second verse in the clarinet part in bar 16 and Shift-clicking the last (whole) bar in the drum part.

2. So that you can transpose the key (as well as the notes), you must convert this passage selection into a system passage. To do so, choose **HOME** > **SELECT** > **SYSTEM PASSAGE**, as shown in Figure 1.93. The passage selection changes from blue to purple (see Figure 1.94), indicating that the whole system is selected. (This allows the key to be transposed.)

Figure 1.93
The System Passage button.

Figure 1.94
The purple highlight indicates that the entire system is selected.

3. To transpose the system selection, choose **NOTE INPUT > NOTE INPUT > TRANSPOSE**, as shown in Figure 1.95. The Transpose dialog box appears.

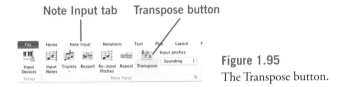

Note Input tab   Transpose button

Figure 1.95
The Transpose button.

4. In the Transpose By section, click the **INTERVAL** option button to select it.

5. In the Transpose by Interval section, click the **UP** option button to select it.

6. Click the first drop-down list in the Transpose by Interval section and choose **MINOR/DIMINISHED**.

7. Click the second drop-down list in the Transpose by Interval section and choose **2ND**. (A minor second, of course, is the same as a semitone.)

8. Leave the **TRANSPOSE KEY SIGNATURES** check box selected.

9. Click the **CHANGE KEY AT START** check box to select it.

10. Click the **USE DOUBLE SHARPS/FLATS** check box to deselect it; in this case, that isn't necessary. Figure 1.96 shows the appropriate settings.

11. Click the **OK** button.

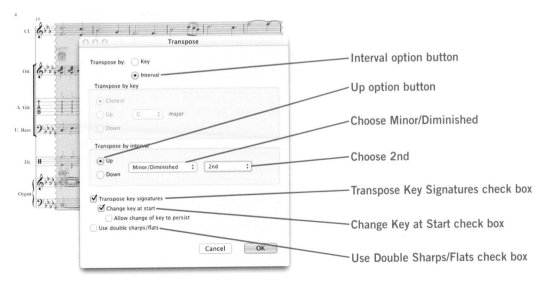

Interval option button

Up option button

Choose Minor/Diminished

Choose 2nd

Transpose Key Signatures check box

Change Key at Start check box

Use Double Sharps/Flats check box

Figure 1.96
The Transpose dialog box, with the correct settings shown.

As shown in Figure 1.97, five flats will be added to the score (apart from in the clarinet part, which now shows three flats if you're viewing a transposing score; you can check in the status bar if you're not sure). Play back from a few bars before the modulation to hear the effect of what you've done.

Figure 1.97
Instruments in the modulated key signature with a transposing score.

Adding the modulation not only created a cheesy "lifting" effect in the music (because it has modulated chromatically upward), it also enables you to see another feature of the Ideas panel in play as we add the second idea, which is called *Strings Amazing Grace.*

To add the second idea:

1. First, you need to add staves for the strings idea. These will be where the string parts will be added. To begin, press **I** to open the Add or Remove Instruments dialog box.

2. Click the **Choose From** drop-down list and choose **Common Instruments**.

3. Click the **Strings** triangle to expand the Strings family.

4. While holding down the **CTRL (COMMAND) KEY,** click the **VIOLIN 1,**
   VIOLIN 2, VIOLA, VIOLONCELLO, and **DOUBLE BASS** entries to select them
   (see Figure 1.98).

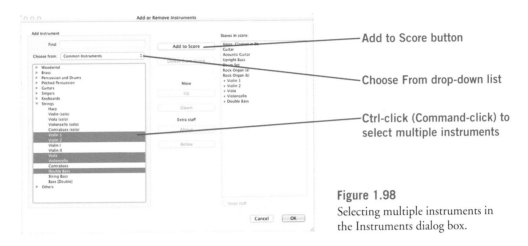

Figure 1.98
Selecting multiple instruments in
the Instruments dialog box.

Note: You may be wondering whether a violoncello is similar to a cello. In fact,
it's the same instrument, it's just that the abbreviation is typically used.
If you think having its full name on the first page of your score and parts
might confuse your players, you can edit the instrument name text just as
you edited other text in your score in the last section—double-click it and
off you go. The same can be said for the difference between double bass
and contrabass; it's the same instrument with a different name. For that
matter, the upright bass in this score is also a double bass, but in the jazz
and popular genres it implies that it will be played *pizzicato* (plucked),
whether indicated or not.

5. Click the **ADD TO SCORE** button to, well, add them to the score.

6. Click the **OK** button. A string section appears in your score.

7. With the string section added, click and hold on the **STRINGS AMAZING**
   GRACE idea in the Ideas panel.

Note: If you're using Sibelius 7 Sounds, there will be a short delay while Sibelius
loads the samples for these string sounds for the first time. Continue to hold
the mouse button down; once the sounds have loaded, Sibelius will give
you a preview of the string arrangement. With a shorter idea, such as a
two-bar drum pattern or guitar riff, Sibelius will noticeably repeat (or *loop*)
ideas when you preview them. When the strings idea begins to play, just
hold the pitch in your head. Some clever things are about to happen!

8. Select bar 17 in the violin 1 part.

9. With the strings idea still selected, click the **PASTE** button in the Ideas panel. The idea is pasted into all five string staves and remains selected (with a blue highlight).

10. Rather than pressing Esc to deselect, press **P** to play from the beginning of the selection.

You should notice three things:

- Most notably, when you pasted the idea from the Ideas panel into the score, Sibelius took note of the fact that you were pasting it after the modulation, and therefore transposed it to fit the new key (see Figure 1.99).

Figure 1.99
The strings idea, transposed to fit the prevailing key.

- When playback began, you only heard the strings playing. In later lessons, you will learn about using the mixer to mute or solo parts, but this can also be done in the score. If you have a passage selected when you begin to play back, Sibelius plays only the instruments highlighted in the passage selection.

- Sibelius has done a spot of arranging. If you compare the idea in the Ideas panel with the playback in the score, you'll notice the violins playing screechingly high, the cellos and violas in mid-range (from about C3 to G4), and the bass on the bottom.

Note: To enable you to quickly refer to pitches in their exact octave, they are numbered according to convention in this book. If you haven't used octave numbers before, doing so is simple—as long as you remember that middle C on a piano is C4. Octave numbers change at each C and count for the next 12 semitones including that C. So, for example, if middle C is C4, then the B below it is B3, and the B above it is B4. The C above it is C5, and the C below it is C3.

By default, when ideas are pasted into the score, Sibelius transposes them by an octave or two so that the majority of the notes fit within the comfortable range of the instrument in question. This is very sensible, because a melodic line originally created in a trombone part would otherwise show many ledger lines if pasted into a piccolo part! In this case, apart from the fact that Sibelius's transposition has taken a few notes out of the viola range (they're the red ones), the strings parts still sound rather lovely when played back. However, if you press Esc to cancel the passage selection and play back from the same entry, the texture will sound stodgy and unclear because there are too many parts playing in the same range as the melody. To rectify this, use the Undo feature repeatedly until the idea has been removed from the score and bar 17 is again selected in the violin 1 part.

To force Sibelius to paste the ideas into the score at their original pitch:

1. Choose **FILE** > **PREFERENCES**. The Preferences dialog box appears.

2. Click the **IDEAS** entry in the list on the left side of the Preferences dialog box.

3. Click the **TRANSPOSE BY OCTAVES TO FIT WITHIN INSTRUMENT RANGE** check box to deselect it, as shown in Figure 1.100.

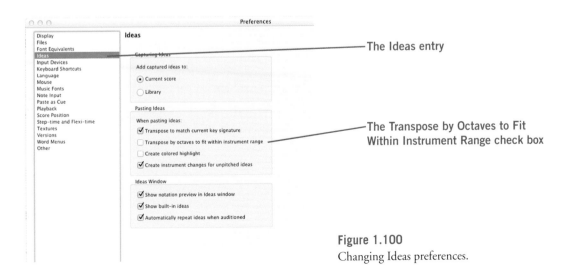

Figure 1.100
Changing Ideas preferences.

4. Click the **OK** button.

5. Assuming the strings idea is also still selected, click the **PASTE** button in the Ideas panel. This time, you will notice even more notes out of range in the lower parts; that's simply because Sibelius has made the transposition down a major 7th instead of up a minor 2nd (which results in the same key).

6. While the passage selection remains, press **CTRL+UP ARROW** (**COMMAND+UP ARROW**) to shift all the notes up an octave.

7. Press **ESC** to cancel the selection. Then play back all instruments. You should find the string balance much better with the ensemble.

I'm surprised at how many Sibelius users think of the Ideas feature as nothing more than a Musical Clip Art feature—fun to play with, but not a tool for serious professional use. You might be surprised to learn that the Sibelius Ideas feature is a powerful scratchpad that has the power to transform the way you work. For example, you can use the Ideas panel for any musical motif. I find it to be an indispensable tool for drum set patterns, which can be time-consuming to enter with their different noteheads and stems up/stems down multi-voice layout. You can also modify an existing pattern or motif. Once in the score, you can modify the pasted music however you'd like without changing the original idea. It's usually worth a quick search to see if anything is close to what you need; in many cases it can be faster than creating something similar from scratch.

Create a new idea by selecting one or more bars of music in your score and pressing Shift+I. Your captured idea can be saved to the library or to the current score for later retrieval. Once it's saved, you can use Edit Info at the bottom of the panel to name it, create tags (keywords) to help you find it quickly, and even color-code it. You can also edit the original idea content by double-clicking the idea in the panel's list to open the Idea Editor if you decide the original idea needs a tweak. While the most obvious elements to copy and save for later recall are notes and rests, articulations, phrasing, and dynamics will also be copied if included. Basically, whatever you have in the staff will be copied as part of the idea. But this is really just scratching the surface!

—**Robert Puff, musician, arranger, and notation expert**

On the Web Robert regularly publishes tutorials, ideas, and other interesting facts about working with Sibelius on his Web sites, www.rpmseattle.com/of_note and www.musicprep.com/sibelius.

It's time to put some finishing touches on the score and to complete the first lesson. You will do two more things to further improve playback.

First, if you look at the start of some of the strings parts, you will notice an unnecessary *arco* marking. (It's unnecessary because string players assume they're going to play *arco*, or *bowed*, unless they're told otherwise.) Edit the word *arco* so that it instead says *pizz.* Then make a passage selection of these three instruments by selecting bar 17 in the viola part, and Shift-clicking the double bass below. When you play these three lines back, Sibelius will change the sound to *pizz.* for you.

The final addition should be a *molto rit.* at the very end for a grand finish:

1. Make a passage selection in the clarinet for the last two bars.

2. Choose **NOTATIONS > LINES > MORE**, as shown in Figure 1.101. (The More button is at the bottom of the three arrow buttons on the right of the Lines group.) The Lines gallery opens.

Notations tab   More button

Figure 1.101
The Lines group.

3. In the Lines gallery, click **MOLTO RIT.** (you may need to scroll down), as shown in Figure 1.102. Because the last two bars were selected, the *molto rit.* appears there.

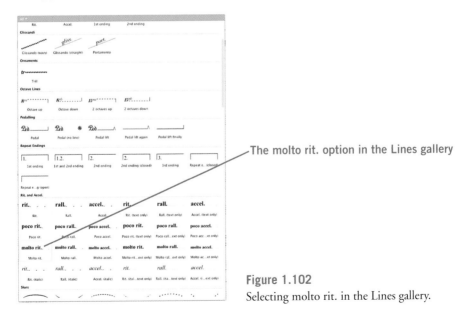

—The molto rit. option in the Lines gallery

Figure 1.102
Selecting molto rit. in the Lines gallery.

Play back your score and enjoy your hard work!

Review/Discussion Questions

1. What keys can be used to navigate the score?

2. Apart from dragging the page, how can you use the mouse to navigate the score?

    a. Click the arrow buttons.

    b. Use the Navigator or mouse wheel.

    c. Triple-click a staff.

3. True or false: The Zoom slider is found in the bottom-left corner of the main Sibelius window.

4. How do you edit text on a score?

    a. In the Ribbon, go to Text.

    b. Select the text, then press Ctrl+T (Command+T).

    c. Double-click the text.

5. True or false: The green playback line shows your current selection in the score.

6. What are the keyboard shortcuts for zooming in and out?

7. How do you make a passage selection?

8. How do you paste an idea from the Ideas panel into your score?

    a. Click Copy in the Ideas panel, then double-click your score.

    b. Click your score, then click Paste in the Ideas panel.

    c. Quick-Copy with the middle button of your mouse.

9. Name two ways to change the pitch of a note.

10. True or false: The shortcut to move notes up or down an octave at a time is Ctrl+Up Arrow (Command+Up Arrow) or Ctrl+Down Arrow (Command+Down Arrow).

Lesson 1 Keyboard Shortcuts

Shortcut	Function
Esc	Cancel selection or mode
Ctrl+Alt+N (Windows)/ Command+Option+N (Mac)	Toggle the Navigator panel on and off
Home	Move the view of your score toward the first page
End	Move the view of your score toward the last page
Ctrl+Home (Windows)/ Command+Home (Mac)	View the first page of your score
Ctrl+End (Windows)/Command+End (Mac)	View the last page of your score
Page Up	Move the view of your score toward the top of the page
Page Down	Move the view of your score toward the bottom of the page
Ctrl+= (Windows)/Command+= (Mac)	Zoom in
Ctrl+− (Windows)/Command+− (Mac)	Zoom out
T	Time Signature
K	Key Signature
Alt (Windows)/Command (Mac)	When nothing is selected, invoke key tips (a series of shortcuts for getting around the ribbon)
Space bar	Start playback from the green playback line or stop play. Only works when there is no selection.
P	Play back from the selection (e.g., from a selected note, barline, or dynamic)
Esc	Stop playback or recording
[	Rewind
]	Fast forward
Ctrl+[(Windows)/Command+[(Mac)	Move playback line to start
Ctrl+] (Windows)/Command+] (Mac)	Move playback line to end
Ctrl+Shift+F (Windows)/ Command+Shift+F (Mac)	Record (Flexi-time Input)
Up Arrow (when note selected)	Move pitch of note up diatonically
Down Arrow (when note selected)	Move pitch of note down diatonically
Ctrl+Up Arrow (when note selected)	Move pitch of note up one octave

Lesson 1 Keyboard Shortcuts

Shortcut	Function
Ctrl+Down Arrow (when note selected)	Move pitch of note down one octave
Ctrl+Z (Windows)/Command+Z (Mac)	Undo
Ctrl+Y (Windows)/Command+Y (Mac)	Redo
Ctrl+Shift+Z (Windows)/ Command+Shift+Z (Mac)	Undo History
Ctrl+C (Windows)/Command+C (Mac)	Copy
Ctrl+V (Windows)/Command+V (Mac)	Paste
Alt-click (Windows)/ Option-click (Mac)	Quick-Copy the selection
Shift+Alt-click (Windows)/ Shift+Option-click (Mac)	Quick-Copy the selection to its closest default position
Shift+P	Toggle Panorama view on and off
Ctrl+I (Windows)/Command+I (Mac)	Italic text (when text is being edited)
Ctrl+B (Windows)/Command+B (Mac)	Bold text (when text is being edited)
Ctrl+U (Windows)/Command+U (Mac)	Underlined text (when text is being edited)

Rearranging a Score

With a pending deadline in your role as arranger for any ensemble you can imagine, how can you quickly rearrange a score and make it your own using the tools that you learned during the "Amazing Grace" lesson?

Media Used: Scarborough.sib (located in the Lesson 1 folder under Core Resources)

Duration: Approximately 30 minutes

GOALS

- Rearrange a file used in the Sibelius 7 tutorials: Scarborough Fair

Ideas to Get You Started

Here are a few ideas to get you started:

- You can add in new instruments or delete existing ones with the Add or Remove Instruments dialog box.

- You can copy and paste music between different instruments or sections.

- You can change the instrument playing each part with the Change Instruments button.

- There are over a thousand ideas available in the Ideas panel; perhaps you can find a different drum beat.

- You can make changes to dynamics or tempo to change the mood of the piece.

Beethoven's 3rd String Quartet, First Movement, Opus 18, Number 3

To complete this lesson, you're going to copy in the first part of the first movement of Beethoven's 3rd string quartet, first movement, opus 18, number 3. If you're studying this course with a teacher, you'll be required to submit the score after it's complete to show that you've learned each of the skills.

Media Used: Beethoven Complete.pdf, Beethoven Complete.sib, Beethoven1.sib, Beethoven2.sib, Beethoven3.sib, Beethoven4.sib, Beethoven5.sib, Beethoven6.sib, Beethoven7.sib

Duration: Between three and six hours

GOALS

- Learn how to set up a score from scratch
- Discover how to input notes with the four main input methods available in Sibelius
- Learn how to add dynamics, articulation marks, and phrasing
- Learn how to produce parts for players
- Find out how to share parts online as PDF files
- Connect and use a MIDI keyboard if you have one
- Learn many shortcuts used in Sibelius for the quickest results

Printing Out the Score

Before you begin, you need a printout of the score to copy. It is included in Appendix B, "Scores Required in this Course." You'll also find it on the CD as a Sibelius file called Beethoven Complete.sib (no, you can't just submit this file to complete the course!) and as a PDF file called Beethoven Complete.pdf in case the computer from which you are printing doesn't have Sibelius installed. To print from Sibelius, choose File > Print, check that your printer is selected, and click the big Print button.

Creating and Exploring a New Score

If you are studying this book without a teacher, watch the video **2.1 Creating and Exploring a New Score** before you read this section. See the section "Accessing the Video Files" in this book's introduction for help finding and viewing the video content.

If you have any open scores in Sibelius, close them now. By default, the Quick Start dialog box will appear, as described in the preceding lesson, in the section "Moving Around the Score." As you learned, the Quick Start dialog box has a number of functions. For example, if you click the Recent tab, you will see the Amazing Grace file you worked on in Lesson 1, "Amazing Grace." If you were to double-click this file, it would open. If you weren't sure whether it was exactly the right file, you could zoom in on it using the Zoom slider at the bottom of the Quick Start dialog box to see it in greater detail. If you click the Amazing Grace file, you'll also see information about the file, including its length in pages and duration (time) and the folder in which the file has been saved, as shown in Figure 2.1. The latter is especially useful if you aren't great about managing your files. (By default, all Sibelius files are saved in the Scores folder in your Documents folder, but it's possible to save them anywhere on your hard drive or on removable media such as USB drives.)

Figure 2.1
The Quick Start dialog box with the Recent tab selected, zoomed in on the completed "Amazing Grace" score from Lesson 1.

Creating a New Score from the Quick Start Dialog Box

In this section, you'll create the Beethoven score from scratch.

To create a new score:

1. Click the **NEW SCORE** tab at the top of the Quick Start dialog box. If the Zoom slider is still all the way to the right, drag the **ZOOM** slider back toward the left to zoom out a little so you can have a good look at the available manuscript papers (see Figure 2.2).

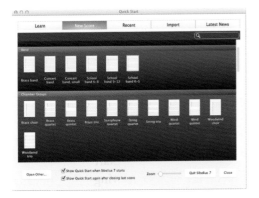

Figure 2.2
The Quick Start dialog box with the New Score tab selected, zoomed out to display many available manuscript papers.

On Sibelius Terminology

The original designers of Sibelius, Ben and Jonathan Finn, are on record saying that when they designed the first version of the software, they didn't examine any other notation software to see how it worked. Instead, they tried to re-create the experience of writing music on manuscript paper as authentically as possible.

The term *manuscript paper* is a good example of how the Finn brothers have tried to use musical terminology rather than computer terminology whenever possible. (In fact, at one time they trademarked the term *virtual manuscript paper.*) In most programs, these would be called *templates*, but in a musical context, it makes much more sense to call them manuscript papers because they are like empty, ready-ruled manuscript, to be written on. Other examples of this abound in Sibelius. For example, what sequencers and other notation programs call *quantize*, Sibelius calls *adjust rhythms* or *renotate performance* (these are subtly different features).

2. Scroll through the manuscript papers. As you do, you'll see that they are grouped by the kinds of ensembles for which they are written—for example, Band, Orchestra, and Jazz. You can expand or collapse these groups by clicking the band that contains their name. For information on using manuscript papers created for worksheets, see Lesson 4, "Worksheets."

3. Although there is a String Quartet option under Chamber Groups, you aren't going to use it just now. Instead, scroll back to the top of the list and click the **BLANK** manuscript paper under **NO CATEGORY**. The New Score wizard will start (see Figure 2.3).

Caution: It's important to single-click rather than double-click the Blank manuscript paper. Otherwise, the New Score wizard won't start; instead, you'll find yourself in Sibelius with an empty score.

Figure 2.3
The New Score wizard.

In the new Quick Start dialog box in Sibelius 7, you will find tabs organizing the manuscript paper by genre. This will help you find the right manuscript paper very quickly. When you export a new manuscript paper, you have the option of adding it to existing categories or creating a new category. I have created a category for my clients. Now you don't have wade through an alphabetical list of all your manuscript papers. There is also a Find box in the Quick Start dialog box to help you find just the right manuscript paper. Do you need the ever elusive Mariachi Band manuscript paper? Just type "mariachi" into the Find box, and there you have it! Again, cool!

—John Hinchey, composer, arranger, and notation software expert

On the Web   Avid expert John Hinchey has written lots more about Sibelius at his Web sites, www.johnhinchey.com and www.hincheymusic.com.

Note: Choosing the Blank manuscript paper will enable you to create a score with any combination of instruments from scratch. The next time you need to create a score, you can choose a manuscript paper that fits your ensemble (assuming there is one) to save yourself a little time.

4. On the left side of the New Score wizard is a preview of your new score, and on the right side is a series of settings you can change. Change the **PAGE SIZE** setting under Document Setup to your country's standard page size, as shown in Figure 2.4. In the U.S. and some other countries, this will be Letter; in the U.K., Australia, and many European countries, it is A4. (The dimensions of these page sizes are similar, with Letter being slightly shorter and wider than A4.)

Tip: **If you aren't sure which option to choose, select Letter, because the catch-up files and completed score provided are set to Letter size.**

Figure 2.4
Choosing the page size
in the New Score wizard.

5. If necessary, click the **PORTRAIT** option button. (If you aren't sure what the difference between Portrait and Landscape setting is, click each one and watch the orientation of the score in the preview pane change.)

Choosing a Paper Size and Orientation

Choosing paper size and orientation is very important, although you can easily change it later. The favored paper size for composers publishing their own large orchestral scores is not A4, Letter, or A3, but B4. This page size is halfway between A4 and A3, but is extremely difficult to find unless you have a specialist paper supplier. You will probably need a special printer, too. If you do source both, make sure the B4 setting in Sibelius matches the exact sizing in your region, as there are differences.

As a general rule, conductors don't like scores—especially scores on large paper sizes like B4 or A3—in landscape orientation. That's because they can flop off the edge of the music stand, are harder to turn quickly due to wind resistance, and are prone to tearing.

The main exception to this rule is in stage band (otherwise known as big band) scores, which are frequently published in landscape orientation to allow the leader to see more bars per page turn. Stage bands are often not conducted anyway (or the leader leads from memory), so these issues are less of a concern.

Finally, you should avoid small page sizes unless you are writing for choir. The Octavo size is the preferred page size for publishers of choral music. Singers benefit from smaller music sizes because they often have to hold their music instead of keep it on a stand, which would block their projection.

6. Click the **CHANGE INSTRUMENTS** button. The Add or Remove Instruments dialog box, which you used in Lesson 1, appears.

7. Add the necessary string instruments to the score. To do so, click the **CHOOSE FROM** drop-down list and choose **COMMON INSTRUMENTS**. Then click the **STRINGS TRIANGLE** to expand the Strings family. While holding down the **CTRL (COMMAND) KEY**, click the **VIOLIN 1**, **VIOLIN 2**, **VIOLA**, and **VIOLONCELLO** entries to select them, and then click the **ADD TO SCORE** button. The instruments are added to your score, as shown in Figure 2.5.

Figure 2.5
Adding the string quartet in the Add or Remove Instruments dialog box.

8. Click the **OK** button. The Add or Remove Instruments dialog box closes, and the preview pane in the New Score wizard shows the instruments and five empty bars, as in Figure 2.6.

Figure 2.6
Instruments added to the score appear in the preview pane on the left side of the New Score wizard.

9. Drag the scroll bar on the right side down to view the Time Signature Setup section. Alternatively, click the **DOCUMENT SETUP** bar to collapse that section and reveal the Time Signature Setup section more fully. Then click the cut common time signature, notated as a C with a line through it. This is shorthand for the 2/2 time signature, with two half note (minim) beats per bar. Directly beneath it are the numbers 4,4, which indicate how eighth notes (quavers) will be beamed together. (See Figure 2.7.)

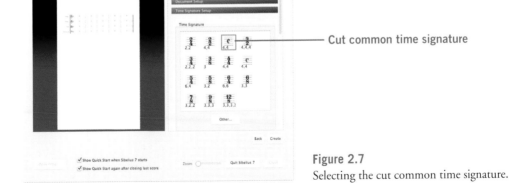

Cut common time signature

Figure 2.7
Selecting the cut common time signature.

10. Usually, the default beaming settings in Sibelius are just what you need. You will need to edit them only if you are writing in an irregular or additive meter. The exception to this rule is with the most common of all time signatures: 4/4, or common time. By default, Sibelius beams the eighth note (quaver)s in 4/4 in two groups of four (written as 4,4 under that time signature in Sibelius, as shown in Figure 2.7), just the same as cut common.

Some publishers and composers of contemporary music prefer for each eighth note (quaver) within each *quarter note* (crotchet) beat to be beamed separately, which would instead be shown as 2,2,2,2 in Sibelius. For clarity's sake, these different ways of beaming the same time signature are shown in Figure 2.8. To set this up manually, click the **Other** button and then click **Beam and Rest Groups**. You can then change the **Group 8ths (Quavers) As** option **4,4** to **2,2,2,2**, as shown in Figure 2.9. Because this isn't necessary for the lessons in this book, you can leave learning those subtleties until your next Sibelius course.

Figure 2.8

Two examples of how the 4/4, or *common* time signature, can be beamed. On the left are two groups of four eighth notes (quavers), which in Sibelius is written 4,4. On the right are four groups of two eighth notes (quavers) (2,2,2,2). Neither is correct nor incorrect. Sibelius does the former by default.

Figure 2.9

The Beam and Rest Groups dialog box, where you can change the default beaming of the 4/4 time signature.

11. Scroll down to the **Tempo** options. Beethoven did not mark this work with a metronome mark, but if he had, you would check the corresponding check box and type a number to signify the number of note lengths per minute—by default, a quarter note (crotchet). There *is* a given tempo marking, however, you can either click the **Tempo Text** combo box and type **Allegro** or select **Allegro** from the list.

12. Scroll down to the **Key Signature Setup** section or click the **Time Signature Setup** bar to collapse that section and reveal the Key Signature Setup section (see Figure 2.10). The key signature of the Beethoven is D major, so click the D major key signature to select it.

Figure 2.10
The Key Signature Setup options.

Understanding Key Signature Options

In this case, you didn't have to change the setting in the Key Signature Setup drop-down menu; by default, it was already set to Major Sharp Keys, so the key signature you needed (D major) was visible. Other options in the drop-down menu include No Key Signature (which should be used only for atonal music or music that is so chromatic, a single key signature does not prevail), Major Flat Keys, Minor Sharp Keys, and Minor Flat Keys.

You may be wondering why Sibelius bothers to make the distinction between major and minor keys in this drop-down menu. After all, whether it's D major or B minor, a key signature of two sharps is a key signature of two sharps—at least in terms of what shows on the page. Well, not quite. There are many instances (such as when you're recording from a MIDI keyboard) when knowing whether the key is major or minor will help Sibelius write accidentals correctly—the sharpened leading note of a minor scale, for example. Therefore, it's always worth checking the key signature of the music you're putting into Sibelius rather than just assuming the major equivalent will suffice.

13. Scroll down to the **SCORE INFORMATION SETUP** section or click the **KEY SIGNATURE SETUP** bar to collapse that section and reveal the Score Information Setup section. It's not essential to enter every bit of information about the score, such as its title, composer name, lyricist, copyright line, and so on. It's a good idea, though, to at least provide a title and composer, because this forms essential metadata for other functions.

In plain English, that means Sibelius will remember this information (you can edit it later by choosing File > Info) and can therefore show it in other useful places such as the Quick Start dialog box's Recent tab and as the title of a Scorch Web page (more on that later). In this case, name the piece STRING QUARTET NO. 3 and attribute the work to Ludwig van Beethoven, as shown in Figure 2.11.

Figure 2.11
It is not necessary to fill in all fields in the Score Information Setup section, but adding a title and composer is advised.

Caution: Be careful not to press the Esc key while completing the New Score wizard; this will cancel it and return you to the Quick Start dialog box's New Score tab. Also, don't click the Create button until you have entered all necessary information, as this closes the wizard and opens the score with the settings you have entered so far.

14. You can resize the Quick Start dialog box—and, therefore, the New Score wizard. To do so, click the bottom-right corner and drag inward or outward to make the window larger or smaller, respectively. Alternatively, click the MAXIMIZE (ZOOM) button to fit the window to the screen, as shown in Figure 2.12. If you're keen to see exactly how your score is going to look before you create it, this is extremely helpful.

15. Now, click the CREATE button!

Note: Of course, you can change each of the settings in the New Score wizard within the score itself—for instance, you can add a key signature by pressing the K key—but it's much quicker to set them all at once when you create the score.

Figure 2.12
The Quick Start dialog box and the New Score wizard set to fill the screen provides a great preview of what the score will look like.

Saving Your Score

Now that you're looking at your score, the first thing you should do is save it. Although Sibelius 7 isn't prone to crashing, like any computer program it may crash from time to time. This is especially true if other applications are trying to use the same resources as Sibelius, if your system has outdated drivers, and so on.

Tip: To prevent crashes, keep your computer in good health. Also, when you're running Sibelius, close all other applications. That is, don't have your e-mail, Web browser, and computer chess game going while you're composing!

With Sibelius, you can use the standard Ctrl+S (Command+S) shortcut to save. You can also choose File > Save or, if you use Windows, click the Save button in the Quick Access toolbar, discussed in Lesson 1.

By default, Sibelius saves scores in the Scores folder it has created inside the Documents folder. If you followed the instructions in Lesson 1, you know all about this folder because you copied all the files needed to complete the lessons in the Core Resources folder there. If you prefer to keep your scores in other folders, you can navigate to those folders within the Save dialog box, just as you would in any other application. Sibelius will track your scores wherever you save them in the Quick Start dialog box's Recent tab (unless you haven't edited them for more than a month).

Once you have saved the file, Sibelius does several important things for you:

- It enables auto-save, meaning it automatically saves your file for you as you work. If your computer crashes for any reason (including your power going out) and you haven't saved the file yourself for more than 10 minutes, Sibelius will prompt you to open a more recent auto-saved version. If you have several scores open when your computer goes down, having the recovered files is invaluable.

- It ensures that on each subsequent save you execute, a backup score is created. That way, if you accidentally delete the file or make disastrous changes to your score on one of those working-through-the-night occasions, you have a backup version from each time you saved. This enables you to track your work getting lousier and lousier as the night went on and, more importantly, to access a better version of the score from before it went south.

To locate the Backup Scores folder, open your Documents folder (accessible from the Start menu in Windows and in a Finder window's sidebar by default in Mac OS). Then open the Scores folder, and you will see it. Figure 2.13 shows the contents of the Backup Scores folder of a user who has been working on Lesson 1.

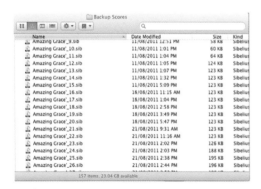

Figure 2.13
The Backup Scores folder in action.

Tip: When you're working in *any* program, you should try to get used to pressing Ctrl+S (Command+S) very regularly, almost as a nervous habit.

Moving Around Your Score

In Lesson 1, you learned a number of ways to quickly get around a score. To review them very quickly, they include the following:

- With nothing selected, you can drag blank parts of the paper as if it were a sheet of manuscript paper on your desk.

- You can use the Navigator. To open the Navigator panel, choose View > Panels > Navigator. (The Navigator panel is not available in Panorama view.)

- Pressing the Home and End keys takes you toward the start and end of your score, respectively, a page or screen width (depending on your zoom) at a time.

- You can press Ctrl+Home (Command+Home) to go to the very start of your score, or Ctrl+End (Command+End) to go to the very end.

- You can press Page Up and Page Down to go up and down the page.

- You can roll the mouse wheel to go up and down the page. Holding down the Shift key while you roll the mouse wheel moves the cursor left and right.

- You can zoom in and out with the Zoom slider on the right side of the status bar to zoom in and out of the score. Alternatively, you can press Ctrl+= (Command+=) and Ctrl+− (Command+−) to zoom in and out, respectively.

You also learned that the pages can be viewed in four different configurations or turned into one infinitely long page in a view called Panorama. The shortcut for Panorama view is Shift+P.

Here are a few more shortcuts you can add to your arsenal:

- When you press the Home, End, Page Up, and Page Down keys, the score moves a page or screen at the time, depending on how zoomed in you are. To move by smaller increments, hold down the Alt (Option) key as you press these keys. This will just nudge the page around.

- This lesson involves a much longer score than Lesson 1. Frequently you will be given an instruction like "Go to bar 42." Rather than always searching for the bar, you can choose Home > Edit > Go To > Go To Bar, as shown in Figure 2.14. (Notice that there is another option, Go To Page, that's slightly less useful.) Alternatively, press Ctrl+Alt+G (Command+Option+G). Although this is a little more complex than shortcuts you've memorized before, it's quite easy if you remember it as "G for go to." Once this dialog box opens, type the number of the bar to which you'd like to jump and click OK.

Figure 2.14
The Go To Bar command on the ribbon.

Try these new shortcuts out, even though you don't yet have much of a score to play with. Where you can, try to get used to using the keyboard shortcuts for moving about your score. As this lesson goes on, you will learn to do just about everything in Sibelius with a keystroke!

Using the Mouse to Populate Your Score

 If you are studying this book without a teacher, watch the video **2.2 Using the Mouse to Populate Your Score**.

Although you will learn how to use your keyboard to perform nearly every task in this lesson, the most intuitive way of exploring Sibelius is still with the mouse. This is even more true with the addition of the ribbon to Sibelius 7; nearly every function of the program is laid out in a logical manner and only a few clicks away.

Using the mouse is much slower than using keyboard shortcuts, but it's a great way to ease yourself into note entry in Sibelius. Even the most experienced Sibelius users—those who can literally "touch type" music—quite often reach for the mouse because it's the closest you can get to *touching* your score until it actually comes out of your printer. (And while that's nice to lay your hands on the final score, it's a little more difficult to edit or play back at that point.)

Tip: There is a catch-up file called **Beethoven1.sib** that you can use if you didn't complete all the steps in the section "Creating and Exploring a New Score," or if you have chosen to begin Lesson 2 at this point. Remember, however, that if you're doing this course with an accredited Avid trainer, the file you hand in needs to be all your own work. (And yes, this can be easily checked!)

Adding Bars

When you start a new score from the Blank manuscript paper in the Quick Start dialog box, only five bars are added to it. Obviously, you'll have a lot more music than that to put into Sibelius! You'll want to begin by adding more bars (which will, if you're in one of the page views, also add more pages once they fill up).

There are a number of ways to add bars to your score. The simplest way to add bars to your score is to use the Ctrl+B (Command+B) (think B for bars) keyboard shortcut. This adds a single bar to the end of your score. Hold down these keys for 10 or 15 seconds, and you'll add a few pages. (If you have the Navigator panel open, you'll see the new pages being added there, too.)

If you'd like a little more control over your bar adding, choose Home > Bars > Add. The Add button is a combo button. Clicking the top half of the button adds a single bar to the end of the score. Clicking the bottom half reveals a menu with three options, as shown in Figure 2.15:

Figure 2.15
The Add combo button on the ribbon.

- **Add Bar At End.** This adds a single bar to the end of the score.

- **Add Single Bar.** This adds a bar at the selected point in the score. If there is no selected point, it turns the mouse pointer blue and waits for you to click.

- **Add Multiple or Irregular Bars.** This opens a dialog box, where you can specify the number and kind of bars or beats to add, and then adds them at the selection point or where you click on the score.

Make sure you have at least 100 bars in your score. (Your score should now be at least four pages long.) Then deselect the bars you just added by pressing the Esc key.

Adding Notes and Rests with the Keypad Panel

If the Esc key is your best friend in Sibelius and Undo is a close second, their old roommate, with whom they enjoy toasting marshmallows around the campfire, is the Keypad panel. By the time you've finished this lesson, you'll have used the Keypad panel more than any other part of Sibelius. The Keypad panel is where notes *and everything attached to them* come from.

The Keypad panel—which you used in Lesson 1 to edit some note lengths—is a panel that you'll keep open all the time unless you've become so pro that you just about live in Sibelius (and there are two more courses to go before you get to that point). Figure 1.54 in Lesson 1 showed the Windows and Mac OS Keypad panels. If the Keypad panel is not visible on your screen, you can display it by choosing View > Panels > Keypad or pressing Ctrl+Alt+K (Command+Option+K).

To use the Keypad panel to input notes, first press the Esc key twice to make sure nothing in the score is selected. (This can be a useful nervous habit, like saving.) Then, with your printout of the Beethoven score in hand, begin copying the second violin part at bar 3. (You'll get to the first violin a little later.)

To input notes with the Keypad panel:

1. The second violin begins with a whole note (semibreve), so click the **WHOLE NOTE (SEMIBREVE)** button on the Keypad panel, as shown in Figure 2.16. Once you move your mouse pointer away from the keypad it turns blue to tell you it's loaded, just as it did when you input the instrument change in Lesson 1. As you drag the mouse over the score, you'll also notice a gray shadow whole note (semibreve). This shadow note shows you where the note will go if you click—not only its pitch, but also its rhythmic position in the bar.

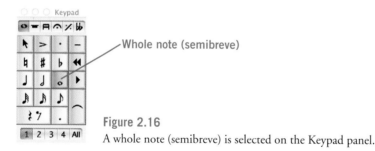

Whole note (semibreve)

Figure 2.16
A whole note (semibreve) is selected on the Keypad panel.

2. Position the mouse pointer over the F sharp that you need to input into bar 3 of the second violin. Note that if you move it left and right along that space in the bar, the shadow note moves to four different positions, showing where four quarter notes (crotchets) would come in the bar. This indicates that the whole note (semibreve) that you have selected on the Keypad panel could begin at any of these positions in the bar. (See Figure 2.17.) Beethoven has that note beginning right at the start of the bar, so figure out where the first beat is—it will be close to the barline on the left, but not right on it, or the note will go onto the fourth beat of the second bar—and then click to enter it in the bar.

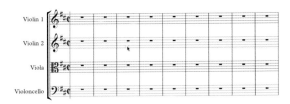

Figure 2.17
A gray shadow note appears under the blue mouse pointer, indicating the pitch and rhythm to the nearest quarter-note (crotchet) position.

Help! I Clicked in the Wrong Place!

If you accidentally click in the wrong place, the best way to fix your mistake is to undo it. Choosing Undo will undo the wrong note and enable you to input it again. If you have the correct rhythmic position but the pitch is wrong, pressing the Up Arrow or Down Arrow key will move the note up or down by step, respectively. That's probably quicker than undoing and inputting the note again.

What *won't* work is trying to click and drag a note to the correct position. If you do try that, you're just going to create another note. For example, suppose you click to create a note and, while it is still highlighted blue, you click again on the same beat. In that case, you'll actually create a chord (two notes on top of one another, whether on the same pitch or not), as shown in Figure 2.18. If you click the beat before or after the first note you clicked and the notes overlap—as they would with a whole note (semibreve)—you'll overwrite or add to the existing note. As shown in Figure 2.19, this can have some confusing results.

Figure 2.18
Clicking repeatedly on the same rhythmic position in the bar in an attempt to drag notes will result in bizarre cluster chords.

Figure 2.19
Trying to adjust the pitch of the first whole note (semibreve) by clicking later in the bar or clicking another pitch results in a strange double stop for the second violin.

Of course, you *can* drag pitches up and down. Before you do this, however, you must press the Esc key once. The status readout in the status bar will change from Create Note to Edit Note, indicating that you can drag the note. Then, when you are ready to input a new note in the next bar, you will need to press Esc again to change the status readout to No Selection before starting over by clicking on a note length in the Keypad panel.

Tip: At this point in your Sibelius career, taking note of what appears on the status bar is more important than ever. The status readout tells you what mode you're in, and what will happen when you click. The color of the mouse pointer is also important, with a blue pointer indicating that the pointer is "loaded."

3. Continue clicking in the notes for the second violin, which are a series of whole notes (semibreves). When you get to the end of bar 9, you'll notice that the A is tied to a quarter note (crotchet) in bar 10. After you input the whole note (semibreve), click the **TIE** button on the Keypad panel, as shown in Figure 2.20. Then select the **QUARTER NOTE (CROTCHET)** button on the Keypad panel, as shown in Figure 2.21, and click that in at the start of bar 10. The two notes will be tied together.

Figure 2.20
The Keypad panel with the Tie and Whole Note (Semibreve) buttons selected.

Figure 2.21
The Keypad panel with the Quarter Note (Crotchet) button selected.

Note: Although you have learned to put the tie in, you won't worry right now about the phrasing (bowing) marks, nor will you worry about the dynamics.

4. Leave two bars empty, and then click the **WHOLE NOTE (SEMIBREVE)** button in the Keypad panel again and continue inputting notes.

5. There is another tie at the end of bar 14 and then a run of eighth notes (quavers). Click the **EIGHTH NOTE (QUAVER)** button in the Keypad panel as shown in Figure 2.22 and click the first eighth note (quaver) into bar 15. Complete the passage in bar 15. Notice that Sibelius now allows you to place the shadow note on the next half of the beat, as shown in Figure 2.23; in this case this is because there is already an eighth note (quaver) on the beat.

Note: As you place shorter notes—for example, quarter notes (crotchets) and eighth notes (quavers)—at the start of a bar, Sibelius inserts rests in the remainder of the bar to ensure that it still adds up in the prevailing meter. If Sibelius didn't do this, you'd have to manually enter the rests yourself, which would mean much more work for you!

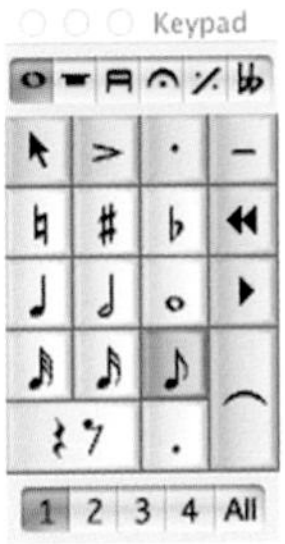

Figure 2.22
The Keypad panel
with the Eighth Note
(Quaver) button
selected.

Figure 2.23
The shadow note appears
on the second half of the
beat when an eighth note
(quaver) is placed in the
first half.

Tip: Although you won't need to do this in the Beethoven score in this lesson, suppose you want to start a rhythm on the second half of the beat. First, make sure nothing in the score is selected. Then click the Eighth Note (Quaver) button in the Keypad panel, followed by the Rest button, as shown in Figure 2.24. Next, click at the start of the beat to create the rest. You can then easily place the eighth note (quaver) on the second half of the beat. Sibelius automatically deselects the Rest button on the Keypad panel, enabling you to continue clicking in notes as normal. (You'll learn more about the subtleties of rest input later in this lesson.)

6. Your next challenge is the double stop in bar 16. The notes are whole notes (semibreves), so to begin, click the **Whole Note (Semibreve)** button in the Keypad panel. The lower note (D) also has an accidental (a sharp) on it; click the **Sharp** button on the Keypad panel, as shown in Figure 2.25, and then click to input the D sharp.

Figure 2.24
The Keypad panel with an eighth
note (quaver) rest selected—a
combination of the eighth note
(quaver) rhythm and the Rest button.

Figure 2.25
Selecting an accidental
(a sharp in this case) on
the Keypad panel.

7. The note above the D sharp is a C natural. Although Sibelius has already dismissed the sharp (Sibelius behaves slightly differently with accidentals and articulations), the whole note (semibreve) selection remains. Click the **Natural** button on the Keypad panel (as shown in Figure 2.26) and then click to input the C above the D.

Figure 2.26
The Natural button is selected on the Keypad panel.

8. Click the **QUARTER NOTE (CROTCHET)** button in the Keypad panel and input the double stop in bar 17. Your score should look like the one shown in Figure 2.27. (This score is shown with pages spread horizontally.) Make sure the quarter note (crotchet) double stop you just input is indeed at the start of bar 17. If you get out by one bar, it won't fit with the other parts as you add them.

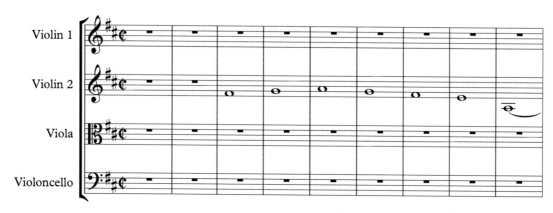

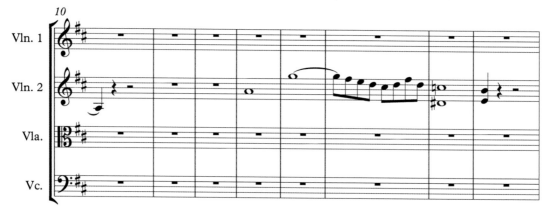

Figure 2.27
The score so far, with the second violin added to bar 17.

9. To practice what you have learned so far, input the viola and cello parts up to the same point. (Leave the first violin part for now; you'll add that soon.) If you're not sure how to read the viola part, see the upcoming sidebar, "The Alto Clef."

10. Play back the score from bar 2. This is an excellent way to audibly "proofread" the score, because any wrong notes will probably stand out! Isn't it lovely to have Beethoven coming out of Sibelius? Not so great to end on an unfinished cadence, but you will progress quickly.

The Alto Clef

You might be wondering what to do if you don't read alto clef, which is the clef that the viola part is written in. The simple answer to this is, learn it! Alto clef is a common clef; many ensembles have string sections, and most string sections have violas. Although viola players also read treble clef (but never bass clef), it is correct to write viola parts in treble clef only when they are playing high pitches for several bars in a row. (By "high," I mean any passage that would be entirely on more than two ledger lines if it were in alto clef. In actual fact, the viola range goes much higher than that. The strings of the viola are tuned to C3, G3, D4, and A4—exactly an octave higher than a cello.)

If you're desperate to move on with the course and don't have time to learn alto clef, there is a workaround:

1. Find and open the Beethoven Complete.sib file in the Lessons folder on the CD.

2. Press Esc twice to make sure nothing is selected.

3. Press the Q key or choose Notations > Common > Clef and select the treble clef. The mouse pointer will turn blue.

4. Change the alto clef right at the start of the viola part to a treble clef by clicking on it. All the notes in the viola part will jump to read correctly in that clef.

5. Print out the score.

6. Change the viola to treble clef in the score you're working on. Then, when you've finished the whole lesson, change it back. Just don't tell anyone how you did it!

Appendix A, "Elementary Music Theory," provides further information about alto clef. Figure 2.28 shows the position of notes in alto clef compared to treble and bass clefs.

Figure 2.28
The same pitch in three clefs. In alto clef, the middle line represents middle C.

Changing the Snap Positions

If you intend to use the mouse a lot with Sibelius, you might prefer to increase the sensitivity of the rhythmic position of the shadow notes as you become more confident. In other words, you can change the way Sibelius displays them to be every eighth note (quaver), or even every sixteenth note (semiquaver) if you really trust your judgment.

To change how shadow notes are displayed:

1. Choose **FILE** > **PREFERENCES** or press **CTRL+,** (**COMMAND+,**). (Yes, that's a comma.) The Preferences dialog box opens.

2. Click **NOTE INPUT** in the list on the left side.

3. Click the **SNAP POSITIONS** drop-down list and choose the eighth note (quaver), as shown in Figure 2.29.

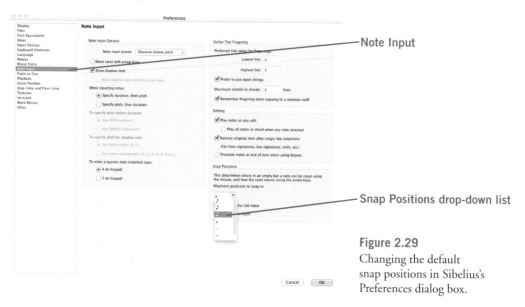

Figure 2.29
Changing the default snap positions in Sibelius's Preferences dialog box.

4. Click the **OK** button.

5. Using your mouse, input a few notes. Notice the change in the shadow notes' behavior. (Be sure to delete the notes you input before you continue to the next section.)

You would definitely need to change this setting if you were doing a lot of mouse input in a piece with a compound time signature. Because every beat would be a dotted quarter note (dotted crotchet), it would make no sense to have note positions snap to a different subdivision of the bar. To make a dotted quarter note (dotted crotchet) display in the Snap Positions drop-down list, click it and select a quarter note (crotchet); then click the drop-down list *again* and select the dot, which appears at the bottom of the list, as shown in Figure 2.30. (Note that the dot is often quite faint on high-resolution displays because it's so small, but it *is* there.)

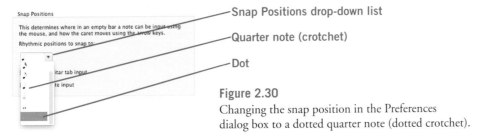

Snap Positions drop-down list

Quarter note (crotchet)

Dot

Figure 2.30
Changing the snap position in the Preferences dialog box to a dotted quarter note (dotted crotchet).

Tip: This technique also works in other, similar drop-down lists with notes in them in Sibelius, such as when an anacrusis (pick-up) bar is created in the Time Signature dialog box.

Using Flexi-time Recording

 As usual, a video covers all the essential points of this section. The video is called **2.3 Using Flexi-time Recording**.

If you completed the previous section, your score should look like the one shown in Figure 2.31. Your next step will be to input the first violin part over the top, which adds the melody to the opening section. You'll do this with Flexi-time recording, which is Sibelius's method of recording in real time from a MIDI keyboard or from another instrument that can output MIDI, such as a special guitar pickup.

"Flexi-time didn't work the first time, so I gave up." It's a familiar phrase from many Sibelius beginners. Recording to a click in tempo is not easy, but remember that Flexi-time is designed to help. Used effectively, it does work. Make sure you set up the Flexi-time options before you record. The minimum note value is key. Ensure you choose only the minimum note value you need—i.e., if your piece involves no notes of smaller value than a quaver, set the drop-down list to a quaver (quarter note). This ensures any rhythms out of time will snap to the relevant quaver in the bar. If you do decide to record with semi-quavers or demi-semi-quavers, beware that you need to be more accurate with your performance.

However, there's more! If the notation of your recording hasn't come out as well as you expected, select the score and use the Renotate Performance plug-in found in the Notes menu. This will do a pretty good job of sorting out many of the errors of timing and some of the errors of notes being in the wrong clef. Using Flexi-time takes practice, but when used to its potential alongside the plug-in, it can be of real help.

—Richard Payne, Sibelius expert

On the Web   **Follow Richard's work with Sibelius on his Web site, www.doublesharptraining.co.uk/.**

Figure 2.31
The score so far.

Note: With Flexi-time recording, which you'll have a chance to experiment with in this section, Sibelius can follow *your* tempo as you play. Speed up, and Sibelius speeds up with you. Slow down, and Sibelius follows along.

If you aren't much of a keyboard player, don't worry. If you have only very elementary skills, you can slow the tempo down and have a go. (For a refresher of which key on the keyboard corresponds to which note, see Appendix A.) If you've never touched a keyboard in your life, follow the instructions in this section anyway; when it's time to play, just key in any old thing so at least you've had a go. You'll just have to use your mouse to copy the actual first violin part into the score.

Tip: If you've chosen to study this section alone, you can use the catch-up file called **Beethoven2.sib** on the CD to save time.

Understanding Input Devices

As mentioned, Flexi-time recording requires some kind of MIDI input. The most common kind of MIDI input is a MIDI keyboard. These come in various shapes and sizes, and can be connected to your computer in a number of ways. The two most common forms of connection are MIDI interface and direct USB connection.

A Word on MIDI

MIDI, short for Musical Instrument Digital Interface, is simply the language that computers and other digital hardware like MIDI keyboards use to talk about music. Broken down, MIDI is literally a series of thousands of messages that say things like "I'm playing C sharp," "I'm playing a note this loudly," or "I'm holding a note for this long."

Each time you play a note, press a foot pedal (if you have one), or change a setting on your MIDI keyboard, the keyboard sends that as a message to your computer. Sibelius can capture these messages and turn them into notation, which is quite a complex process when you think about it! Similarly, when you click the Play button in Sibelius, it can send messages about the music playing in your scores out to your keyboard. If your keyboard has in-built sounds and speakers, it can play it back.

All these messages can also be stored in a file called a MIDI file. This file contains all the information about every note from the start of a piece to the end. MIDI files are very useful because most music software can open and interpret them. This makes them great for e-mailing to friends to share your music if they don't have Sibelius. You'll learn much more about MIDI files in Lesson 3, "Purple".

Some keyboards are not MIDI capable. If you aren't sure whether yours is, refer to the manufacturer's guide or check the back of the unit for five-pin MIDI sockets marked in, out and possibly thru, or for a port marked USB or with the USB symbol. Figure 2.32 shows both MIDI sockets and a USB port, found on the back of an M-Audio AxiomPro 49.

Figure 2.32
Plugs for MIDI.

If your MIDI device has a USB port, connecting it to your computer is as simple as using a single USB cable. This should have been supplied with your MIDI device. If it wasn't, or if it has since been lost, you can easily buy one at a computer or electronics store. Each end of the cable is a different shape, so there is no way you can get it the wrong way round. If your MIDI device has MIDI sockets but no USB port, then you need a MIDI interface to translate the signal to your computer. These can be purchased relatively inexpensively from a good music store. Modern MIDI interfaces have MIDI in and out plugs on one end, a small box in the middle to perform the translation, and a USB plug on the other end. Figure 2.33 shows how your setup should be arranged.

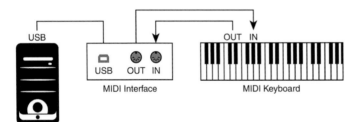

Figure 2.33
Connecting a computer and a MIDI keyboard using a MIDI interface.

Tip: Some older computers may also support a direct connection to MIDI sockets via a special breakout cable, which connects to the joystick port on your computer's sound card at one end and to the MIDI in and out sockets on the other. This is unusual nowadays, but if your computer supports it and it works with Sibelius 7, then great. If it doesn't, then a MIDI interface is your solution.

Regardless of how you connect your MIDI device to your computer, you should always turn on your MIDI device before you run Sibelius. If you don't, they might not be available within the program. In that case, you'll need to restart the program to make them available. Also, be aware that your MIDI device will not work with Sibelius (or any other music application on your computer, for that matter) if you have not installed the appropriate drivers. *Drivers* are small programs that tell your computer how to communicate with the interface. These drivers are available on the CD that came with your MIDI device; in addition, you can download the most recent drivers for the device from the manufacturer's Web site.

Note: Some keyboards, such as many in the M-Audio line, don't require drivers for certain operating systems because they are *class compliant*. That is, the way they work is already supported by the operating system.

After you connect your MIDI device and install the necessary drivers, check to make sure that Sibelius can communicate with it:

1. Choose FILE > PREFERENCES or press CTRL+, (COMMAND+,). The Preferences dialog box opens.

2. Click INPUT DEVICES in the list on the left. A list of available devices will appear on the right, as shown in Figure 2.34. (Note that in the given example the same keyboard appears multiple times because it offers more MIDI options, with the ability to connect another keyboard through it.)

Note: You can use more than one device for input if you have more than one connected. If multiple devices are connected but you don't need them all, you can uncheck them in the Use column.

3. Play a few notes on your MIDI device. The green indicator light marked Test will move up and down.

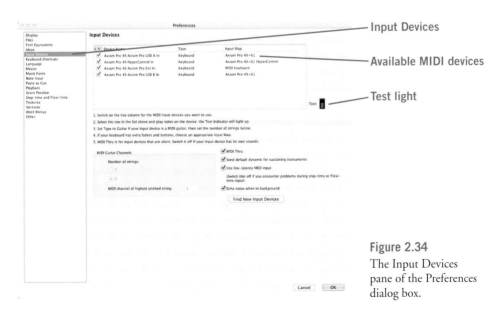

Figure 2.34
The Input Devices pane of the Preferences dialog box.

If the Test light doesn't move, it means Sibelius isn't receiving a signal from the device, even though it might appear in the list of available devices. This is most likely because the MIDI in cable has been connected to the MIDI in socket on your keyboard and the MIDI out cable to the MIDI out socket. In fact, they should be the other way around—out goes to in, and in goes to out. You can swap these cables over while the keyboard and Sibelius are running without any danger.

Using the Sibelius Keyboard Panel

If you don't own a MIDI keyboard, you're probably wondering how on earth you can complete this section of the lesson. Luckily, Sibelius has a solution for you: the Keyboard panel. To display the Keyboard panel, choose View > Panels > Keyboard, as shown in Figure 2.35. The Keyboard panel appears at the bottom of the window (see Figure 2.36).

Figure 2.35
Display the Keyboard panel.

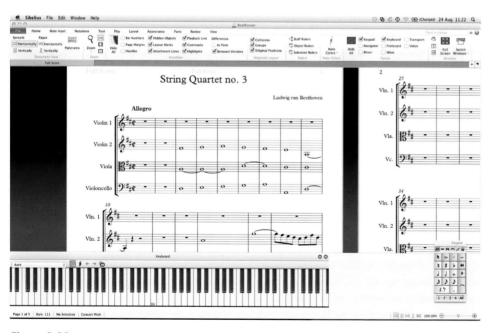

Figure 2.36
The Keyboard panel in its default position, docked at the bottom of the window.

By default, the Keyboard panel is docked, but if you drag it up away from the bottom of the window, it will become a floating panel. You can also drag the right side of the Keyboard panel to the left or right, meaning the Keyboard panel can be as wide as you like (or, put a different way, can show as many octaves as you like). In Figure 2.37, the Keyboard panel is shown floating over the score. You can also adjust the size of the keys in the Keyboard panel. By default, they are set to the middle size; clicking the Change Size button (see Figure 2.38) toggles them first to large, then to small, and finally back to middle.

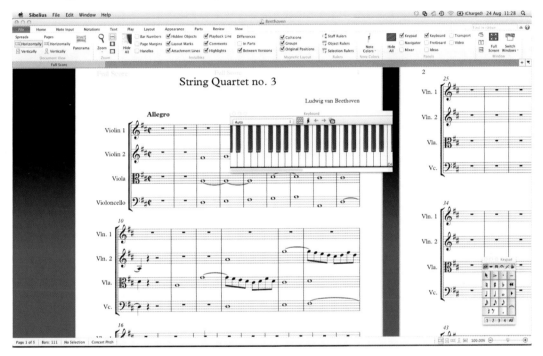

Figure 2.37
The Keyboard panel, set to float above the score and show just three octaves.

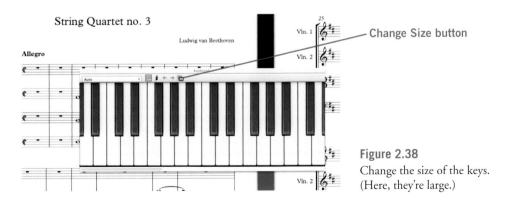

Figure 2.38
Change the size of the keys. (Here, they're large.)

You can use the Keyboard panel to play live music, by clicking its keys. (Before you start playing around with the Keyboard panel in this way, make sure nothing is selected in the score. Otherwise, if you click a key on the Keyboard panel, you will input a note.) This isn't a very easy way to play live music, however. Fortunately, you have another option: You can click the QWERTY Input button on the Keyboard panel, as shown in Figure 2.39, and use the QWERTY keyboard on your computer to play music live. The keys on your computer keyboard map to those on the Keyboard panel as shown in Figure 2.40, with one octave of notes available. To move the octave up or down, press X or Z, respectively.

Figure 2.39
The QWERTY Input button on the Keyboard panel.

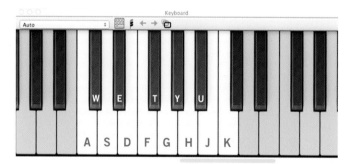

Figure 2.40
Letters on the keys of the Keyboard window show corresponding keys on your QWERTY keyboard for playing in Sibelius.

If you opt to use the Keyboard panel, you will need to do a few workarounds when it comes time to record the first violin part. Specifically, you'll probably want to enter the first bar with the mouse. Bars 2 to 5 fit within one octave, so you can record those using the Keyboard panel. Then, stop recording, adjust the octave range of the keyboard, and record bars 6 to 10. Another workaround is to record the whole part in one octave and then transpose each section by an octave as need be. It's imperfect, but better than nothing.

Tip: You can also use the Keyboard panel to display the notes that are already in your score. To do so, click the Change Size button until the keys are the smallest size. Then click the drop-down menu on the left side of the Keyboard panel and choose All Staves. Finally, play back your score and watch what happens (see Figure 2.41); each note playing back is shown on the keyboard.

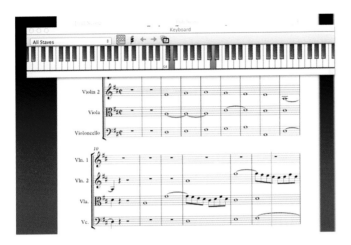

Figure 2.41
The Keyboard panel, reflecting playback of all parts.

Preparing to Record

No doubt, your sense of anticipation is growing as you get closer to the moment when you will record your first solo into Sibelius. There are some settings to check before you begin, however. This may seem laborious, but it will save you a great deal of time in the long run!

To prepare to record:

1. Choose **NOTE INPUT > FLEXI-TIME** and click the dialog launcher button. The Flexi-time Options dialog box opens. Here, you can adjust settings to ensure Sibelius converts what you play into notation as accurately as possible.

Figure 2.42
Clicking the dialog launcher button in the Flexi-time group in the Note Input tab.

2. Click the **FLEXIBILITY OF TEMPO** drop-down list and choose one of the following options, depending on your confidence as a keyboard player:

   ● **None (Non Rubato).** If you don't have much confidence in your keyboard skills, choose this setting, as shown in Figure 2.43. When you choose None (Non Rubato), Sibelius will expect you to play in time with the metronome when recording and will notate how you play according to that and other settings in the Flexi-time Options dialog box.

- **Low (Poco Rubato).** Choose this setting if you're an acceptable keyboard player. With this setting, if Sibelius detects that you are speeding up or slowing down, it will speed up or slow down with you.

- **Medium (Rubato).** Advanced keyboard players should choose Medium (Rubato). As with Low (Poco Rubato), Sibelius will speed up or slow down as you do, but will perceive even finer changes in tempo.

- **High (Molto Rubato).** If you're a highly accomplished keyboardist, this is the setting for you. The higher the setting, the more precisely Sibelius will take lead from your own slight changes in tempo. If you race, it will chase you!

 ———— Flexibility of Tempo drop-down list

Figure 2.43

Setting the Flexibility of Tempo option to None in the Flexi-time Options dialog box.

Note: Don't expect to hit on the correct setting the first time when recording in Sibelius. Like all the other note-entry methods, it takes practice to use Flexi-time to get the results you're expecting. If the notation you end up with looks nothing like you intended, try first recording with the Flexibility of Tempo setting on None and then increasing the flexibility as you have more success. Remember, if your recording is terrible, you can always choose Undo and try it again!

3. Leave the **Existing Music** and **Metronome Click** settings as is.

4. Under **Voices**, uncheck the **Record into Multiple Voices** check box and make sure the **1** option button is selected, as shown in Figure 2.44. (You'll learn why you're choosing this setting and more about voices in Lesson 3.)

5. Click the **Notation** tab at the top of the dialog box.

6. Under **Note Values**, click the **Adjust Rhythms** check box to select it.

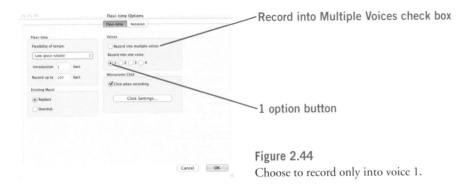

Record into Multiple Voices check box

1 option button

Figure 2.44
Choose to record only into voice 1.

Note: The Adjust Rhythms check box is the most important of all the Flexi-time options. For those who have used a sequencer before, Adjust Rhythms is rather like a pre-quantization. Before you record, you effectively say to Sibelius, "The shortest note length I'm meaning to play is x," where x might be an eighth note (quaver), a quarter note (crotchet), or a sixteenth note (semiquaver). When you record, Sibelius then considers the timing of each note you play. It thinks to itself (insert Finnish accent here), "This human is a terrible player. That note was a thirty-second note (demisemiquaver) early. However, he has told me that he is playing nothing outside the eighth note (quaver) subdivision, so I shall fix his timing for him."

7. When you begin to record into Sibelius, you will notice that the notation is always a few notes behind you, as Sibelius works out what you *meant* to play based on your Adjust Rhythms settings, and fixes it for you. If you look at the Beethoven you're about to perform, the shortest note is an eighth note (quaver), so click the **Minimum Duration** drop-down list and select the **Eighth Note (Quaver)** option, as shown in Figure 2.45.

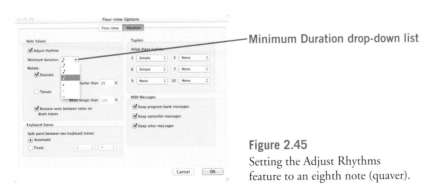

Minimum Duration drop-down list

Figure 2.45
Setting the Adjust Rhythms feature to an eighth note (quaver).

8. Click the **OK** button.

9. You're nearly ready to begin, but there is one more small feature that can make everything easier when you record: the Tempo slider in the Transport panel. To display the Transport panel, choose **VIEW** > **PANELS** > **TRANSPORT**.

10. Start playback in Sibelius from bar 13 so you can hear how fast the eighth notes (quavers) will be. If you don't feel you could play them at that tempo, drag the **TEMPO** slider to the left, as shown in Figure 2.46. Find a tempo that feels comfortable; Sibelius will remember that tempo when you record.

Tempo slider

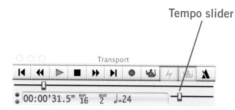

Figure 2.46

Slowing the tempo down with the Tempo slider in the Transport panel.

Recording in Real Time

To begin recording from any position in your score, simply select that bar. In this case, you're going to record from the first bar in the first part. Although this is Sibelius's default, you should get used to the process by selecting the first bar in the first violin so that it is highlighted blue.

As you may have noticed in the Flexi-time Options dialog box, by default, Sibelius gives you a one-bar count-in. That means when you record, you will get two beats in. Don't forget, the time signature is *cut common*, or 2/2. That means there are two half note (minim) beats in the bar. If you find it too confusing to divide the beat and would prefer a 4/4 metronome while you play, make sure nothing is selected, press T for time signature (note that this won't work if you're using your QWERTY keyboard to play in; in that case, choose Notations > Common > Time Signature), choose 4/4 (see Figure 2.47), and click in the first bar. Sibelius will change the time signature. (You'll need to remember to change it back to cut common before you finish.)

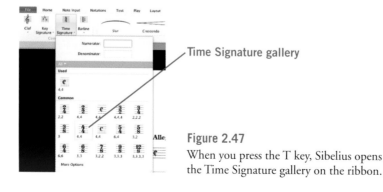

Time Signature gallery

Figure 2.47

When you press the T key, Sibelius opens the Time Signature gallery on the ribbon.

Prepare yourself to begin recording (taking note of the key signature). When you're ready, do one of the following:

- Click the Record button in the Transport panel.

- Choose Note Input > Flexi-time > Record.

- Choose Play > Transport > Record.

- Press the Ctrl+Shift+F (Command+Shift+F) keyboard shortcut.

After a one bar count-in, Sibelius will start recording, and you should start playing. As you play, the playback line (colored red to show you it's recording) will follow the score, adding the notes you play. When you're finished, simply press Esc to stop recording. If your recording didn't go as planned, choose Undo, consider adjusting the Tempo slider, and try again. There is no pressure to get it right the first time!

Note: If you are getting lots of rests between notes that shouldn't be there, it's probably because you're releasing notes a little early and Sibelius is rounding them down to the note length you chose in the Adjust Rhythms setting. Try playing as legato (smoothly) as possible to remedy this problem, holding right to the start of the next beat on long notes at the end of phrases.

Record the violin part up to the end of bar 16. If 16 bars are too much to record at once, you can resume recording from any bar by selecting it first. Don't try for perfection. Leave any small errors for the next section.

Editing Your Recording

Figure 2.48 shows a not-quite-right recording. There are two incorrect pitches in bar 3, and the player has accidentally played two notes at the end of bar 8 and the start of bar 9. The rest of the recording is correct, however; rather than redoing the whole thing, it would be quicker to edit out those slips.

In Lesson 1, you did a lot of basic editing. You clicked and dragged notes to different pitches. You used the Keypad panel to change their rhythmic value (note length). You edited text, transposed selections, repeated, copied and pasted elements of music around the score, and learned how to select passages. Combined with your new knowledge of mouse entry, you now have all the tools you need to do the kind of edit required to the recording shown in Figure 2.48. You can drag the incorrect pitches in bar 3 into position and delete the unneeded F natural at the end of bar 8. The easiest thing to do with the mess in bar 9 is probably to input a new whole note (semibreve) over the top of it on the right pitch. A few other editing tips and tricks will save you time if you have many of these kinds of edits to make. These involve working with the keyboard as well as the mouse.

Figure 2.48
A recording of the violin solo with a few small errors.

To edit your recording:

1. After making sure you have nothing selected in the score, click at the beginning of a passage of notes with some incorrect pitches. Then take your hand off the mouse so you can practice using the keys.

2. Press the **UP ARROW** or **DOWN ARROW** key to adjust the first incorrect pitch. Then press the **RIGHT ARROW** key to move to the next one. In this way, you can move along the passage one note at a time—quicker than picking that mouse up again! If there are multiple bars between the cursor and the next incorrect pitch, hold down the **CTRL (COMMAND)** key as you press the **RIGHT ARROW** key to move forward a bar at a time. In the example shown in Figure 2.48, adjusting the pitches is easily done with the arrow keys alone.

Tip: Even if you played in the solo flawlessly, try pressing the Left Arrow and
Right Arrow keys to move among the notes.

3. Press the **RIGHT ARROW KEY** until you come to the unwanted note
in a chord in bar 8 (refer to Figure 2.48). Then press the **DELETE** or
BACKSPACE KEY. As you move along chords with the arrow keys, Sibelius
selects only the top note of the chord. To select other notes in the chord,
hold down the **ALT (OPTION) KEY** and press the **DOWN ARROW KEY** to
move through the notes of the chord, deleting the ones you don't need.

4. To convert the E sharp in Figure 2.48 into a whole note (semibreve), click
the **WHOLE NOTE (SEMIBREVE)** button on the Keypad panel.

5. To remove the staccato marks added by Sibelius (refer to Figure 2.48),
select each note and then click the **STACCATO** button (not to be
confused with the Dotted Rhythm button) at the top of the Keypad panel
(see Figure 2.49.)

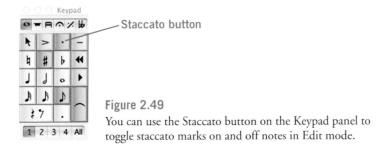

Staccato button

Figure 2.49
You can use the Staccato button on the Keypad panel to
toggle staccato marks on and off notes in Edit mode.

What's That Gray Text?

After recording in Sibelius, you may notice blocks of gray text all over your score, above
the staff you've been recording into. If this happens to you, there's no need to panic. In the
example in Figure 2.50, one such piece of text, which reads "~A 0," has been dragged away
from the group. This is recorded MIDI data from the keyboard—information that couldn't be
adequately recorded on the fly in music notation (such as a swell on a note, a pitch bend, or
a foot pedal). Sibelius doesn't want you to lose any aspects of your real live performance, so
it records these in faint gray text. This text does not print out on your score.

Figure 2.50
Some recorded MIDI data in Sibelius.

If you find the text distracting, or have so much of it that you keep selecting it accidentally, you can hide it by choosing View > Invisibles > Hidden Objects. This, however, may hide other hidden objects that are useful to you. If so you may want to prevent Sibelius from recording this data. To do so, choose Note Input > Flexi-time > dialog launcher button to open the Flexi-time Options dialog box. Then click the Notation tab and deselect all three check boxes under MIDI Messages, as shown in Figure 2.51.

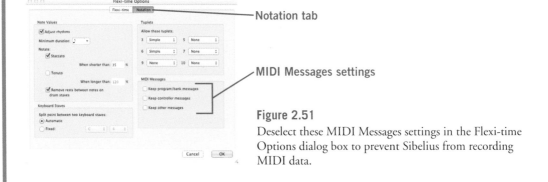

Notation tab

MIDI Messages settings

Figure 2.51
Deselect these MIDI Messages settings in the Flexi-time Options dialog box to prevent Sibelius from recording MIDI data.

Learning Step-Time and Alphabetic Entry

The video 2.4 Learning Step-Time and Alphabetic Entry will demonstrate all the most important aspects of this section. Watch it before you begin this section.

Flexi-time recording represented your first move away from inputting notes with the mouse. You've also developed some essential skills for editing without the mouse. Step-time and alphabetic entry round off this skill set. By the time you have completed this section, there won't be many aspects of note entry and editing that you can't do with keyboard strokes alone or a combination of keyboard strokes and a MIDI keyboard.

Step-time entry requires the use of a MIDI keyboard. If you don't have one, you can simply practice alphabetic entry twice as much; the two are quite similar, with the use of the keyboard for step-time entry being the only real difference. In fact, there are plenty of occasions when you'll choose one over the other, as the mood strikes you. For those copying music that is already written down (as opposed to arranging or composing on the fly in Sibelius), these are definitely the quickest ways to work.

Note: If you are lucky enough to own one of the aforementioned M-Audio keyboards with HyperControl capabilities, it should be noted that this is a variation of step-time entry. This is covered in Lesson 5, "Agent Zero."

Tip: If you're dipping in and out of this book and want to begin this lesson from this point, you can open a catch-up file on your CD called **Beethoven3.sib**. (No, that one isn't the *Eroica*.)

Further Exploring the Keypad Panel

Wouldn't it be useful if there were easy-to-remember shortcuts for everything on the Keypad panel? Well, there are. If you're using a full-sized computer keyboard, you may notice that the numeric keypad on the right side contains exactly the same number of buttons, a long horizontal button along the bottom that looks suspiciously like the Rest button, and a long vertical button on the lower-right side that resembles the size and position of the Tie button. As you may have guessed, that's no coincidence! The Keypad panel maps exactly to the numeric keypad, as shown in Figure 2.52.

Figure 2.52
Sibelius's Keypad panel and the numeric keypad from a Mac and Windows keyboard, side by side.

Caution: While each keyboard's keypad exactly matches the layout on the Sibelius keypad, note that Windows and Mac numerical keypad layouts are subtly different in their arrangement of some of the symbols. For example, on the top row of the keypad, the Num Lock key is the same on both, but then a Windows keyboard has the symbols /, *, and then –, in that order. In contrast, a Mac keyboard has the symbols =, /, and *, in *that* order.

Caution: As with other shortcuts in this book, where two are given, the first is always Windows, with Mac OS shortcuts in parentheses. If this may still not be clear, it will be explicitly stated.

Try this: Make sure you have nothing selected in your score. Then, while keeping an eye on the Keypad panel, type 123456 on the numeric keypad. The note length buttons in the Keypad panel—beginning with the button for the thirty-second note (demisemiquaver) through to the button for the whole note (semibreve)—will turn blue as you press each key, just as if you were clicking on the buttons. This knowledge will come in very handy as you explore step-time and alphabetic entry!

Using a Laptop with Sibelius 7

If you're working on a laptop, unless it's one of the really gargantuan ones with a full-sized keyboard, you may be feeling a little left out by the news that the numeric keypad is so important in Sibelius. Laptops generally don't have these.

On some Windows laptops, the numeric keypad is overlaid on the N, M, J, K, L, I, O, P, 9, 0, and – keys. Holding down the Function key (sometimes labeled "fn") gives you access to the numeric keypad. That means you can still easily access the Keypad panel shortcuts, even if they require two keystrokes instead of one. Unfortunately, however, Apple phased this functionality out of their laptops a number of years ago, so unless you're lucky enough to have a MacBook that's old enough to offer this functionality but still new enough to run Sibelius 7, you won't have this option.

Luckily, there are quite a few other solutions to the problem:

- You can change the behavior of the number keys along the top of the keyboard (above the QWERTY letters), mapping them to mirror the functionality of a numeric keypad— although, of course, you won't get the visual hint that is so obvious when you see them side by side, as in Figure 2.52. To change the keys to work in this manner, choose File > Preferences > Keyboard Shortcuts. This opens the Keyboard Shortcuts tab in the Preferences dialog box. Next, click the Current Feature Set drop-down menu and choose Notebook (Laptop) Shortcuts, as shown in Figure 2.53. Try out the setting by typing 123456; the note length buttons in the Keypad panel will turn blue as you press each key, just as if you were clicking on the buttons.

- You can invest in a separate numeric keypad, which you can connect to your laptop via USB. These are usually available at good computer stores. Be aware, however, that some of these don't map correctly to the Keypad panel in Sibelius. (They actually mirror the wrong keys.) Before you make a purchase, check the Sibelius Help Center (www.sibelius.com/helpcenter) for a list of compatible keypads.

- You can buy a separate full-sized keyboard, which you can connect to your laptop via USB. Although the idea of lugging around something that's as large as your laptop may seem ridiculous, you might be surprised to find how much more quickly that full-sized keyboard will enable you to work in Sibelius!

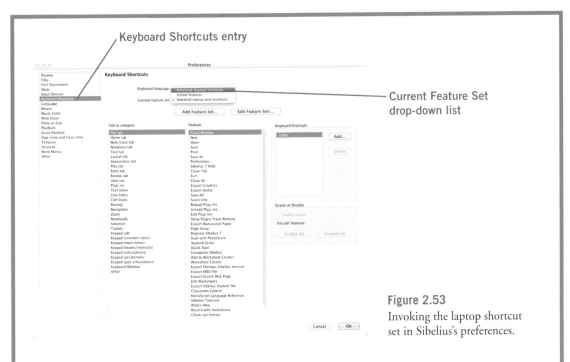

Figure 2.53
Invoking the laptop shortcut set in Sibelius's preferences.

■ You can purchase one of the many apps for your mobile phone to connect it to your laptop and replace the numeric keypad. A few apps even display the Sibelius Keypad panel layout, such as Remote Control for Sibelius for Android phones and NumPad for iPhone (see Figure 2.54).

■ You can purchase the AxiomPro 21. This small MIDI controller keyboard has the Keypad panel mapped to its own numerical pad and communicates with Sibelius via HyperControl. While not every Keypad panel option is available, it does give you a keyboard and numeric keypad in one—and it's shiny, too.

Figure 2.54
NumPad, an app for the iPhone, which mirrors the Sibelius Keypad panel.

Using Step-Time Entry

Now you know how to use the Keypad panel, learning step-time entry will take you only a few minutes. The more you use your numeric keypad, the more you'll automatically remember the location of keys for different note lengths, articulation marks, accidentals, and so on, without having to look at the Keypad panel on the screen.

In this section, you'll input a fair bit of music yourself to practice. The best thing you could do after finishing Lesson 2 is buy a copy of the whole quartet and copy all the rest in. Consider that optional homework!

To input music using step-time entry:

1. Select bar 17 in the first violin part. Then press the **N KEY**. As shown in Figure 2.55, if you have the Note Input tab on the ribbon selected, you will notice that the Input Notes button becomes highlighted. In addition, the readout on the status bar changes to Create Bar Rest. Finally, a blue cursor appears (see Figure 2.56) to show you where the next note will go, similar to the way the blinking cursor in a word processor indicates where the next letter you type will appear.

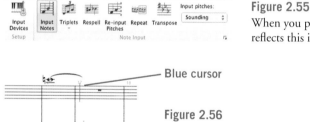

Figure 2.55

When you press N, for note input, the ribbon instantly reflects this if you have the Note Input tab selected.

— Blue cursor

Figure 2.56

When you enter Note Input mode, a blue cursor appears to show you where the next note you input will go.

2. Press the **3 KEY** on your numerical keyboard to select the eighth note (quaver) in the Keypad panel. The violin plays nothing but eighth notes (quavers) for the next 10 bars.

3. Using your MIDI keyboard, play the pitches in the violin part. (Notice that as soon as you play the first note on your MIDI keyboard, the status readout in the status bar changes to Create Note to reflect the mode you have entered.) There is no pressure to perform in time or to play the notes quickly because Sibelius assumes every note is an eighth note (quaver) until you tell it otherwise by selecting something else on the Keypad panel.

Tip: If your MIDI keyboard isn't close to your computer, you may want to re-arrange your workspace.

Note: If you notice that some pitches are spelled incorrectly—for instance, if Sibelius spells the B sharp in bar 24 as a C natural—don't panic. You will learn how to respell enharmonics as soon as you've completed this part.

4. When you reach bar 27, press the **4** KEY on the numeric keypad to change the note length to a quarter note (crotchet) for the D. Then play the D on your MIDI keyboard.

5. To get to the next bar and continue inputting the first violin part, you could repeatedly press the **RIGHT ARROW KEY** until you arrive in the next bar. This method is a little clunky. Instead, enter the rests as they appear. The first rest is a quarter note (crotchet) rest. You already have the quarter note (crotchet) selected from the last pitch you input, so simply press the **0** KEY on your numeric keypad; this corresponds to the Rest button on the Keypad panel. The status reading changes to Create Rest, and the cursor advances.

6. Next is a half note (minim) rest, so press the **5** KEY on the numeric keypad to select the half note (minim), and press the **0** KEY to add it as a rest.

7. Now you're at the start of bar 28. Press the **6** KEY to select the whole note (semibreve) on the Keypad panel, and then play the D and G that follow.

8. By now, you've probably got the idea, so here is another element: Press the **3** KEY on the numeric keypad to choose eighth notes (quavers). Next, play the first two notes of the downward run (G an F sharp). Then, before you play the remaining notes in the run, press the **ASTERISK (*) KEY** on Windows keyboards or the **SLASH (/) KEY** on a Mac's numeric keypad, which corresponds to the Staccato button (see Figure 2.57). Like the note lengths, articulations on the Keypad panel are "sticky." (This is in contrast to the accidentals, which only remain selected while the next note is entered.) You can now play the rest of the eighth notes (quavers) in that bar; each will have a staccato mark.

Figure 2.57

The Staccato button on the Keypad panel corresponds to the asterisk (*) key on Windows keyboards or the slash (/) key on a Mac's numeric keypad.

9. When you reach the end of the bar, press the **4** KEY on the numeric keypad to change the selection to quarter notes (crotchets). In addition, to turn off the staccato articulation, press the **ASTERISK (SLASH) KEY** on the numeric keypad.

Note: Repeatedly pressing the Staccato key toggles staccato on and off, just as it did when you were editing your Flexi-time input. The only difference is that in Create mode, it applies to the note that is *about* to be input, whereas in Edit mode it applies to the note that's *selected*. Now you see why knowing what mode you are in is important to understanding why Sibelius behaves the way it does when you press something on the numeric keypad! To belabor the point, the easiest way to do this is to keep an eye on the status readout on the status bar at the bottom of the window.

10. You're nearly finished with the section in the first violin part. Input another rest in bar 31 and another staccato run in bar 34. (Keen-eyed users will notice that this is just the same phrase repeated up an octave. Although it might be quicker to just repeat it and then transpose it up an octave, you need step-time entry practice, so do it manually.)

11. Finish putting in the violin part after the first two crotchets at the start of bar 35. You will return to this point later in this lesson to learn how to input triplets with step-time and alphabetic entry.

Handling Enharmonics

In the preceding violin passage, there were a number of notes that Sibelius spelled incorrectly. They are the same pitches, but they need to be spelled *enharmonically* to reflect the inherent harmony that Beethoven used.

To handle these enharmonics:

1. Press the ESC KEY twice to cancel Create mode and then Edit mode and return to no selection.

2. The first note that may appear to be input incorrectly is the D natural in bar 21. Beethoven's score does not have a natural here, but Sibelius has added a cautionary because of the D sharp in the bar before. There is nothing wrong with this natural—indeed, many publishers prefer caution-ary naturals, even when the note is in a different octave from the preceding one. But if you'd like to be a purist, select the **D** and then press the **7** KEY on the numeric keypad, which corresponds to the Natural button in the Keypad panel, to toggle it off (see Figure 2.58).

Note: If you resent the extra work Sibelius has created for you by adding that cautionary, be aware that the settings for cautionary accidentals can be changed. Also be aware, though, that this feature also saved you some time in bar 20 by automatically adding a cautionary with which Beethoven agreed. Changing cautionary accidentals is covered in the Expert level.

Figure 2.58
The Natural button on the Keypad panel corresponds to the 7 key on the numeric keypad.

3. The first misspelling in the violin part is the C natural in bar 24, which Beethoven spelled as a B sharp. To change it, simply select IT and press ENTER (RETURN) or choose NOTE INPUT > NOTE INPUT > RESPELL (see Figure 2.59). The note is instantly respelled as B sharp, its enharmonic.

Note Input tab   Respell button

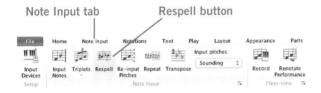

Figure 2.59
Press Enter (Return) to respell notes enharmonically or find the control in the ribbon as shown.

4. Make the same edit to enharmonically respell the F naturals in bars 31 and 35 so they read E sharp.

Practicing Alphabetic Entry

Having gotten used to step-time entry, alphabetic entry will not take you long to learn. It is the ideal note-input method for those who do not own a MIDI keyboard or who do not find using a MIDI keyboard to be a good solution. In alphabetic entry, you still begin by pressing the N key to enter Note Entry mode, and you still choose all note lengths, accidentals, and articulations from the numeric keypad. You also enter rests in the same way as with step-time entry. The difference in alphabetic entry is that you will input pitch from your computer keyboard rather than a MIDI keyboard.

To practice, add the second violin part, starting at bar 20:

1. Select bar 20 in the second violin part and press the **N KEY** to begin note entry.

2. Add the rests at the start of the bar as you would have in step-time entry. When you're finished, leave the quarter note (crotchet) selected on the Keypad panel.

3. To input the E pitch, simply press **E**. Next, to add the tie from the Keypad panel, press **ENTER** (**RETURN**), as shown in Figure 2.60. Finally, press **E** again to add another E on the first beat of the next bar.

Figure 2.60
On the Keypad panel, the Tie button corresponds to the Enter (Return) key on the numeric keypad.

4. To add the F sharp, simply press **F**. There is no need to add the sharp, because Sibelius assumes that you will write within the prevailing key signature, and that you will add an accidental if you need to write at all chromatically.

5. Continue until you come to the G sharp in bar 22. Press the **8** key on the numeric keypad, which corresponds to the Sharp button on the Keypad panel; then press the **G KEY** to enter the pitch. Next, add the tie, and press **G** again. There is no need to add the sharp again because Sibelius (correctly) assumes a tied pitch must be the same. From there, it should be plain sailing until you get to bar 30.

As you get used to alphabetic entry, you'll notice a couple helpful things:

■ It's very comfortable to sit at a computer keyboard with your right hand on the numeric keypad on the right, and your left hand over the A to G keys on the left. There's very little reason to move either hand.

■ Because you're copying music from a printed score, which is probably on the desk next to you, it's very slow to add a note, check that you got it right, go back to the score, and so on. But soon, you can begin to trust your ear as Sibelius plays each pitch you enter. Even if you don't have great aural skills (let alone perfect pitch) you'll find this aural feedback essential. Just remember to look at the screen every few bars to make sure you haven't gotten off beat. (That's experience speaking!)

At bar 30, you will notice something that will likely throw you off your flow. After you input the A on the first beat, you will enter the E, but Sibelius will put it in the wrong octave. (It will also turn it red to tell you a violin can't play that pitch, as shown in Figure 2.61.) There is logic behind this behavior, however.

Figure 2.61
At bar 30, Sibelius incorrectly guesses the octave of the E on the second half of the first beat. There is logic behind this madness, however.

On a MIDI keyboard, you can specify not just accidentals, but the exact octave of the pitch. With alphabetic entry, however, Sibelius has to do some guesswork. If you were to begin from the very first note of the piece, Sibelius would choose the octave closest to the middle line. For example, if you pressed the F key on the numeric keypad in treble clef, Sibelius would choose the F in octave 4 because it's slightly closer to the middle line of the staff than the F in octave 5. This isn't arbitrary; clefs are chosen carefully for each instrument to increase the likelihood that you won't have to use many ledger lines. Instruments that have exceptionally wide ranges or ranges that cross clefs will often use more than one clef. Their principal clef, however, reflects their comfortable range. Therefore, if you say to Sibelius, "I'd like a G, but guess which one," it's going to go for the one most plumb in the middle of comfortable range. Following this logic, you might think that Sibelius would *always* choose pitches closest to the middle of the staff, but it does something cleverer. It chooses the note closest to the preceding one.

Note: There's a whole field of research within the wider fields of psychology and perception that posits that human beings will find a line of music fits their expectations the closer it is to being unison or stepwise. Other rules tell us things like if a melodic line *does* have a leap (a perfect fifth or greater), it will most likely reverse direction—a principle called *registral return*. If such things interest you, look up the names Eugene Narmour and Glenn Shellenberg. If such things bore you to tears, they are at least still at practical work in Sibelius. When you type a subsequent pitch, it's following a rule that is going to be right the great majority of the time. That is, most of the time, the octave of a pitch is probably closest to the last pitch. Even the most complex modernist works often fit to this principle, not least because it's exhausting and terribly difficult to perform music with many large jumps in it.

To better understand this principle, see Figure 2.62. In this example, when the user enters the F, Sibelius chooses the one closest to the middle line of the staff.

The next three pitches are all within the closest octave. Then, when the user enters the C, Sibelius chooses the lower C because it is closer to the preceding F, even though the top C is required; you can press Ctrl+Up Arrow (Command+Up Arrow) to move it up an octave. Finally, the interval from E to B flat is a tritone, so there is no closest pitch. Sibelius takes a stab by assigning the lower pitch.

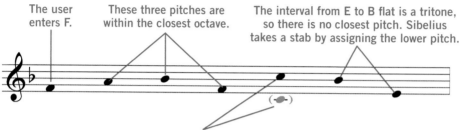

The user enters F.

These three pitches are within the closest octave.

The interval from E to B flat is a tritone, so there is no closest pitch. Sibelius takes a stab by assigning the lower pitch.

When the user enters the C, Sibelius chooses the lower C because it is closer to the preceding F, even though the top C is required.

Figure 2.62
The logic behind pitches chosen in alphabetic entry.

To rectify the aforementioned problem in bar 30, where the E is placed on the wrong octave, move the E pitch to the correct octave by pressing Ctrl+Up Arrow or Ctrl+Down Arrow (Command+Up Arrow or Command+Down Arrow). The pitch will move. Sibelius remains in Create Note mode, meaning you can enter the next pitch and carry on. This will happen again as you complete this bar, so you can practice doing it quickly.

Complete the second violin part to the same bar as the violin part, remembering to toggle the staccatos on where necessary and off again when not. Next, it's time for revision. Input the viola and cello parts using step-time entry or alphabetic entry, or use a combination of the two if you prefer.

Entering Triplets

In Flexi-time recording, eighth note (quaver) triplets you play will be detected as long as you've left the defaults set in the Flexi-time Options dialog box and have the Adjust Rhythms option set to an eighth note (quaver) or shorter. You can also input triplets using alphabetic entry (discussed here), step-time entry, or mouse entry.

Note: In Sibelius, you will see the word *tuplet* from time to time. This word describes all the different divisions—for example, triplets, quintuplets, sextuplets, and septuplets. In this book, you will learn how to input triplets only, but if you choose Note Input > Note Input > Triplets (click the bottom half of the combo button), you will find options for all tuplets.

To input triplets using alphabetic entry:

1. Select bar 35 of the first violin part and add the E sharp and F sharp quarter notes (crotchets) if you haven't already. This will leave a half note (minim) rest filling the bar.

2. Begin note entry here. Add a quarter note (crotchet) rest; then change your selection to eighth note (quaver) on the numeric keypad and enter the first note of the triplet (the A).

3. Press **CTRL+3** (**COMMAND+3**) using the 3 key on the left side of the keyboard rather than the 3 on the numeric keypad, to convert the rhythm of the A and subsequent rest to a triplet, as shown in Figure 2.63.

Figure 2.63
After adding the first eighth note (quaver) of the triplet, press Ctrl+3 (Command+3) to convert it and the remaining rests into a triplet.

Note: The triplet shortcut is typed *after* the first note is input because the initial note defines the length of the triplet. For example, if you added a quarter note (crotchet) to the start of the next bar and then pressed Ctrl+3 (Command+3), you would create a quarter note (crotchet) triplet, which would fill the rhythmic space of two quarter notes (crotchets).

The Auto-Bracket Feature

Sibelius uses an auto-bracket feature to correctly bracket triplets when required. As shown in Figure 2.64, as the first two notes of the triplet are input, a bracket is added with a 3, signifying the triplet, to show that the quavers are grouped into three. If the triplet contains three notes that share a beam, as shown in Figure 2.65, Sibelius knows that the bracket is not needed and removes it, leaving the number 3 on the beam side of the notes. Naturally, the behavior of auto-brackets can be changed (although this is beyond the scope of this book).

Figure 2.64
If the three notes of a triplet are not beamed together, Sibelius adds a bracket to make the grouping clear.

Figure 2.65
If a beam connects all three notes in the triplet, Sibelius removes the bracket.

4. Continue entering notes until you reach bar 47, where there are six triplets in a row. To save you from having to use the triplet shortcut each time, you can turn on Sibelius's Sticky Tuplets feature. To do this, add the C natural eighth note (quaver) that begins the run and press **CTRL+3** (**COMMAND+3**) as before. Then press **SHIFT+ALT+K** (**SHIFT+OPTION+K**) to turn on Sticky Tuplets. A 3 will appear above the cursor, as shown in Figure 2.66. Finally, continue entering pitches (or playing them if you're using step-time entry); each will be a triplet.

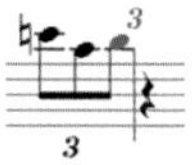

Figure 2.66
The 3 above the blue cursor indicates Sibelius has *sticky tuplets* turned on.

5. When you reach the end of bar 48, press **SHIFT+ALT+K** (**SHIFT+OPTION+K**) to turn off Sticky Tuplets.

6. Finish this section by inputting the violin to the end of the excerpt, which is bar 57.

Note: For help adding a phrase mark over triplets, as is common in much classical and romantic music, see the section "Handling Dynamics and Phrasing."

Entering Pitch Before Rhythm

If you're taking this course on your own, watch the **2.5 Entering Pitch Before Rhythm** video before reading this section.

This section may throw a spanner in the works for some, but will be a great relief to others. The former group will be composed of new users to Sibelius who have just learned alphabetic and step-time entry as well as those who may have been using Sibelius for some time. The latter group will consist of those who are new to Sibelius but have plenty of experience using other notation software, namely Finale.

Like Sibelius, Finale has a number of notation-entry methods; the closest to step-time and alphabetic entry is Speedy Entry. There is one major difference between them, however: in Speedy Entry, the user chooses the pitch first and *then* the note length. It's completely the opposite order of operations to those you've just learned in Sibelius.

Sibelius 7 offers the option of entering pitch before rhythm in both step-time entry and alphabetic entry for those who find this approach makes more sense—in general, people who have experience using Finale (although some new users may prefer being able to think about the pitch before they commit to the note length).

In this section, you can give the alternative a go. If you find it completely confusing—perhaps even detrimental to what you've just learned—then switch back and enter the rest of the music in this section (the remainder of the cello part) using your preferred method.

Tip: If you're dipping in and out of this book and want to begin this lesson from this point, open the catch-up file in the Lesson 2 folder under Core Resources called **Beethoven4.sib**.

Changing Preferences

Before you can try the pitch-before-rhythm approach, you need to tell Sibelius that's how you'd like to proceed.

To indicate that you want to use pitch-before-rhythm:

1. Choose FILE > PREFERENCES > NOTE INPUT or NOTE INPUT > NOTE INPUT and click the dialog launcher button. (see Figure 2.67).

Figure 2.67
The Note Input options in the Preferences dialog box.

2. Click the NOTE INPUT PRESET drop-down list and choose PITCH BEFORE DURATION (see Figure 2.68).

Figure 2.68
Changing the Note Input Preset setting.

Notice in Figure 2.69 that various options have changed. The Move Cursor with Arrow Keys check box is checked, the Specify Pitch, Then Duration option button is selected, and the To Specify Pitch Before Duration settings have become active. In addition, the position of the quarter note (crotchet) on the Keypad panel has changed (don't worry if this is distracting while you're still learning Sibelius's default positions—you can turn these features on or off in any combination). As you will see, other note lengths will shift with it (see Figure 2.70). Naturally, these new positions mirror those used in Finale (although, of course, Finale doesn't actually have a Keypad panel as Sibelius does).

Figure 2.69
The Note Input settings after Pitch Before Duration is selected.

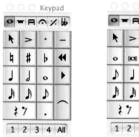

Figure 2.70
Changes to the Keypad panel when Note Input options are changed. Compare the standard Sibelius Keypad panel on the left to the changed one on the right, which matches shortcuts Finale users would be used to.

Entering Notes

In this section, you'll use the pitch-before-rhythm technique to input the cello part, starting at bar 37. (This section assumes you followed the steps in the preceding section, "Changing Preferences.")

To enter notes using the pitch-before-rhythm technique:

Note: If, after a dozen bars or so, you find the pitch-before-rhythm technique too confusing, change the settings in the Note Input section of the Preferences dialog box back to their original state and input the rest of the cello part using whatever input method you prefer.

1. Select bar 37 and press the **N KEY** for note entry.

2. While *holding down* the 0 key on the numeric keypad, press the **5 KEY** (instead of the 4 key) to add a quarter note (crotchet) rest.

3. While *holding down* the C sharp key on your MIDI keyboard, press **5** on the numeric keypad to create a quarter note (crotchet). Repeat this step for the D. You should notice a few things as you go:

    ● When you play a pitch on your MIDI keyboard, it appears as a gray shadow note just to the right of the blue cursor (see Figure 2.71). This even works if you play a chord on your MIDI keyboard; all notes appear as shadow notes until you enter a note length.

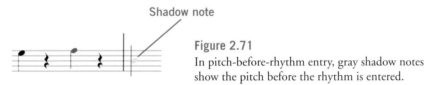

Shadow note

Figure 2.71
In pitch-before-rhythm entry, gray shadow notes show the pitch before the rhythm is entered.

    ● The Left Arrow and Right Arrow keys work differently. Normally, using the Left Arrow and Right Arrow keys to move along existing notes and rests switches you from Create Note mode to Edit Note mode. With pitch-before-rhythm, however, the mode doesn't change. Rather than inputting every quarter note (crotchet) rest, you can simply press the Right Arrow key to move the cursor and recommence input in a position later in the music. Similarly, if you make a mistake, you can use the Left Arrow key to go back and overwrite the notes previously entered.

4. Continue adding the cello part until you reach the end of bar 45. Then, choose **FILE > PREFERENCES > NOTE INPUT** or **NOTE INPUT > NOTE INPUT** and click the dialog launcher button to view the Note Input options in the Preferences dialog box. Under To Specify Pitch Before Duration, select the **USE QWERTY KEYBOARD** option button. Then, select the **USE LETTER NAMES (A–G)** option button under To Specify Pitch for Shadow Note, as shown in Figure 2.72. When you're finished, click **OK**.

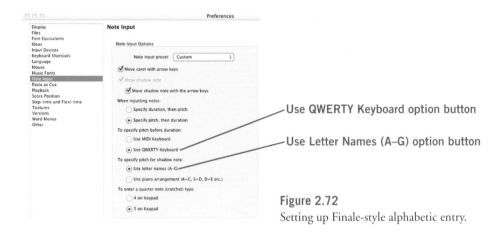

Figure 2.72
Setting up Finale-style alphabetic entry.

5. If the status bar reads Create Note, press the **RIGHT ARROW KEY** as needed to get to the third beat of bar 47. Otherwise, select bar 47, press **N** for note entry, and press the **RIGHT ARROW KEY** twice to move to the third beat of the bar. Finally, to move the shadow note—which appears as an A or a D, depending on whether you restarted Note Entry mode—to F, press the **UP ARROW** or **DOWN ARROW KEY** as needed or press the **F KEY**.

6. Press the **5 KEY** to enter a quarter note (crotchet). The F will appear in the correct space. (Unlike in MIDI-keyboard entry, in this mode, you don't have to hold the F key down.) There's a problem, however: It is supposed to be an F natural (there is a sharp in the key signature), but the Keypad panel doesn't have a Natural button in this mode (because it doesn't in that "other" program it's mimicking)! To transpose the selected note down by a semitone, press **SHIFT+PAGE DOWN**. This works in Sibelius's default alphabetic and step-time entries, as well as in Edit mode.

7. Use the same technique to enter the next F natural. Then press the **RIGHT ARROW KEY** to add rests between the quarter notes (crotchets) in the next few bars.

8. When you reach bar 51, you will discover that adding articulation marks from the Keypad panel works differently in this mode. Select the E at the start of the bar, and press the **4 KEY** for an eighth note (quaver). Then click the **STACCATO** button on the Keypad panel (see Figure 2.73). It is added *after* the note input, not before as it is in standard alphabetic input.

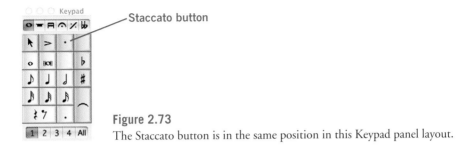

Figure 2.73
The Staccato button is in the same position in this Keypad panel layout.

9. The same is true of accidentals. Although the Natural button is missing from the Keypad panel, the Sharp and Flat buttons are there. To add the G sharp in this bar, press the **G KEY** for the initial pitch; then press the **4 KEY** on the numeric keypad for an eighth note (quaver). You must then click the **SHARP** button on the Keypad panel, as shown in Figure 2.74. Finally, remember to add the staccato once more.

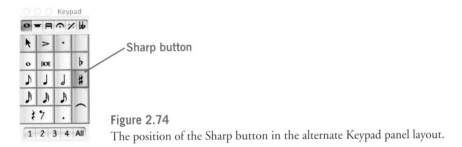

Figure 2.74
The position of the Sharp button in the alternate Keypad panel layout.

10. In alphabetic entry, articulation marks are *sticky*. That is, once you turn them on by clicking the appropriate button on the Keypad panel, they remain selected until you turn them off again. Similarly, if you require several bars of eighth notes (quavers) as you do in this passage, you need only click the corresponding Keypad panel button and then input all the note lengths. To mirror this behavior in pitch-before-rhythm mode, you can press Shift+Alt+L (Shift+Option+L) to lock the selected note value and articulation. Try it here, before adding the next pitch: Press **SHIFT+ALT+L** (**SHIFT+OPTION+L**) and lock in the **EIGHTH NOTE (QUAVER)** button on the Keypad panel, and the staccato (see Figure 2.75). Then finally, play the subsequent pitches. You may find that some of the usual functionality with the arrow keys is lost, but you can toggle the lock on and off as required.

11. Unless you're really bamboozled by this input method, complete the cello part to the end of the excerpt.

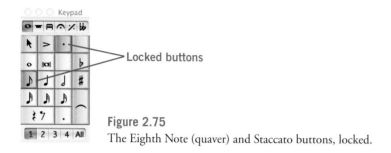

Figure 2.75
The Eighth Note (quaver) and Staccato buttons, locked.

Now it's decision time. If you want to become a really fast Sibelius user, you probably won't want to change between the pitch-before-duration and duration-before-pitch modes very often. My advice? Stick with the one that feels more natural to you. If you aren't sure, go with Sibelius's default mode, duration before pitch. That is the mode used in the rest of this course.

To return to the default layout:

1. Choose FILE > PREFERENCES > NOTE INPUT or NOTE INPUT > NOTE INPUT > DIALOG LAUNCHER BUTTON.

2. Click the NOTE INPUT PRESET drop-down list and choose DURATION BEFORE PITCH (see Figure 2.76).

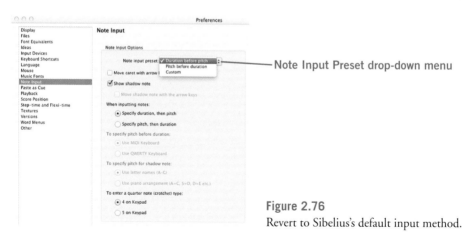

Figure 2.76
Revert to Sibelius's default input method.

Handling Dynamics and Phrasing

As usual, there is a corresponding video, called **2.6 Handling Dynamics and Phrasing**. If you're learning on your own, watch it before completing this section.

There is still one important note entry method, repitch, to learn. You'll get to that in the next section. Before you can do that, however, there are a few more things you need to know.

You've completed two of the four parts of the Beethoven excerpt, but you have skipped over several important score elements to concentrate on learning the note-input methods. Although you did learn how to add an articulation mark (the staccato) during note input, you have so far ignored all other markings, such as those related to phrasing and dynamics. In this section, you'll go back through the music you've added so far and discover how to quickly add these elements in Edit mode. You'll also add the second violin part to the final section to learn how to add these marks as you input the notes.

Tip: If you're dipping in and out of this book and want to begin this lesson from
      this point, you can open the catch-up file on your CD called **Beethoven5.sib**.

Adding Expression Text

To add expression text—in this example, adding the *p* dynamic marking to each part at the opening:

1. Press **CTRL+HOME** (**COMMAND+HOME**) to return to the first page of your score.

2. Select the first note in the first bar of the first violin; then choose **TEXT** > **STYLES** > **EXPRESSION**. (You will notice in Figure 2.77 that the Expression style set is the first one shown in the Styles group. This is because it's the style set most often used in Sibelius. If your ribbon doesn't have enough space to display the gallery within it, you'll find Expression text under Common near the top of the list.)

Expression style set

Figure 2.77
Adding expression text. If your ribbon doesn't have enough space to show the gallery preview, Expression text is found under Common in the resulting list.

3. A flashing cursor appears below the staff. Press the **P KEY**; a rather wimpy-looking dynamic marking appears, as shown in Figure 2.78.

Figure 2.78
Simply typing the letters of the dynamic you need will result in wimpy-like markings like this *p* marking.

By default, Sibelius uses a simple italic font. If you were typing a word—for example, *crescendo*—this font would be perfectly fine. However, in music publishing, the dynamics letters **p**, **m**, **f**, **s** and **z** are typically written in bold to make them stand out and easy to read. They also use a special font.

Delete the marking you just added and begin again. There are two ways to quickly add dynamics markings with this font to your Sibelius score:

■ After you specify where in the score the dynamics marking should go and click Expression in the Text tab's Styles group, right-click at the flashing cursor and choose **p** from the menu of commonly used expression marks that appears (see in Figure 2.79). As shown in Figure 2.80, the selected dynamic appears in your score, looking much better than the dynamic in Figure 2.78. When you're finished entering markings, press the Esc key to switch from Text Input mode to Edit Text mode. (Notice that the text remains highlighted; you'll learn why soon.)

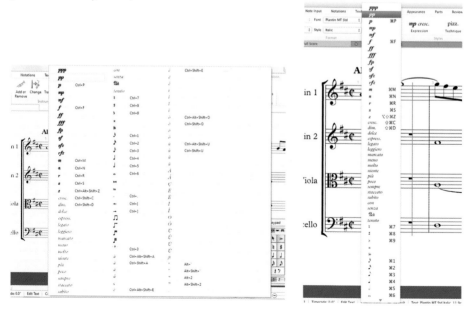

Figure 2.79
The menu that appears when you right-click in Edit Text mode is slightly different in Windows (left) than on a Mac (right).

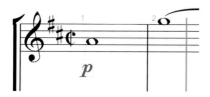

Figure 2.80
Dynamics entered correctly look like this.

■ After you specify where in the score the dynamics marking should go by selecting a note, press Ctrl+E (Command+E) to select the Expression style set in the Text tab's Styles group, and hold down the Ctrl (Command) key as you type the letter for the marking.

Try this second technique on the second violin part:

1. Select the first note.

2. Press **CTRL+E** (**COMMAND+E**).

3. Press **CTRL+P** (**COMMAND+P**) to enter a *p* marking with the special font.

4. For practice, press **ESC** twice; then, to add another piece of expression text, press **CTRL+E** (**COMMAND+E**). Press **CTRL+M+F** (**COMMAND+M+F**) to enter an *mf* marking. That is, hold down the **CTRL** (**COMMAND**) **KEY** as you press the **M KEY** and then the **F KEY**.

5. Create another dynamic for practice. This time, once you have created some expression text, press **CTRL+F+F+F** (**COMMAND+F+F+F**) to enter an *fff* marking. That is, while holding down the **CTRL** (**COMMAND**) **KEY**, press the **F KEY** three times. Then undo both these practice markings.

6. Press **ESC** when you're finished typing.

Note: Because typing them in is the quickest way to add dynamics, you should master the keyboard shortcut for entering expression text rather than relying on the ribbon to find it each time you need it. There are 63 more dynamic markings in this excerpt alone, so it's worth working out how to add them as quickly as possible!

If a score contains many instances of the same marking, there's no need to keep adding it over and over. Another approach is to copy and paste it.

To copy and paste a marking:

1. Select the dynamic that you want to copy so that it is highlighted blue (you don't need to double-click it, which would edit it).

2. Press **CTRL+C** (**COMMAND+C**).

3. Select the note under which you want to paste the dynamic—in this case, select the first note in the viola part. The note becomes blue.

4. Press **CTRL+V** (**COMMAND+V**). The marking is pasted under the selected note.

If you already entered dynamics as regular text rather than the correct dynamics font in one or more scores, don't worry; it's easy to fix using the Change Dynamics plug-in. Choose Text > Plug-ins > Change Dynamics. The Change Dynamics plug-in is very useful for quickly changing the overall dynamic level of a passage of music in your score after the fact, but it also has a little-known yet powerful bonus feature: It enables you to restore your dynamics to the Music Text font.

*When the plug-in dialog box comes up, you can choose to run the plug-in on a region of the piece or on the whole score. Notice the Update the Font of Dynamics That Don't Change option, which is checked by default. Important: In this case, you don't want to change anything but the font of the dynamics, so make sure that the Custom Dynamic Mapping option button is selected. Also, if you have extreme dynamics such as **pppp**, make sure you uncheck the Limit Extremes option.*

When you click OK, the Custom Dynamic Mapping dialog box will open. For now, don't change any values in this dialog box; just press Return or Enter or click OK. The plug-in will run, updating the font of all of your dynamics to the correct one.

—Robert Puff, musician, arranger, and notation expert

Robert regularly publishes tutorials, ideas, and other interesting facts about working with Sibelius on his Web sites, www.rpmseattle.com/

On the Web   **of_note and www.musicprep.com/sibelius.**

Using Quick-Copy

You can also use Sibelius's Quick-Copy feature to copy markings. With a dynamic already selected, simply Alt-click (Option-click) or use the middle mouse button (if you have one) where you want that marking to be pasted.

Be aware, however, that if you use this method, the pasted marking will be placed where you click rather than in its default position. This may not seem like a huge problem, but if you are pasting a dynamic into more than one part (or several dynamics one after another into the same part), they are less likely to be aligned, and therefore your music will be less tidy.

(See Figure 2.81 and Figure 2.82 to compare and contrast markings pasted at their default position versus markings pasted with Quick-Copy.) To fix this problem, hold down Shift as well as Alt (Option) when you click.

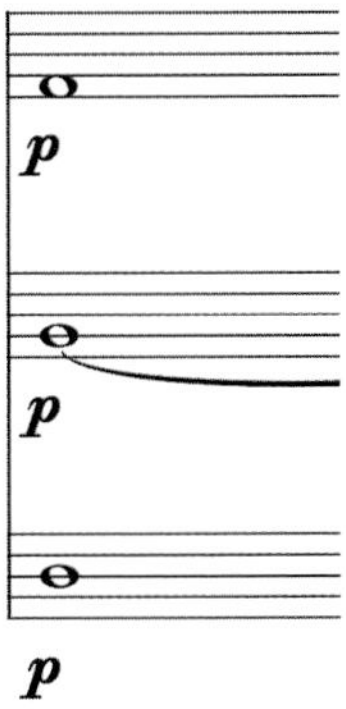

Figure 2.81
Dynamics pasted at their default position (by clicking on the note above first) will retain their default position and line up nicely.

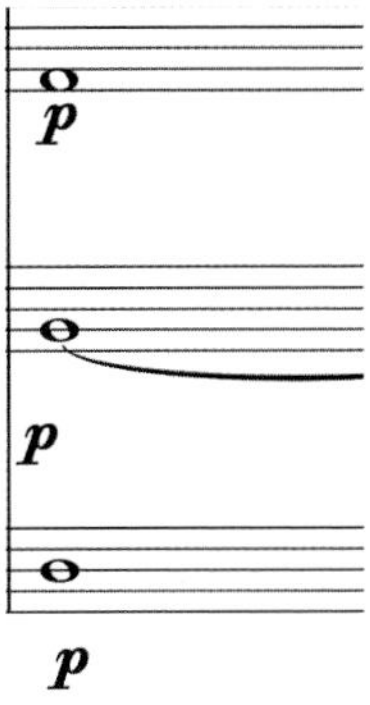

Figure 2.82
Dynamics pasted with Quick-Copy may align badly and make your score look messy.

Notice that at bar 13, the second violin and cello have the instruction *p cresc.*, as shown in Figure 2.83. This requires the use of two fonts: the special font for the dynamic and an italic font for the word *cresc.* (which, of course, is the abbreviated version of *crescendo*, instructing the player to gradually play louder). Fortunately, switching from one font to the other is a simple matter.

Figure 2.83
A mix of fonts is used in this dynamic marking: the special font for the *p* dynamic and plain italics for the word *cresc.*

To switch from one font to another:

1. Select the note in bar 13 of the second violin part under which the dynamic will be written.

2. Press **CTRL+E** (**COMMAND+E**).

3. Press **CTRL+P** (**COMMAND+P**) to insert the *p*.

4. Release the **CTRL** (**COMMAND**) **KEY**, press the **SPACE BAR**, and type **CRESC.** to complete the marking.

5. Add this same marking to the cello part in bar 13 and to the first violin part in bar 15. Also add the **CRESC.** in bar 13 of the viola part.

Using Multicopy

As shown in Figure 2.84, at bar 16, all parts play *f* at once, and at bar 17 they all play *p*. Using Copy and Paste makes it easy to create these dynamics quickly, but it is still relatively laborious to paste each dynamic into each part one by one.

Figure 2.84
The whole string quartet changing dynamics together.

Enter multicopy. Multicopy enables you to copy anything in your score and paste it to fill a new selection. For example, you could copy a one-bar *ostinato*, select another 50 bars, and use multicopy to paste the single bar 50 times to fill the selection. (Eat your heart out, Steve Reich!) Multicopy also works with single elements like dynamics.

For example, to copy a marking in the first violin part to three other parts (the second violin, the viola, and the cello):

1. Enter an *f* marking in the first violin part in bar 16.

2. Press **Esc** once to change to Edit mode. Copy the marking with the usual shortcut: Press **Ctrl+C** (**Command+C**).

3. Select the second violin, viola, and cello parts by selecting bar 16 in the second violin part and then Shift-clicking the cello part below (see in Figure 2.85).

4. Press **Ctrl+V** (**Command+V**). The dynamic is pasted into all three parts at its default position.

5. To practice, copy any *p* dynamic in the score. Then repeat steps 3 and 4 and this time creating a passage selection of all four parts in bar 17 and pasting the dynamic into all four parts at once. It's a huge time saver!

Figure 2.85
The blue highlight in bar 16 in the second violin, viola, and cello parts indicates a passage selection.

Unless you're working on your score in Panorama view, you may have noticed that a dynamic turned red when you multicopied it into the score (see Figure 2.86). Sibelius turns elements of your score red when it can't find space for them (or, in the case of notes, when they're out of range). As you did in Lesson 1, you can fix any problems with spacing between staves by choosing Layout > Staff Spacing > Optimize.

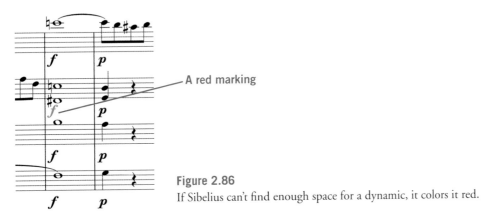

A red marking

Figure 2.86
If Sibelius can't find enough space for a dynamic, it colors it red.

You now have a number of strategies for inputting dynamics using Expression text. Use these to put in the *cresc.* markings at bar 23 and the *p* markings at either side of the barline at bar 26.

Adding Hairpins

The dynamic markings in bars 27 and 28 of the cello part (followed by the other parts in subsequent bars) do not use expression (or any other kind of) text. Instead, they use crescendo and diminuendo lines, which in Sibelius are known as *hairpins* (a term often used to refer to them in jazz and other styles).

To enter hairpins in the cello part:

1. Select the note in the cello part at bar 27 and press the **H KEY** for hairpin. Sibelius draws a hairpin to the end of the bar.

2. Click the first note in the next bar, and press **SHIFT+H** to add the diminuendo line.

3. In the same bar (bar 28), add the crescendos to the first and second violins as shown in Figure 2.87. Notice that when you click the first note for the second violin and press H, the line is drawn only to the next note, not through the whole bar. To space out the line, press the **SPACE BAR**. Each time you press it, the line extends one note. If you extend it too far, just use undo or press **SHIFT+SPACE BAR**, and the line will contract.

Figure 2.87
Crescendo and diminuendo lines in Sibelius. The shortcut is H, which is short for *hairpins*.

If you like, you can even use multicopy to add hairpins to both parts at once. Try this in bar 31 of the viola and cello parts and in bar 32 of the first and second violin parts. To select *both* the crescendo and diminuendo hairpins, hold down Ctrl (Command) key as you click the second line.

To review using multicopy:

1. Select the first crescendo line from the cello part in bar 27.

2. Hold down the **CTRL (COMMAND) KEY** and select the diminuendo line from the cello part in bar 28.

3. Press **CTRL+C (COMMAND+C)** to copy the two lines.

4. Select both the cello and viola parts in bar 31.

5. Press **CTRL+V (COMMAND+V)** to paste the lines into both parts.

6. Select both the first and second violin parts in bar 32 and press **CTRL+V (COMMAND+V)** to perform the multicopy there, too.

Tip: As you can see, you can enter hairpins very quickly with a few shortcuts, and can multicopy them even faster. If you prefer to use the mouse, however, you can. Simply choose **Notation > Lines > Crescendo** or **Decrescendo**, as shown in Figure 2.88.

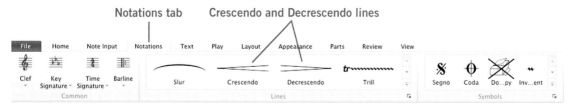

Figure 2.88
The location of the hairpins on the ribbon.

Notice that the hairpins should climax on beat 3 of bar 33 in the second violin (shown in Figure 2.89), not on the first beat.

Figure 2.89
Bars 31 to 33 in the second violin part.

To fix the problem with the hairpins:

1. Click the start of the diminuendo line in bar 33. As shown in Figure 2.90, a blue square handle will appear to let you know it's selected.

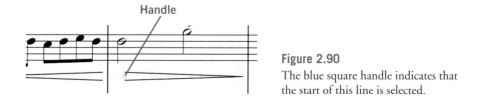

Figure 2.90
The blue square handle indicates that the start of this line is selected.

2. Press the **SPACE BAR** to move the start to beat 3. Alternatively, drag it with the mouse.

You can extend the end of the crescendo in bar 32 in exactly the same way. Do that now.

Adding Phrase Marks and Slurs

Although phrase marks and slurs are subtly different types of music notation, they are drawn the same way, and you input them into Sibelius in the same way.

Note: Phrase marks mean different things to different players—a point worth bearing in mind if you're adding your own phrasing lines to music. To a pianist, a phrasing line shows a small section of music (in fact, a phrase), which should be musically structured like a sentence. To a violinist, a phrasing line shows how many notes should fit under one bow. If no phrasing is present, a violinist assumes each note is a separate bow. In contrast, to a wind or brass player, a phrase mark may suggest a different kind of tonguing or other articulation to create as little a gap between notes as possible.

To add a slur:

1. Click the first note in bar 1 of the first violin part to select it.

2. Press **S** for slur. A slur is added.

Note: There is a distinct difference between a tie (which you've already added via the Keypad panel) and a slur or phrase mark. A *tie* appears between two notes of the same pitch and tells the player to join them together as one note. If you enter a tie in the place of a slur (Sibelius users less expert than you make this mistake often), it will not only look wrong, but it may play back in funny ways, creating held notes that never end.

Bar 3 contains a phrase that extends over the whole bar, as shown in Figure 2.91.

Here's one way to quickly add this line (similar to the process you learned for hairpins):

Figure 2.91
The phrase in bar 3.

1. Click the first note in the bar.

2. Press **S** to add a slur from that first note to the second note.

3. Repeatedly press the **SPACE BAR** to space the line out across the bar.

Note: Remember, if your markings (dynamics, slurs, and so on) don't fit between the staves, Sibelius will color them red. To automatically make room for them, choose Layout > Staff Spacing > Optimize as you learned in Lesson 1.

Alternatively, if you aren't averse to picking up the mouse, simply select the whole bar and press S. The slur will automatically include every note in the selection. (This shortcut works for other types of lines. For instance, you could use the mouse to select the same bar and press H to add a crescendo line spanning the length of the bar.) You can also use the mouse to select the bar and then choose Notation > Lines > Slur.

Adding Dynamics and Phrasing On the Fly

So far, adding dynamics and phrasing has involved first selecting an object. That means even if you have learned the shortcut, you've still had to pick up your mouse and click to begin. To really speed things up, you must learn how to work on your score without clicking. Start by entering the three phrase marks in bars 8 and 9 of the first violin (see Figure 2.92).

Figure 2.92
The three phrase marks in bars 8 and 9 of the first violin.

To explore adding dynamics and phrasing on the fly:

1. Click the first note of bar 8 in the first violin part. (This is the only click in this procedure, I promise!)

2. Press **S** to add a slur from the A to the B. Then press the **SPACE BAR** once to space the slur out farther to the next A.

3. Press the **TAB KEY**. Pressing the Tab key cycles your selection through each object on the staff. Therefore, your selection jumps back to the note you started the slur from.

4. Press the **RIGHT ARROW KEY** three times to move to the start of the next phrase.

Tip: If you need to move through notes more quickly, press Ctrl+Right Arrow or Left Arrow (Command+Right Arrow or Left Arrow) to move one bar at a time rather than one note at a time.

5. Press **S** and then press the **SPACE BAR** two times to draw the next phrase mark.

6. Press the **TAB KEY** to return to the last-selected note; then press the **RIGHT ARROW KEY** four times to move to the start of the next slur.

7. Press **S** one last time to enter the final phrase.

8. Using the mouse as little as possible, enter the phrase markings in the remainder of the excerpt until all that is left to do is complete the second violin and viola lines for the last 20 bars.

Tip: If you're ever unsure what Sibelius is doing, check the status bar. As shown in Figure 2.93, it will indicate when you're editing a line.

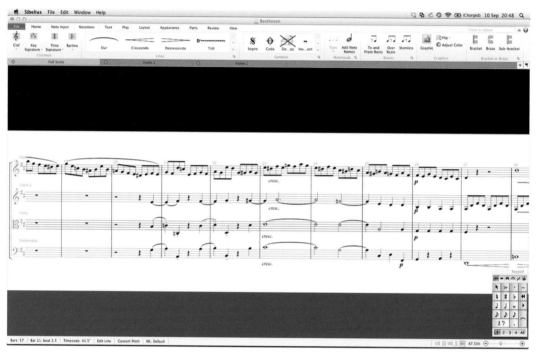

Figure 2.93
The status readout showing Edit Line.

Tip: If a slur appears above the notes when you meant for it to go below them (or vice versa), press X to flip it to the other side. (The easy way to remember this shortcut is to think of an X as a cross, for flipping the slur "across" the staff.)

Note: The new shortcut here is the Tab key. If you've ever used a computer program that allows you to create tables, like a spreadsheet program or even a word processor, you may know that pressing Tab moves you to the next cell in the table. In Sibelius, the Tab key behaves in a similar way: Pressing it takes you to the next element in the score. Try pressing Tab repeatedly; soon you'll notice that you can select dynamics this way or cycle through the notes (like pressing the Right Arrow), too. Pressing Shift+Tab takes you through each element in the opposite order.

So far this might not seem very "on the fly" to you, despite the heading for this section. You're learning fast editing skills, but "on the fly" suggests that you ought to be able to input all these dynamics and phrasing at the same time you create the notes to which they relate, right? Right. Once you've finished editing the existing material, it's time to input the remaining bars of the second violin and learn how to input *everything* in the music as you go. To do this, you'll use alphabetic entry or step-time entry together with the shortcuts you've learned in this section, including the Tab key.

Note: You're probably getting sick of reading how much quicker it is to do every-thing with the keyboard. Of course, that's not *always* true. And anyway, you can use Sibelius however you want. But if you can learn to do many things with keystrokes, you'll input much more music in less time!

To enter more music:

1. Select bar 36 in the second violin part and press **N** for note entry. Then add a G on the second beat of bar 36. Next, press **S** to add a slur. It will hang over the next beat, disconnected, as shown in Figure 2.94.

    Figure 2.94
    A slur is inserted in Create Note mode and hangs into the next beat.

2. Add the F sharp and watch the slur align with it perfectly, as shown in Figure 2.95.

    Figure 2.95
    As soon as a note is added, Sibelius aligns the hanging tie with it perfectly.

3. In bar 37, repeat the same process for the G and F sharp.

4. After typing the F sharp, press **SHIFT+S** to end the slur. (This wasn't necessary in bar 36 because a rest came next. It wouldn't make sense for a slur to go over a rest, so Sibelius ended it for you.)

5. Before you add the lower F sharp, add the staccato marking from the Keypad panel. Then toggle it off so it isn't repeated on the next note.

6. Using the same method for slurs and staccato, input all notes to bar 45.

7. At bar 45, input the C natural on the third beat, press **CTRL+3** (**COMMAND+3**) to create a triplet, and then press **SHIFT+ALT+K** (**SHIFT+OPTION+K**) to turn on Sticky Tuplets.

8. Before you add the next note, press **S** to add a slur. Then enter the next *five* notes and watch the slur extend over all of them as you type.

9. You could add the *sf* under the second C right after inputting it, but this will effectively stop input of the sticky slur and triplets. Instead, after completing the phrase, press the **LEFT ARROW KEY** to go back to the C. Then press **CTRL+E** (**COMMAND+E**), press **CTRL+S+F** (**COMMAND+S+F**) (that is, hold down the **CTRL** or **COMMAND KEY**, press the **S KEY**, and then press the **F KEY**) to enter the dynamic, press **ESC**, and then press **TAB** to return to the note.

10. Press the **RIGHT ARROW KEY** as needed to move to the start of the next bar. Then begin note entry again using the process from step 7. (In fact, the exact same phrase is repeated, so you could just copy and paste it. But it's good practice to enter it normally.) You should end up with two bars that appear just as in Figure 2.96.

Figure 2.96
The completed passage.

Note: You may have noticed that you didn't need to press Shift+S to end the slur, nor did you have to press Shift+Alt+K (Shift+Option+K) to toggle the Sticky Tuplets off. That's because pressing the Right Arrow or Left Arrow key automatically takes you from Create mode to Edit mode, thus cancelling the Sticky Tuplets and slurs.

These steps may seem very elaborate. But in fact, however you inputted the notes, you'd have to create the triplets, add the slurs, and the dynamics. This method allows you to do it all at once!

Note: If you're finding it slow going and a little overwhelming, don't worry. These processes become second nature after you've practiced them for a while. For practice, why not get hold of a copy of the rest of this quartet and input the whole thing?

You've nearly completed the second violin part; there's just one more thing to try out. When you come to bar 55, you can add the crescendo hairpin on the fly.

To add the crescendo hairpin on the fly:

1. Input the staccato B half note (minim) on the first beat of bar 55 and press **H** for a crescendo hairpin.

2. Enter the two A pitches and the G sharp. Watch the hairpin extend automatically as you input.

3. Although the hairpin actually ends under the G sharp, you should input the A in the final bar with it still on. Hairpins automatically extend to the note you're inputting.

4. Because it's your last note, you don't actually need to, but press **H** again to end the sticky hairpin just to get into the habit.

Note: You may be wondering why the input process for some sticky lines is slightly different. For example, to begin a sticky slur while inputting notes, you press S, and to end it you press Shift+S. In contrast, to both begin and end a sticky hairpin, you simply press H. The reason input is different for slurs is that you will sometimes need to have one slur under another—for example, if there were an overarching two-bar phrase with slurred notes underneath it, as shown in Figure 2.97. You could create this by pressing S to begin the overarching phrase, then pressing S again to begin the shorter slur. But pressing Shift+S would only end the last slur that was begun, meaning the overarching phrase would continue until you pressed Shift+S twice. In contrast, you'd never need to have two hairpins at once; it simply wouldn't make sense. So you can toggle them on and off with the same shortcut, just to make it easier.

Figure 2.97
Slurs under an
overarching phrase.

Exploring Magnetic Layout

As you've been working, you may have noticed that every now and then, a slur will jump out of the way of a note or a dynamic will make room for a note on ledger lines below the staff. You may also have noticed that when you select one dynamic, dotted lines and brackets appear that connect it to other dynamics, as shown in Figure 2.98. These little bits of magic show Magnetic Layout at work.

If you've never used notation software before, you're probably thinking that it's fairly obvious that one element of the score should stay out of the way of another. And you'd be right—yet Sibelius is the only music software with such self-awareness.

Figure 2.98
When a dynamic is selected, dotted lines and brackets appear. This is Magnetic Layout at work.

In all other software, and in versions of Sibelius prior to Sibelius 6, not only would you have to manually move things out of the way of each other, but you'd have to do it all over again in the parts when you'd finished the score. Magnetic Layout saves you literally *hours* of time on big projects.

To get an idea of how much work Sibelius does for you, view page spreads horizontally (not in Panorama). Optimize staff spacing if necessary, and then choose Layout > Magnetic Layout > Magnetic Layout to toggle Magnetic Layout off. Figure 2.99 shows bars 27 to 30 with Magnetic Layout off. As you can see, when Magnetic Layout is turned off, hairpins crash into notes and phrasing, and the phrasing in the cello part goes through the accidental in bar 28. In contrast, Figure 2.100 shows the same bars with it turned on again. Everything looks much tidier!

Figure 2.99
Bars 27 to 30 with Magnetic Layout turned off.

You can have a little fun with Magnetic Layout! Choose Layout > Magnetic Layout > Magnetic Layout to toggle Magnetic Layout back on. Then drag a note in the middle of a phrase up or down (depending on the part you choose) until it is on many ledger lines and watch the phrase mark move out of the way, as in Figure 2.101. In addition to trying to keep out of the way of each other, objects also try to stay aligned. As shown back in Figure 2.97, if you select a dynamic that is proximate to other dynamics (the example given is from bar 17), dotted lines and brackets appear that connect it to other dynamics.

Figure 2.100
Bars 27 to 30 with Magnetic Layout turned on.

Figure 2.101
A slur doing contortions just to
keep out of the way of a rogue note.

As long as there is space and they are not forced too far away from the staff, dynamics will try to remain aligned with other dynamics on the same staff (horizontally) and also with dynamics in the same position in other staves (vertically). To witness this first hand, try dragging the C on the first beat of bar 17 down. When it gets to G or F sharp in octave 4, its beam forces the *p* dynamic below to move down and avoid a clash. Note in Figure 2.102 that the dynamics in the two bars before also move down to retain alignment.

Figure 2.102
When one dynamic has to move lower to avoid a clash with a beam, other dynamics in proximate bars move down too, to retain perfect alignment.

Once the note reaches E or lower, there is no longer any room between the staves for that dynamic, so it moves to the left of the barline (also avoiding a clash with the barline). As shown in Figure 2.103, the dynamics in the parts below also move to the left to stay in line.

Figure 2.103
If there is no further vertical space, the dynamic finds a space to the left of the note, and all dynamics below it move with it to maintain alignment.

In the parts for your score, Sibelius takes into account transposition and special engraving rules for page turns, still using Magnetic Layout to keep everything as neat as possible. More on this in later in the section "Working with Parts."

Reinputting Pitches

If you like watching the video before you read each section, this is the time to watch the video **2.7 Reinputting Pitches**.

The score is now nearly complete. The only part remaining is the viola from bar 36. You now have all the skills to input this part quickly, but first a bit of observation: If you compare the viola part in this section of the score to the second violin part, you will find that they are often playing homophonically. Through this passage, the viola does sometimes play independently from the second violin, but the great majority of its part has the same rhythm, phrasing, articulation, and dynamics as the second violin. Enter Sibelius's Reinput Pitches feature.

Tip: There is a catch-up file on your CD called **Beethoven6.sib** if you'd like to do this section but haven't already created the whole score to this point.

Note: Homophonic writing has been used in all genres of music since the medieval period. In homophonic music, two or more parts share the same rhythm but play different notes to create harmony—think horn stabs in big band jazz, broad choral choruses from the Baroque period, or shimmering string writing in film music. In homophonic writing, composers don't just write the same rhythm between parts. They also usually share dynamics, phrasing, and articulation, so the chords sound as one.

Copying Passages: A Review

To use Reinput Pitches, you must first copy passages from the second violin where the viola is playing homophonically.

To copy a passage:

1. Making sure you have nothing selected, select bar 36 in the second violin.

2. Extend this passage selection to the middle of bar 43. To do so, hold down the **Shift key** as you click the D in that bar. All bars in between become highlighted blue.

3. You could use Copy and Paste, but Sibelius's Quick-Copy feature is quicker. To use it, hold down the **Alt** (**Option**) **key** and click bar 36 in the viola part.

Reinput Pitches

Now you're ready to use Reinput Pitches. Because you're leaving the rhythm, articulation, and dynamics as they are, you only need to change the pitches.

To use Reinput Pitches:

1. Select the first note in the passage you just copied into the viola part, beginning in bar 36.

2. To enter Reinput Pitches mode, choose **Note Input** > **Note Input** > **Reinput Pitches**. A dotted blue line appears in front of the note (in Figure 2.104 it is shown between the first and second notes for clarity, after the first note has been changed).

Figure 2.104
The dotted blue line in front of the note shows you that you are in Reinput Pitches mode.

3. Using the alphabetic entry method, input the pitches, this time entering accidentals on the Keypad panel *after* typing the pitch (as though you're in Edit mode rather than Create mode). Alternatively, use a MIDI keyboard, as with step-time entry. You will discover that you don't need to worry about rests. Sibelius knows you're just reinputting pitches; if there are rests, they are ignored. The next pitch you input affects the next note in the staff.

4. When you reach the end of the passage, input the independent viola line to the second half of bar 47, where you can again copy and repitch the second violin part to bar 51.

5. Copy and repitch starting at bar 54 to the end of the excerpt. The score is complete.

Congratulations! Take a well-deserved break and listen to your copy of Beethoven's magnificent work.

Working with Parts

 You can watch the video **2.8 Working with Parts** before reading this section.

If you're old enough to remember copying out parts by hand, you'll know that the greatest asset of even the earliest notation programs was the ability to automate this process, at least to some extent. For the hand copyist, completing the score meant the job was only half done. Every note then had to be copied again—and if the score wasn't a transposing score, transposition had to be done for the parts as they were copied.

As notation programs matured, they became better at making parts. They would count all the bars rest together and make multirests, take care of the transposition, and even look for good places to make page turns. But until Sibelius 5 came along in 2007, all programs *extracted* parts. That is, each part became a separate file. So if you revised a passage, you had to make that change in every part *and* in the score or extract all the parts again.

What modern composers, arrangers, copyists, hobbyists, teachers, and students have with Sibelius 7 are features like Magnetic Layout and Dynamic Parts (more on what makes them dynamic in a second) that save literally *days* of work over hand-copying and even some other notation software. Unless you've lived through hand-copying, you can't begin to imagine how lucky you are!

Tip: If you didn't need to learn entry, but just want to find out how Sibelius's parts work, there is a catch-up file called **Beethoven7.sib** that will give you a complete score from which to work.

Opening a Part

You may have noticed a strip of gray below the ribbon and above the main score. This strip of gray has the words "Full Score" on the left and two buttons—one with a plus sign (+)—on the right. This is the Document Tab bar (see Figure 2.105), another innovation in Sibelius 7, this one drawing on the popular tabbed document interface used by most modern Web browsers (Firefox, Safari, Chrome, et al.). You've only seen one tab open—the Full Score tab on the left—because you haven't yet looked at any parts.

Document Tab bar

Figure 2.105
The Document Tab bar in Sibelius 7.

To look at a part:

1. Click the **PLUS** (+) button on the right side of the Document Tab bar. As shown in Figure 2.106, a menu containing all the parts in the score appears. By default, Sibelius creates one part for each instrument added to the score; in this case, there are four parts.

Figure 2.106
Clicking the plus (+) menu shows a menu of available parts.

Note: Sibelius can support complex combinations of parts, parts that don't show in the score, and instruments in the score that don't have a part. You don't need to worry about such things at this level, however.

2. Choose **VIOLIN 1** from the menu. Sibelius opens a new tab. You can now change between the full score and violin 1 part by simply clicking the appropriate tab.

3. Repeat this process to open tabs for each remaining part—violin 2, viola, and violoncello—as shown in Figure 2.107. If your window isn't wide enough to fit all four tabs, click the Open Tabs button, also shown in Figure 2.107, and choose the desired part from the menu that appears.

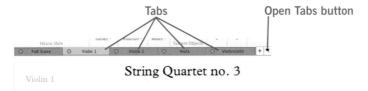

Figure 2.107
Tabs for each part you've opened, in addition to the full score and the Open Tabs button.

Several things should strike you about each part (see Figure 2.108):

■ The part's name appears in the top-left corner, in addition to the title and composer text that you added to the full score. (The part name also appears at the top of page 2.)

■ The four bars that the violin *doesn't* play—bars 11 to 14—have been combined to create one multirest instead of four separate bars of rest.

■ Because it doesn't need to take into account the other three instruments that were in the score, the music has been respaced.

■ Bar numbers have been calculated at the start of each system.

■ At the bottom of the page, Sibelius has added the letters "V.S.," for "Volti Subito." This translates roughly to, "Turn the page quickly"—an indication that Sibelius wasn't able to find an appropriate place for the player to turn the page (for example, where they had some rests).

■ The page color is subtly different. The cream color serves as a reminder that you're looking not at the score, but at a part (in case you wondered where all the other staves went).

Naturally, there's a keyboard shortcut to quickly jump between the full score and a part: the W key. (Why the W key is the shortcut for switching between the full score and a part isn't immediately obvious; this one might need writing down somewhere.)

To try the keyboard shortcut, return to the full score, and then do the following:

1. Select any note or passage in any part so it is highlighted blue.

Figure 2.108
The violin 1 part, with some automated formatting by Sibelius.

2. Press the **W** KEY. Sibelius switches you not only to the part in which you made the selection, but to the same note or passage so you won't lose your place (see Figure 1.109).

Figure 2.109
The full score and violin 1 part, open in separate windows. Note that the selection in the full score exactly mirrors the selection in the part.

3. Press **W** again to jump back to the score.

Note: If you use the W shortcut with nothing selected, Sibelius assumes you want to return to the most recently open part.

The Parts tab on the ribbon includes various advanced options (see Figure 2.110). You don't need to trouble yourself with these now, but it's worth taking a quick look at them. Now that you have a broad understanding of what parts are and how they work, you may find some of these options to be self-explanatory.

Figure 2.110
Options available in the ribbon's Parts tab.

Understanding How Parts Interact with the Full Score

To get an understanding of how what you add in the full score interacts with a part (and vice versa), you will perform the sacrilegious act of adding a few performance directions to Beethoven's score that he didn't intend. Performance directions for individual instruments (that is, that will affect just the instrument to which they are directed) are written in Technique style unless there is a special style just for that instruction. Examples of performance instructions that should be written in Technique style appear in Table 2.1. (Note that this is not an exhaustive list by any means.)

Table 2.1   Italian Performance Directions Requiring Technique Style

Instruction	Meaning
con sord.	Play with a mute.
pizz.	Play plucked. Short for pizzicato.
arco	Play with the bow.
legato	Play smoothly.
sul pont.	Play on (or rather close to) the bridge. Short for sul ponticello.
sul tasto	Play on the fingerboard.
normale	Play in the normal bowing position.
tremolo	Play the note tremolo (repeated).
divisi	Divide the part between more than one player.
l.v.	Allow the note to ring.

Typically, these directions should go over the top of the staff, which is where Sibelius places technique text by default. Sibelius understands and interprets many translations of these terms in English, French, German, and other languages. You will learn more about what Sibelius can interpret in Lesson 5.

Tip: If you aren't sure which text style to use for which instruction in Sibelius, Expression or Technique style will be the answer the majority of the time. If those don't seem appropriate, choose Text > Styles > More to open the full gallery. Not only do you get an example of what the text will look like, but you'll also see an example of what kind of thing is written in that text. For another clue as to whether you've chosen an appropriate text style, try adding the text to the score; then right-click it to reveal a context-sensitive menu of commands appropriate to that text.

Suppose you want the players to play pizzicato from the end of bar 35.

To add the appropriate technique text:

1. Click the **FULL SCORE** tab to go back to the full score. Select the first note of the triplet at the end of bar 35 in the violin 1 part.

2. Press **CTRL+T** (**COMMAND+T**) to add technique text. Just like when you added expression text, a flashing cursor appears—but this time *above* the note, which is the correct position for playing techniques to be written.

3. Type PIZZ.

4. Press **ESC** twice.

5. Play back the score from this point. The violin will play with a pizzicato sound.

6. Add the same instruction to the other three parts in bars 36 and 37, as shown in Figure 2.111.

Figure 2.111
Adding pizzicato markings that Beethoven didn't intend.

7. Again, play back the score from this point. Beethoven might not be very happy, but it's a fun edit!

8. Press **W** to switch to the violin 1 part, or click on its tab. Note that the *pizz.* marking has been automatically added to bar 35.

9. Select the first note of the triplet passage in bar 47, press **CTRL+T** (**COMMAND+T**), to add technique text, and type ARCO.

10. Press **W** to go back to the full score. The *arco* marking appears at bar 47 in the full score in the first violin part. Of course, it plays back too.

So, any score element—technique text, notes, articulations, phrasing, and so on— can be added in the full score and will automatically show in a part (or vice versa). Editing is the same, but with one difference.

To edit score elements:

1. Press **ESC** twice to make sure nothing is selected.

2. In the full score, drag the *arco* text in the first violin part to the start of bar 46.

3. Press **W** to switch to the violin 1 part. Notice that the text has moved there, too.

4. Again, press **Esc** twice to make sure nothing is selected.

5. Still in the violin 1 part, drag the *arco* text back to the start of the triplet passage in bar 47. Notice that the text turns orange, and a dotted red line drawn back to the prior position in bar 46 appears, as shown in Figure 2.112.

6. Press **W** to return to the full score. Notice that the *arco* text has not moved from its position in bar 46.

Figure 2.112
The *arco* text in the part turns orange, and a red dotted line appears to show its position in the score.

This behavior might seem a little confusing, but in fact, it's ingenious. As discussed earlier in this lesson, many instruments in orchestras, bands, and jazz ensembles transpose. For instruments like the bass clarinet, tenor saxophone, and French horn, the transposition involves the notes moving a long way. For example, compare the excerpt of an untransposed tenor sax solo in Figure 2.113 with the same excerpt transposed in Figure 2.114. The transposed version uses Sibelius's Magnetic Layout and the Layout > Staff Spacing > Optimize command to avoid all collisions.

Figure 2.113
An excerpt from a tenor saxophone solo at concert pitch.

Figure 2.114
The same excerpt from a tenor saxophone solo, transposed.

Thanks to Sibelius's Magnetic Layout, if notes in the part are a lot higher than they were in the score due to transposition, other elements (for example, phrasing and technique text) will jump out of the way. Sibelius will fix collisions in your score in the most logical way the majority of the time, but occasionally circumstances will require you to move, say, some text marking a beat earlier in the part. If moving it in the part meant it also moved in the score, you would then have the text in an incorrect position in the score, and you'd have to choose one or the other: a marking that's correct in the score or one that's correct in the part. Obviously, this is not an acceptable way of working.

Sibelius solves this problem by making any movement in the part an *offset* of the score position. So, if you move something in the score, it moves in the part. Move it in the part, however, and Sibelius turns it orange to tell you it's offset. If you move it much more than a beat, it may actually change the music, so Sibelius draws a red dotted line to its original position (refer to Figure 2.112) to remind you where it would be by default. An example of when an offset might be useful appears in Figure 2.115, where the word *growl* has been moved to the left of the note, allowing the *rit.* line to also move down. This is in contrast to Figure 2.114, in which the word *growl* has been moved up so far above the transposed note, the *rit.* line has in turn moved to a point where it may not be noticed. (In Figure 2.113, the word *growl* is in an appropriate position.)

Figure 2.115
The word *growl* is offset, and the *rit.* line moves down.

Proofing Parts

Although Sibelius does an incredible job of formatting parts for you, you should always quickly proofread them before distributing them to your players. The most common errors are collisions between notes and other objects on the score, and text that isn't properly attached.

You can almost always solve collisions by running Layout > Staff Spacing > Optimize on the whole part. Once Sibelius has enough space between the staves, it can usually sort everything else out. As you've discovered, only occasionally should you need to offset text or another object in a part. Even more rarely, you may need to drag a whole staff out of position—but try to avoid this if you can.

Attachment problems are a little more difficult to fix, especially if you weren't aware of them when you created your score (which, in this example, is most likely the case). *Attachment* refers to the connection of a staff object to its staff in the full score, and is shown by a faint dotted gray arrow (see Figure 2.116). (It may be difficult to see the gray attachment lines unless you zoom in on your score.)

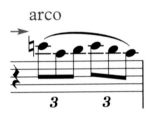

Figure 2.116
The light gray line between the *arco* text and the note below shows they are attached.

To fix an attachment problem:

1. Back in the Beethoven full score, drag the *arco* in bar 46 back to the position it had in bar 47. As you do this, the faint gray arrow moves along the notes and rests below it. You are changing the attachment position of the text.

2. In the same bar in the second violin part, add more technique text. Press CTRL+T (COMMAND+T) and type ARCO again, as shown in Figure 2.117.

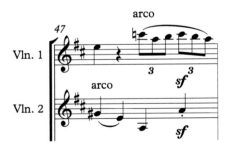

Figure 2.117
Adding more text.

3. When you're done, press **Esc** twice to switch from Edit Text mode to No Selection mode.

4. Drag the new *arco* marking until it touches the Violin 1 staff. Then drag it back down to halfway between the staves.

5. Look at the second violin part. The *arco* marking is nowhere to be seen. Check the first violin part, and there it is, hanging below the staff as shown in Figure 2.118. When you dragged it onto the first violin staff, you not only changed its rhythmic position, you changed the staff to which it was attached. If you look closely, you can see this reflected in the faint gray attachment line, as shown in Figure 2.119.

Figure 2.118
The first violin part now has the *arco* text from the second violin part attached to it.

Figure 2.119
The gray attachment line confirms that this text is attached to the wrong staff.

This is a very common error for inexperienced Sibelius users. If you input dynamics using the shortcuts you have learned, it's much less likely to happen, but if you frequently copy (and especially quick-copy) or drag dynamics or other text with the mouse, you'll probably have this problem at some time. Fortunately, you can see all attachments in your Sibelius files by choosing Home > Select > All or by pressing the standard Windows and Mac shortcut, Ctrl+A (Command+A).

Last but not least, you've seen that Sibelius will try to find a good place for players to make a page turn. If it can't, it adds the V.S. instruction to the part. It also draws an orange "bad page break" symbol on the score, as shown in Figure 2.120.

Figure 2.120
The "bad page break" symbol.

If you have found a better place for a page turn than the one Sibelius chose, you can force a page break. Although it's a ridiculous example, you could add one after the four-bar multirest in the first violin part.

To move the page turn mark:

1. Switch to the violin 1 part.

2. Select the barline after the four-bar multirest. It will turn purple to show it is selected.

3. Press **CTRL+ENTER** (**COMMAND+RETURN**) on the main part of your keyboard (not on the numerical keypad) to insert a system break. Sibelius will be pleased that you found a page break of which it approves and will award you a "good page break" symbol, as shown in Figure 2.121.

Figure 2.121
The "good page break" symbol.

Printing and Exporting PDFs

As usual, there's a video with the same name as this section (2.9 Printing and Exporting PDFs), should you like to watch it. You've nearly completed the lesson!

The final section in Lesson 2 is a short one because printing and exporting PDF files is remarkably simple in Sibelius 7. When it's time to share your score and parts with a conductor and players, you're almost always going to print it (unless they all have iPads running Avid Scorch, but that's a story for Lesson 3, where you'll learn about other useful formats in which you can share files). There are occasions, however, when you need to share a score or part with someone online—for example, to send it to them quickly in advance of a rehearsal.

Of course, if your players have Sibelius, you can simply share your Sibelius file. But if you don't want to give access to the whole file, or if they don't have Sibelius, then PDF is the next best thing. PDF is a good solution because PDF files can be opened on any computer, regardless of operating system, with a free PDF reader installed. Most current systems include a free reader by default, or you can download one from the Internet.

Tip: There is no catch-up file for this section of Lesson 2 because nothing required here was added in the last section. If you need a file to work with, open **Beethoven7.sib**.

Printing

To print in Sibelius, choose File > Print. (On a Mac, note that this refers to the File tab, not the File menu, which doesn't contain a Print option.) You can also use the standard shortcut, Ctrl+P (Command+P). A preview of what your printed document will look like plus a whole host of options appears, as shown in Figure 2.122. Check that your printer is selected and adjust other settings as required. Sibelius will even help you print double-sided scores and parts by telling you when to turn the page over.

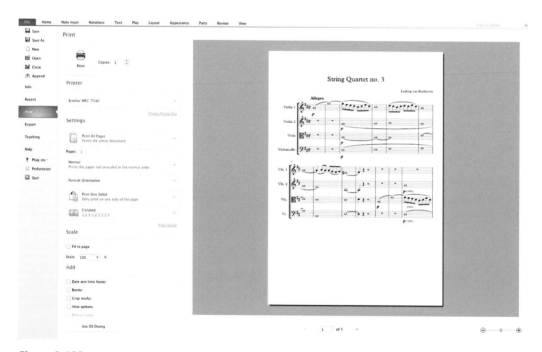

Figure 2.122
The printing options in Sibelius.

Tip: On a Mac, if some of the printing options available for your printer don't seem to be available in Sibelius, click the Use OS Dialog button. This opens your usual Print dialog box. (Note that this will override any of Sibelius's special settings.)

If you need to print parts, there are a few ways to go about it:

- Choose Parts > Print > Print All Parts.
- Open a part and choose File > Print.
- Open a part and press Ctrl+P (Command+P).

This shows nearly exactly the same options as before, but adds options for printing combinations of parts, as shown in Figure 2.123.

Parts

Figure 2.123
Extra options are available when you print parts.

Notice that if you chose Parts > Print > Print All Parts, all parts will be selected in the list shown in Figure 2.123. If you chose to print while viewing a part, just that part will be selected. Either way, you can change your selection. To print a single part, simply click it in the list. To toggle a part on or off, Ctrl-click (Command-click) it. To print multiple copies of a part, double-click the number in its Copies column, and type the desired number of copies (up to 99), as shown in Figure 2.124. This isn't so useful for a string quartet score, but if you have a school concert band with 43 flutes, it's a great time saver at the photocopier later on.

Parts

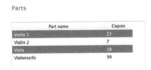

Figure 2.124
Setting different numbers of copies for each part and any combination of parts to print.

Whether you're printing scores or parts, once you have the settings as you need them, simply click the big Print button at the top of the screen, as shown in Figure 2.125.

Exporting PDFs

Exporting PDFs is just as easy as printing in Sibelius 7. Unlike previous versions of Sibelius, there is no need to rely on separate PDF maker applications (or in the case of Mac OS, the built-in service, which doesn't always embed fonts as needed).

Figure 2.125
Click the Print button.

To begin, choose File > Export > PDF. You'll see a number of simple but powerful options, as shown in Figure 2.126. The options are self-explanatory, but their benefits may not be:

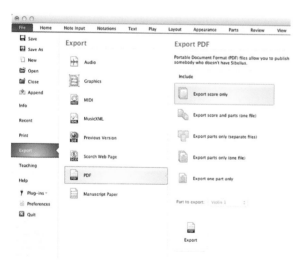

Figure 2.126
Sibelius 7's Export to PDF options.

■   Being able to export the score and parts into one file is the best way to archive your work in a single file, which anyone would be able to use to retrieve a copy of the score (by using the Print Range options in their PDF reader).

■ Exporting the parts as separate files is very handy if you need to send specific parts to particular players. Try this now with the string quartet. Select Export Parts Only (Separate Files) and then click Export. Sibelius will ask you where to save the PDF files; consider creating a new folder in which to keep them, as shown in Figure 2.127. (This figure shows a Mac OS Finder window; a Windows Explorer window will look slightly different.)

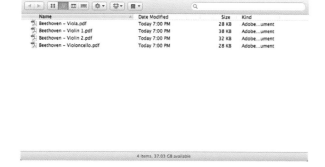

Figure 2.127
A folder of PDF files for the parts of the Beethoven string quartet that you have copied into Sibelius.

■ If you need just one part as a PDF—for instance if one player misses a rehearsal and you need to email just that part—choose Export One Part Only. Then choose the part from the drop-down menu, as shown in Figure 2.128.

Figure 2.128
Selecting only one part to export as a PDF.

You've completed Lesson 2! If it felt like this lesson was much tougher than Lesson 1, that's because it was. But don't worry—it was also much tougher than Lessons 3, 4, and 5. That's because you learned not only all the main methods of note entry, but also how to add dynamics, articulation marks, and phrasing, as well as how to format parts and print your project. When you think about it, that's all of the essential knowledge you need to use Sibelius to make scores and parts. It only leaves out worksheets (Lesson 4) and highly complex scores (see the Expert level)!

The next three lessons will give you an opportunity to consolidate all that knowledge as well as to practice those note-entry skills. And, they'll introduce a whole load of cool features to augment what you can already do.

Review/Discussion Questions

1. Why can't you drag the page while the mouse pointer is blue?

2. True or false: The shortcut for clef is Q.

3. MIDI keyboards can connect to your computer via which of the following?
   a. Bluetooth
   b. USB
   c. Firewire

4. Why is alphabetic entry called alphabetic entry?

5. True or false: You can nudge the score around in small increments with the shortcuts Shift+Home/End/Page Up/Page Down.

6. How does Magnetic Layout save you time?
   a. It keeps everything grouped together like a magnet.
   b. It makes the layout of parts exactly the same as the score.
   c. It prevents objects from colliding by making them jump out of the way of one another.

7. Why is the Tab key important in Sibelius?

8. True or false: In Sibelius, a shadow note shows you where a note will go if you click the mouse.

9. Why is PDF is a good format for sharing your Sibelius scores?
   a. You can open a PDF in a free PDF reader on both Mac and Windows computers if you don't have Sibelius.
   b. PDFs play back and transpose into any key you need.
   c. PDF is a good format to import into other notation programs and sequencers.

10. If you're working in Panorama view, how will you know what your score will look like when you print it?

Lesson 2 Keyboard Shortcuts

Shortcut	Function
Ctrl+S (Windows)/Command+S (Mac)	Save
Alt+Home/End/Page Up/Page Down (Windows)/ Option+ Home/End/Page Up/Page Down (Mac)	Nudge the page around in small increments
Ctrl+Alt+G (Windows)/ Command+Option+G (Mac)	Go to bar
Ctrl+B (Windows)/Command+B (Mac)	Add bar (to the end of the score)
Ctrl+Alt+K (Windows)/ Command+Option+K (Mac)	Keypad panel
Ctrl+, (Windows)/Command+, (Mac)	Preferences
Ctrl+Shift+F (Windows)/Command+Shift+F (Mac)	Flexi-time Record
N	Note entry (enter Create mode)
Ctrl+Up Arrow (Windows)/ Command+Up Arrow (Mac)	Transpose selected note up an octave
Ctrl+Down Arrow (Windows)/ Command+Down Arrow (Mac)	Transpose selected note down an octave
Ctrl+3 (Windows)/Command+3 (Mac)	Triplet
Ctrl+E (Windows)/Command+E (Mac)	Expression text
Ctrl+P/M/F (Windows)/Command+P/M/F (Mac)	Create special dynamics font (must be in expression text)
Ctrl+Right Arrow/Left Arrow (Windows)/ Command+Right Arrow/Left Arrow (Mac)	Move forward/backward one bar (requires a note or rest selection)
Ctrl+Enter (Windows)/Command+Return (Mac)	Insert page break (requires bar selection)
Ctrl+P (Windows)/Command+P (Mac)	Print
Shift+Page Down (Windows)/ Shift+Page Down (Mac)	Transpose a note down chromatically
Shift+Page Up (Windows)/Shift+Page Up (Mac)	Transpose a note up chromatically
Shift+Alt+L (Windows)/Shift+Option+L (Mac)	Lock Note Values

Lesson 2 Keyboard Shortcuts

Shortcut	Function
S	Slur (sticky)
Shift+S	End slur
X	Flip an object across the staff
Q	Open the Clefs gallery
T	Time Signature
Enter/Return	Respell accidentals (requires a note selection)
H	Hairpin (crescendo)
Shift+H	Hairpin (diminuendo)
Space bar	Extend line (the end of a line must be selected)
Shift+space bar	Contract line (the end of a line must be selected)
Tab	Next object
Shift+Tab	Last object
Shift+Alt+K (Windows)/ Shift+Option+K (Mac)	Sticky Tuplets
Ctrl+T (Windows)/Command+T (Mac)	Technique Text
W	Switch between the selected part and the full score
Alt+Up Arrow/Down Arrow (Windows)/ Option+Up Arrow/Down Arrow (Mac)	Move selection up or down through notes in a chord

Practicing Entry Methods

Having copied some music of a great composer, travel back in time and copy the music of another. In the Lesson 2 folder you will find the file Brandenburg5.pdf, which is a PDF of the first five pages of J.S. Bach's fifth Brandenburg concerto. You'll also find it in Appendix B. Print it out and copy it. Consider the four note-entry methods you've learned and decide which entry method suits you the best; then practice it as much as possible to become faster.

Media Used: Brandenburg.pdf

Duration: Approximately one to two hours

GOALS

■ Practice all the skills you learned in this lesson

Purple

In this lesson, you're going to piece together a rock song called "Purple," written in honor of the color scheme the Avid suite of products has going right now! You'll use many different kinds of media. By the time you've completed this lesson, you'll be rocking out to some very different music from the Beethoven string quartet you just copied!

Media Used: Purple1.sib, Purple2.sib, Purple3.sib, Purple4.sib, Purple5.sib, Purple6.sib, PurpleProToolsSibelius.sib, PurpleSequencer.mid, PurpleSequNotGM.mid, PurpleNotation.mid, PurpleLogicMP3.mp3 (unquantized draft), PurpleProToolsMP3.mp3 (unquantized draft), PurpleSibeliusMP3.mp3 (final edited song), PurpleMIDItoPT.mp3 (final edited song sent to Pro Tools as MIDI)

Other Files Used: Folder: Purple Pro Tools Session, which includes the Pro Tools session file PurpleProTools.ptf

Folder: Purple Logic, which includes the lesson file PurpleLogic.logic

Purple1.mxl, Purple1.mus, which is a Finale 2010 file that you can use to test the entire MusicXML conversion (if you have both programs),

PurpleLyrics.txt, PurpleNotationScore.pdf, PurpleXMLExport.pdf

Duration: Between two and three hours

GOALS

- Import and export MIDI files to and from Sibelius
- Discover the advantages of MusicXML over MIDI
- Gain new note-entry skills
- Input lyrics into a vocal part
- Create all kinds of repeats
- Export your Sibelius files as audio and convert them to MP3
- Send a Sibelius score to Avid Scorch for iPad as well as publish a score on the Internet

Notes on the Media Used

To help you learn the many skills covered in this lesson, a range of special files have been created for you. Each of these files contains different versions or parts of the rock song "Purple." They are organized on the previous page by file type. You will find all files (not including the videos) in a folder called Lesson 3 inside the Core Resources folder, which you copied into your Scores folder.

For a start, you'll work with MIDI files created in different programs and even with a Sibelius file generated by Pro Tools. MP3 files are also provided to enable you to compare how differently each program plays back the same MIDI data. The samples are different, and no quantizing has been applied to the draft version so the rhythmic playing is often not in time.

The files listed under "Other File Formats" can be opened on any computer. The MIDI and MusicXML files are supplied because they can be opened in Sibelius, but they have been exported from several other professional music programs including Pro Tools, Logic, and Finale. These file types are provided here in case you own this software and want to try the export process before importing to Sibelius (you can compare playback with the MP3s above even if you do not have these programs).

If you own another sequencer, such as Cubase or Sonar, you could still import the PurpleSequencer.mid MIDI file into those programs to practice cleaning up and exporting, even without the correct lesson file.

Please be aware that the MIDI file imported into Sibelius, PurpleSequencer.mid, has had General MIDI channels and appropriate program numbers applied to it before exporting from any of the listed programs, and this process would need to be repeated (refer to the relevant user guide for your preferred sequencer).

A Few Key Terms

This lesson naturally involves talking a lot about software other than Sibelius. There are three terms with which you should be familiar:

- **Sequencer.** A *sequencer* is a computer program used to record and edit music. All modern-day sequencers enable you to record both MIDI and audio, which is real sound (almost always recorded through a microphone, but sometimes through a direct input—for example, a guitar plugged straight into an audio interface). Sequencers have been around for more than 30 years and began life as separate machines. As computers have become more powerful, almost all sequencers run on them (with the exception of drum machines, which usually include on-board sequencers and are used by DJs at parties).

■ **DAW.** As mentioned in Lesson 1, "Amazing Grace," DAW stands for *digital audio workstation*. Nowadays, a DAW does everything a sequencer does, but the history of the term refers to the fact that DAWs originally had a lot of dedicated hardware. Even if your DAW ran on a computer you needed to plug in a special sound card or interface for a special mixing desk. There used to be another difference, which was that DAWs were particularly good at editing audio (thanks to the hardware, which had special computer chips for adding effects like reverb), while sequencers were particularly good at editing MIDI. Now, these features have been merged; even the most powerful DAWs, like Pro Tools 10, can run on a computer without any dedicated hardware.

■ **Notation software.** Sibelius is an example of notation software. There are other notation programs in the market. (Naturally, by the time you've completed this course, you'll know Sibelius is the best!) Although notation programs may have quite advanced MIDI input and playback features, and the ability to record or sync audio, these are distinguished from sequencers by their main focus being the final product of printed music. In other words, if you want to record the next number-one single, use a sequencer/DAW. If you want to write the next big Hollywood soundtrack to be performed by a symphony orchestra, you need notation software.

Importing MIDI Files

 As ever, there is a video that will take you through the key features of this section. Its name is **3.1 Importing MIDI Files.** See the section "Accessing the Video Files" in this book's introduction for help finding and viewing the video content.

If you have any open scores in Sibelius, close them now. By default, the Quick Start dialog box will appear, as described in the section "Moving Around the Score" in Lesson 1. You are going to begin by importing a MIDI file made in a sequencer.

On MIDI Files and General MIDI

In the section "Using Flexi-time Recording" in Lesson 2, "Beethoven's 3rd String Quartet, First Movement, Opus 18, Number 3," you learned that MIDI is the language that computers and MIDI keyboards use to send messages about the music being recorded or played back. When you make a Flexi-time recording in Sibelius, it captures the MIDI data from your keyboard and reinterprets it as notation. You also learned that all the MIDI data used in a piece of music can be saved as a MIDI file. Sibelius is not unique in being able to import and export MIDI files—just about every kind of music software can. Plus, there are free MIDI players included in both Windows and Mac OS standard installations.

To understand the issues when dealing with MIDI files, you need to know just a little more about MIDI. When MIDI was first invented, there was no standard for how MIDI worked from one manufacturer to the next. So in the 1980s, if you plugged in a Roland keyboard, you might need setting 13 for a guitar sound, but if you plugged in a Yamaha keyboard, you might need setting 84. A lot of time was spent reading manuals!

To solve this problem, a standard called General MIDI was established in 1991. In General MIDI, or GM for short, the setting (or program change, as it's called) for acoustic grand piano is always 1, the program change for shakukachi is always 78, and so on. Now, you could plug your sequencer into any keyboard or sound module that had a GM setting and know you'd get the right playback sounds straight away.

Another limitation of MIDI was that it had only 16 channels on which to operate. That meant you could only have 16 different instrumental sounds at any one time (although workarounds to this eventually became available). In the General MIDI specification, all channels except channel 10 use the instrument patch map of pitched instruments. Channel 10 was reserved for the percussion key map of unpitched percussion instruments such as drums, shakers, and cymbals.

Nowadays, you very rarely have to worry about any of this because many instruments used for playback are virtual instruments—like Sibelius 7 Sounds, the computer actually generates the playback—and these do not have the limitations of MIDI devices and GM. However, when you start exporting and importing MIDI files, this information from the 1990s suddenly becomes very useful again because using GM program changes are one good way to keep playback consistent between programs. Sibelius always offers to do this for you and will always import a MIDI file best if it has been exported with GM settings.

On the Web **To manually set each sound to its correct GM program change, you need to know the number for each sound. A complete list is provided on the MIDI Manufacturers Association Web site at www.midi.org/techspecs/gm1sound.php. There is also a lot of other interesting information about MIDI there.**

In Sibelius, the quickest way to begin the import of a MIDI file is to click the Import tab of the Quick Start dialog box, and then select the Open MIDI File button as shown in Figure 3.1. If you're already working on a score, you can also click the File tab in the ribbon and then choose Open, as shown in Figure 3.2. The resulting dialog box will enable you to open any file format that Sibelius can read.

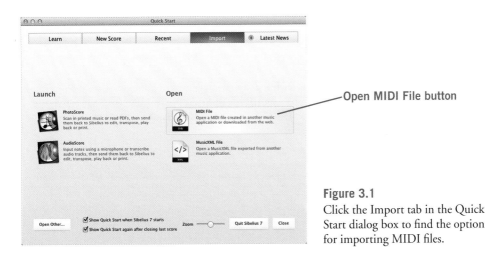

Open MIDI File button

Figure 3.1
Click the Import tab in the Quick Start dialog box to find the option for importing MIDI files.

Figure 3.2
MIDI files (and any other kind of file Sibelius can read) can also be opened from the File tab.

After clicking the Open MIDI File button in the Quick Start dialog box, you will be prompted to choose the MIDI file. In this case, you're going to choose the MIDI file PurpleSequencer.mid, which is found in the Lesson 3 folder inside the Core Resources folder that you copied to the Scores folder at the start of Lesson 1. Click Open to begin the process.

As will be seen, being able to import the same MIDI file several times can be useful so that the data of several imports can be merged. To this end, it is also useful to be able to open MIDI files in Sibelius directly from your operating system. The process is similar in both Windows and Mac OS.

Importing MIDI Files on a Windows PC

Importing a MIDI file on a Windows PC is a simple matter.

To import a MIDI file in Windows:

1. Locate the MIDI file you wish to open on your desktop or in a Windows Explorer window.

2. Right-click (or Control-click if you do not have a two-button mouse) the MIDI file and choose **OPEN WITH**. If Sibelius is listed, you can choose it, and the MIDI file import will begin. If Sibelius isn't listed, click **CHOOSE DEFAULT PROGRAM**, as shown in Figure 3.3.

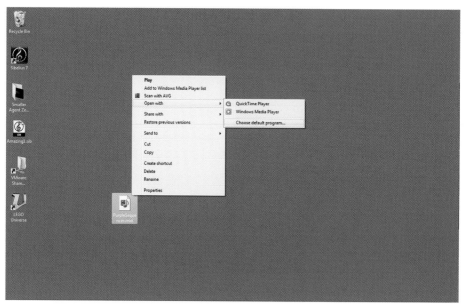

Figure 3.3
Importing MIDI into Sibelius right from the operating system in Windows.

3. The Open With dialog box opens. Click the down arrow to view various programs that may be able to open MIDI files.

4. If Sibelius is available in the list, click it to select it, and click **OK**. If it isn't, click **BROWSE** instead, as shown in Figure 3.4. (You'll only have to do this once, so don't be exasperated if this seems like a long process.)

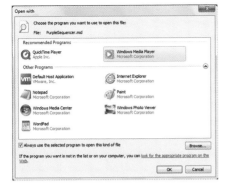

Figure 3.4
Setting a new default program to open
MIDI files in the Open With dialog box.

5. Another Open With dialog box appears, asking you to locate Sibelius 7.
By default, it (correctly!) displays the contents of the Program Files folder.
Find and double-click the **AVID** folder to open it (see Figure 3.5).

Figure 3.5
Locating Sibelius 7, which is in the Avid
folder under Program Files.

6. Double-click the **SIBELIUS 7** folder, as shown in Figure 3.6.

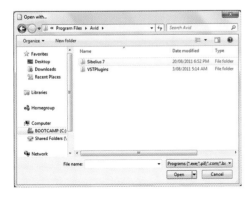

Figure 3.6
Opening the Sibelius 7 folder to locate
the application itself.

7. Click the **SIBELIUS.EXE** icon once to select it, as shown in Figure 3.7; then click the **OPEN** button.

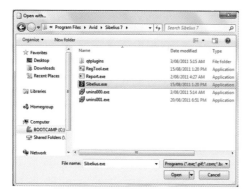

Figure 3.7
Selecting Sibelius as the default application for opening MIDI files.

8. Sibelius will now appear in the Open With dialog box, as shown in Figure 3.8. Make sure the **ALWAYS USE THE SELECTED PROGRAM TO OPEN THIS KIND OF FILE** option is selected. Then simply click **OK**, and Sibelius will proceed to import the MIDI file.

Figure 3.8
Sibelius now appears, selected, in the list of available applications.

Sibelius is now the default application for opening MIDI files in Windows. Next time, you can just double-click the MIDI file directly. You'll also see it now appears under the Open With option when you right-click (Control-click) any MIDI file, as shown in Figure 3.9.

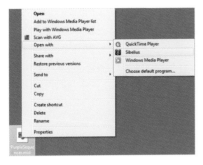

Figure 3.9
Sibelius also now appears by default in the
list of available Open With applications.

Importing MIDI Files on a Mac

To import a MIDI file on a Mac:

1. Locate a MIDI file on your desktop or in a Finder window.

2. Right-click (Control-click) the file, choose **OPEN WITH**, and select
   SIBELIUS 7, as shown in Figure 3.10.

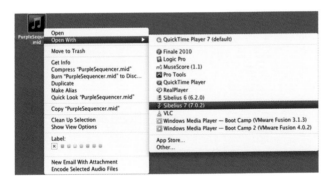

Figure 3.10
Right-clicking (Control-clicking) a MIDI
file in Mac OS gives the option to open
with Sibelius 7.

3. If you would like to use Sibelius as the default application every time you
   double-click a MIDI file, select the file and press **COMMAND+I** (the shortcut for Get Info).

4. In the Get Info dialog box, click the **OPEN WITH** drop-down list and
   choose **SIBELIUS 7**, as shown in Figure 3.11.

Figure 3.11
Selecting Sibelius as the default application to open MIDI files with in Mac OS.

5. Click the **CHANGE ALL** button. As shown in Figure 3.12, the Finder will ask you to confirm that you want all MIDI files to be opened by Sibelius; click **CONTINUE**, and then close the Get Info dialog box. A restart may be required for the change to take place, depending on what version of Mac OS you have.

Figure 3.12
Confirming that Sibelius will now open all MIDI files double-clicked in the Finder.

Using the Import Settings

The Open MIDI File dialog box (shown in Figure 3.13) that appears should be immediately familiar to you. It's nearly identical to the Flexi-time Options dialog box that you opened from Note Input > Flexi-time > dialog launcher button before you recorded MIDI from your MIDI keyboard in Lesson 2, in the section "Using Flexi-time Recording."

Figure 3.13
The MIDI File tab of the Open MIDI
File dialog box.

If you think about it, this makes complete sense. Because a MIDI file is simply a record of every note from the start to the end of a piece—which note is played, how loudly, how long it is held, and so on—Sibelius needs to apply the same logic it would to an incoming live performance.

The MIDI file PurpleSequencer.mid has deliberately been performed rhythmically loosely into Pro Tools. Apart from the drum track, quantization has not been applied. In other words, the rhythms are not exactly on the beat or on fractions of the beat. This is exactly the state that you would find many MIDI files shared by musicians or available for download online. As it is, it simply represents initial sketches of the first chord pattern of a rock song "Purple" that you'll be working on throughout this lesson. As mentioned, this song is an homage to the shades of purple used in the icons for Sibelius, Pro Tools, and Media Composer (see Figure 3.14).

Figure 3.14
The icons for Sibelius, Pro Tools, and Media
Composer, all shown in Avid's magnificent deep
shades of purple.

The only editing that has been done before exporting this MIDI file from Pro Tools is to map the MIDI channels and program changes to conform with GM standards. Sibelius will use these numbers to make sure it identifies the instruments correctly, and chooses the right number of staves, clef, and the playback sound.

If a file conforms to GM standards and has been heavily quantized, Sibelius won't have to interpret very much about it at all. On the other hand, if it hasn't, Sibelius will have to work pretty hard.

Let's assume (wrongly!) that we can import this file as is:

1. As shown in Figure 3.13, you know that the MIDI file uses a General MIDI sound set, so you can leave the first option in the MIDI File tab of the Open MIDI File dialog box as its default. You can also trust the rest of Sibelius's defaults here: Timecode isn't relevant, as this isn't a film lesson (you'll learn about that in Lesson 5, "Agent Zero"), and the document and transcription settings are fine.

2. Click the **NOTATION** tab. As shown in Figure 3.15, uncheck the **ADJUST RHYTHMS** check box so that you can see the file in its original glory. Because it *isn't* quantized, it's going to be ugly, but it can be good to look at it first like this just to confirm this setting does need to be on.

3. Confirm that the **REMOVE RESTS BETWEEN NOTES ON DRUM STAVES** check box is checked, as it makes drum notation look much neater. Also leave the Tuplets options at their defaults, allowing triplets and sextuplets, as shown in Figure 3.15. (If you *really* trusted the quantization of the MIDI file, you could change all these settings to Simple or Moderate.) Finally, leave the MIDI Messages settings as is.

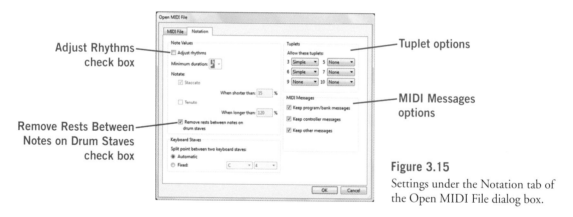

Figure 3.15
Settings under the Notation tab of the Open MIDI File dialog box.

Tip: Always leave the MIDI messages on. They will affect the playback of your score so you get something as close as possible to what the composer originally intended. MIDI messages will appear as light gray text in your score (or if they can be imported as notation, won't appear in text at all), won't print out, and can be completely hidden if you prefer.

4. One last warning: This is not going to be pretty! Click **OK**.

To call what appears an illegible mess is an understatement, as shown in Figure 3.16. It would be completely useless if it were not for the fact that at least its playback gives you an idea of what the piece *should* look like on the score. While every note is off the beat, a general sense of rhythm can be heard, so it should be possible to rescue much of the music.

Figure 3.16
With Adjust Rhythms turned off, the score created by importing the MIDI file is illegible.

There are a few other promising elements to the MIDI file import. Sibelius has correctly recognized the instruments and set up appropriate staves (a grand staff for the piano and rock organ, for example) and clefs (a percussion clef for the drum part, for example). It's also plainly obvious that the drum part was quantized before being exported from Pro Tools, as it has by far the most precise rhythmic notation.

Close this file (when Sibelius asks you if you want to save changes, you should probably click *No!*). Then import the same MIDI file again, but this time, change a few things.

To import the same MIDI file again:

1. In the Notation tab of the Open MIDI File dialog box, check the **ADJUST RHYTHMS** check box.

2. You can't be sure exactly how much you want Sibelius to adjust the rhythm to the nearest beat or fraction of a beat. Listening to the playback of the file, it sounded like most rhythms used simple subdivisions of 4/4. If so, an eighth note (quaver) may not be overkill, so let's try a sixteenth

note (semiquaver) first and see how it turns out. Open the MINIMUM DURATION drop-down list and choose the SIXTEENTH NOTE (SEMIQUAVER).

3. Leave all other options at their defaults, as shown in Figure 3.17, and click OK.

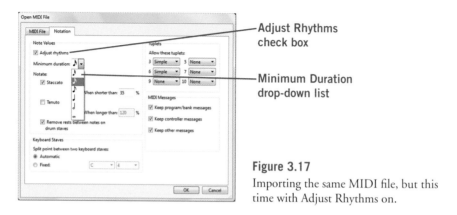

Adjust Rhythms check box

Minimum Duration drop-down list

Figure 3.17

Importing the same MIDI file, but this time with Adjust Rhythms on.

Immediately you can see that Sibelius has done a terrific job cleaning up the score. Not only is every part more legible, but most could be immediately used to perform (with the exception of the acoustic guitar and rock organ, which both require some editing first). You can also quickly improve any clashes between staves by choosing Layout > Staff Spacing > Optimize.

While the guitar part needs some work, you can see the Use Multiple Voices option in the Open MIDI File dialog box at work: The moving part on the bottom E string is written rhythmically separate from the other notes, with stems down. You'll learn much more about writing with voices in the section "Discovering Drum Notation" later in this lesson.

Save this file with a name that will help you remember what you did—for example, MIDISixteenth.sib.

Faced with the decision of whether to work on this file now and clean it up or to try the import again with yet more different settings, you might be tempted to decide that this is good enough. But it's much more sensible to import the file again—even two or three times more. Consider why:

■ Not only can you copy and paste between one part of your score and another, but you can copy and paste between any number of Sibelius files. So, if most of the parts are perfect now but another part can be improved, you can import again and copy just the improved part into this one.

■ There are a lot of triplets in the acoustic guitar part (and possibly the rock organ, depending on your system), as shown in Figure 3.18. Like those shown, some of them go over the middle beat of the bar, so it's not easy to read. It might be worth trying import with all tuplets turned off.

Figure 3.18
The acoustic guitar part at bars 3 and 4 showing triplets that are very difficult to read. The quarter-note triplet in bar 3 crosses the third beat of the bar, which is a no-no in music publishing.

■ The left hand of the piano and the electric bass parts sometimes use two voices when one would be enough. It might be worth trying an import with multiple voices turned off, even though this will make the guitar and drums less legible.

■ The piano part uses a lot of sixteenth (semiquavers) notes and rests in the left hand, which would make more sense notated as eighth notes (quavers).

■ Similarly, the acoustic guitar part has quite a few hanging sixteenth notes (semiquavers), which could possibly be cleaned up. Examples of both are shown in Figure 3.19.

Figure 3.19
The acoustic guitar and piano parts use sixteenth notes (semiquavers) and rests when eighth notes (quavers) would suffice.

Try the import two more times:

1. In the MIDI File tab of the Open MIDI File dialog box, uncheck the USE MULTIPLE VOICES check box, as shown in Figure 3.20.

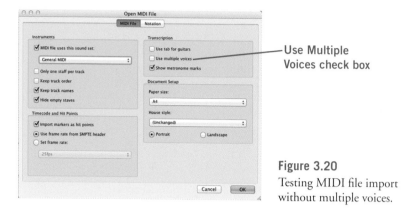

Use Multiple
Voices check box

Figure 3.20
Testing MIDI file import
without multiple voices.

2. In the Notation tab, in the Tuplets section, open the drop-down lists for both triplets and sextuplets and choose **NONE**. (All tuplets should now be set to None, as shown in Figure 3.21.) Other settings, including the Adjust Rhythms check box and the Minimum Duration drop-down list, remain the same.

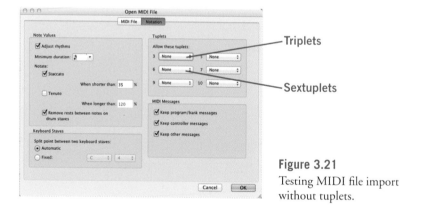

Triplets

Sextuplets

Figure 3.21
Testing MIDI file import
without tuplets.

3. Click **OK**.

4. Save this import with a suitable filename, such as **MIDISIXTEENTHNOTUPLETS.SIB**, and immediately import the MIDI file again.

5. In the MIDI File tab of the Open MIDI File dialog box, check the **USE MULTIPLE VOICES** check box.

6. In the Notation tab, leave **TUPLETS** set to **NONE**, and open the **MINIMUM DURATION** drop-down list and choose the **EIGHTH NOTE** (**QUAVER**), as shown in Figure 3.22.

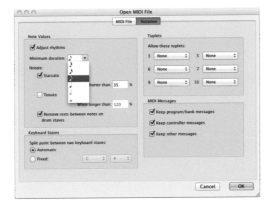

Figure 3.22
Testing MIDI file import with the Minimum Duration drop-down list set to an eighth note (a quaver).

7. Click **OK**.

8. Save this import with a suitable filename, such as **MIDIEIGHTHS.SIB**, and it will be time to compare.

Now it's time to compare your three MIDI imports and decide which elements of each gives you the best start at a score you can use. Assuming you have all three scores open at once, try View > Window > Tile Vertically to compare them. (On a small laptop screen, this may not be practical, but on anything 13 inches or bigger it should be useful.) To make the comparison as easy as possible, try to look at the same bars in each of the three versions, as shown in Figure 3.23.

Figure 3.23
The three imported scores, ready to be compared.

Using a Larger Monitor

Incidentally, Figure 3.23 was shot on a 22-inch monitor, which shows the benefit of working with Sibelius on a larger monitor. Your productivity can increase exponentially because you can see so much more of your scores (or in this case, multiple scores)! Until recently, large LCD monitors were prohibitively expensive. Nowadays, you will find 22-inch and 24-inch monitors nudging under the $200 mark, with occasional special deals even closer to $150. Online auction sites often have second-hand large monitors for under $50.

If you use a laptop, don't think this counts you out. In fact, you need to be using both your laptop screen and a secondary monitor if your laptop supports it (most built in the last five years do), with mirroring turned off. That means you can have one score on one screen and one on the other, or you can move Sibelius's floating panels like the Keypad, Navigator, and Ideas panel off your main score and onto another screen. Couple a second monitor with an external full-sized keyboard and a mouse, and your laptop will work like a desktop!

To achieve the best import from this file, you simply need to consider which file gives the best results for each part. With some parts, it's very easy to decide, while with others it's a little more tricky.

So that you work with the same edits as will be described here in the next part of the lesson, these are the choices that will be made:

- **Drum.** The drums are definitely easiest to read in the first good import, when multiple voices were allowed and the Minimum Duration setting under Adjust Rhythms was set to sixteenth notes (semiquavers), as shown in Figure 3.24 (although there isn't much difference with the last import, either).

Figure 3.24
The drum part in the sixteenth note (semiquaver) import with multiple voice is the best.

- **Piano.** Apart from the odd place where two voices make a bit of a mess, the piano part is clearest in the eighth-note (quaver) import of the file, as shown in Figure 3.25. If you are feeling particularly pedantic, you could consider importing the file again just for the piano part, but turn multiple voices off.

Figure 3.25
Apart from the odd issue with voices, the eighth-note (quaver) import of the piano part is best.
Your score may have a few minor differences, depending on your operating system.

■ **Acoustic guitar, distorted electric guitar, and electric bass.** As shown in
Figure 3.26, these three parts are also much clearer in the eighth-note (quaver) import, although the acoustic guitar part does get simplified to such a
degree rhythmically speaking that you might not get quite the same performance from a guitarist you give the resulting part to.

Figure 3.26
These three parts are also cleanest in the eighth-note (quaver) import.

■ **Rock organ.** This part is clearly better in the sixteenth-note (semiquaver)
import with *no* multiple voices, as shown in Figure 3.27. The repeated pattern in the right hand is much closer here to correct notation of what plays
back than any of the other imports.

Figure 3.27
The rock organ's main motif uses sixteenth-note rhythms. When multiple voices are turned
off, it's very clean.

Because the eighth-note (quaver) import that was done last has the highest number of parts that will be used, the drums and rock organ should be copied from the other two files into that one. (Alternatively, you could start a new score with all the instruments to copy them into.)

To copy entire parts from one score to the other, beginning with the drum part:

1. In the sixteenths score with the best drum part in it, triple-click anywhere in the drum part. As you learned in Lesson 1, this creates a passage selection of the entire drum part.

2. Press **CTRL+C** (**COMMAND+C**) to copy the passage selection.

3. In the eighths score, select the first bar in the drum part.

4. Press **CTRL+V** (**COMMAND+V**) to paste the passage selection *over the top of* the existing drum part, replacing it.

5. Repeat this process for the rock organ part from the sixteenth-notes (semiquavers) score with no tuplets or multiple voices into the eighth-notes (quavers) score. To select both staves in the rock organ part, select the first (triple-click) and then Shift-click the second to extend the passage selection.

6. If you've found the process of having so many scores open at once a bit confusing, choose **FILE** > **SAVE AS** and save the final improved score with a suitable name such as PurpleMIDICombined.sib. Close all other scores.

If you compare the resulting score with the very first import that you did with Adjust Rhythms turned off, you can see you've come a long way. There's a minimum of editing to do. But before you get into editing the resulting score, how about playing back your hard work? Do that now, and you'll notice something interesting. While you've fixed up much of the strange rhythmic notation in the Sibelius score, the inaccurate rhythmic playing is still there. It doesn't sound better at all!

Naturally, there is a reason for this. Just as it does when you record into Sibelius, the original performance MIDI data is kept separate from the notes (unless you actually delete the notes, at which point it will also be deleted). So while you've fixed the notation, you're still hearing the live performance. To turn off the live performance and hear what the score itself sounds like, choose Play > Live Playback > Live Playback. This will toggle Live Playback off, as shown in Figure 3.28.

Live Playback button

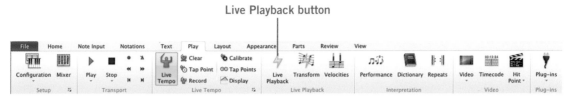

Figure 3.28
Turning off Live Playback in the ribbon.

Played back without Live Playback, the piece does sound a little less musical. Some of the rhythms have been vastly simplified and are perhaps a little insipid. But the performance is much more together.

In actual fact, you don't know exactly how far you've come because the first bit of work—making sure the program changes and MIDI channels were GM standard—was done for you. If you want to see what a complete mess this could have been, import the file PurpleSequNotGM.mid, which was exported directly from Logic sequencing software without the necessary changes. Even with Adjust Rhythms turned on, you're going to have a mess on your hands.

Surprisingly, taking MIDI data from any sequencing program to another can create problems—or at least starkly different results. One final comparison you can do with this little draft file is to compare the two MP3s also included in the Lesson 3 folder: PurpleProToolsMP3.mp3 and PurpleLogicMP3.mp3. It's exactly the same, unquantized MIDI data, but played back with varying virtual instruments and effects.

Editing Imported MIDI Files

You learned plenty of editing skills in Lessons 1 and 2, so you should be able to simply practice them now. In addition, you'll learn about some new features in Sibelius to continue expanding your knowledge.

One of the options not discussed in the first part of this lesson was Hide Empty Staves on the MIDI File tab of the Open MIDI File dialog box, shown in Figure 3.29. This feature is most often used in large orchestral scores, where publishers show every instrument on the first system of the score, but after that show only the instruments that are playing on any given page. This serves two purposes: It saves publishers money by using less paper, and it saves conductors from having to look down for page turns quite as often.

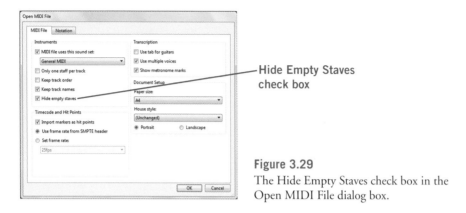

Hide Empty Staves check box

Figure 3.29
The Hide Empty Staves check box in the Open MIDI File dialog box.

This feature is turned on for MIDI files by default because some sequencers export bits of music that have been copied and pasted along one track as *separate* tracks instead of single tracks with empty bars. Therefore, a five-minute song might have 100 tracks, which means 100 staves in your score! For this reason, Sibelius hides any staves that have no music in them to keep the import clean. In this score, the distorted electric guitar part is hidden until a staff includes its entry in bar 13. You can tell that something is hidden by the faint dotted blue line between the acoustic guitar part and the electric bass part, as shown in Figure 3.30.

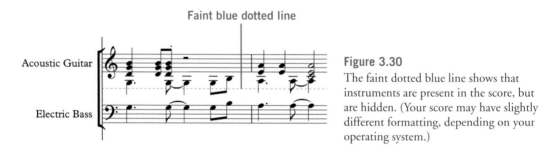

Faint blue dotted line

Acoustic Guitar

Electric Bass

Figure 3.30
The faint dotted blue line shows that instruments are present in the score, but are hidden. (Your score may have slightly different formatting, depending on your operating system.)

To show hidden staves:

1. In any part, at bar 10, make a passage selection for the part of the piece in which you'd like to show the hidden staves. (Just one bar will suffice in this example.)

2. Choose LAYOUT > HIDING STAVES > SHOW EMPTY STAVES, as shown in Figure 3.31. The Show Empty Staves dialog box appears, as shown in Figure 3.32.

Show Empty Staves button

Figure 3.31
The Show Empty Staves button on the ribbon.

Figure 3.32
The Show Empty Staves dialog box.

3. You could specify the distorted electric guitar part now by selecting it, but because all staves are selected and going to be shown anyway, simply click **OK**. The three empty bars of the distorted electric guitar part appear as shown in Figure 3.33, but are not present in earlier sections of the score because you selected only one bar in step 1.

Figure 3.33
The empty distorted electric guitar staff is now shown.

4. There are other places where staves are hidden—for instance, the electric bass and electric guitar parts at bar 21. To show all empty staves through-out the whole piece, simply press **CTRL+A** (**COMMAND+A**) to select the entire score, again choose **LAYOUT** > **HIDING STAVES** > **SHOW EMPTY STAVES** to open the Show Empty Staves dialog box, and click **OK**.

5. If your score is looking a little crowded, choose **LAYOUT** > **STAFF SPACING** > **OPTIMIZE** to fix any clashes.

While you're dealing with the overall look of the score, you may have noticed that every staff has the full instrument name. If you hark back to the Beethoven score in Lesson 2, you will remember that Sibelius wrote the full names of instruments in the first staff and abbreviated names thereafter (see Figure 3.34).

Figure 3.34
The standard display for instrument names is full names at the start of the score, with shortened names in subsequent systems.

If you double-click each instrument name in any system after the first, you will be able to edit the name. This will then change it for every use except the first system in the score. There are several standard short names for instruments. In fact, depending on your nationality and publisher, there could be several names for your instrument! As shown in Table 3.1, Sibelius uses popular English abbreviations in the English language version. Changing each of the names to their abbreviations will save lots of space in your score.

Table 3.1   Instrument Name Abbreviations

Instrument Name	Abbreviated Name
Drum	Dr.
Piano	Pno.
Acoustic guitar	A. Gtr. (but if there were only one guitar, Gtr. would suffice)
Distorted electric guitar	E. Gtr. (the distortion effect should be written above the staff, not in the name)
Electric bass	Bass (E. Bass if it isn't clear, but in a rock band, "bass" means "electric bass")
Rock organ	Organ (settings should be written above the staff)

Another way to save space in your score is to make the staff size a little smaller. Sibelius measures everything in your score relative to the staff (if you decide to complete the Sibelius Professional and Expert levels in this series, you'll learn an awful lot more about this), so if you make it smaller, the notes, text, and so on will become proportionately smaller too. To make the staff size smaller, go to Layout > Document Setup > Staff Size and click the Staff Size down arrow to gradually make the staff size smaller, as shown in Figure 3.35. As the size moves toward 5.5 mm, two systems can fit on all pages at once, even with all instruments showing.

Staff Size down arrow

Figure 3.35
Making the staff size (and everything else) smaller in Sibelius.

Making staves smaller is a great way to save paper, but can also make your score difficult to read (especially if your eyesight isn't that great). Don't make your staff smaller than 5 mm; it might be too small to read easily. In Sibelius, it can be difficult to realize exactly how small the staff is. After making changes, print your score to see what it looks like:

Caution: As you progress further into advanced editing, it's important that you understand the difference between a staff and a system. If you're not sure, check out Appendix A, "Elementary Music Theory."

Time for some simpler edits. When you imported the MIDI file, one of the options under Adjust Rhythms was to notate short notes as staccato. In retrospect, it might have been better to leave this off, as there are now some notes that unnecessarily have staccato marks on them, such as the eighth notes (quavers) in the left hand of the piano, as shown in Figure 3.36.

Figure 3.36
Notes in the left hand of the piano part have been marked staccato by the MIDI import.

You could select each of these notes and turn the staccato off by clicking its button on the Keypad panel, but there's a quicker way: the advanced editing technique of filtering.

To use filtering:

1. Select either the whole score (if you want to also remove all other staccatos, such as those in the guitar part) or just the left hand of the piano part (by triple-clicking it).

2. Choose **HOME > SELECT > ADVANCED**, as shown in Figure 3.37. The Advanced Filter dialog box opens.

Figure 3.37
Selecting the Advanced filter.

3. In the Articulation section of the Advanced Filter dialog box, click the **ANY OF THE SELECTED** option button and check the **STACCATO MARK** check box (the second articulation in the list), as shown in Figure 3.38.

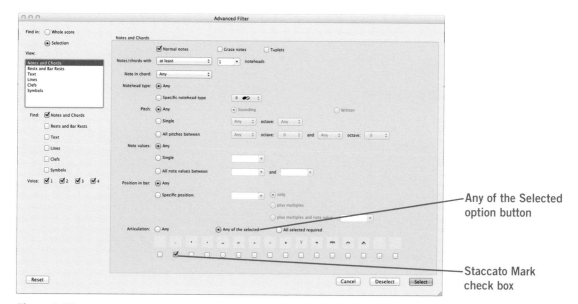

—Any of the Selected option button

—Staccato Mark check box

Figure 3.38
The Advanced Filter dialog box, set up to filter all notes that have staccato marks.

4. Click **SELECT** to return to the score. As shown in Figure 3.39, every note that has a staccato mark is now highlighted; click the **STACCATO** button on the Keypad panel to turn the staccato marks off.

Figure 3.39
Notes with staccato marks are highlighted.

The rock organ part provides another opportunity to use the Advanced Filter dialog box to tidy up. In its four-bar pattern, shown in Figure 3.40, the rhythmic import is very good, but there are some sixteenth notes (semiquavers) and rests that it would be more neatly combined as eighth notes (quavers).

Figure 3.40
The rock organ part could do with a little cleaning up too; its rhythms are sometimes messy.

In the excerpt shown, three subtly different problems have emerged. In the left hand in bar 5, the F sharp should probably be written as an eighth note (quaver) instead of a sixteenth note (semiquaver). In the next bar, the syncopated G sounds good, but when compared with other instruments playing the bass line, it's clear that it should be a quaver on the beat. Finally, in the right hand, the G tied between bars 5 and 6 and the A tied between bars 7 and 8 are silly. The first beat should consistently be a quarter note (crotchet) rest. Two of these problems are easy to fix with the filter, and one will have to be done another way.

To fix the problem with the F sharp in the left hand:

1. Make a passage selection of the entire left hand of the rock organ part by triple-clicking it.

2. Open the Advanced Filter dialog box by choosing **HOME > SELECT > ADVANCED**.

3. The easiest method to grab all the F sharps is to filter that exact pitch. Luckily, there aren't any other F sharps in that part. Therefore, you can simply click the **SINGLE** option button under Pitch, open the corresponding drop-down list, and choose **F#**, as shown in Figure 3.41.

4. If necessary, click the **ANY** option button in the Articulation section. This ensures that Sibelius won't retain the staccato filter from your last advanced filter operation.

5. Click **SELECT** to return to the score. All the F sharps in the left hand of the rock organ part are highlighted; simply click the **EIGHTH NOTE (QUAVER)** button on the Keypad panel to turn them all instantly into eighth notes (quavers). Problem solved!

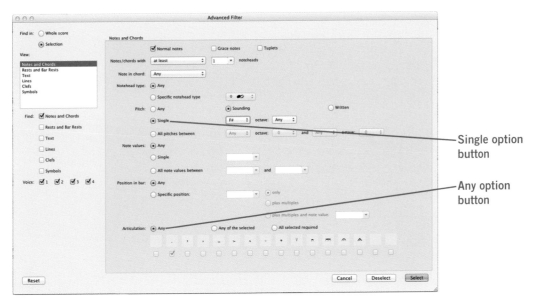

Single option button

Any option button

Figure 3.41
Using an advanced filter to select all notes with the pitch of F sharp.

Note: If there were other uses of the pitch F sharp in this selection, you may have still been able to use the advanced filter. If you look at the options in Figure 3.41, you can see that not only can you specify the F sharp in any particular octave, but you can even specify a certain rhythmic position in the bar.

You could apply a similar filter to the G in bar 6, but the problem is that you need to *move* it onto the beat, not turn it into an eighth note (quaver), which would overwrite the B that follows it. Therefore, you will use a different approach to fix this note. You have learned that in Sibelius, rather than using a quantize operation to move rhythms closer to the beat or subdivision of the beat, you set up Adjust Rhythms *before* you record and before you import MIDI. In actual fact, it is possible to perform simple quantizing in Sibelius, which re-interprets the performed or imported data according to the rules you apply.

To perform simple quantizing:

1. If it isn't already selected, triple-click the left hand of the rock organ part to select it.

2. Choose **Note Input > Flexi-time > Renotate Performance**, as shown in Figure 3.42. The Renotate Performance dialog box opens.

Renotate Performance button

Figure 3.42
The Renotate Performance button on the ribbon.

3. In the Renotate Performance dialog box, open the **QUANTIZATION UNIT (MINIMUM DURATION)** drop-down list and choose **LONGER: 1/8 NOTE (QUAVER)**. Leave all other options on their defaults, as shown in Figure 3.43.

Figure 3.43
The Renotate Performance dialog box.

4. Click **OK**, and watch the rhythm problems be magically fixed.

The third problem—the hanging sixteenth note (semiquaver) ties in the right hand—is also simple enough to fix with the advanced filter, but this time it will need to be run twice.

First, to remove the ties:

1. Make a passage selection of the entire right hand of the rock organ part by triple-clicking it.

2. Choose **HOME > SELECT > ADVANCED**.

3. As shown in Figure 3.44, click the **ANY** option button under Pitch. Then, under Position in Bar, click the **SPECIFIC POSITION** option button.

4. To select the correct position in the bar, open the **SPECIFIC POSITION** drop-down list twice. The first time, choose the **HALF NOTE (MINIM)**. The second time, choose the **EIGHTH NOTE (QUAVER)**. Rather than replacing the half note (minim), the two are added together, giving the rhythmic position of the notes with the ties that you want to remove. (This is also shown in Figure 3.44.) If this doesn't make much sense to you, see the upcoming tip.

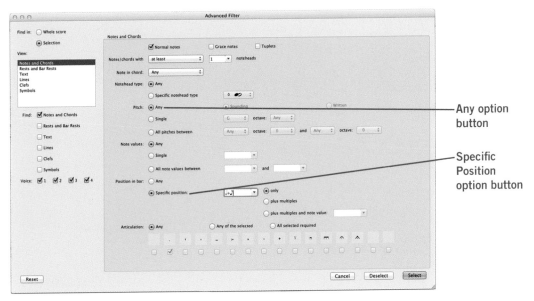

Any option button

Specific Position option button

Figure 3.44
Another advanced filter, this time selecting all notes on a specific beat of the bar.

5. Click **Select** to return to the score. All the dotted quarter notes (dotted crotchets) at that position of the bar are selected—although not all these notes have a tie.

6. Click the **Tie** button in the Keypad panel to first give *all* the selected notes a tie. Then click the **Tie** button a second time to turn them all off at once. Presto! All ties are removed!

The second step is to delete those sixteenth notes (semiquavers) at the start of bars 6 and 8 (and similar ones right through this part). This can be done with just one more filter.

To use a filter to delete the sixteenth notes:

1. Make a passage selection of the entire right hand of the rock organ part by triple-clicking it once more.

2. Choose **Home** > **Select** > **Advanced**.

3. This time, you want to select every note on the first beat of the bar. Begin by deleting the note lengths in the Specific Position field, as shown in Figure 3.45. To do so, click the note lengths and press **Delete** or **Backspace**.

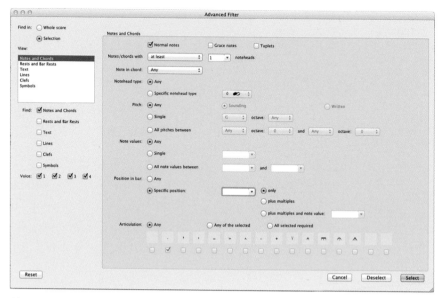

Figure 3.45
Deleting all note lengths from the Specific Position field on the first beat of the bar.

4. Click **SELECT** to return to the score. All the sixteenth notes (semiquavers) on the first beat of the bar are selected.

5. Click the **QUARTER NOTE** (**CROTCHET**) button on the Keypad panel to change the selected sixteenth notes (semiquavers) to quarter notes (crotchets). Then click the **REST** button on the Keypad panel to turn them all into rests.

Tip: If the specific position selection isn't making much sense to you, it's understandable. You might think that to choose the first quarter-note (crotchet) beat in the bar, it would make sense to have a quarter note (crotchet) in the drop-down list. The best way to think of it is as an offset from the start of the bar. So, the start of the bar is beat 1. If nothing appears in that drop-down list, you'll just select beat 1. To select beat 2, you need to offset that by a beat, so you'd add a quarter note (crotchet). In other words, the position you select is beat one *plus* whatever note lengths you input.

If you count these small problems in this four-bar passage multiplied through the piece, you'll find you just fixed dozens of errors with three quick processes. And these processes are simple to customize for similar problems you may have when importing MIDI files in the future. Figure 3.46 summarizes the improvements you've made.

Figure 3.46
In three quick operations, this passage has been made much more easily readable thanks to the power of Sibelius's advanced filter and Renotate Performance tools.

The whole score looks much cleaner now. In fact, if you compare the score you're looking at now with the first import in Figure 3.16, you'll likely think it's incredible that both are imports of the same MIDI file! Using the editing skills you learned in Lessons 1 and 2, manually edit any remaining notes that might be wrong. Consider the following:

- ■ The repeated F sharp accidentals in the score are unnecessary. Add an E minor key signature by pressing K (for key signature) with nothing selected and then clicking at the start of the very first bar.

- ■ You can select any note and change its length or articulation by clicking the appropriate buttons on the Keypad panel.

- ■ You can repitch any selected notes by dragging them with the mouse, moving them up and down with the Up Arrow and Down Arrow keys on your keyboard, or overwriting them with your keyboard or MIDI keyboard.

- ■ You can add dynamics and phrasing to practice those skills.

- ■ You can delete notes by selecting them and pressing Delete or Backspace.

- ■ You may be able to filter any repeated errors that you discover with an advanced filter.

When you've completed this cleaning up, save the file again and close it and any other open scores. You will now import several more files for the same song, "Purple."

Sending to Sibelius from Pro Tools

If you're lucky enough to own Pro Tools, there is another option for you to import your MIDI data into Sibelius. Pro Tools enables you to view and edit your MIDI data in its own Score Editor window. If you think the beautiful font and spacing you get in Pro Tools's scores is strikingly similar to Sibelius, then you're realizing the benefits each of these products is getting from working together under the Avid banner!

Not only has decades of development in producing beautiful notation from MIDI data found its way from Sibelius to Pro Tools, but there is a path back again too. This will be of great interest to musicians who:

- Work in education, where sequencers are often taught in music technology class before notation software and as a progression toward it

- Work in film music, where high-quality audio mockups are an important part of the creative flow of working with your director and producers

- Want to add audio tracks onto their Sibelius score, such as recording a real vocalist singing the vocal line instead of using a sampled or synthesized voice sound

- Are composers or arrangers who prefer to work creatively in a sequencer and only go to the score late in the compositional process

In Figure 3.47, you can see the original, rough arrangement of the "Purple" sketch that you've been working on. The MIDI was exported from Pro Tools and into Sibelius after each track had been given GM standard settings to help Sibelius correctly identify each instrument.

Figure 3.48 shows Pro Tools's Score Editor in action. Note that in the Notation Display Track Settings dialog box, the Display Quantization setting effectively does the same thing as Sibelius's MIDI import: It retains the timing of the original performance in playback while adjusting the rhythms of the notation to the nearest specified note length. Notes can also be dragged to change pitch and even (unlike Sibelius) rhythmic position.

Figure 3.47
The rough draft of "Purple" in its original form as a Pro Tools session.

Figure 3.48
Pro Tools's Score Editor in action.

On its own, the Score Editor is powerful enough to produce scores and parts or lead sheets. With some careful quantization of the individual playback elements as well as the visual quantization, you can get a very neat-looking score. However, you don't have the tools in Pro Tools to do anything approaching professional standard notation work. Even if you've made the score look good in Pro Tools, you'll want to be able to send it to Sibelius. Doing this is as simple as choosing File > Export > Sibelius, as shown in Figure 3.49. The score will be exported with the settings you've established in the Score Editor. (In fact, if you haven't yet opened the Score Editor, Pro Tools grays out the option to export to Sibelius to make you have a look at what you're going to export first!)

Figure 3.49
Exporting a Sibelius file from Pro Tools.

If you have Pro Tools, the Pro Tools session folder has been saved in the Lesson 3 folder under Core Resources. It is called Purple Pro Tools Session, and the Pro Tools session inside it is called PurpleProTools.ptf. You can play around with the Score Editor (and quantizing the performance in the Edit window too, if you like) and try the Export to Sibelius option.

If you don't have Pro Tools, don't worry. You haven't been wasting your time going through this process. The exported Sibelius file, with display quantization set to sixteenth notes (semiquavers), is also in the Lesson 3 folder. It's called

PurpleProToolsSibelius.sib. Open it and have a look. (Sibelius may ask you to update from a previous version—that's just because of support for Sibelius 6 too.)

In the Avid Learning Series

If you want to know more about Pro Tools, you need *Pro Tools 101*. It's part of the same series as this book, the Avid Learning Series. The Send to Sibelius feature is covered in Lesson 2.

If you use another sequencing program, some general principles of exporting MIDI for Sibelius have already been discussed—namely, setting the export to GM standards and quantizing the file before export.

If you're composing in a sequencer as well as in Sibelius, you have more control over the MIDI files you export. Getting good, clean MIDI file conversions from your sequencer into Sibelius is an important technique to learn, and is easy once you know the steps. The MIDI cleanup starts in your sequencer program. Here are examples for two popular sequencing programs—Logic and Digital Performer—although these same basic types of "clean-up" operations apply to most any sequencer.

In Logic, quantizations are made permanent, and notes are forced to be legato, so there are no spaces between two note events (unless an obvious rest is intended). To export MIDI files in Logic, follow these steps:

1. *Normalize region parameters. (This ensures all the transpositions that were applied are in the actual MIDI content and not just a playback parameter.)*

2. *Delete all muted events. Shift+M is the default keyboard shortcut, but that may be different depending on the user.*

3. *Make sure the first note event starts in bar 1. It can't start in bar 0. This can also be buggy if the first event is after bar 1, beat 1. To be safe, you can add a random dummy note event on bar 1, beat 1.*

4. *Select all and export to a Type 1 MIDI file.*

To export MIDI files in Digital Performer, follow these steps:

1. *Quantize the music by choosing Region > Quantize or Region > Smart Quantize. Make connected notes legato, so there are no spaces in between two note events (unless an obvious rest is intended).*

2. *Set a default patch for each instrument/track so you won't have to reassign instruments in Sibelius after import. It also helps to have the tracks for your orchestral instruments named with "real" instrument names.*

3. *Remove all unused controller data and other events, and either uncheck Play for tracks that you don't want exported or delete them before export.*

4. *Make sure the first note event starts in bar 1. It can't start in bar 0. This can also be buggy if the first event is after bar 1, beat 1. To be safe, you can add a random dummy note event on bar 1, beat 1.*

5. *Select all and export to a Type 1 MIDI file, deselecting the Save Track Names as Plain Text option.*

—Robert Puff, musician, arranger, and notation expert

Robert regularly publishes tutorials, ideas, and other interesting facts about working with Sibelius on his Web sites,
On the Web **www.rpmseattle.com/of_note and www.musicprep.com/sibelius.**

Importing MIDI Files from Other Notation Programs

The last thing you will experiment with in MIDI file importation is with a MIDI file made in another notation program. Generally speaking, MIDI exported from notation programs will be cleaner than MIDI from sequencers, simply because notes added to the score with note-entry methods such a alphabetic or step-time entry are automatically conforming to exact subdivisions of the beat.

This example also serves to illustrate the exact difference between importing MIDI and importing MusicXML, which you will try in the next part of this lesson. The file you are now going to import is another draft of the song "Purple."

To import another draft of the song "Purple":

1. In Sibelius, choose **FILE > OPEN** or, from the Quick Start dialog box, choose **MIDI FILE** in the Import tab. Then find and open the **PURPLENOTATION.MID** file in the Lesson 3 folder.

2. In the Open MIDI File dialog box, in the MIDI File tab, leave all options at their defaults (or change them back to their defaults, if your changed settings from earlier in the lesson have been remembered), as shown in Figure 3.50.

Figure 3.50
The MIDI File settings for this import.

3. In the Notation tab, uncheck the **ADJUST RHYTHMS** check box. It will be interesting to see whether the notation-input file needs adjusting. Leave all other options set to their defaults, as shown in Figure 3.51.

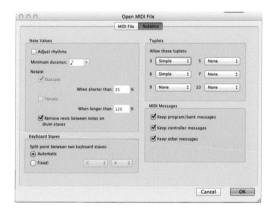

Figure 3.51
The notation settings for this import.

4. Click **OK**.

Several elements of the imported score don't work well. The most obvious is the drum kit, which has for some reason imported on a single line staff with notes in no discernable order bunched around it.

To fix this problem, use the advanced filter to move the notes where you think they should be:

1. If your Drum Set is hidden in bar 1, use **SHOW EMPTY STAVES** to show it now.

2. With no selection, choose **HOME** > **INSTRUMENTS** > **CHANGE** and choose **DRUM SET (ROCK)** from the list. (Search for it if necessary.) Then click **OK**.

3. With the blue, loaded mouse pointer telling you that you can insert the instrument, click the left side of the first bar in the drum part. The staff will change to a five-line staff. The normal noteheads now line up with where the snare drum sound should be (much more detail on that in the section "Discovering Drum Notation" later in this chapter), but the other noteheads don't do much.

4. The process from here is to filter each pitch (Sibelius assumes that the pitches in the drum staff are equivalent to treble clef) and move it to wherever you think the best sound is. For example, you could filter the cross noteheads on the D5 pitch and move them up to G5, which is the correct space for a hi-hat using the settings shown in Figure 3.52.

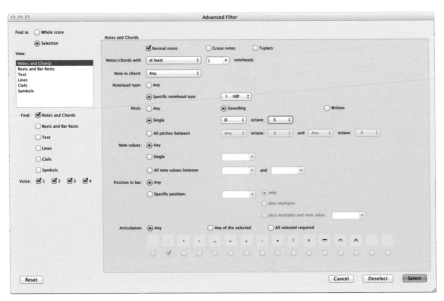

Figure 3.52
Optional settings to filter drum notation to move rhythms to their correct position on the staff. Note that the notehead type is set to cross noteheads, and the pitch to D5.

Sibelius has guessed the instruments correctly, but its left- and right-hand split point (the point where Sibelius decides which notes go into the left and right hands in parts in a grand staff) aren't always the best for the rock organ player. For example, in bar 11, there is a 9th stretch for the right hand when the bottom A could easily be played by the left hand. To change how Sibelius splits the right and left hand of keyboard parts, change the Split Point Between Two Keyboard Staves in the Notation tab of the Open MIDI File dialog box (see Figure 3.53) from Automatic to Fixed. When a pitch (for instance, middle C) is fixed, all pitches above it go into the top staff and all pitches below it into the bottom staff.

Figure 3.53
Changing the split point in a MIDI file import.

This is very useful if Sibelius's automated split point isn't giving you great results, but only if the range each hand plays doesn't change very much. Usually, the default setting, Automatic, will give you the best results. There are also some great plug-ins for fixing up little problems once you've completed a keyboard staff import:

■ Note Input > Plug-ins > Plug-ins > Change Split Point enables you to change where the split point is for a short selection. For example, if you set select bar 11 in the rock organ part, and then run the plug-in with the split point set to C4, it makes the changes shown in Figure 3.54.

■ Note Input > Plug-ins > Plug-ins > Move to Other Staff takes the selected note(s) and moves it to the other staff. For example, you could select the low A in the right hand in Figure 3.54, run this plug-in, and get the same result as running the preceding plug-in.

Figure 3.54
Using the Change Split Point or Move to Other Staff plug-in can fix problems with keyboard staves arising from MIDI import or Flexi-time recording.

These kinds of problems are less severe than those from the sequenced import. There certainly wasn't the need to requantize or import the same file multiple times. However, if you were producing a score and parts from what you've finished now, you'd still have a lot of editing work to do to make it performable. For example, there are no dynamics, articulation marks, or phrasing through the entire piece.

Provided for you in Appendix B, "Scores Required in this Course," and also as a PDF called PurpleNotationScore.pdf in the Lesson 3 folder, is a copy of an excerpt of the score from another notation program that you have just imported as MIDI. Compare it to what you see on the screen. As well as the general elements discussed previously, there is greater detail that is missing, including the following:

- Tempo marking

- Metronome marking

- Grace notes

- Performance instructions (e.g., "First Time Only")

- Lyrics

- Accuracy of writing in two voices in guitar and drums

Even if you get a good MIDI file import, these elements are always going to be lost, simply because MIDI files don't support that level of detail. As discussed, the data in MIDI files is just about the notes—when they start, when they finish, how loud they are, and so on. Sibelius does a lot of work to *interpret* that when you import a MIDI file.

Doesn't it seem a bit ridiculous, then, that if you want to share data between another notation program and Sibelius, there isn't another file format that can include not only the note information but also all this extra data about exactly what you want the notation to look like? Good question. That's where MusicXML comes in.

Importing MusicXML Files

MusicXML is a file format that is supported by more than 40 different music-notation programs, including Sibelius. MusicXML import was introduced in Sibelius 4, but until Sibelius 7, you needed a separate plug-in to export MusicXML. Now you can export a MusicXML file from Sibelius and send it to a colleague, student, or friend with completely different software, and the minimum possible data will be lost.

 Before you read this section, you might like to watch a video that will give you a thorough overview. It is called **3.2 Importing MusicXML Files.**

Sharing Music Between Different Notation Programs

If you need any persuading that this is a valuable subject to give some time, read what John Hinchey has to say about it.

If you don't know about MusicXML, you really should! Some users still believe MIDI is the only way to share music files between applications. The problem with MIDI is it's designed for music performance, not music notation. So yes, you can export a Finale file as a MIDI file (also known as a Standard MIDI File) and open it in an earlier version of Finale or in Sibelius. But all you are going to get is meter, key, and notes. And if you've ever done this, you know that the rhythmic translation can be a real mess sometimes.

MusicXML was developed to create a format that would include all the information MIDI provides plus, lyrics, dynamics, chord symbols, etc. With recent developments in MusicXML, you now also get Guitar TAB, jazz markings, page formatting, and much more. I could do a whole series of blog posts on MusicXML, and perhaps at some point I will. As with many things in life, you don't have to know all the inner workings to get the full benefit. If you want more information on MusicXML, I suggest stopping by Michael Good's site, Recordare (www.recordare.com/musicxml). He is the leader in MusicXML programming, and there is a lot of great info on that site.

—**John Hinchey, composer, arranger, and notation software expert**

On the Web   **Avid expert John Hinchey has written more on MusicXML and Sibelius at his Web sites, www.johnhinchey.com and www.hincheymusic.com.**

In this lesson, you will continue work on the song "Purple." Instead of working from one of the imported MIDI files, however, you'll work with an imported MusicXML file, which will give you a much greater head start. In fact, it's going to be from the exact same file on the exact same notation program that the last imported MIDI file came from, so you'll be able to do a direct comparison between the results you get with MIDI and with MusicXML.

Importing MusicXML into Sibelius

To begin afresh, close all open scores, which should take you back to the Quick Start dialog box. Just like MIDI files, you can import MusicXML from the Import tab of the Quick Start dialog box, as shown in Figure 3.55. Alternatively, you can choose File > Open if you already have another score open.

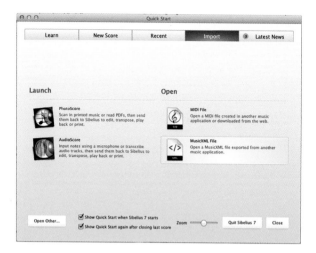

Figure 3.55
Importing MusicXML in Sibelius's
Quick Start dialog box.

There are two different types of MusicXML files: XML and *compressed* XML. The main differences between these two types of files is that compressed XML files are smaller (and so easier to email to people you're collaborating with) and can contain embedded graphics (while normal XML files can't).

Sibelius imports and exports both kinds of MusicXML, so the only limitation on what kind of file you should use is if you're sharing with someone who has a program that doesn't support compressed XML. Compressed MusicXML files have the file extension .mxl, while uncompressed MusicXML files have the extension .xml.

The file Purple1.mxl has been provided in the Lesson 3 folder for you to import. As mentioned, it is an export of the exact same score as the last MIDI file you imported, from another music notation program. After opening it, Sibelius will give you a few options, as shown in Figure 3.56.

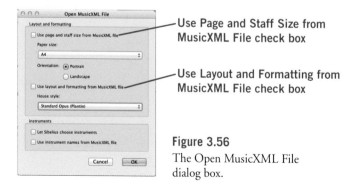

Use Page and Staff Size from
MusicXML File check box

Use Layout and Formatting from
MusicXML File check box

Figure 3.56
The Open MusicXML File
dialog box.

Make the following selections in the Open MusicXML File dialog box:

1. While keeping all defaults may be the best way to get a resulting score that looks closest to the original, it also stops Sibelius's spacing rules from cleaning up your score. Therefore, uncheck the USE PAGE AND STAFF SIZE FROM MUSICXML FILE check box. Set the paper size to the standard size for your country (probably Letter or A4) and set the orientation to PORTRAIT.

2. For exactly the same reason as in step 1, uncheck the USE LAYOUT AND FORMATTING FROM MUSICXML FILE check box. (If you'd like to import it twice to compare the difference, go for it!) Because you've unchecked this option, you don't need to worry about the House Style drop-down list.

3. As shown in Figure 3.56, uncheck the LET SIBELIUS CHOOSE INSTRUMENTS check box. In actual fact, Sibelius would do a good job of this if you left it checked, but unchecking it will allow you to fix one small problem with drum kit playback (more below), and give you a chance to look at the Choose Instruments dialog box.

4. Uncheck the USE INSTRUMENT NAMES FROM MUSICXML FILE check box to ensure that the instruments you choose in the next dialog box coincide with the names on the score. Click **OK**, and the Instruments dialog box will appear, as shown in Figure 3.57.

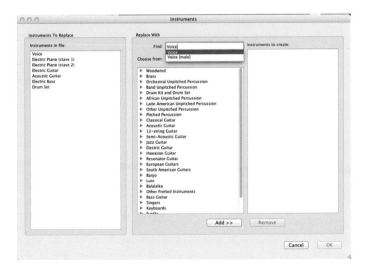

Figure 3.57
The Instruments dialog box.

This Instruments dialog box is very similar to the Change Instruments dialog box, so it should immediately seem familiar. The difference here is that the list of identified instruments in the MusicXML file is provided on the left, and you need to match it with the instruments you'd like to use on the right. The easiest way to do this is to use the search function.

To use the search function:

1. For the first instrument in the list, the voice, simply type VOICE in the Search box.

2. As you type, words that match what you're typing appear below, as shown in Figure 3.57. You can press the DOWN ARROW KEY to select the preferred instrument, and then press ENTER or RETURN to select it in the list.

3. Click the ADD button to add the instrument to the list on the right. Alternatively, simply press ENTER or RETURN a second time, since it's selected.

4. Instead of electric piano, you should use the same rock organ you used in the MIDI file import. There are many options for the various the guitars and drum sets, too. Table 3.2 serves to help you choose for the best results. When you're finished, check that the INSTRUMENTS TO CREATE list matches the imported INSTRUMENTS IN FILE list (or double-check it against Figure 3.58). Then click OK to open it in Sibelius.

Table 3.2   Instruments to Create

Instruments in File	Instruments to Create
Voice	Voice
Electric piano	Rock organ
Electric guitar	Electric guitar [notation]
Acoustic guitar	Acoustic guitar [notation]
Electric bass	Electric bass [notation]
Drum set	Drum set (rock)

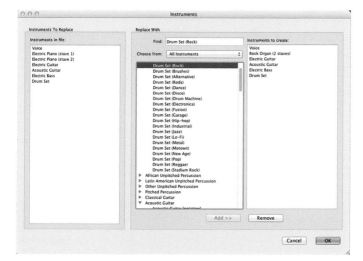

Figure 3.58
The list you have created on the right should match the one shown. Note that there are seven items in the list on the left and six on the right because of the electric piano showing the left and right hand staves separately.

The score will open. Immediately, you will discover a much more detailed score than you could ever have gotten from MIDI. A nice way of looking through it might be to play it back, so do that now.

Editing Imported MusicXML

As you played through the imported score, you probably found very few things that need to be fixed, which means that this final part of the lesson will be quite short. The three most obvious things are the odd colliding dynamic in the guitar part (which you can fix simply via Layout > Staff Spacing > Optimize), the long lyric melisma line from bar 16, and some of the text (such as the title) being in strange positions.

To fix the text-position oddities:

1. Press **CTRL+A** (**COMMAND+A**) to select all.

2. Choose **APPEARANCE** > **DESIGN AND POSITION** > **POSITION**, thereby moving all selected objects back to Sibelius's default positions (*resetting* them).

3. If you didn't already, choose **LAYOUT** > **STAFF SPACING** > **OPTIMIZE** while everything is already selected.

To fix the long melisma line at the end of the lyrics in bar 16, double-click the final syllable ("ple"), press the space bar twice, and then press Esc. You're going to learn everything about how lyrics work in the section "Creating Lyrics" later in this lesson, but this may whet your appetite somewhat.

One other thing you *may* notice is that Sibelius's notation actually looks slightly different than usual. The most obvious example of this is that the percussion clef could have two thin, longer lines instead of Sibelius's usual two short thick ones (see Figure 3.59 for a comparison).

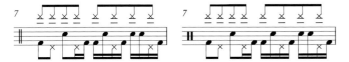

Figure 3.59
If your computer has the font installed that the original notation program used, Sibelius will use it and the percussion clef will appear as on the left. If not, Sibelius substitutes it with its own music font, and it appears as on the right.

You will only see this difference if you have the font installed that the original file used, because it's different from Sibelius's. If you don't have that font installed, Sibelius simply substitutes it with its own font. If you have a good eye, you may also notice subtle differences in the notehead shapes between the two preceding examples, because all elements drawn by fonts are different.

That covers just about anything that could be considered wrong with the imported score. If you compare it to the provided score printout in Appendix B or in the included PurpleNotationScore.pdf, you can see that all the detail has been captured.

Fonts

Wondering what fonts have to do with music notation? Wondering what fonts are at all? You're probably used to thinking about fonts when you're using a word processor. Similar to what you see in Sibelius's Text tab, in a word processor you can change the text between one of the popular fonts like Times New Roman, Arial or even (if you're feeling daring) Comic Sans, or choose something more obscure. Most computers these days come with many fonts installed on them, so you have plenty of choice.

Music software is just the same. As well as fonts for text, it also uses fonts for things like noteheads, accidentals, articulations, and so on. In fact, most of the things you see on the staff itself are drawn with fonts, the exception being things like lines.

There are lots of different music fonts available: Sibelius comes with four, and can change to use any more that you might install on your system, including some fonts designed for specific genres such as early music. You can see which music fonts you have installed and what your score will look like with them by choosing Text > Format, clicking on the dialog launcher button, and clicking the Main Music Font drop-down list.

On top of the rhythmic and pitch notation that you battled to import cleanly from a MIDI file, you have the following:

■ Slurs/phrase marks

■ Lyrics

■ Dynamics

■ Performance directions

■ Further text, such as title, composer, and tempo

■ Accurate writing in two voices in the guitar and drum parts

■ Correct noteheads and note positions in the drum part

There really isn't all that much left to do. You might as well get on with completing this song!

Exploring Guitar TAB and Chord Symbols

 As usual, there's a video to step you through the essentials of what you'll learn in this section. It's called **3.3 Exploring Guitar TAB and Chord Symbols**. Watch it before you begin reading so that you can move ahead as quickly as possible.

In Lesson 1, you edited a score that contained some guitar notation and some guitar tablature. You learned that the six lines represent the six strings of the guitar (from bottom E on the bottom line to top E on the top), and that the numbers represent the frets on which fingers should be placed. You also created guitar chord symbols the easy way: by getting Sibelius to analyze the harmony and write them out for you. In this section, you'll learn not only how to create guitar tablature and guitar chords from scratch, but also lots more new information about writing in voices and editing chord symbols.

Tip: You've just imported a MusicXML file that has the skeleton of the song's structure and more than half its final ingredients. In this case, you should only need the catch-up file Purple1.sib if you missed out on the preceding section. However, you will also find playback has been slightly improved in the Sibelius file since the MusicXML import, so feel free to open it and work from that in either case. If you *do* open Purple1.sib, Sibelius will prompt you with the question shown in Figure 3.60. There are hidden comments in the file that will help you locate where to put repeats later in this lesson, in the section "Using Repeats and Repeat Bars." You don't need those now, so click No.

Figure 3.60

If Sibelius asks you if you want to show hidden comments, click No.

Inputting Guitar Tablature in Alphabetic Entry

If you cast your mind back to the playback of the original, loosely performed (for want of a better term) MIDI file that you started with, you'll remember that there was a distorted guitar playing big power chords. Without any intention to generalize or be at all prejudicial, imagine that you have a rock-God guitar hero coming to join your band, but despite his excellent bandana-wearing skills, he doesn't actually read traditional music notation. What he needs is a guitar tablature part!

To add a guitar tablature staff:

1. Press the **I** key to open the Instruments dialog box.

2. Type **ELECTRIC GUITAR** in the search field. From the options that appear, choose **ELECTRIC GUITAR, STANDARD TUNING [TAB]**, as shown in Figure 3.61. Then click **ADD TO SCORE**.

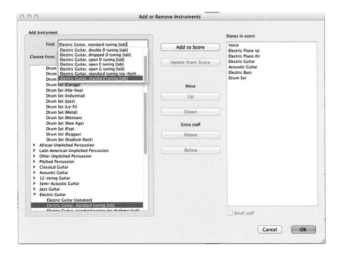

Figure 3.61

Selecting Electric Guitar, Standard Tuning [Tab].

3. The guitar is added to the top of the list, but our rock band isn't written in orchestral score order (what with it not being an orchestra). Click the new guitar part and then click the **DOWN** button twice so the new guitar appears above the other guitars in the score, as shown in Figure 3.62.

Figure 3.62
Move the new guitar down so it is above the other guitars.

4. Click **OK** to return to the score with the tablature staff showing.

At this point, Sibelius may ask you if you'd like to decrease the staff size to make more music fit on your score. Quite often, when it suggests this, it's a very good idea. In this case, however, there is probably plenty of space already, so you can click No.

As you've probably noticed, like all the best rock songs, this song is made up of just two four-bar chord progressions. Therefore, while there's quite a lot more guitar music to put in, much of it will be repeats. You will begin with the first four-bar phrase, which is shown in Figure 3.63.

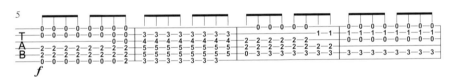

Figure 3.63
The first four-bar phrase in the guitar tablature part, which begins at bar 5.

To input these four bars with a variation of alphabetic entry:

1. Select bar 5 of the guitar tablature staff and press **N** to begin note entry. Remember that when you did this in traditional notation, the blue caret extended from the top to the bottom of the staff to show you where the next note would go. In this case, it appears only on the bottom string, as shown in Figure 3.64.

The blue caret

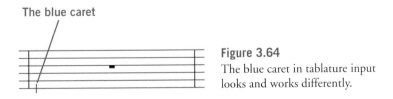

Figure 3.64
The blue caret in tablature input looks and works differently.

2. The notes in this guitar part are all eighth notes (quavers), so click the **EIGHTH NOTE** (**QUAVER**) button on the Keypad panel (or press **3** on the numeric keypad).

3. Looking again at Figure 3.63, you will notice the bottom string has a 0 to show that it is to be played open (no fingers on frets). The blue caret is in front of that string already, so press **O** on the main part of the keyboard (above the letters O and P) rather than on the numeric keypad. The 0 appears on the staff as shown in Figure 3.65, and Sibelius also plays an E so you can hear the pitch you just input.

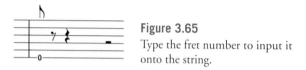

Figure 3.65
Type the fret number to input it onto the string.

4. There are more notes to be strummed above the E you just input. Press the **UP ARROW KEY** once. Instead of moving that note up, it moves the blue caret up to the string above. Now you can type **2** to input a note on the second fret of the A string.

5. Press the **UP ARROW** and the numbers **2**, **0**, and **0** to input three more notes into the chord until it appears as shown in Figure 3.66.

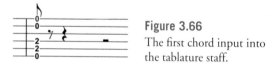

Figure 3.66
The first chord input into the tablature staff.

6. Press the **RIGHT ARROW KEY** to move the blue caret from the top note you just input to the next eighth note (quaver) part of the beat, as shown in Figure 3.67. When inputting tablature, the Right Arrow and Left Arrow keys do not cancel the input mode, which is always set as if editing.

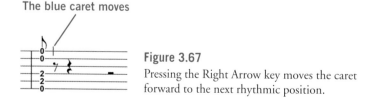

The blue caret moves

Figure 3.67
Pressing the Right Arrow key moves the caret forward to the next rhythmic position.

7. Press the **O KEY** for the top note of the chord. This time, press the **DOWN ARROW KEY** and numbers **0**, **2**, **2**, and **0** to add the notes of the chord from top to bottom.

8. You now have two strums of the E minor chord. You could press the Right Arrow key to move to the second beat and begin inputting the chord from the bottom again. Instead, press **R** five times to repeat the chord another five times until it appears as shown in Figure 3.68.

Figure 3.68
Press R to repeat a chord.

9. With the chord on the fourth beat still selected as shown in Figure 3.68, press the **UP ARROW KEY** repeatedly until the caret is over the fourth string (B) and then press **O** to complete the chord.

10. Press **R** to repeat that chord. Then press the **UP ARROW** or **DOWN ARROW KEY** to select the bottom string and press **2** to change its fret number. You should now have completed the first bar, as shown in Figure 3.69. Subsequent bars are shown in gray to save you flipping back to Figure 3.63 as you complete the next three bars to finish the pattern.

Tip: Should you ever need to delete a fret number entirely, simply select it and press Delete or Backspace. You can delete an entire chord by double-clicking it and then pressing Delete or Backspace. You could have guessed that, right?

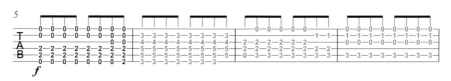

Figure 3.69
The first bar of chords input into the tablature staff, and the remaining three bars to put in shown in gray.

Once you've completed this four-bar pattern, you can copy it into the other two places where it is used in the song "Purple."

To copy the four-bar pattern:

1. Make a passage selection of all four bars.

2. Press **CTRL+C** (**COMMAND+C**) to copy the selection.

3. While they are still highlighted, press **R**, because these four bars are repeated immediately.

4. Select bar 27 in the guitar tablature part and press **CTRL+V** (**COMMAND+V**) to paste the pattern there.

There is one remaining pattern, which is used at bar 39. To do that, you'll learn another method of tablature input.

Inputting Guitar Tablature with the Fretboard Panel

In the last lesson, you learned about Sibelius's onscreen keyboard, which can be used to view the music playing back or even as an input device itself. Sibelius also includes a Fretboard panel, which does exactly the same thing but with an interactive guitar or bass fretboard. To turn it on, choose View > Panels > Fretboard. The Fretboard panel will appear at the bottom of the screen, docked. You can drag it away from the bottom of the screen if you don't want it to be docked, and it can reside on a second monitor if you have one. You can also resize it using the Change Size button shown in Figure 3.70.

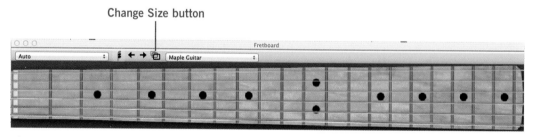

Figure 3.70
The Fretboard panel in Sibelius.

A drop-down list on the right side of the panel enables you to change the fretboard—not just between guitar and four- and five-string electric bass, but even the kind of wood used on the fretboard, as shown in Figure 3.71. Do be aware, however, that Sibelius automatically chooses the right fretboard to suit any selection you make on the score, so if you select a bass guitar and then click the guitar tab staff, Sibelius will switch the Fretboard panel back to a guitar layout. It also won't allow you to select a fretboard, which contradicts the selection in the score!

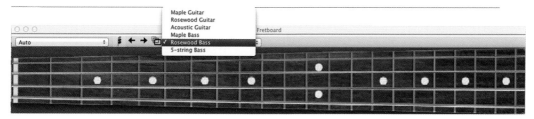

Figure 3.71
Changing the kind of fretboard in the Fretboard panel.

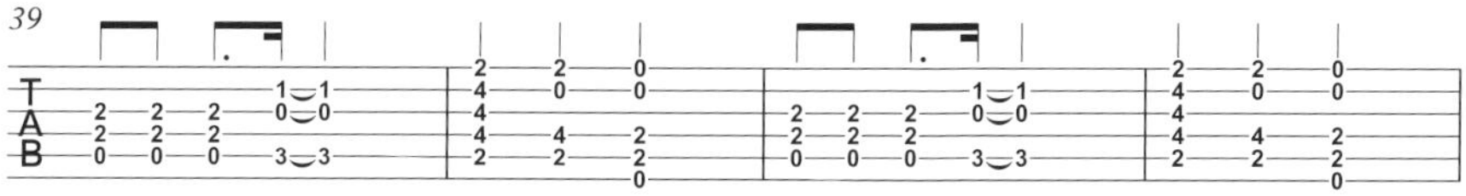

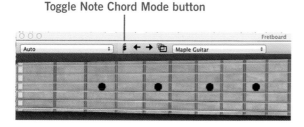

Figure 3.72
The chord pattern to be input into the tablature part at bar 39.

Figure 3.72 shows the chord pattern, this time with much more interesting rhythm than the last, to be input at bar 39 in the tablature part.

To input this pattern using the Fretboard panel:

1. Select bar 39 in the tablature part and press **N** to begin note entry.

2. You're going to input chords, so select the **TOGGLE NOTE CHORD MODE** button in the Fretboard panel. It will appear blue, as shown in Figure 3.73.

Toggle Note Chord Mode button

Figure 3.73
Select the Toggle Note Chord Mode button to input chords.

3. Choose the **EIGHTH NOTE** (**QUAVER**) button on the Keypad panel.

4. On the fretboard, click the three strings to be played at their relative positions in the first chord in the bar. For the open string, click the very left end (called the *nut*), as shown in Figure 3.74. Note the chord plays as you click, so it's easy to tell if you mistakenly click the wrong string or fret (unless you're writing atonal guitar music, that is).

Nut

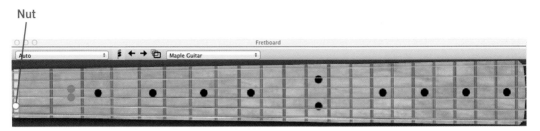

Figure 3.74
The chord pattern to be input into the tablature part at bar 39.

5. Click the **MOVE FORWARD** button, as shown in Figure 3.75.

Move Forward button

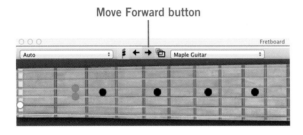

Figure 3.75
The Move Forward button.

6. Click in the same chord, then click **MOVE FORWARD** again.

7. This time, click the **EIGHTH NOTE (QUAVER)** and **RHYTHM DOT** buttons on the Keypad panel. (Note that you're not in Create mode, so the eighth note [quaver] isn't kept on each time you click Move Forward.) Then click the same chord once more. Finally, click **MOVE FORWARD** again.

8. The note length of a sixteenth note (semiquaver) is automatically selected in the Keypad panel because the rest was there, so you can click in the new chord. After you click in each note, click the **TIE** button on the Keypad panel. When you've done all three notes, click **MOVE FORWARD** again.

9. To complete the first bar, click in the same chord. Your first bar should appear as shown in Figure 3.72.

10. Click in the second bar of the pattern.

The third and fourth bars of the pattern are exactly the same as the first two, so you could highlight them and press R for repeat. However, there are a few more tricks than can be learned that may make your Fretboard panel input even faster.

To explore tricks that make Fretboard panel input even faster:

1. With bar 41 selected, press **N** to begin note entry and click the **Eighth Note** (**Quaver**) button on the Keypad panel. Click in the notes of the first chord as you did before.

2. Instead of clicking Move Forward, press **R** for repeat.

3. The same chord now needs to repeat again, but with a different note length. Press **R**, then click the **Rhythm Dot** button on the Keypad panel.

4. You could do exactly the same again, but instead, click **Move Forward**, then play the chord shown in Figure 3.76 on your MIDI keyboard.

Figure 3.76

Play this chord on your MIDI keyboard and watch Sibelius notate it in tablature.

That's right. Sibelius notates the chord instantly in tablature. You can continue by clicking the Tie button on the Keypad panel and playing the chord again, but you can choose how you'd like to complete putting in this passage.

Sibelius can do more than just input from the Fretboard panel into tablature and from a MIDI instrument onto tablature. If your first instrument is guitar, you can use the Fretboard panel to input notes into any staff of traditional notation, such as a piano or flute staff. Extending MIDI input one level further, you can also purchase MIDI guitars or pickups for normal guitars that convert what you play into MIDI data and enable you to play from your guitar straight into Sibelius. This process is a little out of the scope of this section, but Sibelius supports it with clever features like the ability to ignore a note below a certain level (velocity) so you don't get accidentally strummed strings in your transcription.

This pattern doesn't appear again in the song, so once you've copied all four bars, you're finished.

Changing Guitar Sounds

As you've experienced, Sibelius does a great job of turning what you write in the score into realistic musical playback. Now that you've learned a little about the complexities of MIDI files and MIDI input, you can probably better appreciate the work Sibelius generally does for you automatically. One example of this is that when you added the guitar tablature part, Sibelius automatically loaded the correct sound for playback of that guitar. If you're using Sibelius 7 Sounds, the guitar will sound extremely realistic, too. If your computer isn't fast enough to run Sounds, you should still be able to hear the difference in timbre between the bass guitar, acoustic guitar, and electric guitar because General MIDI provides set program changes for each of these instruments. If you do have Sibelius Sounds installed, you can call on extended samples just by writing them on the score.

To call on extended samples by writing them on the score:

1. Click any note in the first chord in the guitar tablature part at bar 39. Then press **CTRL+T** (**COMMAND+T**), the shortcut for Technique Text.

2. A cursor will flash above the staff. Type **DELAY** to tell the guitarist to use a delay pedal.

3. Select the same bar in the same part (to solo it, so you don't hear any other parts) and press **P** for play. Sibelius adds a delay effect to the guitar part.

You can double-click the text to edit it and try the following effects. All are supported by Sibelius 7 Sounds, and some may be supported by a General MIDI sound set too. (If you don't hear the sound change, they're not supported on your setup.)

- Flange
- Harmonics
- Muted harmonics
- Mute
- Overdrive
- Distortion

This guitar part is intended to be played with a distortion pedal (it goes with the guitarist's bandana), so unless it really offends you, insert the distortion instruction in bar 5 when the guitar begins playing. Listen to it back with the rest of the band "playing" and see if you think it has the intended effect.

Adding Chord Symbols

Chord symbols are often included not just in guitar parts, but also in any part that might comp or improvise a solo. Sibelius is extremely flexible with what you can do with chord symbols put into any part. Begin by putting the chords into the electric piano/rock organ staff. The pattern to input is shown in Figure 3.77.

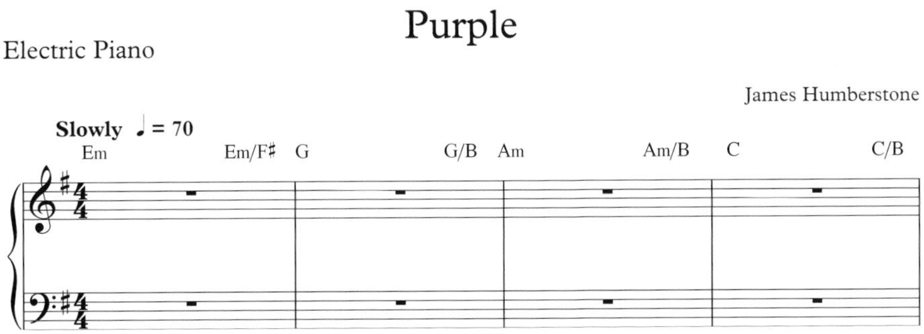

Purple

Electric Piano

James Humberstone

Figure 3.77

This pattern is to be input into the keyboard part.

To input the chord pattern:

1. Select the first bar in the keyboard/organ part and press **CTRL+K** (**COMMAND+K**), the shortcut for Chord Symbols.

2. A cursor will flash above the staff. The first chord is E minor, so simply type Em, and then press the space bar. Sibelius will change the font to look like chord text.

3. Pressing the space bar moved the cursor to the next beat of the bar. The next chord change doesn't happen until beat 4, so press the space bar two more times.

Note: The convention for musicians reading from chord progressions rather than written-out scores is that each chord persists until the next. You don't need to repeat the chord every beat. When a part involves playing and stopping, slashes are added in the staff to show when it plays and rests when it rests.

4. Type Em**/F#**, where the sharp sign is simply the hash sign (Shift+3). Then press the space bar. The hash magically turns into a sharp, and aligns itself nicely in superscript to the letters.

5. The rest of the process is obvious. Type the **G** and **G/B** chords as they appear in Figure 3.77, aligning them with the first and fourth beat of each bar, using the space bar to move between each one. Simple.

6. As ever, there's more. The next bar has the Am and Am/B chords. With the flashing cursor in the correct position, play these chords on your keyboard (they are written in Figure 3.78 in case you're not used to playing from chord symbols). Sibelius will even work out the harmony of what you play during chord input!

Figure 3.78
How to play the chords (as simply as possible) in bars 3 and 4.

7. Use either method and the space bar to complete the fourth bar with the C and C/B chords (also provided in Figure 3.78 for your reference). Piece of cake.

These text chords are great for your keyboard player, and they'd be useful if you had someone coming along to solo for you on any instrument. (By the way, copy them into a transposing instrument and Sibelius will take care of that transposition for you.) But what about creating chord *diagrams* for your guitar player—the grids you learned about in Lesson 1 that also show how each chord is fingered? Well, luckily, you've already done it.

Editing and Copying Chord Symbols

Sibelius doesn't consider chord symbols that just have text or chord symbols with guitar chord diagrams as two separate things. As far as it's concerned, they're one and the same.

Try this for another "Eureka!" moment:

1. Make a passage selection from bar 1 to bar 4 in the right hand of the keyboard/organ part.

2. Choose HOME > SELECT > FILTERS > CHORD SYMBOLS to filter out just the chord symbols.

3. Press CTRL+C (COMMAND+C) to copy the chord symbols.

4. Select the first bar in the acoustic guitar part and press CTRL+V (COMMAND+V) to paste the chord symbols in. What do you notice?!

5. If the score is a little squashed for space with the chord symbols (they will turn red to indicate that Sibelius can't fit them in), choose LAYOUT > STAFF SPACING > OPTIMIZE to make space.

Sibelius automatically created chord symbols for the chords you wrote. If you need to change the chords for any reason, you can just double-click them to edit them. But you can also edit the chord diagrams themselves.

While the guitar notation provided in both the acoustic guitar and tablature parts is designed to give an indication of what might really be performed (for instance, the fact that every note isn't sounded in each chord to reflect the way a human strums), the chords generally provide the best fingering for most of those chords. But say you want to be pedantic and tell your guitarist not to play the top string on the G chord, which is what you have notated in the part below: You would need to change the chords in bar 2 from those shown in Figure 3.79 to those shown in Figure 3.80—a subtle difference.

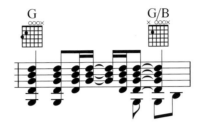

Figure 3.79
Chord diagrams in bar 2 as Sibelius has written them by default.

Figure 3.80
Chord diagrams in bar 2 as they should be written to exactly reflect the chords in the notation.

To make these changes:

1. Click the first chord (G major) and choose **Text** > **Chord Symbols** > **Revoice Chord Diagram**. This control is a tiny little button, but you can check its location in Figure 3.81. The chord is revoiced to the chord shown in Figure 3.82, but that's not the same chord as the once shown in Figure 3.80, so it's not the one you want.

Revoice Chord Diagram button

Figure 3.81
The (very teeny!) Revoice Chord Diagram button.

Figure 3.82
After clicking the Revoice Chord Diagram button, the chord is changed, but it doesn't match the one in Figure 3.80 that you need.

2. Luckily, Sibelius knows dozens of different fingerings for most common chords, so you can simply click the **Revoice Chord Diagram** button until you get a match. In fact, three more clicks on that button will get you the exact chord shown in Figure 3.80.

3. You can arrive at the correct chord diagram for the G/B chord with *14* clicks on the Revoice Chord Diagram button, but it is also possible to just edit the chord diagram. To do this, click TEXT > CHORD SYMBOLS > EDIT CHORD DIAGRAM, another small button, shown in Figure 3.83.

Edit Chord Diagram button

Figure 3.83
The Edit Chord Diagram button.

4. The Edit Chord Diagram dialog box appears. If you're going to be writing a lot of guitar music, you may like to spend some time playing around with how this works. Click anywhere in the diagram to add a dot and drag a line to create a barré. You can mess up the chord symbol, and then click CANCEL so that you don't keep the changes.

5. The only change you actually *need* to make is to change the top E string to be silent, which is notated with a cross above the string. To toggle between the open and silent string symbols (an o for open and a × for silent), press the SHIFT key as you click in the space above the string, as shown in Figure 3.84. You will need to click twice.

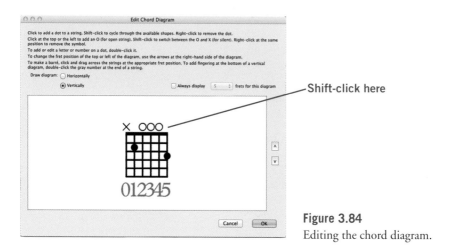

Figure 3.84
Editing the chord diagram.

6. Once changed, the dialog box should appear as shown in Figure 3.85. Click OK to finish editing the chord diagram.

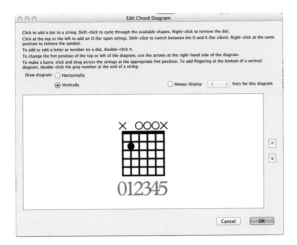

Figure 3.85
The edited chord diagram.

Tip: If you took note of the screen tip as you used the **Revoice Chord Diagram** button, you would have seen that you can save some time finding it in the ribbon
by pressing **Ctrl+Shift+Alt+K** (**Command+Shift+Option+K**). That's a pretty
tough-to-remember shortcut unless you're spending a *lot* of time working with
chord diagrams. Instead, try right-clicking (Control-clicking on a Mac) any
chord diagram and choosing **Chord Symbol** and then **Edit** or **Revoice Chord
Diagram** from the menu that appears (see Figure 3.86).

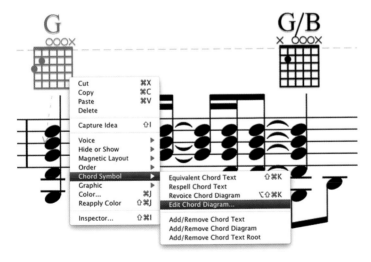

Figure 3.86
Right-clicking (Control-clicking)
a chord symbol gives you
options to edit it.

Discovering Drum Notation

 If you're taking yourself through this course rather than studying it with an Avid Training Partner, you should certainly watch the video **3.4 Discovering Drum Notation** before you read the following section.

Although drum notation is one of the common things people call upon Sibelius to do, it's also one of the most complicated notations you'll learn. This isn't because of any shortcoming in Sibelius; it's simply because drum notation itself is complex.

On the Web

John Hinchey, one of the experts you've been getting tips from throughout this book, has written about the issue of drum notation extensively on his blog. If you need more detail than is provided in this lesson, check out www.johnhinchey.com.

The reason drum notation is complex is that it covers so many different instruments (and ways of playing those instruments) all at once. Consider the scale on the piano in Figure 3.87. Each note is played on a different pitch, but on the same instrument.

Figure 3.87
A piano scale.

Now consider the excerpt of a percussion section from an orchestral score shown in Figure 3.88. Each line of an orchestral percussion section is to be played by a different player. Their rhythms and timbres combine to make an exciting percussion sound, and some extensive parts will ask them to play more than one instrument in the course of a work, but essentially the score is simple because it shows you who is playing each instrument at once.

Now take the percussion section that is a drum set. You have the snare, cymbals, and bass drum that you see in the orchestral percussion section, yet the poor drummer has to play them *all at once!* Not only that, but even a simple student set has several different kinds of cymbals—some played with the feet and some played with the hands—and at least two or three different-sized toms.

Figure 3.88
The percussion section in an orchestra.

Larger kits will include a wider range of percussion sounds, including the tambourine from our orchestral section, wood blocks, cow bells, triangles, and so on. And many of these percussion instruments can be played in a number of ways. So that's at least 20 different sounds to be incorporated in the poor drummer's part.

Unlike the piano scale and orchestral excerpt, where each staff represented one instrument, the drummer's staff has to include those 20 or more available sounds. So it's no wonder that drum notation looks as complicated as what you have from bar 4 of "Purple," shown in Figure 3.89.

Figure 3.89
The opening drum notation in the song you're working on, "Purple."

Each of the lines and spaces in the drum staff tells the drummer to play a different sound on the kit. Some instruments are played in several ways, so they have more than one position or notehead—hence the use of noteheads that have cross, triangles, or diamond shapes.

To further complicate matters, music publishers subtly vary the way they position these noteheads and the way they lay out the notation. If you're not a drummer, you're probably feeling quite relieved about it now. But unfortunately, you still need to know how to write for drums!

To try to make things as consistent as possible, Sibelius has based its drum notational system on the recommendations of the Percussive Arts Society, which are laid out in Norman Weinberg's book, *Guide to Standardized Drumset Notation*. Sibelius's standard drum set map appears in Figure 3.90.

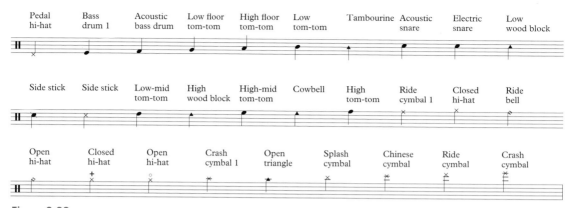

Figure 3.90
Sibelius's standard drum map.

Note: This drum map is slightly different from the one published in the *Sibelius Reference*. The noteheads shown here include the full range of Sibelius's standard drum staff mapping so that you know exactly how to get all these sounds without changing any settings. It's possible that you might not consider some of these notes and positions *standard*, but they are the best compromise and starting position. If you study the expert level, you'll learn how to build your own drum maps.

The next challenge in reading and writing drum notation is the use of voices. You are probably wondering what voices have to do with drums—no one is going to be singing, right? In actual fact, when you write two different sets of rhythms on *any* one staff, you will always show one with stems pointing up and the second with stems pointing down for clarity. In Sibelius, *voices* refers to these different rhythmic layers (which is what some other programs call them) on one staff, as shown in Figure 3.91. In the trumpet excerpt, voice 1 notes are colored blue and have their stems up, while voice 2 notes are colored green and have their stems down. The same is true in the drum excerpt.

Figure 3.91
Two examples of voices in use.

In orchestral scores, it's quite normal to write two parts on one staff to save space in the score. The two trumpets in the first excerpt are rhythmically independent, but because they don't cross over, they can clearly be written as two voices and it's easy to follow one part or the other (or both!).

In the drum excerpt in Figure 3.91, different sounds have been written in different voices so it's easier to see their exact beat position. If you compare the note position on the staff and noteheads used with the map in Figure 3.90, you can work out that in voice 1 (shown in blue with stems pointing up), there is a closed hi-hat playing on every eighth note (quaver) and a snare drum on beats 2 and 4. In voice 2 in the drum excerpt, there is a bass drum (played with a foot pedal), strengthening beats 1 and 3. It's a typical rock beat.

The use of voices in the drum excerpt is *nearly* standard. In just about every drum score you'll see, hi-hats are written in the space above the staff and with their stems pointing up, while the bass drum is written in the bottom space with its stems pointing down.

There is a little debate about which direction the stems of the snare drum should point. Some write it as shown in Figure 3.91 in voice 1, while others write the snare with stems down—in voice 2—as shown in Figure 3.92. While some drummers and publishers strongly prefer one or the other, neither is *wrong*. If you're composing or arranging for a client or a publisher, you should see how they do it.

Figure 3.92
The same drum beat written with the snare drum in voice 2 (green notes).

Finally, there are a few further variations. Some publishers prefer to show no rests in voice 2 or even either voice if the beat is clearly visible in the other voice; an example of this is given in Figure 3.93. Some publishers consistently put all notes played by the hands in voice 1, and all notes played by the feet in voice 2.

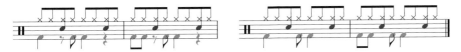

Figure 3.93
The same drum beat, first with rests shown and then with rests hidden.

If you can bear the two following things in mind, you'll go fine with drum notation:

■ The notes do not stand for pitches. Each note is a different sound, representing a different percussion instrument. Noteheads also change the sound to be played. If you're not sure which sound refers to which line or space on the staff, refer to Figure 3.90, Sibelius's drum map.

■ The use of voices varies from drummer to drummer and from publisher to publisher. Begin with the bass drum in voice 2, stems down, and the hi-hats in voice 1, stems up. (You'll learn how to do this in a moment.) From there, the important thing is just to be consistent.

Tip: If you're dipping in and out of this book, and just want to try this out, use the catch-up file Purple2.sib, which you'll find in the Lesson 3 folder under Core Resources. It has all of the work to this point already complete! If you *do* open Purple2.sib, Sibelius will prompt you with the question shown in Figure 3.60. There are hidden comments in the file, which will help you locate where to put repeats in the section "Using Repeats and Repeat Bars" later in this lesson, but you don't need those now, so click No.

Starting Quickly: The Ideas Panel

"Purple" has a very exciting and relatively complex drum beat that begins in bar 5 and continues until the first verse starts at bar 13. It uses a number of common drums including the snare and bass drum as well as pedaled hi-hat and splash, ride, and hi-hat cymbals played with drum sticks. (Of course, you can work this all out from Figure 3.90.)

Making a drum pattern this detailed can take a while, and yet this one was created in less than a second. If you're particularly sharp, you can probably guess how: It was copied into the score from the Ideas panel.

To copy the drum pattern in for the rest of the verse and chorus:

1. Choose VIEW > PANELS > IDEAS to open the Ideas panel.

2. In the Search field, type DRUM, as shown in Figure 3.94. Then press ENTER (RETURN).

3. To preview each of the drum beats, click and hold on it. You may be able to work out that the one used is Rock Drum Kit 9 just by listening to them.

Figure 3.94
Type drum in the Search field.

Note: If you like, you can choose a different drum beat for the song. Just remember that the song is relatively slow, so if you choose a rhythm that was originally recorded at a fast tempo, it may sound odd at the slower tempo. When it comes to the description of modifying the given beat, you'll need to invent similar changes to your own.

4. Click the Rock Drum Kit 9 idea (or the idea you'd rather use).

5. Select the drum set part in bar 13. Then click the **PASTE IDEA** button on the Ideas panel.

6. When this drum beat was used in the introduction, a change was made. Drag the ride cymbal down to the position of splash cymbal, as shown in Figure 3.95. Well done, you just composed a drum beat!

Edit this note by dragging it down

Figure 3.95
Editing a drum beat from the Ideas panel.

It might seem a little ridiculous to refer to what you just did as *composing*, but starting off with one of the provided ideas and editing it is a way some arrangers work. Very often, drum beats are derivations of one simple style (e.g., rock, Latin, reggae, and so on), so starting with an established pattern and editing it is a good way to begin.

To further edit this drum beat to match the rhythm used in the chorus:

1. Make a passage selection of the four bars you just added.

2. Press **R** two times to repeat them. Figure 3.96 shows the same drum pattern at bar 21 with the cymbals rhythm edited to match the rhythm of the rest of the band.

Figure 3.96
Edit the drum part at bar 21 to change it as shown.

3. To edit the drum part to create this pattern, select the first note in voice 1 (the cymbal with the cross notehead and stem pointing up). Use the Keypad panel to add a rhythm dot and an accent so the part appears as shown in Figure 3.97.

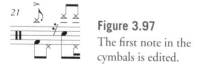

Figure 3.97
The first note in the cymbals is edited.

4. There are a number of ways to create the next note. Press **R** to repeat the note you have selected; this will save you from having to re-create the cross notehead.

5. Press the **DOWN ARROW KEY** to move the pitch down one step. Then use the Keypad panel to change the rhythm to a sixteenth note (semiquaver) and then add a tie.

6. Press **R** to create the next note and use the Keypad panel to change its note length to a dotted eighth note (dotted quaver). You should now have what is shown in Figure 3.98.

Figure 3.98
The first three notes in the cymbals are now edited.

7. Again, press **R** to create the next note. Then press the **UP ARROW KEY** to nudge its pitch up. Finally, use the Keypad panel to change the note to a sixteenth note (semiquaver) then add a tie and add an accent.

8. To complete bar 21, press **R** once more and use the Keypad panel to change the note to a half note (minim). You should now have the complete bar, as shown in Figure 3.99.

Figure 3.99
Bar 21 in the drum part, complete.

9. From completing bar 21, you should have learned enough to change the cymbals in bar 22 to match those shown in Figure 3.96. Do this now.

10. The rhythm of bars 23 and 24 is exactly similar to bars 21 and 22. Make a passage selection of those bars and press **R** one more time.

At this point, the drum part meets up with a six extra bars of patterns that were already in the song when you opened it. In the final section, it's time to learn how to make your own drum part from scratch.

Manually Creating Drum Parts

The next empty drum bars come at bar 31. The pattern you're going to build from scratch is shown in Figure 3.100.

31

Figure 3.100
The drum pattern you will create from bar 31.

This is quite a complex pattern, but it is going to be broken down into very simple stages for you. First, you will input the voice 1 part only. As you've discovered, the voice 1 part is written on top of voice 2, with stems pointing up. In Figure 3.101, the voice 1 notes are shown in blue, and the voice 2 notes in green.

Figure 3.101
The same drum pattern, but with voice 1 and 2 clearly distinguished by color.

To make it even easier, Figure 3.102 shows the pattern with voice 2 deleted and with all the voice 1 noteheads changed to the normal shape that you're more acquainted with. Note that without the voice 2 notes in the staff, the voice 1 stems point down as they normally would.

Figure 3.102
Voice 1 shown alone, with normal noteheads.

With voice 1 so simplified, you should now be able to input it without step-by-step instruction. Use alphabetic entry and imagine that it was in treble clef, so the first notes you will input are G and A. (Remember, in alphabetic entry you can press G to add the G and then press 2 to add a note a second above it.) Don't worry if you hear no sound as you put notes in; that's just because you have to include the correct notehead, which you'll do soon.

In bar 34, there is a big tom-tom fill, but to you it's as simple as putting in a series of two-note chords. Input all notes until you have what is shown in Figure 3.102. Next, you can input voice 2. To make it simple to focus on voice 2, Figure 3.103 shows its rhythm with voice 1 hidden. Inputting voice 2 with alphabetic entry is also very simple, as long as you begin the right way.

Figure 3.103
The same drum pattern, but with voice 1 hidden so you can concentrate on inputting voice 2.

To input voice 2:

1. Select bar 31 in the drum part.

2. Press **N** for note entry.

3. To select voice 2 for input, press **ALT+2** (**OPTION+2**), where the 2 is on the main keyboard, *not* the keypad. You should notice several things: The blue caret is now green; any selected notes on the Keypad panel are now green; and a number 2 (also green) at the bottom of the Keypad panel is high-lighted, as shown in Figure 3.104. All these green shadings are visual reminders that you're about to input notes in voice 2.

Figure 3.104
When you change to voice 2, any visual selections become green to serve as a reminder.

4. Click the **SIXTEENTH NOTE** (**SEMIQUAVER**) button on the Keypad panel and press **F** to create the note. (Remember, Sibelius thinks of drum notation in treble clef for the purposes of alphabetic entry.) Sibelius will choose the top note, so press **CTRL+ARROW DOWN** (**COMMAND+ARROW DOWN**) to move the note down an octave.

5. Using the Keypad panel, change the note length to a dotted eighth note (dotted quaver). Then press **F** again to add the next note.

6. Using the Keypad panel, change the note length by turning the rhythm dot off. Then press **C**. Again, the note appears in the wrong octave, so press **CTRL+UP ARROW** (**COMMAND+UP ARROW**) to move the note up an octave. The process is now identical for the remainder of voice 2. You should be able to complete it from here on your own.

Note: Did you notice that as soon as you started entering notes in voice 2, Sibelius automatically made all the voice 1 notes you inputted earlier flip their stems up? This will always work automatically as long as you write voice 1 *above* voice 2. If the parts overlap for more than a note or two here and there, it will become confusing quickly.

When you finish entering the voice 2 pattern, you should have a complete pattern as shown in Figure 3.105.

Figure 3.105
The pattern as you have copied it so far.

The only finishing touches needed now are to change the noteheads for the cymbals. Because the majority of the cross noteheads happen on the position of G5 (if you check back to the drum map in Figure 3.90 you'll see it means closed hi-hat), you can begin by changing all of those at once to save time.

To change the noteheads for the cymbals:

1. Make a passage selection of all four bars.

2. Use the advanced filter to select the pitch G5. To begin, choose **HOME** > **SELECT** > **ADVANCED**.

3. Click the **SINGLE** option button under Pitch. Then click the corresponding drop-down lists and choose **G** and **5**, as shown in Figure 3.106. Finally, click **SELECT**.

4. All the G5 pitches are now highlighted blue. Choose **NOTATIONS** > **NOTEHEADS**, click the lower half of the **TYPE** button, and choose **CROSS**, as shown in Figure 3.107. All selected notes change to the cross notehead.

5. Press **ESC** so you can change the remaining notes that still need alternate noteheads. Next, click the A on the first beat of bar 31; then choose **NOTATIONS** > **NOTEHEADS** > **TYPE** > **CROSS** again. Repeat this for the A at the start of bar 33.

6. Some of the G5 pitches should be set to open diamond noteheads (which means they are open hi-hat notes). Select these in turn—or Ctrl-click (Command-click) to select them all—and choose **NOTATIONS** > **NOTEHEADS** > **TYPE** > **DIAMOND**.

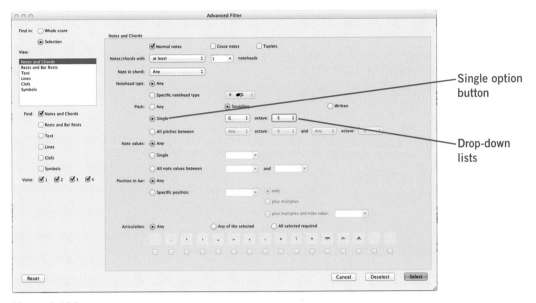

Figure 3.106
Settings for the advanced filter to select the pitch G5.

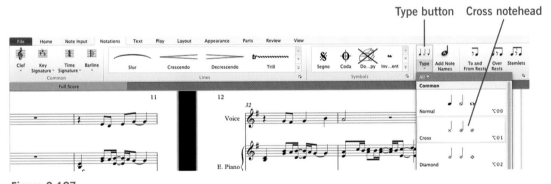

Figure 3.107
Changing the selected noteheads to cross noteheads.

You're done! Select bar 31 in the drum part and press P to play it back and hear your hard work. (Remember, if you select a staff before you start playback, it is soloed.) Pretty cool, eh?

The next four bars of the drum pattern are the same, so you can repeat these if you like. Alternatively, you can input them manually to practice the process. You may also like to vary your method a little following the advice of one of our experts....

Instead of using your computer keyboard or mouse to enter notes on the drum kit stave, you can speed things up by using a MIDI keyboard. It's quicker with a MIDI keyboard because the noteheads are automatically entered in the correct way (i.e., hi-hat parts will automatically have cross-noteheads). To set this up, choose File > Preferences and select Step-Time and Flexi-time from the list on the left. Next, under Percussion Staves, check the MIDI device's drum map if it isn't already. That means you'll be using the inbuilt MIDI percussion instruments in your keyboard to enter notes on the drum kit stave.

—Katie Wardrobe, teacher, arranger, and copyist
with extensive experience in Sibelius training

On the Web   Katie shares (free of charge!) dozens of tutorials on all kinds of music software, including Sibelius, at her Web site: www.midnightmusic.com.au.

If you'd like to follow Katie's advice:

1. Select bar 35 of the drum part.

2. Press **ALT+1** (**OPTION+1**) if you're not set to voice 1.

3. In the Keypad panel, click the **EIGHTH NOTE** (**QUAVER**) button.

4. Instead of typing pitches, play the drums on your MIDI keyboard. For help finding each drum sound, see Figure 3.108.

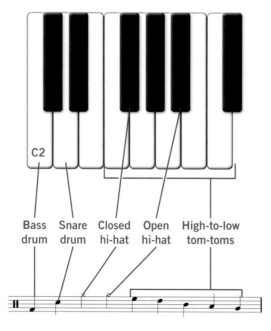

Figure 3.108
Finding each drum sound on your MIDI keyboard.

Note that the C at the bottom of the keyboard in the figure is C2—two octaves *below* middle C. The splash cymbal isn't included in this drum map, and will need to be added manually later.

To complete the drum part for the entire song, copy and paste the four-bar drum pattern from bar 21 into the empty bars at bar 39 (where the chorus material returns). You only need to paste it once, because the song ends as it begins, with a solo acoustic guitar.

Adding Your Own Ideas to the Ideas Panel

Having put some effort into creating your own drum pattern from scratch, you may like to keep it for future use as a starting point for more patterns, in the same way you can use the patterns that are already in the Ideas panel.

To add an idea to the Ideas panel:

1. To open the Ideas panel (if it isn't open already), choose VIEW > PANELS > IDEAS. If "drums" still appears in the Search field, delete it, and press ENTER (RETURN).

2. In your score, make a passage selection of your four-bar drum pattern (from bar 31).

3. In the Ideas panel, click the CAPTURE IDEA button (shown in Figure 3.109) or press SHIFT+I. Your idea will appear at the top of the list of ideas, as shown in Figure 3.110. If you can't see it, make sure you've deleted your search and pressed Enter (Return), and scroll to the top of the list manually.

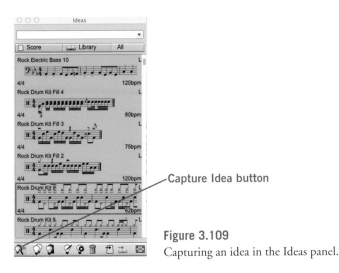

Capture Idea button

Figure 3.109
Capturing an idea in the Ideas panel.

Figure 3.110

Your idea is added to the Ideas panel at the top of the list.

4. Just like the existing ideas, you can click and hold on your idea to hear it play back. If you wanted to, you could paste it into your score at another point just as you've already learned to do.

5. Click the **LIBRARY** tab, as shown in Figure 3.111. Your idea will disappear. This is because although you've captured your idea, by default it's just stored in this score, and not in the library of ideas that came with Sibelius. (Click the **SCORE** tab to see the idea alone, as it is the only idea captured in this score thus far.)

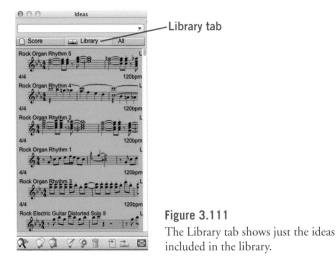

—Library tab

Figure 3.111

The Library tab shows just the ideas included in the library.

6. To be able to use the idea in future scores, you need to add it to your library. After clicking the Score tab, make sure your idea is selected, and then click the **ADD TO LIBRARY** button, as shown in Figure 3.112. Now, if you start a new score and search for your idea with the word Purple, you'll be able to find it and use it.

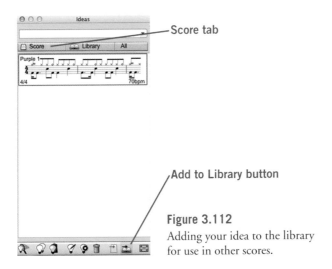

Score tab

Add to Library button

Figure 3.112
Adding your idea to the library for use in other scores.

As you can see, the Ideas panel can be used in more than one way. In Lesson 1, you used ideas that had been specially created for that arrangement. In this lesson, you've used an existing idea that ships with Sibelius 7, and you've added your own idea to the Ideas panel. You've also learned that when you paste ideas from the panel, they transpose themselves into the prevailing key. Believe it or not, there's still more that the Ideas panel can do, and you'll come to some of that in Lesson 5. For now, you can close the panel.

Creating Lyrics

 You may like to watch the corresponding video, 3.5 Creating Lyrics, right now.

After the relatively complex processes of creating guitar tablature and drum notation from scratch, you will be relieved to know that the remaining topics—entering lyrics, entering repeats, and exporting various formats—are very simple and quick. In this section, you'll learn to enter lyrics into your score in a number of ways, all of them nice, quick, and easy.

Tip: If you've jumped ahead in the course to this point, or you just like dipping in and out of the bits that are most useful to you, you can use the catch-up file **Purple3.sib** to start from the right point of progress. Just note that when you open the file, it will point out that there are hidden comments; you should choose to keep them hidden for now.

Typing Lyrics

The first few lines of the first verse in the song you're working on, "Purple," already have the lyrics added. You will take over from bar 17. You'll find all the lyrics in the following sidebar, and in a text file in the Lesson 3 folder under Core Resources. It's called PurpleLyrics.txt. You'll be using this file later on.

The simple procedure with lyrics follows the rules of music publishing. That is that only one syllable can be sung under one note (if you want to squeeze in more syllables, add shorter notes!), and hyphens should join syllables together so the words can be easily read. Whenever a syllable is held over several notes (this is called a *melisma*), multiple hyphens should be used. Alternatively, if it is the last syllable of a word, a line should be drawn from the end of the word to show that the sound is held while more notes are sung.

"Purple" Lyrics

Verse

I made my color,
Made it strong for you,
It was Purple
We were playing cards,
It was your turn,
To be Purple.

Chorus

Oh yeah,
Flowers and pretty things,
Oh yeah,
Butterflies and stuff.

Second Chorus (Variation on First)

Oh yeah,
Sunshine on a rainy day,
Oh yeah,
Ribbons in your hair.

Verse

I went swimming,
On a sunny day,
Not much Purple.
I went rhyming,
What can rhyme with purple?
Only Purple.

Chorus

Oh yeah,
Flowers and pretty things,
Oh yeah,
Butterflies and stuff.

If you're not sure how best to split syllables in words, follow the sage advice of Sibelius guru Daniel Spreadbury, here quoted from the *Sibelius Reference*:

> When you split a word of lyrics with hyphens it's important to split between the correct letters, otherwise the syllables can be hard to read. A rule of thumb (though there are exceptions) is as follows:
>
> ■ Put standard prefixes and suffixes (e.g., un-, -ing, -ed, -ly) as separate syllables.
>
> ■ If there is a single consonant between two syllables (e.g., labor), split *before* it (la-bor).
>
> ■ If there are two consonants between two syllables (e.g., better, Batman), split between them (bet-ter, Bat-man).
>
> As there are exceptions, if in doubt, ensure that each syllable can be read and pronounced correctly on its own; for example, "laughter" should be split "laugh-ter" rather than "laug-hter" because "laug" doesn't produce the right sound when read on its own.

You can see examples of all these rules in the lyrics that are already in the file.

To enter the rest of the first verse of lyrics:

1. Select the first note in bar 17 of the vocal part. Then press **CTRL+L** (**COMMAND+L**) or choose **TEXT** > **LYRICS** > **LYRICS** (click the top half of the Lyrics button).

2. A flashing cursor appears under the note. Type the first two words, **WE WERE**. As usual, press the space bar after each word.

3. To write "playing" over the next *three* notes, type **PLAY**, then press the **HYPHEN KEY** (also known as the minus sign). Sibelius will move the cursor to below the next note. Next, type **ING** to complete the word. Because the note is tied to the next one, press the space bar *twice*, once for each note the syllable covers.

4. To complete the bar, type **CARDS**, and press the space bar.

5. The next bar introduces the first melisma—two notes sung on the single syllable "It," as shown in Figure 3.113. To create it, type **IT** and press the space bar twice. Now you can add the words "was your turn" with one note for each word.

It＿was your turn

Figure 3.113
The second bar of lyrics to be added with a short melisma.

6. Melismas are indicated in the score not just with extended lines or hyphens, but also with a phrase mark over the held notes. Press Esc to cancel lyrics entry, click the first note in bar 18, and add an **S** phrase mark, for slur. The slur will be added below the notes, but for vocal music, it's best to have it over the top (out of the way of the words), so press **X** to flip it ("a-cross" the staff).

7. Continue adding lyrics to match the settings shown in Figure 3.114. Make sure you add all phrasing as well as the text.

Figure 3.114
Input all these lyrics, taking care to include phrase marks.

The repeat structure for this song is not yet in place, so it might not be clear where the second chorus alternate lyrics go. They begin in bar 21. For these, you will use Sibelius's lyrics line 2 text style.

To use the line 2 text style:

1. Select the first note in the vocal part in bar 21 and press **Ctrl+Alt+L** (**Command+Alt+L**) or choose **Text > Lyrics > Lyrics > Lyrics Line 2**. The second line is automatically below the first, and Sibelius will respace the music to make both sets of lyrics align beautifully with the notes.

2. Enter the second chorus lyrics, as shown in Figure 3.115 (and the ones that follow!).

Figure 3.115
Input the second chorus using the Lyrics Line 2 style.

If you sing in a church choir, you may be used to a different convention to show when a syllable is held over more than one pitch. In some music, separate beams on each note show separate syllables for each note while joined beams show melismas. Figure 3.116 shows the same passage changed to use this beaming convention with chorus 1. If you'd prefer to use this convention, it's easy. Simply select staves with lyrics in them and then choose Text > Plug-ins > Plug-ins > Traditional Lyrics Beaming, as shown in Figure 3.117. The plug-in (Figure 3.118) will change the beaming for you.

Figure 3.116
The same passage with the traditional lyrics beaming convention.

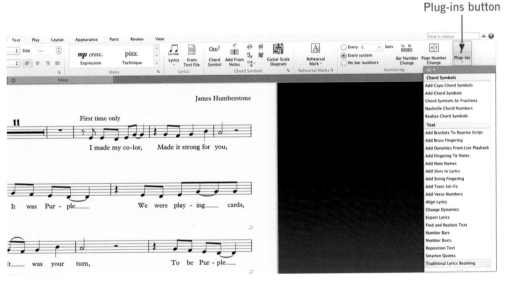

Figure 3.117
Opening the Traditional Lyrics Beaming plug-in.

Figure 3.118
The Traditional Lyrics Beaming plug-in.

Importing and Exporting Lyrics

If you just so happen to have all of the lyrics for your score in a handy text file, you can import them directly into Sibelius. You can now use the provided text file to import the rest of the lyrics into your score.

First, to edit the file to remove the words you've already put in:

1. Open the text file PurpleLyrics.txt in your operating system's default text editor.

2. Delete lyrics from the opening title ("Purple") to the point up to which you have added lyrics to your score ("Ribbons in your hair.") and everything in between. This should leave two verse parts, beginning "I went swimming" and a final chorus ending "Butterflies and stuff."

3. Save the file. (If you'd rather keep the original lyrics in one piece, do a Save As.)

Next, to import the lyrics:

1. Make a passage selection in the voice part from bar 31 to bar 42, where it stops singing.

2. Choose Text > Lyrics > From Text File. The Create Lyrics from Text File dialog box, shown in Figure 3.119, will open.

Figure 3.119
The Create Lyrics from Text File dialog box.

3. Click Browse and select the edited text file.

4. Make sure the rather wonderfully named Automatically Syllabify Ambiguous Words check box is selected. This feature attempts to work out how you would like words to be broken up when it isn't clear. Leave the other options set to their defaults, and click OK.

You will probably find what Sibelius does is quite remarkable. It divides the text, applies it to the music, and respaces it all to fit. It can even do this in six languages, including French, German, Latin, Italian, and Spanish, in addition to English.

Exporting lyrics is just as easy from Sibelius.

To export lyrics:

1. Choose TEXT > PLUG-INS > PLUG-INS > EXPORT LYRICS.

2. Leave the settings on their defaults and click **OK**. Sibelius will export a text file with all the lyrics in it into the same folder that the Sibelius file is saved in.

Using Repeats and Repeat Bars

 As usual, you can begin this section by watching a video of it. The video is called **3.6 Using Repeats and Repeat Bars** and will give you a thorough overview of everything you need to know.

If you've played back your score recently you'll have discovered that it goes for about 2 minutes and 45 seconds. In actual fact, it's longer than that, because there are repeats missing. By the time you've put them in, the song will be over a minute longer. (Isn't it amazing how much material you can get out of two four-chord progressions?)

Music contains lots of different kinds of repeats. There are repeat bar shorthand notations, used most in jazz and popular music notation. There are repeat bar-lines for repeating sections, sometimes with first and second time bars. And there are larger structural repeat instructions such as *da capo* or *coda* instructions. Sibelius reads and plays back all of these, and in this section, you'll learn how to create them.

Tip: A catch-up file called **Purple4.sib** will give you the lesson progressed to this point should you want to just do this lesson on its own. If you're still working from the MusicXML import at the beginning of this lesson, you may prefer to transfer to this Sibelius file simply because it has comments in it confirming where to put the repeats. If you want to keep all your hard work in one file, you can simply open two files and swap between them with View > Window > Switch Windows.

Repeating Shorthand and More About the Keypad Panel

Repeat bars shorthand is not considered suitable for genres of music other than popular music and jazz. If you're writing orchestral parts, for instance, you shouldn't use this form of shorthand. With repeat bars, parts with lots of repetition can show the repetition more clearly, meaning performers need not read and count every bar. Because this is a rock score, any time the repeat function was used to repeat some bars, you could also have used this shorthand.

Exploring the repeat bars symbols also enables you to explore the Keypad panel in greater detail, because the marks reside on the Keypad panel but are currently hidden. The important Next Keypad Layout button on the Keypad panel, shown in Figure 3.120, enables you to rotate through six different layouts to access all that the Keypad panel can offer. You can also use the F7 to F12 function keys on your computer to change quickly between the six different layouts (unless they have been ascribed to other functions by the operating system or your computer manufacturer).

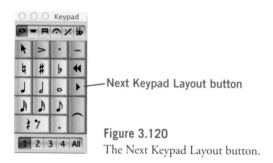 —Next Keypad Layout button

Figure 3.120
The Next Keypad Layout button.

Each Keypad panel layout offers different items to attach to the notes in your score. You are already very familiar with the first Keypad panel layout because you've used it extensively. The remaining keyboard layouts are as follows:

- **More Notes.** The second Keypad panel layout, More Notes, shown in Figure 3.121, includes even longer and shorter note lengths than are available on the first layout, as well as grace notes, extra rhythm dots, and some miscellaneous functions such as creating a bar rest, putting a note in brackets, and making notes cue sized.

- **Beams/Tremolos.** The third Keypad panel layout, Beams/Tremolos, shown in Figure 3.122, is all about beaming. Buttons at the top of the Keypad panel change the beaming away from the defaults, while buttons at the bottom allow for the creation of different kinds of tremolos and rolls.

Figure 3.121
The More Notes Keypad
panel layout.

Figure 3.122
The Beams/Tremolos Keypad
panel layout.

Figure 3.123
The Articulations Keypad
panel layout.

■ **Articulations.** The fourth Keypad panel layout, Articulations, shown in Figure 3.123, contains more articulation marks than can be found on the first layout, including marks for bowing and harmonics. It also contains pauses (fermatas), and three buttons with squares on them that can be user-defined. (Unfortunately, that's the kind of advanced feature that you'll meet in the higher levels.)

■ **Jazz Articulations.** Figure 3.124 shows the fifth Keypad panel layout, Jazz Articulation, which is the one you're about to use. Articulations in this layout include not only repeat bar shorthands, but also scoops and falls found in jazz music and arpeggiation lines.

■ **Accidentals.** The sixth and final Keypad panel layout, Accidentals, is shown in Figure 3.125. It contains not only the accidentals in the first Keypad panel layout, but also double sharps and flats and quarter-tones. There are also useful buttons for bracketing accidentals if Sibelius's automated cautionary accidentals don't quite do the job for you, and for cancelling both accidentals and any brackets around them.

Figure 3.124
The Jazz Articulations Keypad
panel layout.

Figure 3.125
The Accidentals Keypad
panel layout.

One more button must be highlighted as you begin to unlock the true power of the Keypad panel: the First Keypad Layout button shown in Figure 3.126. Because everything you use most often (the most common note lengths, accidentals, articulation marks, tie, and rest buttons) are on that layout, this button serves to get you back to it in one quick keystroke.

Now to put the Keypad panel to work! Before you put in the first articulation, change the orientation of the page to Landscape. Otherwise, forcing four-bar repeats into one stage will squash much of the music. (Although you could just make the staves much smaller, switching to Landscape mode enables you to learn how to change the page orientation.) Simply choose Layout > Document Setup > Orientation > Landscape. You might also want to optimize staff spacing once more.

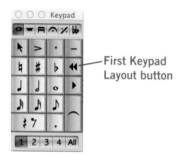

First Keypad Layout button

Figure 3.126
The First Keypad Layout button.

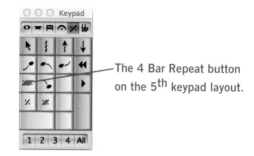

The 4 Bar Repeat button on the 5th keypad layout.

Figure 3.127
The location of the 4 Bar Repeat button on the Keypad panel.

You know that the opening four-bar drum pattern is repeated three times, so highlight bars 9 to 20 in the drum part. Then click the 4 Bar Repeat button (shown in Figure 3.127) on the Jazz Articulations (fifth) Keypad panel layout. A page of music with the repeats in should now look like Figure 3.127.

There are plenty more opportunities to use four-bar repeat signs in the song if you so choose, although they should be used to make the parts *easier* to read. You may find that overusing them makes it difficult to remember what is going on.

If one part (such as the drum part) uses a lot of repeat bars, you can assist performers in counting the bars by numbering each bar that is repeated. That way, performers can just count bars rather than follow the repeats in their part.

To number the bars:

1. Make a passage selection in the drum part for the duration of the repeat signs.

2. Choose Text > Plug-ins > Plug-ins > Number Bars, as shown in Figure 3.129. The Number Bars dialog box opens.

Figure 3.128
The score, including a four-bar repeat in the drums.

Figure 3.129
Running the Number Bars plug-in.

3. In the Number Bars dialog box, type **1** in the Number Every Nth Bar Where N Is field, as shown in Figure 3.130, thus asking Sibelius to number every bar.

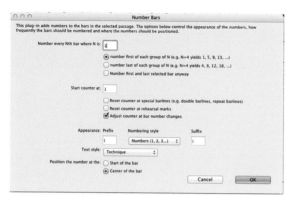

Figure 3.130
The Number Bars plug-in dialog box.

4. Leave all other options as default, and click **OK**.

If you jump into the drum part now, you will see exactly how it will be easier for the drummer to count the bars of repetition, as shown in Figure 3.131.

Figure 3.131
An excerpt of the drum part, with repeats numbered.

Adding Repeat Barlines and First and Second Time Bars

If you're working in one of the Sibelius catch-up files and can't yet see the yellow sticky notes, or comments, on top of the score, choose View > Invisibles > Comments. If they're still not there, open the file Purple5.sib from the Lesson 3 folder (Sibelius will prompt you to show them) and carry on working from there (or use that file as a reference).

Begin by putting in repeat barlines. In Sibelius, the repeat barline that tells you to go back in the music is called an *end repeat barline*, as shown in Figure 3.132. You need one of these at the end of bar 24, as marked by the comment on the score.

To add an end repeat barline:

1. Select the barline at the end of that bar. (It will turn purple.)

2. As shown in Figure 3.132, choose **NOTATIONS** > **COMMON** > **BARLINE** > **END REPEAT**.

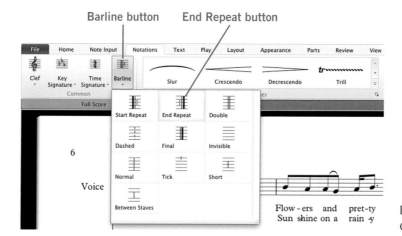

Figure 3.132

Creating an end repeat barline.

3. This repeat is not supposed to go right back to the beginning, so you also need a start repeat barline at the start of bar 13. One way to add this is to make sure you have no selection, and then choose **NOTATIONS** > **COMMON** > **BARLINE** > **START REPEAT**. You will see the loaded blue mouse pointer; click with this pointer at the start of bar 13.

4. These repeats are also designed to have first and second time bars (which explains why bars 24 and 25 are so similar!). Select bar 24 in any part and press **L** to see the full Lines gallery.

5. Select **1ST ENDING**, as shown in Figure 1.133. The first time ending line is added to the score.

6. Select bar 25 in any part, press **L** to open the Lines gallery again, and choose **2ND ENDING** (*not* **2ND ENDING CLOSED**, which won't play back properly).

7. If the first ending line overlaps the second ending line, delete any comments that are in the way (just click them and press Delete or Backspace), zoom in, and carefully grab the arm of the line. (Even if it's right behind the number 2, this is possible.) Then drag it to the left.

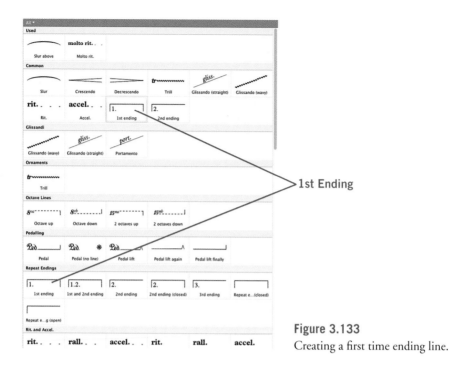

1st Ending

Figure 3.133

Creating a first time ending line.

Time for a bit of a break. Your repeat structure should play back. Play back from the start (or at least from the start of the first verse) and see if the first and second time bars work as you'd expect.

Adding Written Repeats (*D.S. al Coda*)

Naturally, you can't get enough of this song, so let's squeeze a few more seconds out of it by adding an overarching *D.S. al coda*. If you haven't met this before, a *D.C.* (*da capo*) instruction in a score tells the player to go from the top—in other words, to repeat from the start. A *D.S.* (*dal segno*) instruction tells the player to play from the sign. The sign can be written as a capital S, but is usually ornamented and appears as shown in Figure 3.134. The other common structural instructions are used in combination with these. The first is *al coda*, which means "to the coda," a final section (marked with the word *coda* and sometimes the sign also shown in Figure 3.134) for the ending of the piece. The second is *al fine*, which means play until you reach the *fine* (finish) marking.

𝄋   𝄌 **Coda**

Figure 3.134

The segno and coda signs.

These elements can be strung together. For instance, you might get *D.C. al fine*, which would mean you return to the start of the piece and play until you reach the word *fine*. Or, as you're going to put in your score, you could get *D.S. al coda*, which slightly more complicatedly means repeat back to the sign and, when you get to the words "to coda," jump forward to the final section marked "coda." If this is all new to you, it will probably make more sense when you see it in action!

To put in the repeat instructions in the order they will happen in the music:

1. At bar 42, there is a comment with the instruction that a *D.S. al coda* should be put at the end of this bar. Delete the comment. Then, with no selection, choose Text > Styles > More > Repeat (D.C./D.S./To Coda), as shown in Figure 3.135.

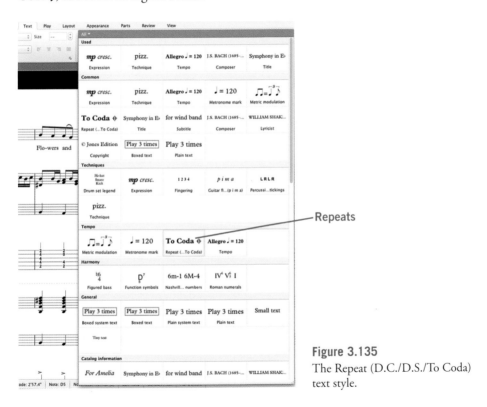

Figure 3.135
The Repeat (D.C./D.S./To Coda) text style.

2. The mouse pointer will become blue, or loaded. Click at the end of bar 42 to make a flashing cursor appear.

3. Rather than typing in the text, right-click (Control-click) anywhere on the score to open a context-sensitive menu (this can be terribly useful for entering things like notes in metronome marks and similar elements) and choose **D.S. AL CODA**, as shown in Figure 3.136. Then press **ESC**.

Figure 3.136

Right-clicking (Control-clicking) when editing any text style makes a context-sensitive menu full of useful text and symbols pop up.

4. The music will now repeat to the segno. Select bar 5 and again choose **TEXT > STYLES > MORE > REPEAT (D.C./D.S./TO CODA)**. Then right-click (Control-click) and this time choose the segno illustrated in Figure 3.134. Press **ESC** and move it back to the start of the bar if it does not assume the correct position.

Tip: If you'd like to make the segno bigger, you can use the Text > Format group controls as you did in Lesson 1 to edit it as you see fit.

5. The next instruction required is to tell the players when to go to the coda. A comment on the score marks the end of bar 12 for this purpose, so select bar 12, then choose the **REPEAT (D.C./D.S./TO CODA)** text style again, right-click (Control-click), and choose **TO CODA**. Again, press **ESC** to finish editing the text.

6. The final instruction required is the coda itself. The players will jump forward from the To Coda instruction to the coda marking, which should be at bar 43 (if you're having problems locating bar 43, change to panorama so that every bar is numbered). Select bar 43, then choose **TEXT > STYLES > MORE** and choose **REPEAT (D.C./D.S./TO CODA)**. Note that this time, as well as being in its usual position, the Repeat (D.C./D.S./To Coda) is also near the top of the list because it is a *used* style in this score. Sibelius does this to help you locate text styles that you're using a lot. After inserting the text style at the start of bar 43, right-click (Control-click), choose the Coda sign (refer to Figure 3.134), and then type **CODA**.

It's probably tempting to play back the song again straight away (unless you're getting sick of it by now!), but there is one more little thing to do to get the playback just perfect. And you'll do that right now.

Changing Playback on Repeats

You may have noticed at bar 13 that the vocalist has the instruction "First time only," and then "Both times" at bar 21. In contrast, there is a guitar solo written between bars 13 and 20 that is marked "Second time only." The idea in this kind of structure is that on the repeat, the vocalist takes a break for the guitarist, who similarly doesn't play the first time through while the singer is singing. To make this work, you get to play for the first time with Sibelius's Inspector. To access this handy floating panel, choose Home > Edit > Inspector (see Figure 3.137).

Figure 3.137
Opening the Inspector.

The Inspector changes to suit the context of what you have selected. If you have nothing selected, it simply says "Nothing Selected" and offers you no further options. However, select a passage of music (for instance, try selecting the vocal part on that first repeat from bars 13 to 20), and it offers all sorts of exciting possibilities, also shown in Figure 3.137.

To use the Inspector to add the appropriate instructions:

1. To make the vocalist part perform the first time through but not the second time, with bars 13 to 20 of the vocal part selected, uncheck the **2** check box under Playback and Play on Pass, as shown in Figure 3.138. Note that when you change selection, the Inspector disappears (unless you click the "pin" button to keep it), and you'll need to select it again in the ribbon next time you need it.

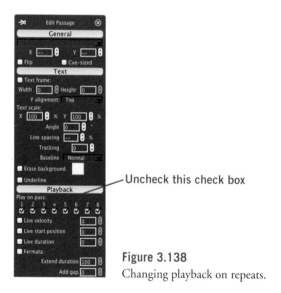

Uncheck this check box

Figure 3.138
Changing playback on repeats.

2. Make an identical passage selection, but in the guitar part.

3. Display the Inspector. Then uncheck the **1** check box under Playback and Play on Pass.

There is a lot more that you can do with the Inspector, but that's all you'll try for now. It will be back in Lesson 4, "Worksheets."

If you play back your score now, you should hear all the repeats in combination and the alternating vocal and guitar lines on the first and second times through. The song is complete! Now it's time to share your hard work.

Exporting and Sharing Online

 There is a video, called **3.7 Exporting and Sharing Online**, that goes with this section.

Following your experience with MIDI file and MusicXML import, you can see the advantages in being able to grab files from other programs and make beautiful scores out of them in Sibelius. It's also quite likely that at some point in your Sibelius career, you'll want to share a file with someone who doesn't have Sibelius. Obviously, the best solution is to remedy them of their ailment and persuade them to buy the world's fastest, smartest, and easiest notation software! But failing that, you might need to think about which format is best for sharing. In addition, you might want to promote your music to a wider community in a number of formats.

PDF is one that you've already seen, and that's a great way for sharing scores and parts with players via e-mail or a Web site where you might allow them to download. PDF is not so good for playback, though, so if you want people to not only see but also *hear* your music, you're going to need one of a number of other formats. Having some experience with MIDI, you can see that's a good universal format for a bit of playback and the ability to import into a number of other programs, but it's by no means the only—nor necessarily the best.

Tip: If you didn't actually work on the song in this lesson, you won't have a file to work with, which will hold you up somewhat. Find the Sibelius file **Purple6.sib** in the Lesson 3 folder under Core Resources and use that.

Exporting XML

Exporting MusicXML from Sibelius is even easier than exporting PDF. You would choose MusicXML if you wanted the person receiving your music to actually be able to edit your file in another notation program, create parts, make changes, and so on. Because there are some basic, free notation programs that can open MusicXML files, this could be a good way to openly share your creative work.

To export "Purple" as a MusicXML file:

1. Choose FILE > EXPORT > MusicXML.

2. There is only one choice to make: compressed or uncompressed XML. If you're not sure what software the person you're sharing the file with is using, and if you haven't embedded any graphics in your score, click UNCOMPRESSED. Otherwise, always choose COMPRESSED, especially because it will also make the file smaller to e-mail.

3. Click **Export**. Sibelius will prompt you to choose where to save the MusicXML file.

4. If you don't have another notation program to try this on yourself, open the **PurpleXMLExport.pdf** file in the Lesson 3 folder, which was created by another notation program after importing the Purple6.sib MusicXML file.

Exporting MIDI

Exporting MIDI from Sibelius is as simple as exporting MusicXML. To make this experiment a bit more interesting, this section will step you through importing the MIDI file in Pro Tools and allocating some instruments to each track. An MP3 will be exported so you can see how much of Sibelius's playback survived the export and import process (exactly the opposite to what you tried in the section "Importing MIDI Files" earlier in this chapter).

To export a MIDI file in Sibelius:

1. Choose **File** > **Export** > **MIDI**. Nearly every time you do this, the default settings, shown in Figure 3.139, will work best.

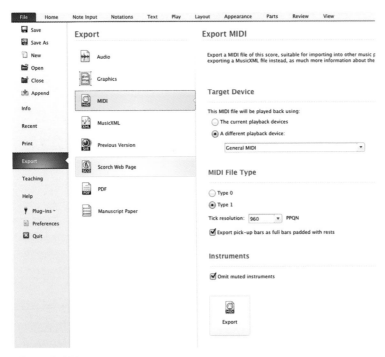

Figure 3.139
The default settings on MIDI export are usually the best.

2. Click **EXPORT**.

3. In your chosen sequencer or DAW, import the MIDI file. As an example, the process in Pro Tools is outlined here. To import a MIDI file in Pro Tools, choose **FILE** > **IMPORT** > **MIDI**. Use the default settings in the MIDI Import Options dialog box, shown in Figure 3.140.

Figure 3.140
The MIDI Import Options dialog box in Pro Tools.

4. In Pro Tools, each MIDI track has been loaded, but because it is not yet allocated to an instrument, it is grayed out (see Figure 3.141). Choose **TRACK** > **NEW** and add an Instrument track for each MIDI track (although in practice, several MIDI tracks can be ascribed to each instrument), as shown in Figure 3.142.

Figure 3.141
The MIDI tracks are imported. Because they're not allocated a playback instrument, they are grayed out.

Figure 3.142
Add multiple instrument tracks to allocate the MIDI tracks. Seven is actually overkill; XPand2 instruments can handle four at once.

5. In each virtual instrument, choose a suitable sample for each MIDI track as shown in Figures 3.143 (Boom) and 3.144 (XPand2).

Figure 3.143
Choosing an instrument setting in Boom.

Figure 3.144
Choosing instruments in XPand2.

6. As you allocate each MIDI track to each instrument, the track in the Edit window turns into color as shown in Figure 3.145. After each track is ascribed, balance the mix in the Mix window, and you're all done. To see how the Sibelius MIDI file sounds playing back in Pro Tools 9, open **PurpleMIDItoPT.mp3**.

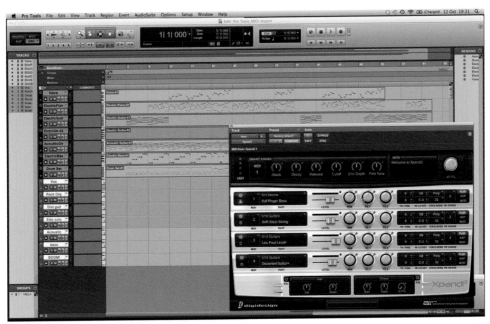

Figure 3.145
With each MIDI track now allocated to an instrument for playback, Pro Tools looks much more colorful. It sounds better, too!

7. Play the file. Notice that Sibelius included all the repeats you wrote in the score in the exported track, recalculating the bar numbers and so on. The next stage in Pro Tools is, of course, to delete the vocals MIDI track and record a real vocalist singing over the top!

In the Avid Learning Series

If you'd like to know more about importing MIDI files into Pro Tools, there is a section on it in the *Pro Tools 101* course that is part of this Avid Learning Series. Refer to Lesson 6.

Exporting Audio

While all things audio are usually the tricks of programs like Pro Tools, Sibelius has a few up its sleeve too. Exporting audio directly will work as long as you're using virtual instruments for playback. (There's much more to learn about virtual instruments in general, but you'll get to that in Lesson 5.) Sibelius 7 Sounds is a virtual instrument, so if you're using it to play back "Purple" and like what you hear, you can export that as an audio track easily and quickly.

You're most likely to want to share your Sibelius score as audio when giving a preview of what it would sound like is important, and when you think the playback you've set up is a good representation. Of course, if you send someone a MIDI file and they play it back on a 20-year-old MIDI keyboard, it's probably not going to sound great.

Sibelius exports audio in an uncompressed format on both Windows and Mac platforms. Windows users will export a WAV file, while Mac users will export an AIFF file. You don't need to know anything technical about these files except that they will probably be too large to email and not of sufficient quality to make available for download. Unless they're just for your listening pleasure, you'll want to convert them to a compressed format such as the very popular MP3. This section will give you a couple of ideas for making the conversion.

Begin by exporting an audio file of "Purple" from Sibelius. If you don't have a virtual instrument installed, follow it through on the video.

To export a file in Sibelius:

1. Choose FILE > EXPORT > AUDIO, as shown in Figure 3.146.

Figure 3.146
Export Audio settings in Sibelius.

Note: If you use several virtual-instrument configurations, Sibelius will enable you to export using any of these even if it isn't currently loaded. You shouldn't change to a different configuration from the one you're using unless you've already previewed it by playing it back in Sibelius, however.

2. The Playback Line section gives you the option to start the export at any point of the file. (Sibelius will export to the end of the file, but if you only want an excerpt, find a clever way—e.g. a fine—to stop playback.) Usually you'll want to export the whole piece, so leave EXPORT FROM START selected.

3. Leave the BIT DEPTH set to its default (probably 16-bit) unless you're going to use the resulting audio in something rather impressive like a surround-sound video soundtrack. As you can see, at 3 minutes and 50 seconds, the file is going to be nearly 39 MB. The limit on file size for e-mails is usually 10 MB at the most, which is why if you want to e-mail this audio file, you'll need to convert it (discussed momentarily).

4. Click EXPORT and select a location to save the file. (If you're not great at remembering where you file things, use the desktop now and delete it later.) Sibelius renders audio offline, which means it can export your recording in a fraction of the time it would be able to play it.

If you have a sequencer or a DAW like Pro Tools, you can then import the AIFF or WAV file and then export it back out as MP3. In Pro Tools, choose File > Bounce To and follow the prompts to name your MP3 file. If you don't have a sequencer, don't despair; there is a lot of free software available that can do the conversion for you. One of the most popular free music library programs is iTunes.

In the Avid Learning Series   Naturally, audio file conversion, including MP3 export, is also covered in the *Pro Tools 101* course.

On the Web   You can download iTunes free of charge from www.apple.com/itunes.

To convert your Sibelius audio files to MP3s in iTunes, you will need to make a change to the iTunes preferences. (Note that you only need to make this change once, not every time you use the program to convert your files.)

To change your preferences in iTunes:

1. On a Windows PC, with iTunes open, choose EDIT > PREFERENCES. On a Mac, with iTunes open, choose ITUNES > PREFERENCES.

2. Under General, click IMPORT SETTINGS, as shown in Figure 3.147.

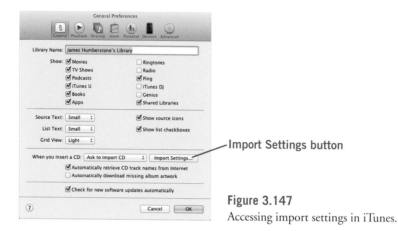

Import Settings button

Figure 3.147
Accessing import settings in iTunes.

3. Click the **IMPORT USING** drop-down list and choose **MP3**, as shown in Figure 3.148. The other settings are also good formats, but not necessarily as widely used as MP3, which is therefore the safest choice for sharing your music. You can also click the **SETTING** drop-down list and choose **HIGHER QUALITY**.

Figure 3.148
Import Using settings in iTunes.

4. Click **OK**, then click **OK** again.

As mentioned, you will only need to set those preferences once. The process after that for converting your Sibelius audio files to MP3 is very simple.

To convert your Sibelius audio files to MP3:

1. Drag your Sibelius file to the Library section in iTunes, as shown in Figure 3.149.

2. The file will appear in the Library (and may start playing). If you can't find it, type the file name in the Search field in the top-right corner of the iTunes window. When you can see it, right-click (Control-click) the file and choose **CREATE MP3 VERSION**, as shown in Figure 3.150.

Figure 3.149
Importing your Sibelius audio file into iTunes by dragging it onto the Library.

Figure 3.150
Converting to MP3 is as easy as right-clicking (Control-clicking) the file and choosing Create MP3 Version.

3. A second copy of your file will appear in the iTunes library. This is the MP3 version. Simply drag it out to the desktop to use it as you see fit. (In this case, the MP3 of "Purple" is 5.6 MB, so no problems e-mailing it to all of your friends or posting it on Facebook!)

Exporting to the Internet

All the file formats you've exported so far are very useful for posting on the Internet. PDF, MIDI, and MP3 can all be shared on Web sites, including social networking sites.

Sibelius also has its own format for publishing your scores to the Internet, called Scorch. Scorch is actually a plug-in for most popular Web browsers (for instance,

Internet Explorer, Firefox, and Safari) that enables them to open Sibelius files. People browsing Sibelius files on your Web site using the free Scorch plug-in can leaf through the pages, play the score back, transpose it into different keys, and even print or save the Sibelius file if you allow them.

There is an online community for sharing and selling your Sibelius scores called Score Exchange, which—funnily enough—you'll find online at www.scoreexchange.com. At Score Exchange, you can set up a profile page with information about you and the music you write. You can upload scores and give them away or even sell them and start earning straight away. Or if you're after music you can browse on the Web site by instrumentation, genre, difficulty, and so on.

On the Web

You can try out Scorch on your computer without needing to delve straight into creating a Web site. Here, you will make a Scorch Web page for "Purple." First, make sure you have the free Scorch plug-in installed. If not, you will find it on your Sibelius installation DVD; alternatively, you can download it from the Sibelius Web site.

Download the free Sibelius Scorch plug-in from www.sibelius.com/scorch.

On the Web

To export the score as a Scorch Web page:

1. Choose FILE > EXPORT > SCORCH WEB PAGE. The settings available are shown in Figure 3.151.

Figure 3.151
Exporting a Scorch Web page in Sibelius.

2. Choose the Classic template to begin with. (You can export the Web page any number of times.)

3. Increase the default width of the Score Size. Sibelius is quite conservative by default, and you can usually increase to 900 pixels without any problems. (Nowadays, Web designers build Web sites with a 900-pixel width by default.) To do so, repeatedly click the **WIDTH** up arrow or type **900** in the **WIDTH** field.

4. Check the **KEEP ASPECT RATIO** and **ALLOW PRINTING AND SAVING** check boxes. (You can always re-export with different settings later on.)

5. Click **EXPORT**. Sibelius will ask you where to save the Web page; choose your desktop or another folder you'll easily be able to access. (Don't choose the Core Resources folder, because that will create a second copy of your "Purple" score.) Sibelius exports two files with nearly identical names. One is an HTML file (the kind of file Web browsers read) and one is a copy of your Sibelius file, as shown in Figure 3.152. These two files need to be kept in the same folder for the Web page to work, as one refers to the other.

Figure 3.152
Two files are saved when you export a Scorch Web page: an HTML (Web page) file and another copy of your Sibelius score.

6. Double-click the HTML file to open the score. (The HTML file will have the same icon as your default Web browser. The one in Figure 3.152 shows an Internet Explorer icon.) The score appears.

Note: If the score doesn't appear, you may not be using a supported browser or operating system. As browser versions change often, you should check the Scorch Web site (www.sibelius.com/scorch) to see if your browser is supported. If not, there are plenty of free browsers that are.

7. The options available from the toolbar, shown in Figure 3.153, include playback, transposition, printing, and buttons for flicking through the pages. Click the **TRANSPOSE** button; the Transpose dialog box shown in Figure 3.154 opens, inviting you to transpose the piece.

8. You can also play back from any point in the score by simply clicking on it. Try this now: Click in the score to play back from that point.

Playback controls   Tempo slider   Transpose button   Save and Print buttons

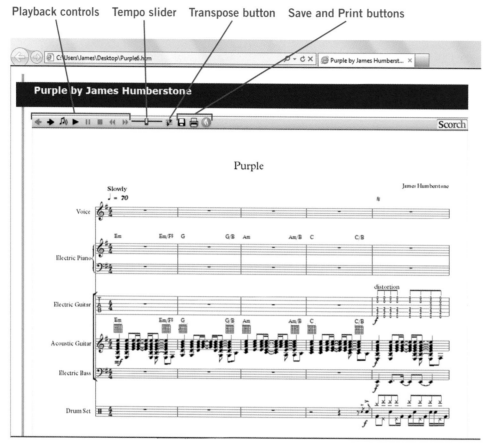

Figure 3.153
"Purple" as a Scorch Web page, and options.

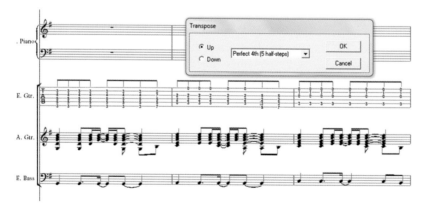

Figure 3.154
The Transpose dialog box in the Scorch plug-in.

Exporting to iPad

The final way of sharing your Sibelius files is probably the most exciting—at least, if you have an iPad! Avid Scorch for iPad is a recent release and enables you to view, play back, and do much more with Sibelius files on your iPad. In fact, the word *exporting* is a bit misleading, because there is no exporting to be done. Scorch for iPad reads Sibelius files with no change to the file format at all. You simply drag them into the Scorch application through iTunes. Figures 3.155 to 3.161 provide a visual description of how "Purple" looks and works in Scorch for iPad.

Scorch for iPad is an incredibly versatile tool. When you start to think about your whole band playing from them, it gets pretty exciting! That's a good, futuristic way to end this third lesson.

Figure 3.155
A page of "Purple" on Avid Scorch for iPad, with the blue playback line. It looks nearly identical to the score in Sibelius, and fits the iPad's screen beautifully.

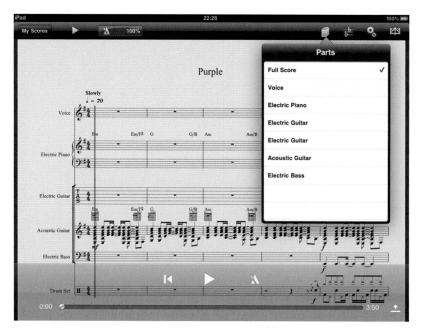

Figure 3.156

The Parts button enables you to jump into a part quickly from the score. (And you can play along while Scorch accompanies you by playing back the rest of he band!)

Figure 3.157

Scorch works in either orientation, and has a fantastic full-screen mode for when you're performing right from the iPad.

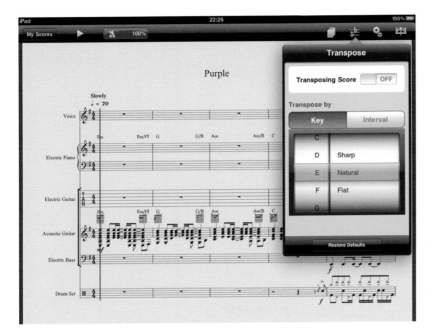

Figure 3.158
Despite being billed as a viewing app, Scorch has some pretty powerful editing features, including the ability to transpose the score…

Figure 3.159
…or you can change a staff on the score to a different instrument (transposition automatically supported!)—here, the voice has been changed to trumpet in B flat.

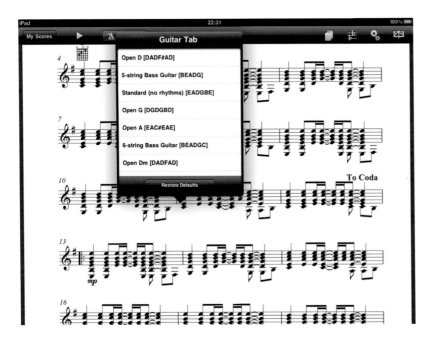

Figure 3.160
Scorch even has the option to convert normal notation to guitar tab.

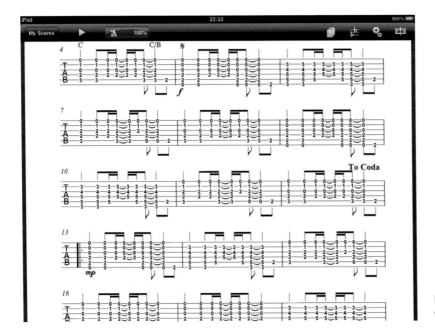

Figure 3.161
The resulting guitar tab.

Review/Discussion Questions

1. What does GM stand for?

2. How many MIDI channels are there in the GM specification?

3. On what channel do unpitched percussion instruments go in the GM specification?

   a. 1

   b. 5

   c. 10

   d. 16

4. True or false: MusicXML can include elements of a score such as phrasing, articulation marks, and text that MIDI can't.

5. What do the numbers on the lines mean in guitar and bass tablature notation?

6. What is the keyboard shortcut for entering the minor chord symbol?

   a. Shift+M

   b. Ctrl+Shift+M (Command+Shift+M)

   c. M

   d. MIN

7. True or false: When inputting guitar chord symbols, you can press the Tab key to move to the next note or beat.

8. How do you divide words up into syllables when writing lyrics?

9. Why does drum notation have so many unusual noteheads in the staff?

   a. Because the same line or space can mean making different sounds depending on the notehead

   b. Because cross noteheads are used when playing the hi-hats

   c. Because the stems show whether the drummer should use his feet or his hands, and the noteheads show how loudly he should do it

   d. Stemless noteheads are used most frequently for plan chant notation with no rhythm. Cross noteheads are for hi-hats and diamond noteheads are used to notate harmonics.

10. True or false: The Keypad panel has six different layouts so that you can easily add slurs and dynamics.

Lesson 3 Keyboard Shortcuts

Shortcut	Function
Ctrl+A (Windows)/Command+A (Mac)	Select All
Ctrl+T (Windows)/Command+T (Mac)	Technique text
Ctrl+K (Windows)/Command+K (Mac)	Chord symbols
Ctrl+Shift+Alt+K (Windows)/ Command+Shift+Option+K (Mac)	Revoice Chord Diagram
Ctrl+I (Windows)/Command+I (Mac)	Capture Idea
Ctrl+L (Windows)/Command+L (Mac)	Lyrics text
X	Flip selected object
Ctrl+Alt+L (Windows)/Command+Alt+L (Mac)	Lyrics Line 2
L	Lines gallery

Rearranging a MusicXML File

In this exercise, you will rearrange a MusicXML file of the song "Ha_gma_" by the band The Trobes as creatively as you can. In the Exercises folder in the Lesson 3 folder, you will find a MusicXML file of a basic transcription of the song and a lead sheet to get you started. Before you begin, check out the original song online. You can watch its music video on YouTube at www.youtube.com/watch?v=LVWj3Y1xZ_g or download it from the iTunes store at http://itunes.apple.com/au/album/ha-gma-single/id418971484. The song is very catchy and a great way to finally get "Purple" out of your head!

Media Used: Ha_gma_Lead Sheet.pdf (PDF file), HAGMA.xml (MusicXML file), HAGMA.mus (Finale file, if you'd like to export the XML yourself)

Duration: Approximately one hour

GOALS

- Create your own arrangement of this song, making it as individual as you can

Ideas to Get You Started

Not sure where to start? Here are a few ideas to get you going:

- Listen to the original song on YouTube to get a better idea of how it sounds than you can from the MusicXML file!

- Add a drum beat by choosing one in the Ideas panel and modifying it, or write your own from scratch.

- Create a bass line from the notes of the chords.

- Create several guitar lines, including one that uses tablature.

- Change the instruments that are already in there with instrument changes.

- If you have access to a sequencer, export the MIDI when you're done in Sibelius and try adding a vocal line of your own in the sequencer.

- If you think you made a good version of the song, why not e-mail it to The Trobes and let them know how much you like their work?

On the Web   The Trobes' Web site (www.thetrobes.com) is the best place to go for information about The Trobes.

Worksheets

In this lesson you'll learn all sorts of advanced layout skills, usable in many kinds of music notation, but in this case centered around the creation of worksheets.

Media Used: Test1.sib, Test2.sib, Worksheet1.sib, Worksheet2.sib, Worksheet1.pdf, Worksheet2.pdf, misc. graphics files

Duration: Approximately two hours

GOALS

- Learn about the 1,700 resources included in Sibelius's Worksheet Creator
- Learn how to customize the provided templates
- Learn how to create your own worksheets from scratch
- Learn advanced text handling
- Learn how to import graphics into Sibelius files
- Learn how to export music from Sibelius into software such as word-processing programs

Exploring the Worksheet Creator

If you're not a teacher, you may be wondering why making worksheets gets its own lesson in this book. The reason is that worksheets are the most common example of complex layout that Sibelius needs to be able to handle.

Consider that the easiest job for Sibelius is a one-instrument score in 4/4 and C major. (These are what Sibelius defaults to if you don't choose a time or key signature.) This easy piece uses just quarter notes (crotchets) and the notes stay within the staves. The spacing is easy, as is calculating page layout to avoid collisions. There are no settings to change; Sibelius just gets everything right.

Now consider a worksheet that asks five questions about intervals. Each one is in its own fragment of a staff, with a gap between each question. There is no time signature because there isn't a need for one. Bar numbers shouldn't show. The notes don't even need stems, let alone rhythms. Text needs to align underneath for students to provide answers…and so on. Each of these requirements means you have to change the default way Sibelius does things—so you're immediately into advanced layout.

Other examples of advanced layout include graphic scores, cutaway scores, musical samples for student essays, special academic notations such as Schenkerian analyses, and musical illustrations for books. These are things that composers, students, publishers, arrangers, and all sorts of other Sibelius users need to be able to make, and the essential skills for those scores are also taught in this lesson. So don't be put off making worksheets; what you'll learn is valuable to everyone.

A video called **4.1 Exploring the Worksheet Creator** will step you through the content for this section of the lesson. I recommend that you watch it before you begin, especially if you're reading this book on your own. See the section "Accessing the Video Files" in this book's introduction for help finding and viewing the video content.

Before you learn to make your own worksheet from scratch in Sibelius, it's possible that the Worksheet Creator will save you some time. Inside it are some 1,700 worksheets, flash cards, pieces of music, fact sheets, templates and much more. Even if the exact sheet you need isn't there, you can modify the existing ones.

The Worksheet Creator is one of the few things you can't get to directly from the Quick Start dialog box. If you don't have a file open, open one you've been working on. Alternatively, start a new blank score with no instruments in it.

To explore the Worksheet Creator:

1. Choose FILE > TEACHING > WORKSHEET CREATOR, as shown in Figure 4.1. The first screen of the Worksheet Creator wizard appears. The defaults are as shown in Figure 4.2.

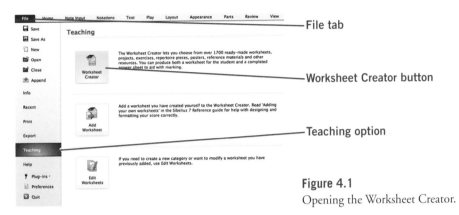

File tab

Worksheet Creator button

Teaching option

Figure 4.1
Opening the Worksheet Creator.

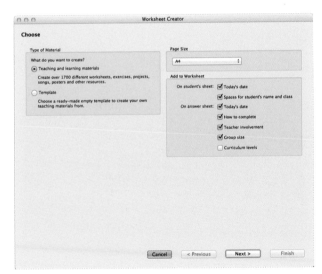

Figure 4.2
The first screen of the Worksheet Creator wizard.

2. Leave the TEACHING AND LEARNING MATERIALS option button selected, and change the page size to suit the default in your country (if it isn't already).

Note: The Add to Worksheet options are self-explanatory. Information such as How to Complete or Group Size can be entered elsewhere within the wizard, so they don't need to be included in your final answer sheet unless you're going to refer to printed versions in the future.

3. Click **NEXT** to move to the next screen of the wizard, shown in Figure 4.3. Options in this screen enable you to narrow down the available selections. In this case, you need to see all available worksheets, so leave as defaults shown.

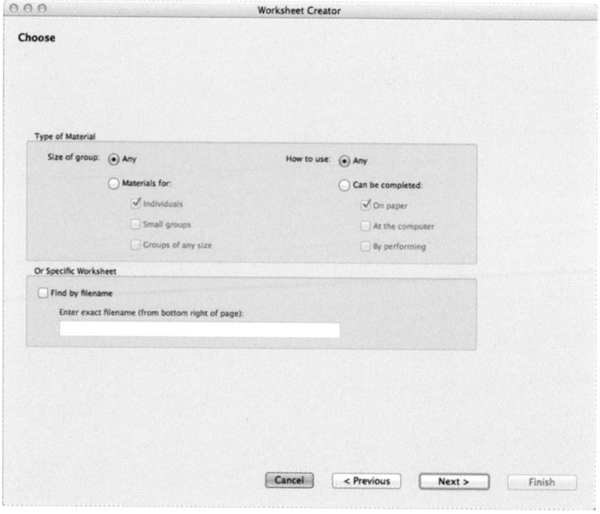

Figure 4.3
The second page of the Worksheet Creator wizard.

Note: It's worth also noting that the Change Type of Material button in the next part of the wizard offers most of the same options as are found in this part, so you don't need to start over to filter the results further.

4. Click **NEXT**. The remaining screens of the Worksheet Creator wizard serve as a folder structure for an awful lot of content. You can navigate back and forth through the different sections by clicking the Next and Previous buttons, choosing selections from the list on the left. Each section is numbered to make it easier to find, and breadcrumbs at the top (shown in Figure 4.4) remind you how you navigated to the list you're looking at.

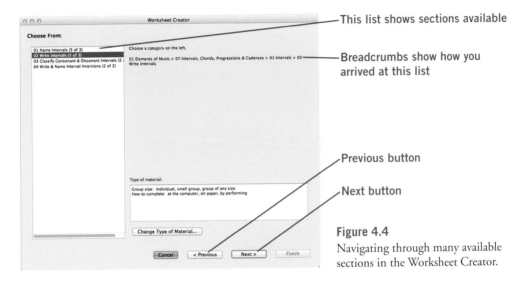

This list shows sections available

Breadcrumbs show how you arrived at this list

Previous button

Next button

Figure 4.4
Navigating through many available sections in the Worksheet Creator.

To describe every available part of the Worksheet Creator would take a lot of pages. It's probably much more effective for you to explore and discover what might be useful to you. The first-level sections are as follows:

■ **01 Elements of Music.** This includes 463 worksheets to test students' knowledge of music theory, including everything from key signatures and understanding of meter to score analysis and sight reading. This is probably the section you'll use the most if you're a classroom teacher because it's great for testing concepts you've already taught in class. You'll look at an intervals worksheet from this section in a moment.

■ **02 Writing and Creating Music.** This includes more than 100 worksheets on correctly notating music as well as arranging, composing, and improvising. There are many beginning points for composers here.

■ **03 Selected Repertoire.** This includes nearly 500 pieces of copyright-free music, which you may print out or use in Sibelius for any purpose you like. The collection is particularly rich in traditional children's songs in many languages, making it ideal for primary school teachers. It also contains a wide range of piano repertoire, including 50 scores by J.S. Bach. It is worth noting that this repertoire is often referred to in worksheets as examples of concepts such as tonality and meter. So, if you're studying a concept, you've got a musical example to back it up.

■ **04 Reference.** This includes an enormous collection of scales and modes that are all referred to in the Worksheet Creator. In addition, it includes some other reference material that may be useful, such as instrumental and vocal ranges.

■ **05 Posters, Flashcards & Games.** This includes, well, posters, flashcards, and games. The 180 posters of things like clefs and instrumental families (see Figure 4.5) are very useful for printing on large paper sizes and sticking to classroom walls, while the games include bingo sheets to print out.

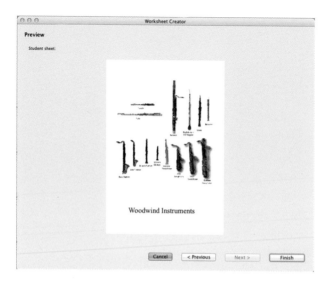

Figure 4.5
A poster of the woodwind family that can be printed out.

■ **06 UK KS3 and GCSE Projects.** These include materials written specifically for the most recent UK curricula, but may be of interest to teachers in other regions, as well.

While there is a separate section for UK materials in the Worksheet Creator, it is worth pointing out that the materials were prepared to cover the knowledge required in all syllabuses of America, Australia, Canada, and New Zealand, in addition to the UK.

On the Web   The structure and majority of content for the Worksheet Creator was conceived and made by widely published freelance author and composer Mary Elizabeth, who is also a coauthor of the *Groovy Music* series. If you are looking for help embedding the wide range of content found in the Worksheet Creator into your teaching programs, support in creating worksheets, or additional materials created to spec, you can contact her via e-mail at edreinvented@edreinvented.com. Mary Elizabeth's Web site is found at http://edreinvented.com, and you can see a list of all of her published work at www.amazon.com/Mary-Elizabeth/e/B001HD37VS.

Making an Intervals Worksheet

To create an intervals worksheet in the Worksheet Creator:

1. Choose **01 ELEMENTS OF MUSIC** > **07 INTERVALS, CHORDS, PROGRESSIONS & CADENCES** > **01 INTERVALS** > **02 WRITE INTERVALS** > **03 COMPLETE, GIVEN TONIC, NUMBER & QUALITY.** The hardest of the three complete intervals worksheets, this level asks students to write the top note of major, minor, perfect, augmented, or diminished intervals. To help you choose the right level of worksheet for your students, the contents of each sheet is explained in the Description field as shown in Figure 4.6.

2. Open the **NUMBER OF QUESTIONS** drop-down list and choose the number of questions to be included on the worksheet, from 1 to 144 (what a gross worksheet!). This is also shown in Figure 4.6.

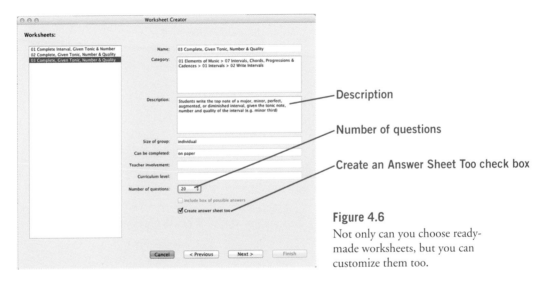

Figure 4.6
Not only can you choose ready-made worksheets, but you can customize them too.

3. If you're a qualified music teacher you probably don't need an answer sheet to help you mark student work, but these can be extremely useful if you need to leave work for a class when you're away. With an answer sheet, the poor science teacher covering your music class doesn't have an excuse not to mark the work you left! Leave the **CREATE ANSWER SHEET TOO** check box checked, so you can see what this looks like, and click **NEXT**.

4. Sibelius displays a preview of the student sheet and the answer sheet side by side, as shown in Figure 4.7. If you left any options such as Spaces for Student's Name and Class selected on the first screen of the wizard, you will notice these elements also included in the preview now. Click **FINISH**.

Figure 4.7
The preview of your worksheet and answer sheet.

When you have chosen an answer sheet as well as the worksheet, you will always view the answer sheet first after clicking Finish. To change between the answer sheet and the worksheet while both are open, choose View > Window > Switch Windows and choose the worksheet. You can also save the exported worksheets if you think you'd like to reuse them at some point, although of course it will only take you a minute or two to locate them in the Worksheet Creator again.

Note: You may notice some grayed-out clefs and brackets on the exported worksheets. These won't show when you print, and are part of the advanced formatting that you're about to learn to do yourself.

Now you've seen how easy it is to get great content out of the Worksheet Creator, you might like to spend a little more time exploring. Before you leave the safety of the Worksheet Creator and venture out to make worksheets of your own from scratch, run it one more time (File > Teaching > Worksheet Creator) so you can have a look at the available templates. These are the perfect midway point, because you can customize them to create the exact content you need.

Select the Template radio button on the first page of the wizard and then click Next. In the list are templates for manuscript paper (apparently it *is* still possible to write music with paper and pencil), games like bingo, flashcards, and a range of worksheet layouts like the one seen in Figure 4.8.

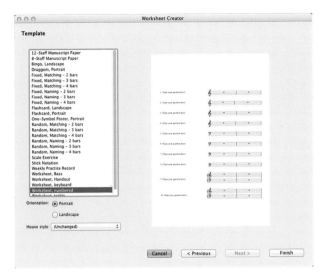

Figure 4.8
Templates available to customize in the Worksheet Creator.

It's very quick to make customized worksheets using the templates. In the Lesson 4 folder on the CD, you'll find a PDF and Sibelius file called Worksheet1.pdf or Worksheet1.sib, which you can make in just a few minutes. Print it out, or refer to the copy of it in Appendix B.

To use a template to create the worksheet yourself:

1. In the Template section of the Worksheet Creator, choose **WORKSHEET, NUMBERED** in the list and click **FINISH**.

2. Choose **TEXT > STYLES > MORE** and, under Catalog Information in the Styles gallery, choose **TITLE**, as shown in Figure 4.9. Finally, click in your score and type the title (in this example, "Compose Answer Phrases").

3. Double-click the text for question 1 and change it to **COMPOSE THE ANSWERING PHRASE**. Repeat this for questions 2 to 8. (You can save time by copying the text while editing it, then pasting it over each other block of text as you edit that.)

4. Make sure you have no selection. Each two-bar example needs a time signature and key signature. You can add these from the Notations tab of the ribbon, but it may be quicker to press the respective shortcut **T** or **K**. This displays their galleries, as shown in Figures 4.10 and 4.11.

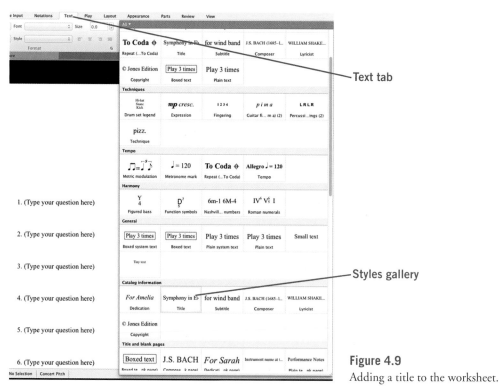

Text tab

Styles gallery

1. (Type your question here)

2. (Type your question here)

3. (Type your question here)

4. (Type your question here)

5. (Type your question here)

6. (Type your question here)

Figure 4.9
Adding a title to the worksheet.

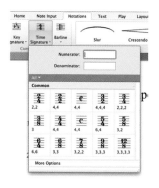

Figure 4.10
The Time
Signature gallery.

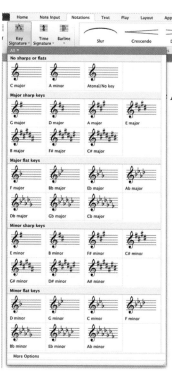

Figure 4.11
The Key
Signature gallery.

5. In each case, after typing the shortcut, you will need to click **MORE OPTIONS**, because in a worksheet you need to change some of the default options as explained in the next two steps. Clicking More Options opens the full dialog box.

6. In the Time Signature dialog box, shown in Figure 4.12, uncheck the **ALLOW CAUTIONARY** check box. Otherwise, a cautionary time signature will appear at the end of the previous question, which is not needed (since this isn't a piece of music to be performed). Now add the time signatures in the same order as the completed worksheet.

Figure 4.12
The full Time Signature dialog box.

It's much faster to copy and paste a time signature than to create it from the More Options dialog box. So once a time signature has been used once, the quickest thing to do is to select it and Alt-click (Option-click) or chord-click where you want to paste it. This will carry with it the non-cautionary property as well, so it's quite safe. The same goes for pretty well any object that doesn't have a keyboard shortcut—e.g., symbols, barlines—and even some things that do, like key changes, if they are available in the score nearby.

—**Neil Sands, founder of Chichester Music Press and Sibelius expert (in fact, the technical editor of the very book you're reading!)**

On the Web Chichester Music Press publishes the music of contemporary British composers and, like most of the world's top music publishers, uses Sibelius. It has an especially extensive catalog of contemporary choral music, which you can browse online at www.chichestermusicpress.co.uk.

Note: If you don't really understand what the Allow Cautionary check box is doing, try putting in a time signature at the start of question 2 without changing it, and look at the end of question 1. This is known as a *cautionary* because it shows at the end of a system when a change of time signature is coming up at the start of the next, to help a performer who is sight-reading.

7. Again, make sure you have no selection. After clicking More Options in the Key Signature gallery, you will see the full Key Signature dialog box, as shown in Figure 4.13. For the same reason as the time signature, check the HIDE check box. Select the E minor key signature (all key signatures are minor on this worksheet), click **OK**, and click the score to place the key signature. Repeat this process for each of the questions.

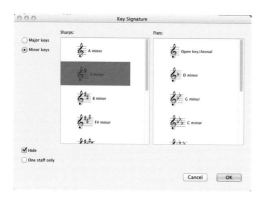

Figure 4.13
The full Key Signature dialog box.

8. If you look down the right margin, you will see gray key signatures, reflecting the hidden option you chose. These are shown in Figure 4.14. Now copy the music as shown in the first bar of each question using any note entry method you like.

Figure 4.14
The hidden key signatures.

9. Those completing this worksheet could finish it in Sibelius, but suppose you're going to print it out and give it to them. You will need to have an empty bar, which means removing the default bar rest. To do this, right-click each empty bar and choose **HIDE OR SHOW** > **HIDE OR SHOW** or press **CTRL+SHIFT+H** (**COMMAND+SHIFT+H**).

10. You don't need the remaining bars numbered questions 9 and 10. Make a passage selection for these four bars, and then choose **HOME** > **BARS** > **DELETE** or press **CTRL+DELETE/BACKSPACE** (**COMMAND+DELETE**). Sibelius will ask you if you're sure; click **YES**. It may also ask you if you want to completely remove the staff from your score (see Figure 4.15); click **YES**.

Figure 4.15
If you delete all the music from one staff, Sibelius will ask you if you want to remove it from the score. This is a good idea, unless you know you'll use it later, because it eliminates empty parts, unclear formatting, and so on.

11. The worksheet is essentially finished now. You can make it look a little better by manually adjusting the layout. Some of the bars in 4/4 take up so much room, it might be difficult for the student to write an answer into the remaining space (see Figure 4.16 as an example, which shows the default spacing of question 7). To override Sibelius's spacing, make a passage selection (in this case, just the first bar of question 7) and press **ALT+SHIFT+LEFT ARROW** (**OPTION+SHIFT+LEFT ARROW**) to contract the spacing, as you should know, or **ALT+SHIFT+RIGHT ARROW** (**OPTION+SHIFT+LEFT ARROW**) to expand it. After you contract it six times, the spacing will appear as in Figure 4.17—a great improvement.

Figure 4.16
The spacing of the first bar of this question takes up too much room.

Figure 4.17
After you press the contract spacing shortcut six times, there is much more space to write in the second bar.

12. The final adjustment you may like to make to layout is to realign the text for each question, which has gotten out of alignment as shown in Figure 4.18. The reason for this is simple: In actual fact, the text is still the same distance from the start of the bar to which it's attached, but the key signature has moved the start of the bar in some cases. To help you realign the text, you can change the texture of your score to graph paper. Choose **FILE** > **PREFERENCES** and click **TEXTURES**, as shown in Figure 4.19.

13. Click the **PAPER** drop-down list and choose **PAPER, GRAPH**. Click **OK**, then align the text to one of the stronger lines on the graph paper, as shown in Figure 4.20.

Figure 4.18
The text for each question is now out of alignment.

Figure 4.19
The Textures page of the Preferences dialog box.

Figure 4.20
With a graph-paper background,
you can easily align text by eye.

When you've finished, you may want to change the graph-paper background back
to one of the white textures, before it starts to give you a headache!

Tip: When you're aligning elements of your score by eye, try clicking on them and
then using the arrow keys for precise movement rather than dragging them
with the mouse. You'll find it much easier.

These kinds of procedures—changing the spacing, hiding elements, aligning text,
and so on—are typical of advanced score layout. At first they can seem a little fiddly—indeed, advanced layout *is* fiddly—but once you understand conceptually
what you're doing, you can work very quickly to achieve the results you need.

Making Your Own Worksheet from Scratch: Formatting

As ever, a video is available that shows you the myriad of things
you'll learn in this section. It's called **4.2 Making Your Own
Worksheet from Scratch: Formatting**.

To learn a range of advanced layout skills, you're going to create a complex work-sheet from scratch. To begin, print out the Worksheet2 Sibelius or PDF file within the Lesson 4 folder under Core Resources, or photocopy it from Appendix B. (It's not wise to try to copy it from there and read this chapter at the same time, but you could if you have no other option.)

Planning Your Layout

In this lesson, you have a finished piece of work to copy. That means the impor-tant first step has been done for you. Whenever you do your own advanced lay-out, begin by sketching out the layout of the score or even by writing out the whole worksheet by hand. Because the layout is complicated in Sibelius, looking at what staves you'll need, how much space you'll need for text, and so on is impor-tant to consider in advance. If you don't spend time doing it first you'll probably spend a lot of time trying to re-jig your work later on.

To begin, start a new score using the blank manuscript paper:

1. Add the instrument called Unnamed (Treble Staff) to the score.

2. Leave the time signature as 4/4.

3. Change the key signature to **OPEN KEY/ATONAL**.

4. Name the piece **VERY DIFFICULT MUSIC TEST** (or something else if you prefer). Then, in the Composer field, type **NAME:** _____ (using the underscore key next to 0).

5. Click **CREATE**.

So far, so good. At this point of the process, you need to focus on the music and not worry too much about text and graphics. That said, there are a few text issues you can fix up straight away. The score does not use the standard Sibelius 7 font (Plantin) but instead uses the Arial font. As you know, you can change any text in your score by going to the Text tab on the ribbon. However, in this case you want to change *all* text to use Arial.

To change all text to use Arial:

1. Choose **TEXT > FORMAT**.

2. Click the dialog launcher button to open the Edit All Fonts dialog box (shown in Figure 4.21).

3. Click the **MAIN TEXT FONT** drop-down list and choose **ARIAL**. Then click **OK**. As soon as you're back in your score, you'll notice that the title and composer text change. Any further text you add to the score will also use this font.

Figure 4.21
The Edit All Fonts dialog box.

Even though you can count very few bars on the worksheet, it's best to work with lots of extra bars at first. This gives you more control over the staves. In addition, while you'll need lots of bars, you don't need bar *numbers* to show on the worksheet—this isn't a piece of music to be performed, after all.

To add extra bars:

1. To add many bars at once, choose HOME > BARS > ADD > ADD MULTIPLE OR IRREGULAR BARS, as shown in Figure 4.22. (To access the Add Multiple or Irregular Bars option, click the lower half of the Add button.)

Figure 4.22
Selecting Add Multiple or Irregular Bars from the Add button.

2. In the Create Bars dialog box, type **100** in the Number of Bars field, as shown in Figure 4.23, and click **OK**. If you didn't have any selection in your score you will need to click in any bar to add them.

Figure 4.23
Adding 100 bars at once to your score.

3. You'll now see bar numbers at the start of every system apart from the first. To turn this option off, simply choose **TEXT** > **NUMBERING** > **NO BAR NUMBERS.**

To finalize the layout and get on with the job of putting the music and text in, you should create the correct number of bars on each system. To do this, you'll use a system break. The first question has four separate bars, each with a note in them. To add a system break, click the barline at the end of the fourth bar and press Enter or Return. (This is also found in Layout > Breaks > System Break, but the shortcut is so easy to learn you won't need to remember this!) That barline immediately jumps to the end of the system, and the blue system break icon reminds you that it is in effect (see Figure 4.24). (You can click the icon and press Delete to remove it, or click the barline again and toggle it off.)

Figure 4.24
The blue system break icon.

The second question has no barlines, and so requires only one bar. Click the barline at the end of the first bar of the second system and insert another system break. The third system should have two bars, and finally the fourth system (for question 5) should have seven bars. Once correctly set up, your score should match the one in Figure 4.25.

To make sure the staff is big enough to write into with pencil, you can also make it a bit bigger. Choose Layout > Document Setup > Staff Size and make it 8 mm. Now you're ready for some really advanced stuff.

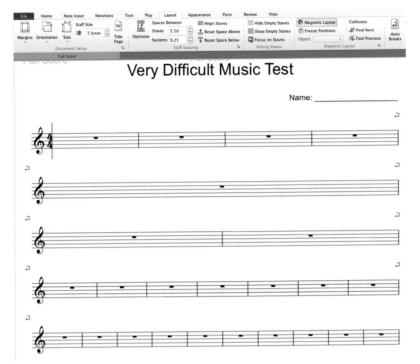

Figure 4.25
The page layout so far.

Re-creating the Intervals Questions from Scratch

As mentioned, you won't worry about the text part of the questions nor the graphics until you've got the music in. Cast your mind back to the intervals questions from the Worksheet Creator and you will remember that they were just like the ones given in question 1 here: There is a gap between each "bar" of music and the student must write in the named interval above the given note. Begin by putting the clef changes into bars 3 and 4.

To add a clef:

1. Make sure you have no selection.

2. Press **Q** for clef. (You could choose Notations > Common > Clef, but pressing Q is a lot easier!)

3. Select the **Bass Clef** from the Clef gallery as shown in Figure 4.26.

4. The mouse pointer should be blue to tell you that it's loaded. Click at the start of bar 3 to add the bass clef.

5. Repeat the process to add a treble clef at the start of bar 4. Don't worry about the fact that it doesn't look the same as the worksheet you're copying yet; you have more work to do!

Figure 4.26
The Clef gallery.

Next, put in the pitches. Each note is a whole note (semibreve), and will appear musically correctly at the left side of the bar. (In the worksheet it needs to be centered, but you'll come back to that.) First you need to split up the bars so that they have the space between them.

To split up the bars:

1. Click the barline at the end of bar 1 and choose **LAYOUT** > **BREAKS** > **SPLIT SYSTEM**.

2. Repeat for the barlines at the end of bars 2 and 3.

3. The notation now looks right, but there are extra cautionary clefs at the end of bars 2 and 3 (see Figure 4.27). To hide each one, click it and press **CTRL+SHIFT+H** (**COMMAND+SHIFT+H**).

Figure 4.27
The cautionary clefs at the end of bars 2 and 3 need to be hidden.

To complete the intervals question, you just need to center the notes in each bar. The time signature will also have to be removed. You can do that first: Simply click it and press Delete. Sibelius will ask you if you want to rewrite the music; in this case, you can click Yes or No, because it won't make any difference.

To center the notes:

1. Make a passage selection of all four bars.

2. Choose **HOME** > **EDIT** > **INSPECTOR** to open the Inspector. (Because you may need to use the Inspector a few times to get the following notes in correct positions, you can "stick" it on using the pushpin button shown in Figure 4.28.)

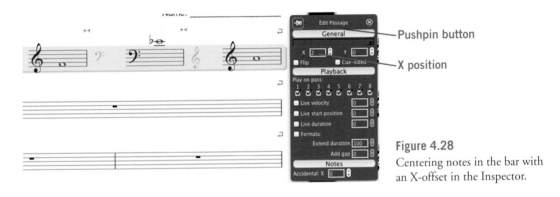

Figure 4.28
Centering notes in the bar with an X-offset in the Inspector.

3. In the X field, under General, type **2** to offset everything to the right by two spaces. The notes should now appear centered in the bars.

Creating Empty Manuscript Paper

Question 2 is extremely simple to set up. In fact, now that you've added the system break, it's nearly ready now. This question *does* need a time signature, though.

To add a time signature:

1. With no selection, press **T** to open the Time Signature gallery.

2. Click **MORE OPTIONS**.

3. Make sure Allow Cautionary *isn't* checked, and click **OK**.

4. Click right at the start of the bar to make sure you place the time signature in the correct position.

Add the A quarter note (crotchet) at the start of the bar, and then hide the rests in the remainder of the bar. You can do this quickly by selecting them and then using the shortcut Ctrl+Shift+H (Command+Shift+H). All that is needed now is the double barline at the end of the bar. To input this, click the existing barline and choose Notations > Common > Barline > Double. If, like most manuscript paper, this stave didn't have a barline on the end at all, you'd go to Notations > Common > Barline > Invisible instead.

Customizable Manuscript

Making your own manuscript paper is very easy in Sibelius, but you have to think of it just like making a worksheet, because it is an advanced layout. If you have access to a large paper size printer (A3, for instance), try printing 7–8 mm staves landscape for big sheets to work on.

You already know how to use system breaks to put just one bar per system and how to hide barlines and rests. For maximum flexibility, choose the blank clef from the Clefs gallery so your staff is completely blank. Top it off with your name or Web site address at the foot of the sheet for real individualization!

If you're thinking to yourself, "But now that I have Sibelius, I don't need manuscript paper!" then that's great. Here's one more trick that will make your day: Next time you're sketching ideas at the start of a project, select an empty bar and capture it as an idea in the Ideas panel. Double-click the idea to edit it, and then add as many bars as you need—virtual manuscript paper for your project that doesn't get in the way of the main score itself, with the extra bonus of being able to copy and paste the good ideas straight in!

Indenting Systems

Question 3 is a lot trickier to set up. In addition to having to add another staff to create a grand staff (piano staff), the bars themselves are indented from the left and from the right.

To add the extra staff:

1. Double-click the third system to select both bars.

Note: It's important you make this passage selection before you proceed to the next step because it ensures the extra staff will be added for only these two bars. If you forget to do this, it will be added throughout, and you'll have to hide the bars you don't need.

2. Press **I** to open the Add or Remove Instruments dialog box.

3. Rather than adding another instrument, click the existing **[UNNAMED (TREBLE STAFF)]** in the **STAVES IN SCORE** list. Then click the **BELOW** button under **EXTRA STAFF**. This is shown in Figure 4.29.

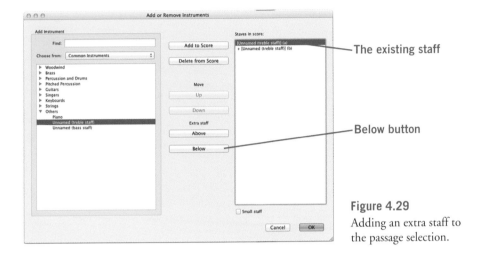

The existing staff

Below button

Figure 4.29
Adding an extra staff to the passage selection.

4. Click **OK** to finish.

5. The system requires a brace. Press **ESC TWICE** to make sure you have no selection. Then choose **NOTATIONS > BRACKET OR BRACE > BRACE** and click right at the **START** of the new system to add the brace.

6. Press **Q** to open the Clefs gallery again and add a bass clef to the left hand.

7. To finish it off, you need to connect the barlines between the right and left hands. Click at the very bottom end of either barline in the right hand, and a handle will appear as shown in Figure 4.30. Drag it down to the staff below to connect them with the one barline.

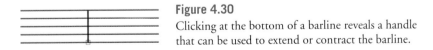

Figure 4.30
Clicking at the bottom of a barline reveals a handle that can be used to extend or contract the barline.

Input the music. Note that you'll need to remember how to put two voices into the second bar of the right hand, as you did in the drum part in Lesson 3, "Purple." A double barline is also required at the end of the second bar.

Indenting the staff from the left can be done by dragging or, if you want to align a series of systems and have absolute control of their alignment, through the Inspector.

To indent the staff using the Inspector:

1. Click the line that joins the staves at the left side (technically, this isn't a barline, but it is referred to as one from time to time in the program).

2. To open the Inspector (if it isn't already open), choose **HOME** > **EDIT** > **INSPECTOR**. (Remember, you can keep the Inspector open by clicking the pushpin button.)

3. The Inspector is context sensitive, meaning the information it shows is relevant to whatever you have selected at any time. Because you have a barline selected, options to do with bars are available, as shown in Figure 4.31. Type **34** in the **GAP BEFORE BAR** field and watch it indent from the left.

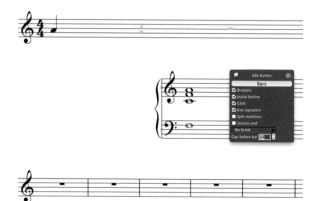

Figure 4.31
The Inspector showing bar options.

There is no such option for indenting from the right, but luckily there are some very useful tools to help you if accuracy is what you're after. The first and most important thing to know is *not* to try to drag the barline in from the right. This actually changes the spacing of the barline itself, and will make a mess. (Try it just to find out if you like it, and then promptly click Undo.)

In fact, there is a rather mystical element to indenting from the right, which is that in order to do it you need to have had the story of the super-magic-secret-hidden handles passed down to you from a wise one. Luckily in your case it's your Avid Training Partner, the video on the Web, or this next sidebar.…

The Story of the Super-Magic-Secret-Hidden Handles

In the beginning, there was Sibelius for Acorn. Written entirely in machine code by two genius twins and running on a blindingly fast (for its time) RISC-OS, Sibelius was unlike any notation program that had come before. But something was missing—only one thing: the ability to indent individual staves from the right.

Several years later, Sibelius 1.1 for Windows (and later Sibelius 1.2 for Mac) was delivered unto the user, and it was good. And there was now a workaround for the important indentation problem: Change thy staff type to Invisible, and have empty bars at the end of the staff that couldn't be seen. This was called "The Workaround."

Another four years later came Sibelius 3, and a brilliant and proper solution had been found. But in their wisdom, the creators (programmers) of Sibelius did not want any old simpleton user to find it, and so they created the super-magic-secret-hidden handles as the only way to truly indent unto the right side of your score. The hidden location is only given to those who have proven themselves worthy of such software insight by completing most of this book (or those who actually read every page of the Reference)....

To discover the location of the super-magic-secret-hidden handles, you need to click in line with the middle line of either staff, a short distance to the right of the end of the system. Unfortunately, it's not as easy as saying "2 mm" (although often it's about 2 mm) because your zoom level and monitor resolution might mean it's quite different for you.

The thing is, until you click them, they're invisible. And unfortunately, to the uninitiated, clicking on something invisible isn't always that easy. So hold in your mind's eye the mystical secret, click approximately the place you expect them to be, and hope. Figure 4.32 shows the relative position of the super-magic-secret-hidden handles at a 200 percent zoom at a 1,680×1,050 pixel resolution.

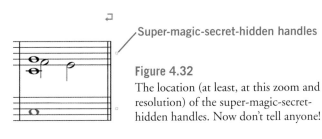

Super-magic-secret-hidden handles

Figure 4.32
The location (at least, at this zoom and resolution) of the super-magic-secret-hidden handles. Now don't tell anyone!

Once you've found the SMSHHs, you can drag them in to the left to indent the system from the right. Because there isn't a dialog box in which you can type an exact measurement, aligning multiple staves with right indents is a little more difficult, but luckily there is one more useful tool.

Choose View > Rulers > Staff Rulers. Measurements appear in special blue text (which won't print out, if you're worried), as shown in Figure 4.33. Drag the indent in or out, and the measurements update immediately. Note that the staff rulers also show the distance between each staff, so if you're trying to visually align staves vertically, you can use these rulers to help you. (Optimize Spacing is much quicker, though.)

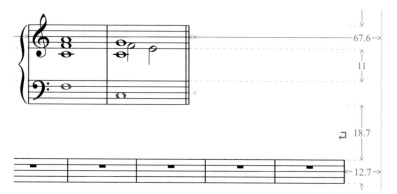

Figure 4.33
Using staff rulers.

Drag the indent until it's between 67 and 68 mm and then turn the rulers off again by toggling the same button (View > Rulers > Staff Rulers).

Breaking the Music!

Because what you're creating is not a piece of music to be performed, you've had to work extra hard at changing it from Sibelius's defaults—for example, changing the spacing of the notes in the bars to center them, or hiding elements in the score to create empty staves.

In question 5, the student is required to circle and describe rhythmic errors—bars that don't add up to the meter given in the time signature. As you know, Sibelius automatically makes sure each bar adds up. When you add a note at any position in the bar, Sibelius changes the remaining rests so that it all still makes sense.

In this case, you don't want Sibelius to fix your mistakes. You want to break the rules of music so that the student can identify the mistakes. To do this, you will actually begin by setting out bars of different lengths as shown in Figure 4.34. Make sure the initial 3/4 time signature does not allow cautionary.

Figure 4.34
Begin question 5 by setting up these time signatures.

Next, add the key signature, again making sure you hide the cautionary. Then input the music as shown in Figure 4.35. (This includes information such as the quarter note rest in the fourth bar that you won't get if you copy directly from the worksheet.)

Figure 4.35
Add the music as shown, leaving the strange time signatures in.

The question is relatively easy to create now:

1. Delete each time signature (except the initial 3/4). To do so, select a time signature and press **DELETE** or **BACKSPACE**. When you do, Sibelius will ask you if you want to rewrite the following bars (as seen in Figure 4.36); click **NO**.

Tip: If you select all the time signatures at the same time by Ctrl-clicking (Command-clicking) to add each to the selection, you can press Delete once to delete them all—and you don't get asked if you want to rebar.

Figure 4.36
Sibelius will offer to rewrite the music for you to make sure the bars add up. In this case, you don't actually want it to, so click No.

2. Click the quarter note (crotchet) rest at the end of the fourth bar and press **CTRL+SHIFT+H** (**COMMAND+SHIFT+H**) to hide it.

3. This example shows you two ways of making the bar not add up. First, the last two bars have simply used a 2/4 time signature, so they have no extra space for the rest. Second, while in this bar you've hidden the rest, but space is still allowed for it. Either may be appropriate, depending on your

project. You can contract spacing or even just drag the barline to the left if you think there is too much space.

4. Now you've put in all of the music in your score, delete the remaining bars. To do so, make a passage selection of them and press **CTRL+DELETE** (**COMMAND+DELETE**). (If you just press Delete, you'll delete the *contents* of the bars, but not the bars themselves.)

In some worksheets or educational music following the Kodály method, stick notation is used—that is, rhythms written without noteheads (except for minims and semibreves), as shown in Figure 4.37. To create stick notation in Sibelius, start a new score with a treble staff. Input notes as usual; for a rhythmic example, use the A space below the middle line of the staff.

Figure 4.37
Stick notation, as described by Sibelius expert Katie Wardrobe.

Next, remove (hide) the stave lines by choosing Home > Instruments > Change, typing No Instrument in the Find box at the top of the window, and choosing No Instrument (Barlines Shown) from the list that appears. Uncheck the Add Clef and Announce at Last Note of Previous Instrument options and click OK.

Click in the score just to the left of the treble clef to make the change. You may see some residual staff lines and a blue vertical box that indicates the position of the instrument change; you can drag the blue box to the left of the treble clef to make the staff lines disappear completely.

Finally, you can remove the noteheads by selecting the bar (or multiple bars) containing the notes you want to change. Choose Notations > Noteheads > Type, and select the Stick Notation noteheads in the "special" section of the gallery. (Make sure you scroll down to Stick Notation style, not to be confused with the Headless style.)

—Katie Wardrobe, teacher, arranger, and copyist
with extensive experience in Sibelius training

Katie shares (free of charge!) dozens of tutorials on all kinds of music software, including Sibelius, on her Web site,
On the Web **www.midnightmusic.com.au.**

Using Advanced Text Options

 If you're studying this book without the aid of an Avid Learning Partner, I recommend you watch the video **4.3 Using Advanced Text Options**.

Respacing Staves

You should now have all the musical elements in your score. What is left to do is to space the staves out, and to add the text and the graphics. Making space for text involves a little thought about how staff spacing works in Sibelius.

Note: If you've jumped ahead to this point of the course to learn about text, you can open the catch-up file Test1.sib, which is included in the Lesson 4 folder under Core Resources.

Whenever you've been short of space in the last three lessons, you've used Optimize Staff Spacing to get Sibelius to automatically make enough space for you. Like Magnetic Layout, Sibelius thinks not just about space but also about other publishing rules such as alignment and consistency, which give your scores a professional look. In this worksheet, however, the spacing is anything but aligned and consistent! So again, you need to override Sibelius's default settings—another example of why this worksheet is advanced score layout.

You can move staves in Sibelius relative to one another by simply dragging them. Try not to do this in a regularly laid-out score, because Sibelius will probably do a better job automatically, but in this case you need to. Click the question 2 staff and drag it down. Notice that its position moves relative to the staff above—all staves below move with it, while the staff above stays in the same position. This is consistently how Sibelius works, unless you hold down the Shift key while you drag, in which case Sibelius moves the staff you're dragging and leaves those above and below in position.

As you drag the second staff farther and farther down the page, you will notice a point where the staves "jump." That is, they respace themselves automatically to fit to the bottom of the page. This is called *staff justification*, and Sibelius does it to avoid having staves where about three-quarters of the page are full and there's an empty space in the rest; it just looks better for the page to be full of music. In this case, though, you want to have absolute control over the spacing, so you need to turn staff justification off.

To turn off staff justification:

1. Choose **LAYOUT** > **STAFF SPACING** and click the dialog launcher button.

2. Under Justification, change the **JUSTIFY STAVES WHEN PAGE IS AT LEAST** setting to **100% FULL**, thus telling Sibelius not to justify the staves at all. This is shown in Figure 4.38.

Figure 4.38
Turning staff justification off. (It won't come into effect ever if it is set to 100 percent).

3. Click **OK**.

You can now drag the staves to positions that will allow the text to be put in. You can do this by eye, or if you'd like to reproduce the exact spacing from the score you're copying, turn on the staff rulers again and move the staves as follows:

- From the top of the page to the top of the question 1 staff is 50.8 mm.

- From the bottom of the question 1 staff to the top of the question 2 staff is 30.8 mm.

- From the bottom of the question 2 staff to the top of the question 3 staff is 31.8 mm.

- From the bottom of the question 3 staff to the top of the question 5 staff is 103.6 mm.

Adding Plain Text

Now the staves are in place; you can begin to add text. You've already discovered Sibelius includes many different text styles, all of which have specific uses. For instance, expression text is used for dynamics, technique text is used for performance techniques, repeat text is used for repeat structures, and so on.

If you choose Text > Styles > More to open the Text Style gallery, you will see the full list of available text styles. Incidentally, each has its own intelligent default position (for instance, expression text will always go under the staff unless it's a vocal staff, in which case it knows dynamics should be above the staff) and each has a context-sensitive menu (so if you right-click in expression text, you'll get a list of dynamics)....

In this case, the text you want isn't musical; it's plain text for asking questions and giving spaces for answers. Therefore, with no selection, choose Plain Text in the General section of the gallery.

Click above question 1 to place it (you can always move it when you've finished typing if you don't place it exactly right) and copy in the text of the question (or, if you're feeling perverse, change it to make the question more difficult). Because you changed the default font to Arial before, note that the new text uses that font.

When you've finished typing, press Esc and adjust the position of the question if you need to. Then repeat the process four times, but each time for one of the intervals under the notes. As you put each interval in, make sure its attachment line connects it to the staff above, not the staff below.

To align the four pieces of text visually, you can turn on object rulers by choosing View > Rulers > Object Rulers, resulting in more onscreen measurements as shown in Figure 4.39. Don't forget that to move objects in very small increments, it's easier to click them and use the arrow keys than to drag them around.

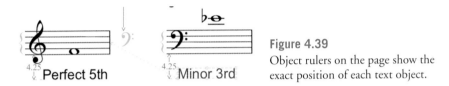

Figure 4.39
Object rulers on the page show the exact position of each text object.

Even better than this, however, is to automatically align them in a row:

1. Select each piece of text. To do so, click the first piece; then, Ctrl-click (Command-click) each subsequent one. Alternatively, perform a lasso select with the mouse. To do so, hold down the **SHIFT (COMMAND) KEY** and click just below and to the left of the first piece of text, then drag to just above and to the right of the last bit of text. This creates a lasso that selects everything inside it, as shown in Figure 4.40.

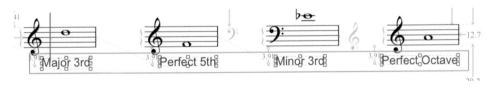

Figure 4.40
The gray rectangle around the text shows a lasso selection in progress. Note all selected text becomes blue to show it's highlighted.

2. To align the selected objects in a row, press **CTRL+SHIFT+R** (**COMMAND+SHIFT+R**) or choose **APPEARANCE > ALIGN > ROW**, as shown in Figure 4.41. The text jumps immediately into an exact line. If one or more pieces of text jump into a strange position, one of them is attached to the staff below by mistake. Undo and check.

Appearance tab   Row button

Figure 4.41
The Row button in the ribbon.

3. While the text is still highlighted, you can nudge its vertical position in relation to the staff above up and down with the arrow keys.

Add the text for questions 2 to 5 in the same way. For the answer lines, use the underscore button (Shift+-). In question 4, you may find it difficult to align the text exactly until you have the graphics in place, so put the text in an approximate position and re-align them once you've completed the section on graphics.

Adding Boxed and Justified Text

The only text that needs to behave differently is the boxed text to the right of the staff in question 3. This text is unique not only because it has a box around it, but also because the text is justified within the box.

To create the text box:

1. With no selection, choose TEXT > STYLES > MORE and choose BOXED TEXT in the General section.

2. To give yourself as much space as possible to add the text, click wherever has the most space in your score. Start typing, but stop *when the text reaches the edge of the page*, not when you've finished typing all the text that goes in the box. This is shown in Figure 4.42.

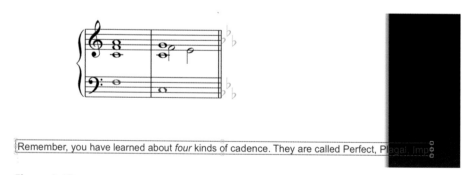

Figure 4.42
Once the text starts to go off the page, press Esc to deselect it so you can resize the text box.

3. Press **Esc** and drag the text box so you can see all four of its corners.

4. Drag the bottom-right corner of the text box in to the left and down, creating an approximate square shape that has space left to continue typing into, as shown in Figure 4.43.

Caution: It's important you don't type too much text before resizing the text box. Once the text is off the page, you can't click those corners to resize the text box. And although you can click other corners, you'll have to keep dragging the text back onto the page afterward. Once it's an appropriate size, you'll work much faster.

Figure 4.43
Resizing the text box by dragging
the bottom-right corner.

5. To finish adding the text, double-click the text to edit it (you can also click it once and press Enter/Return). Note that you can add the italic words on the fly; to do so, press **Ctrl+I** (**Command+I**) to toggle italic text on and off, just as you would in a word processor. Or, you can select a word and click the **Italic Text** button in the ribbon.

6. Select the text; then, to justify it, choose **Text** > **Format** > **Justify Text**, as shown in Figure 4.44. The text will respace to align with both the left and right sides of the text box, as shown in Figure 4.45.

Text tab   Justify Text button

Figure 4.44
The Justify Text button on
the ribbon.

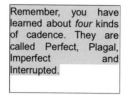

Figure 4.45
The text in the text box is now justified.

7. Resize the text box again so the text fits into it snugly and move it to the right of the stave, where it appears in the completed worksheet you're copying.

Note: You may sometimes wonder why you can't select a text box in the Boxed Text style. If you've made the box quite big, so that there is plenty of space to write into, you can't select the text box by clicking on the white space or on three sides of the box itself. To select it, you must click the actual text, or click the top line of the box.

Changing Advanced Text Settings

In addition to the text settings found in the ribbon, you can make advanced changes through the Inspector. Select the boxed text you've just completed and open the Inspector (in the Home tab). Advanced text options become available as shown in Figure 4.46.

Figure 4.46
Advanced text editing options in the Inspector.

The first check box in the Inspector to do with text is Text Frame. By default, text in Sibelius is not placed inside a text frame. That's why when you keep on typing, it just goes in a long line. As soon as you dragged the corner to resize the text, Sibelius turned the Text Frame option on, which then forced all text to stay inside the frame.

You learned to do this with the Boxed Text style because that makes it easy to see what is going on, but in fact you can use text frames with any text style—even dynamics. If, after dragging the dimensions of the text box, you decide you'd like the text not to have those restrictions, you can turn the option off here. You can also manually edit the dimensions of the frame.

Other options in the Inspector include the following:

- Scaling the text on an X or Y axis (useful for squashing into tight spaces!)

- Changing the angle of the text

- Increasing or decreasing the default space between lines of text

- Increasing or decreasing the tracking, which is the space between each letter

- Using superscript and subscript instead of normal text

- Erasing the background, which can also be used to fill the text frame with any color you like

- A check box to underline the text (bold and italic are found in the ribbon)

The text-editing options are much more powerful in Sibelius 7 than they have been in previous versions of the software. Experiment with these settings so you can see what each one does.

Importing Graphics

 A video called **4.4 Importing Graphics** steps you through the stages described in this section.

Question 4 asks students to recognize instruments visually. Apart from this kind of question, there are many instances in which you might want to import graphics into a score. If you work in a school, the school crest or logo might be a good way of identifying exam papers, manuscript paper, and more.

Scores with graphics on the cover page look great. (There's a lot more information on presentation in the next course in this series.) If you're a composer or arranger, you might like to include a graphic to draw attention to a link to your Web site or phone number.

Those composing contemporary music may want to incorporate graphic notation into otherwise conventional scores, and the ability to import graphics (along with a number of other useful features) makes almost anything possible within Sibelius.

What you learn in this section is more than enough to get you started with graphics.

Note: If you've jumped straight to this section of the lesson, there's a catch-up file called **Test2.sib** in the Lesson 4 folder in the Core Resources folder to get you up to speed.

Importing graphics is remarkably straightforward, thanks to improvements in Sibelius 7. Table 4.1 shows you which formats you can import as graphics and, in case you're not sure what formats you have graphics in, what the file extension is. (For example, if you have a file called image.jpg, its extension is .jpg, and its format is Joint Photographic Experts Group, abbreviated JPEG).

Table 4.1   Graphics Formats That Sibelius Can Import

Full Name	Abbreviation	File Extension
Windows Bitmap	BMP	.bmp
Graphic Interchange Format	GIF	.gif
Joint Photographic Experts Group	JPG or JPEG	.jpg (sometimes .jpg)
Portable Network Graphics	PNG	.png
Scalable Vector Graphic	SVG	.svg (sometimes .svgz)
Tagged Image Bitmap	TIF or TIFF	.tiff (sometimes .tif)

To import the first graphic (the saxophone):

1. Make sure you have no selection. Then choose **NOTATIONS** > **GRAPHICS** > **GRAPHIC** to open the Choose Graphic File dialog box, as shown in Figure 4.47.

Notations tab   Graphics button

Figure 4.47
The Graphics button on the ribbon.

2. Click the **FILES OF TYPE** drop-down list. You'll see the same available formats as listed in Table 4.1. This serves as a good reminder if you don't have this book handy.

3. Browse to the **CORE RESOURCES** folder, then to **LESSON 4**, then to the **GRAPHICS** folder. Select the **SAXOPHONE.TIF** file and click **OPEN**.

4. Click to place the graphic in the space that you need it. (See the worksheet you're copying if you're not sure.) It will be slightly too big for the space you've left, as shown in Figure 4.48.

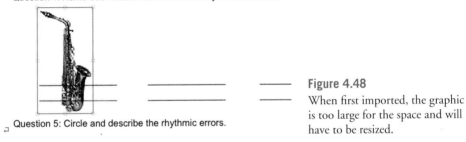

Figure 4.48
When first imported, the graphic is too large for the space and will have to be resized.

5. Shift-click the bottom-right corner of the image and drag upward to make the image smaller. Holding down the Shift key as you click allows you to scale the picture proportionately. (If you don't understand what this means, try dragging it without holding down the Shift key and see the funny sizes of saxophone you end up with!)

6. Once you've got it at just the right size, click inside the image and drag it into the desired space. (Alternatively, once the image is selected, use the arrow keys.)

7. Repeat for the other two images. If you like, instead of repeating steps 1 to 4, you can simply open the folder with the images in it in an Explorer (Finder) window and drag them onto the page in Sibelius.

Tip: When you're dragging the image around, be careful you don't accidentally drag the rotate handle, located directly above the center of the image. If you do, you'll end up with something like Figure 4.49. Don't worry if you do, though—you can simply undo and try again!

Question 4: Name each instrument and the family it comes from.

Figure 4.49
Images can be dragged to any angle with the rotate handle, but be careful you don't do it accidentally when meaning to move the image.

By default, Sibelius embeds the graphic into your document, which is great if you want to be able to share the file. However, there is also an option to link the graphic to an external file, which you might want in certain cases—for instance, if you have a logo or some type of graphic you use across a lot of scores, or that might be date critical.

To do this, right-click the graphic and choose Graphic > Change Link Source. Uncheck the Link to External File option. If you unlink the external file, or if you open the file on a second machine without the graphic, Sibelius does its best to keep an embedded copy of the graphic visible.

—Robert Puff, musician, arranger and notation expert

Robert regularly publishes tutorials, ideas, and other interesting facts about working with Sibelius on his Web sites,
On the Web **www.rpmseattle.com/of_note and www.musicprep.com/sibelius.**

You may choose to move the text around a little until you have the spacing as even as on the worksheet you're copying. Remember, you can align blocks of text or even the three images using the Align in a Row shortcut, Ctrl+Shift+R (Command+Shift+R).

Your worksheet should now be complete. But there is one more section of this lesson, because sometimes your projects, including worksheets, won't be completed in Sibelius....

Exporting Graphics

The video **4.5 Exporting Graphics** will step you through the processes explained in this section. If you're taking yourself through the course, it's highly recommended that you watch the video before reading the text.

If you are producing a worksheet, exam paper, or graphic score, or even writing an essay or a thesis, Sibelius may not be the best program in which to produce your work. That may sound like a strange thing to say in a Sibelius course, but this is not to suggest you won't still be using Sibelius to create any music. Instead, the point is that if you are producing a document or a score that is more text than music, you should use a program made to handle text such as a word processor (the most popular being Microsoft Word).

You then need to be able to get the music you make in Sibelius into that document, and place it amongst the words as required. There are a number of ways to achieve this. The quickest is as simple as copy and paste.

To copy and paste music from Sibelius into another program:

1. In Sibelius, double-click any bar in question 1 to select the whole system.

2. Press **ALT+G** (**OPTION+G**), which is the shortcut for Select Graphic, or choose **HOME** > **CLIPBOARD** > **SELECT GRAPHIC** as shown in Figure 4.50.

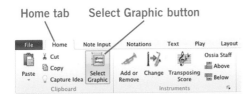

Figure 4.50
The Select Graphic button on the ribbon.

3. Sibelius draws a blue dotted selection box around the system, as shown in Figure 4.51. To adjust it, drag the square handles so the box includes the text below but not the text above.

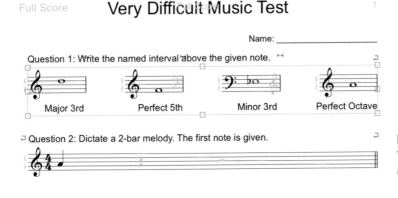

Figure 4.51
The blue dotted box shows the area to be exported as a graphic.

4. Press **CTRL+C** (**COMMAND+C**) to copy the selected area.

5. Open your favorite word-processing software, place the cursor where you'd like the music to appear, and press **CTRL+V** (**COMMAND+V**) to paste the graphic in. Figure 4.52 gives an idea of what this would look like in a word-processing program.

Written exam part 3

In part 3, students will answer a number of music theory questions related to the set work. Students must show that they have understood the theory components by applying this knowledge in answers to questions about the excerpts played. Scores are provided and each excerpt will be played 17 times.

Begin by answering the following questions.

3.1 Write the named interval above the given note:

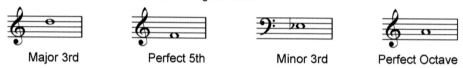

| Major 3rd | Perfect 5th | Minor 3rd | Perfect Octave |

3.2 Perform both a Schenkerian and a Pitch Set analysis on Ferneyhough's *Etudes Transcendantales IX*. In your answer, explain how your analysis extends the communication of Ferneyhough's aesthetic and extemporize on whether you think Ferneyhough is capable of writing melody or whether his music should even be mentioned

Figure 4.52
Question 1 from your worksheet, placed into a more text-heavy exam in a word-processing package.

If you're preparing musical examples for someone else to embed in a document, or for placement in a professional desktop-publishing package (such as Adobe InDesign), you will prefer more control over the export of graphics.

Before exporting graphics files to other programs, decide whether you want to export every page of your score, a single page, or part of a page. Remember that images can be cropped in graphics programs, so if you're not sure, export the whole page and crop in the graphics program for maximum control over page layout.

If you do want to export just part of the page, the Select Graphics feature can be used as outlined previously. Also note that if you have no selection when you press Alt+G (Command+G), you can then draw the selection with the mouse.

If you want to export one of several systems, you can also select that system before exporting the graphic, and Sibelius will make the crop for you. The important thing to think about is what you're exporting *before* you export.

To export the whole page:

1. Begin by making sure you have no selection. Then choose FILE > EXPORT > GRAPHICS, as shown in Figure 4.53.

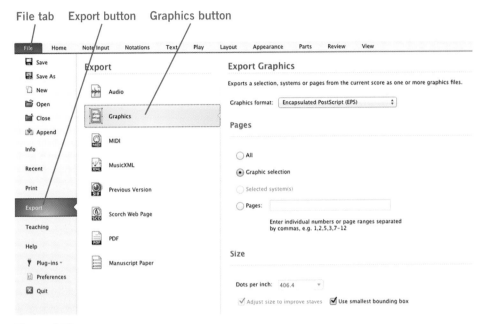

Figure 4.53
The Export Graphics options.

2. A number of options are displayed for exporting your graphic. Click the GRAPHICS FORMAT drop-down list and choose PORTABLE NETWORK GRAPHICS (PNG) from among the six different options, as shown in Figure 4.54. This is a good transferable format, is usable by most programs, and also displays well in Web browsers on Web sites. If you are working with a professional typesetter, they are more likely to ask you for EPS or PDF formats.

Figure 4.54
Choosing the file format to export.

3. You are going to export the whole page, so leave the **PAGES** setting on the default (**ALL**), but it is worth noting that if you had a multi-page score (e.g., the scores you've made in Lesson 1, "Amazing Grace," Lesson 2, "Beethoven's 3rd String Quartet, First Movement, Opus 18, Number 3," and Lesson 3, "Purple"), you could export a range of pages very easily by changing the Pages setting.

4. As shown in Figure 4.55, under Options are some settings to do with color and how the image is drawn. Monochrome means a black and white image, which will have a smaller file size (so good for e-mailing), but may also not appear as "smooth," so leave the **MONOCHROME** check box unchecked for now. (The other options are outside the scope of this book.)

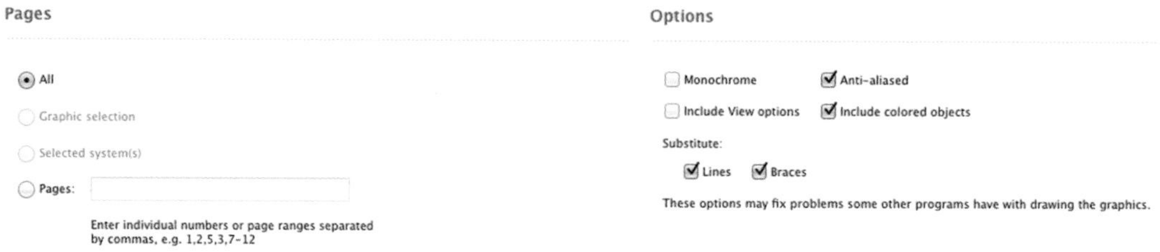

Figure 4.55
Pages and Options in Graphics Export.

5. Under Size are a number of options, shown in Figure 4.56. One of the most important settings in the whole of Graphics Export is Dots per Inch (DPI). For exam papers you're making yourself in a word-processing program, choose **300**. For a professional DTP program, choose **600** or higher. (It's easy for a graphic designer to reduce the resolution of the images you provide, but they can't increase them in any meaningful way.) If your image is for the Internet, choose **72** DPI because that is screen resolution, although it can be useful to export at double that to allow resizing later.

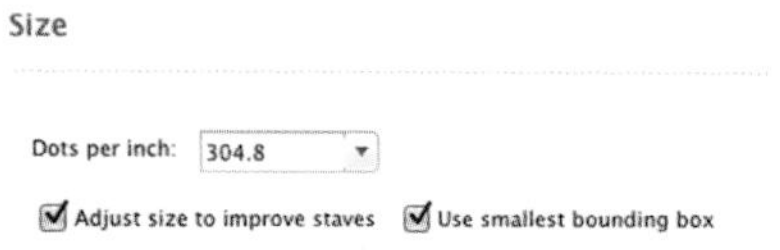

Figure 4.56
Options to do with the size of your graphics export.

6. Still under Size, leave the **ADJUST SIZE TO IMPROVE STAVES** check box checked. This is a good option unless you're a graphics expert and really know what you're doing. The Use Smallest Bounding Box check box is also useful (Sibelius will crop your image right to the edge of the music), but in this case, uncheck the **USE SMALLEST BOUNDING BOX** check box so you can see your full page in all its glory.

7. Last but not least, you can choose a name for your exported file, specify the location where you'd like to save it, and if you're exporting a number of pages, check the **CREATE SUBFOLDER** option, which will collect all the exported files in one folder (otherwise you might end up with 40 files on your desktop). These options are shown in Figure 4.57.

Folder

Filename: My graphics export

Save to folder: /Users/jhumberstone/Desktop   Browse...

☐ Create subfolder:

My graphics export

Export

Figure 4.57
Naming your
exported file.

8. When you're finished, click **EXPORT**, and the file will be quickly created.

Locate the file in the folder that you exported it to, and double-click it to open it. Most modern word processors and design packages will allow you to simply drag the file onto them, but you may need to look for options to insert or place an image.

Graphics export can also be used in highly graphic scores. If you have musical elements that will be surrounded by more graphical elements, you should create them in Sibelius, and then place them into a graphic-design or image-editing program where you can draw the graphics alongside them.

Review/Discussion Questions

1. Why are the skills involved in making a worksheet important even if you're not a teacher?

2. True or false: Ctrl+Shift+H (Command+Shift+H) is the shortcut for hide, and Ctrl+Shift+S (Command+Shift+S) is the shortcut for show.

3. What are super-magic-secret-hidden handles?

   a. Invisible handles you need to find to indent a staff from the left

   b. Found by clicking and hoping just to the right of the end of any staff

   c. The path to enlightenment

4. How do you split a system?

5. True or false: To insert a system break, you click a barline and press Enter/Return.

6. Which of the following graphics *can't* be imported into Sibelius?

   a. EPS PostScript

   b. BMP Bitmap

   c. SVG Vector

7. Is it possible to change the look of all of the text in your score at once?

8. True or false: You can import images into Sibelius, but you can't edit them.

9. Clefs are hidden by:

   a. Clicking on them and pressing the hide or show shortcut Ctrl+Shift+H (Command+Shift+H)

   b. Clicking on them and pressing Delete/Backspace

   c. Selecting Blank Clef from the Clef gallery

10. When would you choose to make a musical worksheet or exam paper in a word processor instead of in Sibelius?

Lesson 4 Keyboard Shortcuts

Shortcut	Function
T	Time Signature
K	Key Signature
Ctrl+Shift+H (Windows)/Command+Shift+H (Mac)	Hide or Show
Ctrl+Delete (Windows)/Command+Delete (Mac)	Delete bars (passage selection required)
Alt+Shift+Left Arrow (Windows)/Option+Shift+Left Arrow (Mac)	Contract note spacing (passage selection required)
Alt+Shift+Right Arrow (Windows)/Option+Shift+Right Arrow (Mac)	Expand note spacing (passage selection required)
Enter (Windows)/Return (Mac)	System break (requires a barline to be selected first)
Q	Clef gallery
Ctrl+Delete (Windows)/Command+Delete (Mac)	Delete bars (requires passage selection first)
Ctrl+Shift+R (Windows)/Command+Shift+R (Mac)	Align in a row
Alt+G (Windows)/Option+G (Mac)	Select graphic

Creating a Worksheet

Create a worksheet or graphics-based document that will be of use to you in your professional life or your study. For example, if you're a composer, try some of the layout techniques you've learned to create new layout for an existing score. Add text and graphics to make your score more attractive and easy to read. If you're a student, create some musical excerpts or analyses and import these into a sample of your writing (for instance, an essay you've already written). See if you can get the text to wrap around a graphic nicely. If you're a teacher or lecturer, make a worksheet, test, or exam for an actual class that you've got coming up soon.

Media Used: No media is required for this exercise. However, in the Graphics folder (found in the Lesson 4 folder inside your Core Resources folder) are a number of images of instruments that you may like to use.

Duration: Approximately 30 minutes (the essay or score layout exercises) to two hours (a detailed exam paper)

GOALS

- Create one of the documents outlined

Agent Zero

This final lesson is a lot of fun, and you'll also learn much more about playback of your scores than you have in prior lessons. It focuses on the creation of a film score for the Avid promotional movie *Agent Zero*, which was made using Avid Media Composer in collaboration with Sony. Along the way, you'll learn how to use PhotoScore Lite, which came with your copy of Sibelius, and what the Review tab (which you haven't looked at whatsoever yet) in the ribbon is for.

Media Used: Zero1.sib, Zero2.sib, Zero3.sib, Zero4.sib, Beethoven.sib, Timpani.pdf, Agent Zero Segment Large.mov (QuickTime movie), Agent Zero Segment Small.mov (QuickTime movie), Agent Zero Segment Small.avi (AVI movie suitable for Windows computers with no QuickTime Player installed), Beethoven Garritan.mp3, Beethoven Sibelius 7 Sounds.mp3, Beethoven Synful.mp3, Beethoven Vienna Dry.mp3, Beethoven Vienna.mp3, Tchaikovsky Romeo and Juliet Garritan.mp3, Tchaikovsky Romeo and Juliet Sibelius.mp3, Tchaikovsky Romeo and Juliet Synful.mp3, Tchaikovsky Romeo and Juliet Vienna.mp3

Duration: Between one and two hours

GOALS

- Use PhotoScore Lite to scan or import PDFs
- Explore AudioScore Lite
- Import a video and synchronize it with your score
- Create hit points and write music to match the action
- Use Sibelius to develop your musical ideas
- Learn how the Versions feature is useful for collaboration and also in education
- Learn much more about controlling playback in Sibelius
- Input music with HyperControl on an Axiom 49 or 61 keyboard
- Use third-party virtual instruments in Sibelius

Before You Begin...

If you're a budding film composer and jumped straight into this lesson without reading the others first, not only will you find it a bit tough because there is a lot of assumed knowledge from the four prior lessons, but you will also need to make sure that you have copied the Core Resources folder to your hard drive as described in Lesson 1, "Amazing Grace."

Also be aware that this lesson involves synchronizing a video with your Sibelius score. If you attempt to sync the video directly from your CD, you will encounter serious performance issues (stuttering playback, failing playback, and lack of synchronization between the music and the video).

Learning PhotoScore Lite

 If you are studying this book without a teacher, watch the video **5.1 Learning PhotoScore Lite** before you read this section. See the section "Accessing the Video Files" in this book's introduction for help finding and viewing the video content.

On your Sibelius DVDs (or included in your download, if you downloaded Sibelius 7 directly from Avid) are a number of goodies that you may not have installed when you first installed Sibelius. Two of these are PhotoScore Lite and AudioScore Lite. If you're not sure whether you installed them, look in your Start menu (Windows; you can simply type in the Start menu's Search field if you're not sure where to look) or your Applications folder (Mac). If you can't find them in these locations, insert the first Sibelius DVD and follow the prompts to install them now.

Both of these programs are made by Neuratron, a company that has worked closely with Sibelius for more than 15 years to create complementary software. PhotoScore enables you to scan out-of-copyright printed scores and into an editable form. You can perform basic editing within PhotoScore, but it's in combination with Sibelius that PhotoScore is most powerful, enabling you to take your scanned scores and repurpose them (for example, rearrange them) in Sibelius.

 A history of Neuratron's development and lots more information about the products they make can be found on their Web site,
On the Web **www.neuratron.com.**

PhotoScore has any number of uses. For example, you can:

- Take a piece for one ensemble (e.g., string quartet) and quickly change the instrumentation—including transposition—for another (e.g., wind quartet).

- If you lose a part for a piece, scan the score and create the part again.

- Conversely, if you lose a score, scan each part and then combine them in a new score.

- Arrange piano pieces easily for multiple instruments.

- Take choral works and combine multiple vocal parts for a piano or organ reduction.

- Create great quality extracts from old scores for inclusion in essays or presentations.

Caution: Scanning music that is in copyright is illegal. Copyright laws vary from country to country; it is your responsibility to be aware of the laws that govern copyright where you live. Be aware that while music may be out of print, or the composer who wrote it may have been dead over 50 or 70 years, that the publisher may still hold copyright to that *edition* (the editorial markings and layout), and so even an old score could still possibly be covered by copyright.

As you might have guessed by its name, PhotoScore Lite is a cut-down version of the full PhotoScore, PhotoScore Ultimate 7. PhotoScore Lite gives you a great taste of the power of the Ultimate version but does not scan all elements of your score. Figure 5.1 shows a splash screen that appears each time you run PhotoScore Lite (unless you uncheck the Show This Next Time check box) that compares the features of the Lite and Ultimate versions.

Figure 5.1
This splash screen compares the features of PhotoScore Lite with PhotoScore Ultimate.

The only features that really affect the import of the part you're about to do are the ability to scan in text (which means you'll have to add all the dynamics manually afterward) and articulation marks. Other great features of PhotoScore Ultimate are that it can read handwritten music and it includes all the musical elements on your score, including phrasing. It's also faster and is much less limited in terms of how many staves you can scan at once.

Note: Should you really enjoy using PhotoScore Lite, you might consider upgrading to PhotoScore Ultimate 7. To do this, speak to the music store where you bought Sibelius or visit the Neuratron Web site (www.neuratron.com).

Because not everyone taking this course will have a scanner attached to their computer, you will learn to use PhotoScore by importing a PDF file. However, if you were to scan, this part in the process would be nearly identical; you'd just be greeted with your scanner's software first. This software is vastly different depending on the manufacturer of your scanner, but if you'd like to try it now, print the PDF out and scan it in by using the Scan Pages button in PhotoScore Lite with the following settings:

- Set the resolution at 300dpi (600dpi will also work, but it's unnecessarily high for this simple part and will slow the process down).

- Set the image type to Grayscale (sometimes called Black and White Photo, but not just Black and White, which will create too much contrast).

Importing PDF Files

By default, as soon as you import a PDF file into PhotoScore Lite, the program will read it. It does a number of things at this point: checks that the page is the right way up, makes sure the staves are level (scanned scores are often slightly off from perfectly horizontal because it's difficult to get a book completely straight on a scanner), detects the five lines of the staff, and then reads the pitches on them.

To import a PDF into PhotoScore Lite:

1. Click the **OPEN PDFS** button, shown in Figure 5.2.

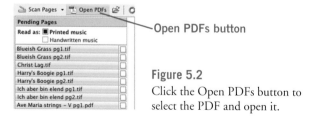

Open PDFs button

Figure 5.2
Click the Open PDFs button to select the PDF and open it.

2. Locate the **TIMPANI.PDF** file, which is in the Lesson 5 folder within your Core Resources folder. Then double-click the file. If Sibelius asks you what the resolution is, choose **300DPI**, which is a safe setting for clean imports. A number of progress dialog boxes flash by—one is shown in Figure 5.3—showing you what PhotoScore is doing.

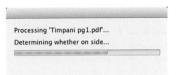

Figure 5.3

This progress dialog box tells you that PhotoScore is seeing whether you scanned your score on its side (in this case, you didn't!).

As mentioned, by default, PhotoScore is set to read your score as soon as it's imported, so you will see the Timpani.pdf file appear in the Pending Pages list and a green progress bar (shown in Figure 5.4) tells you that it is being read. Once read, PhotoScore opens its Output window, ready for you to proofread and edit the file as shown in Figure 5.5.

Figure 5.4

The green progress bar indicates that the Timpani.pdf file is being read.

The original PDF/scanned image

PhotoScore's read score

A close-up view (follows your mouse)

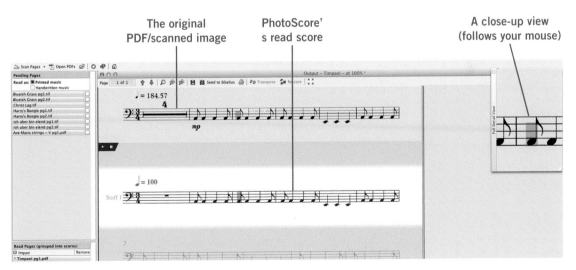

Figure 5.5

PhotoScore's Output window, ready for you to proofread and edit your imported score.

Figure 5.5 also shows you exactly how PhotoScore helps you proofread your score. The top section, colored like buff manuscript paper, shows the original scanned or imported PDF score. Below that, in white, is the score as PhotoScore has read it, ready for you to edit. On the right is the Full Detail view, which shows a close-up of the original score (in case you can't easily make out the notation).

As you move your mouse over the read score, you will notice several things happening:

- Only one staff of the score at once is highlighted white—the one you're hovering the mouse over.

- The original score above adjusts to show the corresponding score as you move the mouse up and down.

- The Full Detail view also follows your mouse pointer.

- As you hover your mouse pointer over a note, it is highlighted purple in all three places at once, to allow you to compare the read score with the original even more quickly (see Figure 5.6). Note that you can also play back the score, which gives another way to quickly proofread it—audibly.

Figure 5.6
Purple highlights are placed over the note the mouse is hovering over in all three views.

Editing the Read Score in PhotoScore Lite

Proofread your score. You will probably find that the pitches are all correct, but if they are not, you can simply drag notes to the correct pitches. Just like in Sibelius, you can also move them up and down by step with the Up Arrow and Down Arrow keys.

It's also likely that your score has no rhythmic errors. If it does, you'll see an indicator from PhotoScore, as shown in Figure 5.7. (Simply delete a note out of any bar to see this if your score has no mistakes.) The red lines above and below the bar serve to highlight that there is a problem (PhotoScore can tell the bar doesn't add up), and the blue rhythmic values at the end of the bar tell you what durations are missing (or extra, if the bar had too many beats).

Figure 5.7
Bars that do not add up to the prevailing meter are highlighted red, while missing or extra note durations are shown in blue.

Adding notes to the score in PhotoScore is simple. In fact, it's nearly identical to Sibelius. You've probably already noticed that, just like Sibelius, PhotoScore has a Keypad panel at the bottom right of the screen (it is shown in Figure 5.8) with all the corresponding shortcuts available in your computer's numerical keypad. To add notes, simply press Esc to make sure nothing is selected, click on the duration you need in the Keypad panel (or press the shortcut, now you know these), and click in the score to create the note.

Figure 5.8
A reflection of how closely Neuratron works with Sibelius; it has a Keypad panel that is nearly identical.

Note: In more complex scores, you may find that the spacing doesn't look great in a bar to which you have to manually add a bunch of notes. Don't worry about this; Sibelius will fix it up when you import it.

As you click the missing pitch in the score, the views of the original PDF still follow your mouse position. That means if you're not sure what pitch you should be adding, you only need to quickly glance up.

The only real error in the score (apart from the missing text and articulation marks, which PhotoScore Lite doesn't read) is that the multirests are missing. While this is another limitation of the Lite version, it has a knock-on effect, which is that the bar numbers are therefore all out. Luckily, this is also simple to fix.

To add the multirests:

1. Press **Esc** to make sure you have nothing selected and that you can see the first bar in the score.

2. Choose **Create** > **Bar Rest** > **Multirest**. The dialog box shown in Figure 5.9 will appear.

Figure 5.9
PhotoScore's Multirest dialog box.

3. Press **4** and click **OK** or press **ENTER** (**RETURN**).

4. Position the mouse pointer over the rest in the first bar so that it is high-lighted purple, as shown in Figure 5.10.

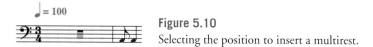

Figure 5.10
Selecting the position to insert a multirest.

5. Click right on top of the rest, which will be replaced with the multirest as shown in Figure 5.11.

Figure 5.11
Your four-bar multirest is created.

6. Repeat this process for the other three missing multirests in the part.

Your part should now be as close to the original as possible. Because you're using PhotoScore Lite, you can't add the missing elements such as dynamics or articulation marks until you send the file to Sibelius, but you could do this in PhotoScore Ultimate (or you may not need to, because they would be read automatically). Therefore, sending the score to Sibelius is the next step.

Note: The editing required on this score is minimal. If you try importing another score into PhotoScore, you may find that there is more to fix. In scores with many small errors, try scanning at a higher resolution. If that doesn't work, focus on fixing just the rhythmic errors so that at least when you send it to Sibelius, the bars will add up.

Sending Your Score to Sibelius

To send the score to Sibelius:

1. Click the **SEND TO SIBELIUS** button in the toolbar, as shown in Figure 5.12. If Sibelius isn't already open, you'll soon hear that familiar start-up music. When loaded, the Open PhotoScore or AudioScore File dialog box will appear, as shown in Figure 5.13.

Send to Sibelius button

Figure 5.12
The Send to Sibelius button on the toolbar.

2. The defaults, shown in Figure 5.13, will do the job just fine, but click the
    Choose Instruments option button so you can tell Sibelius it's a timpani
    part. You're not working on a transposing score, but you can imagine how
    useful it is to be able to tell Sibelius whether or not there are transposing
    parts in the score instead of having to transpose them all to concert pitch
    manually before you begin!

Figure 5.13
The Open PhotoScore or AudioScore
File dialog box.

3. Click OK. The Instruments dialog box will open.

4. In the Find field, type TIMPANI. Then choose **Timpani [no key]** from the
    drop-down list.

5. Timpani are now selected in the list, so click the **Add** button. A Timpani
    entry appears in the Instruments to Create list on the right, as shown in
    Figure 5.14.

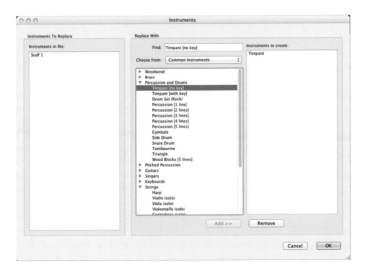

Figure 5.14
The Instruments dialog box,
with a timpani added.

6. Click **OK**.

7. If Sibelius asks you if you want to change playback configuration, click **No**.

The score is essentially correct, but you can clean it up by adding the missing elements and by fixing one small problem at the start. The one small problem is that the (incorrect) metronome mark that PhotoScore inserted has attached itself to bar 4, thus breaking the four-bar multirest at the start.

Note: If you don't have the metronome mark text, you may be using a different version of PhotoScore. In this case, you can just ignore the next steps and move on.

To fix the metronome mark:

1. Click the grayed-out metronome mark and press **Delete/Backspace** to remove it. The multirest will reform to four bars.

2. Insert the missing dynamics. These is an **mp** at bar 5 and an *f* at bar 40.

3. The long D at the end (bars 44–46) should have a trill written over it. (This is one of two ways to write a roll in a drum part.) To add this trill, select the bars, press **L** to open the Lines gallery, and select the **Trill** entry, as shown in Figure 5.15.

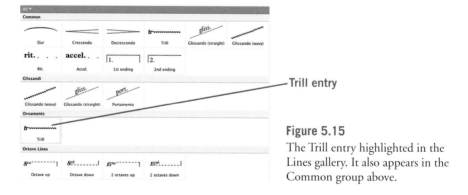

Trill entry

Figure 5.15
The Trill entry highlighted in the Lines gallery. It also appears in the Common group above.

While this import into Sibelius was a simple one, it's enough to show you the power and open up the possibilities of using PhotoScore in your work. Save this timpani part, because you're going to add it to a big film score in the next part of this lesson. First, though, a quick look at AudioScore Lite.

Introducing AudioScore

Only 10 years ago, doing what AudioScore does as well as AudioScore does it was the stuff of science fiction. There were university departments researching this subject, trying to work out how to separate out the sounds of a recording or a live ensemble and extract individual threads to be used on their own.

Early mic input features on some commercial programs were so weak as to be considered unusable for practical work, but AudioScore has surpassed those problems and now offers the real possibility of input into Sibelius from a non-MIDI instrument.

Of course, this technology is much more complicated than MIDI input, so errors *are* still more likely to occur. With MIDI input, messages about the notes travels directly to Sibelius and is re-interpreted as notation. In AudioScore, sound is recorded and mapped to MIDI pitches, from where it can be sent to Sibelius.

If you don't have an instrument with you, try using AudioScore simply by singing into it. It will work, even through basic computer microphones (you are heavily encouraged to wear headphones, though).

When you run AudioScore, you'll be greeted with a splash screen that tells you about extra features you can gain if you upgrade to AudioScore Ultimate (shown in Figure 5.16). The feature most likely to make you consider getting your wallet out is the ability to import MP3s into AudioScore Ultimate. Being able to have a computer program transcribe your music collection is quite an attractive prospect.

Figure 5.16
AudioScore Lite's splash screen extols the virtues of the Ultimate version.

After dismissing the splash screen, click the Record New Track button as shown in Figure 5.17. Options for recording the track are shown in Figure 5.18. You can leave most of these as default, but to achieve the highest degree of success in your first attempt at AudioScore, change the Tempo setting to Adagio. Just as when you recorded MIDI from the keyboard the first time, slowing the tempo will allow you to perform with greatest accuracy, and this can be sped up again later on.

Record New Track button.

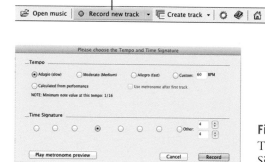

Figure 5.17
The Record New Track button in
AudioScore's toolbar.

Figure 5.18
The Please Choose the Tempo and Time
Signature dialog box.

When you click Record, AudioScore will give you a one-bar count in and then begin recording. For best results:

- Wear headphones.

- Think of a simple melody to record. For example, you could sing the "Amazing Grace" melody from Lesson 1.

- In contrast to recording MIDI, make the articulation at the start of each note clear, even with a slight gap after the last one.

- If singing, try a consonant on the start of each note (words aren't important!)—for example, singing "Do" repeatedly.

- If singing, make sure you've thought of the range in which you're singing in advance. Sing in the strongest part of your range. If you have a bass voice, sing higher in your range.

As you sing, AudioScore gives you instant feedback, as shown in Figure 5.19:

- The Sound Level window shows the level of input from your microphone: too low and Audio can't detect any pitch; too high and it may be distorted.

- Along the left side of the window is a keyboard and list of pitches that AudioScore can detect.

- In the main part of the screen, colored lines show the exact pitches being recorded from the microphone.

As you record, you are also reminded that you are recording in the toolbar and at the bottom right of the screen, as shown in Figure 5.20. Simply press the space bar to stop recording.

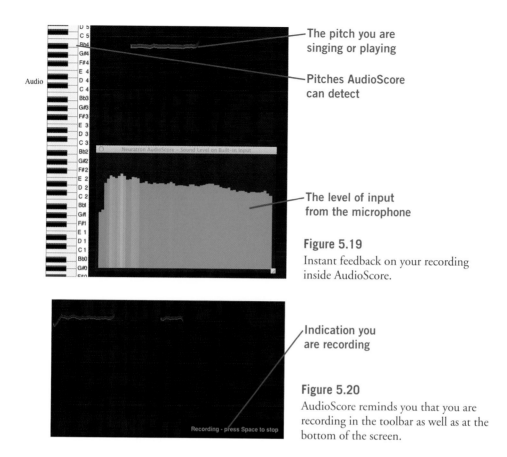

The pitch you are
singing or playing

Pitches AudioScore
can detect

The level of input
from the microphone

Figure 5.19
Instant feedback on your recording
inside AudioScore.

Indication you
are recording

Figure 5.20
AudioScore reminds you that you are
recording in the toolbar as well as at the
bottom of the screen.

When you finish recording, you need to give AudioScore a few seconds (or more, depending on how much music you recorded) to convert what you played or sang into MIDI data. As this happens, the Record button on the toolbar reads Cancel Processing, as shown in Figure 5.21. That way, if it is taking too long (or if you want to trash that attempt and try again), you can cancel the process.

Figure 5.21
If you didn't like your performance, you can
cancel AudioScore processing it and try again.

Once complete, your recording shows at the top of the screen and the MIDI pitches below. There are two Play buttons—one to listen to your recording again, and one to listen to AudioScore's transcription—as shown in Figure 5.22.

Play your   Play AudioScore's   The waveform of   Each bar represents the pitch and
recording   transcription   your recording   duration of each note performed

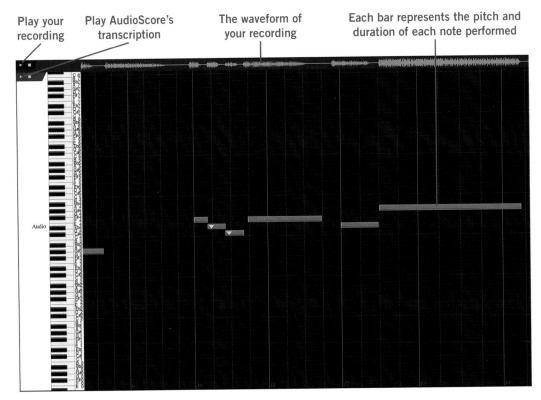

Figure 5.22
A completed transcription.

Notes in the transcription can be edited by hand here, or you can add, delete, or change notes once they are in Sibelius. To change pitches, simply drag them up or down. To change the duration of a note, click the end of the bar and drag it left or right. To change the rhythmic position of a note, click in the middle of the bar and drag it left or right.

If you're happy with AudioScore's transcription, choose Notes > Transcribe, and then finish this quick introduction by clicking the Send To Sibelius button. You will be greeted by the same dialog box you saw when you imported a PhotoScore file. This time, stick with the defaults, and just click OK to view your score and do any further editing as required.

When you've finished, close the file you imported from AudioScore—you won't need it—but keep the timpani file open, as you will need that in the next section.

Adding Video and Hit Points

 If you are studying this book without a teacher, watch the video 5.2 Adding Video and Hit Points before you read this section.

The timpani part you successfully imported via PhotoScore is, as mentioned, part of a bigger film score. Open the film score now by finding the file Zero1.sib in the Lesson 5 folder in Core Resources. You'll notice a sticky note, or *comment* as they're called in Sibelius, above the timpani part in bar 1 (this is shown in Figure 5.23). It reminds you that the timpani part is missing.

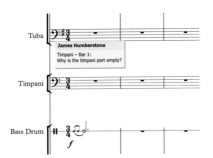

Figure 5.23
A comment at the start of the score reminds you that the timpani part is missing. Luckily, you imported it via PhotoScore.

To add the timpani part:

1. To go back to the open timpani part, choose **VIEW** > **WINDOW** > **SWITCH WINDOWS** > *FILE NAME* (if you haven't saved it, it will be called Untitled).

2. Select the music. To do so, click in the first bar and then Shift-click the last bar. Then press **CTRL+C** (Windows) or **COMMAND+C** (Mac) to copy the whole part.

3. To go back to the *Agent Zero* score, choose **VIEW** > **WINDOW** > **SWITCH WINDOWS** > **ZERO1.SIB**.

4. Select the first bar of the timpani part, then press **CTRL+V** (Windows) or **COMMAND+V** (Mac) to paste the part in. This will paste the whole part in and overwrite the comment, too.

5. Press **ESC**; then play back the score to hear it complete with the timpani part.

Later in this lesson, you will learn how the Versions feature in Sibelius works and can be used for collaboration on scores and in education. Right now, you should create your first version so that you have some breadcrumbs to trace back later on.

To create a new version of the score:

1. Choose REVIEW > VERSIONS > NEW VERSION, as shown in Figure 5.24.

Figure 5.24
The New Version button in the ribbon.

2. The New Version dialog box appears. In the COMMENT field, type a comment that indicates you've added the timpani, as shown in Figure 5.25, then click OK.

Figure 5.25
The New Version dialog box.

Note: For now, you only need to know how to add versions; you'll learn what the other buttons in this tab of the ribbon do soon.

You've already played back the score, but that only tells a small part of the story. As you might guess from the title and the style of the music, *Agent Zero* is a film in the James Bond tradition about an undercover operative and lots of naughty people who would quite like to kill him. In this first scene from the film, we see Agent Zero jump from a helicopter and face some of his foes in hand-to-hand combat while his HQ are trying to contact him via radio.

To add the video footage to Sibelius:

1. Choose PLAY > VIDEO > VIDEO > ADD VIDEO and then locate the AGENT ZERO SEGMENT SMALL file. If your computer is able to open the MOV (QuickTime Movie) version, double-click it. Otherwise, double-click the AVI version.

2. The movie will open in its own panel inside Sibelius. Play the score again from the beginning, balancing the sound on the video with the volume of your score by dragging the slider as shown in Figure 5.26.

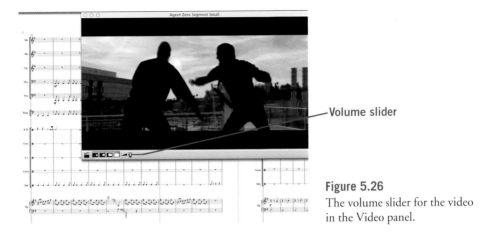

Volume slider

Figure 5.26
The volume slider for the video
in the Video panel.

*The Video window allows you to open video format files such as AVI, MPG,
and MOV in Sibelius. When you play back the score, you can hear the Sibelius
playback sounds and the audio from the video file. What many users don't realize is that you can also open audio file formats such as MP3, AIFF, or WAV in
the Video window. (I'll refer to the audio file as MP3 from here on out, but it's
the same for any of the audio formats.) Simply go to Play > Video > Add Video;
this will open a dialog box so you can find the MP3. Select it, and click Open.
The Video window pops up in a smaller size that shows just the audio volume
control. Now when you start playback of Sibelius, the MP3 will play along.*

—**John Hinchey, composer, arranger, and notation software expert**

**Avid expert John Hinchey has written more on MusicXML and Sibelius
at his Web sites, www.johnhinchey.com and www.hincheymusic.com.**

On the Web

You should find that the video and the music are well synchronized. If you use the
[and] keys to rewind and fast forward playback in your score, the video will be
scrubbed so that the film matches the position of the green playback line on the
score.

A few new shortcuts—and some you've already learned for revision's sake—are
useful at this moment. They are shown in Table 5.1.

Try moving through the video with these shortcuts and other playback shortcuts
that you know. You may find it useful to open the Transport if it isn't open already
(choose View > Panels > Transport), as this also has additional playback controls
that you've learned.

Table 5.1   Playback Shortcuts

Keyboard Shortcut	Description
Y	Clicking a note in any bar and then pressing Y makes the green playback line (and video) jump to that point in the score.
[	Rewind.
]	Fast forward.
Shift+[	Scrubs backward in time by one frame or .1 second (depending on preferences).
Shift+]	Scrubs forward in time by one frame or .1 second.
P	Plays from the note selected.
Space bar	Starts and stops playback when there is no selection.

The tools film composers use to write music that closely matches the action in the film are *hit points* (also known as cues or markers). These are points in the score that show you where the action will happen, as shown in Figure 5.27 (taken from bars 30 to 34).

Figure 5.27
The boxes above the score are hit points, which show the location of specific moments of action in the video.

The clever thing about Sibelius's hit points is that they are linked to time rather than to any particular bar in your score. Try this: At the start of the score, double-click the metronome mark to edit it, and change it to 60 beats per minute. As soon as you press Esc, all the hit points are recalculated. At the slower tempo, fewer bars are needed to move through time, so the hit points all move toward the start of your score. Use Undo to put the music back to its original tempo.

Information in the hit-point boxes also helps the conductor and recording engineer make sure the recording is made to exactly fit the action. The information is labeled in Figure 5.28.

Timecode ⎯ 00:00:30:05
Bar and beat position ⎯ 32.1.05
Hit-point name ⎯ Throw 2

Figure 5.28
Information provided in a hit-point box.

If you try selecting a hit point and dragging it, you won't have much success. This is because it's essential that hit points remain locked to the time to be of any use. Therefore, Sibelius draws them on the score, and you cannot move them without explicitly changing the hit-point timecode—which you'll learn to do very soon.

Before you do that, you should create some hit points of your own and do a little film orchestration. Hit points are created in the Video panel itself. You've learned what the slider on that panel is for (the volume), but not the use of the other buttons. These are shown in Figure 5.29. Notice that in addition to being able to add hit points to the score, you can change the Video panel size with these buttons.

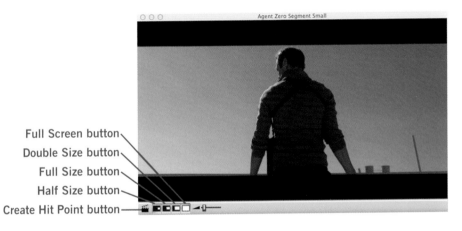

Full Screen button
Double Size button
Full Size button
Half Size button
Create Hit Point button

Figure 5.29
The buttons on the Video panel.

To create hit points at these moments of impact:

1. Move the playback line to the start of bar 18. To do so, select any note at the start of that bar and press **Y**.

2. Press **SHIFT+]** to move the playback line forward one frame at a time until you locate the exact frame where the contact is made.

3. Click the **CREATE HIT POINT** button on the Video panel.

4. Move forward to the next two or three impact points and add hit points for those, too.

5. By default, your hit points have been named simply Hit 01, Hit 02, and so on. To rename them, choose **PLAY > VIDEO**, click on the lower half of the **HIT POINT** button, and choose **EDIT HIT POINTS**.

6. The Edit Hit Points dialog box will appear, as shown in Figure 5.30. Double-click the name of each hit point to edit it; then click **OK**.

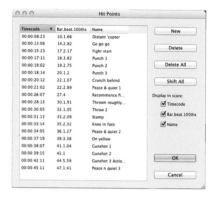

Figure 5.30
The Edit Hit Points dialog box.

Note: While you're looking at the Edit Hit Points dialog box, notice that you can also turn on and off the information that is displayed in the hit-point boxes here. This is also where you can manually edit the position of an existing hit point, by double-clicking its timecode.

7. The names of your hit points will be updated on the score. Their rhythmic position will help you line up chords to match those points in the action, but there's an even easier way to do it. Choose **NOTE INPUT** > **PLUG-INS** > **COMPOSING TOOLS** > **ADD HIT POINT STAFF**, and Sibelius will add a special staff to the top of the score that shows the rhythmic position of each hit point, as show in Figure 5.31.

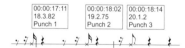

Figure 5.31
The hit-point staff shows the rhythmic position of each of the newly added hit points.

8. Where hit points show up at strange points, it's up to you to choose whether you want to put them at the closest beat or half beat, or put them right on that point. Add a chord at each of the new hit points, using the majority of the percussion instruments and at least the trombone and tuba. If you're not sure what pitches to use in the brass parts, just use unison A.

9. Mark the chords with a dynamic of $\boldsymbol{f}$.

10. When you're finished, watch the film again with your new orchestration at work.

11. When you're happy with your work, you can remove the hit-point staff in the Add or Remove Instruments dialog box (shortcut I).

12. After all this hard work, you should save another version. Choose REVIEW > VERSIONS > NEW VERSION and, under COMMENT, type a comment describing what you just did in the score. Congratulations, you're a film composer!

When searching for footage to use in film-scoring projects, the key is to look for very short videos. One of the videos I use most frequently in workshops is just 16 seconds long! You also need to consider copyright implications, which I've written about on my Web site. Some of my favorite places to find video follow:

■ *The Moving Image Archive (www.archive.org/details/movies). This is a fantastic source of Creative Commons video material. Jump straight to the collection of brick films, which are stop-motion animation videos featuring Lego people (www.archive.org/details/brick_films), the Prelinger archives (www.archive.org/details/prelinger), or the vintage-cartoon collection (www.archive.org/details/classic_cartoons).*

■ *The Australian Centre for the Moving Image Free Media Library (http://generator.acmi.net.au/library). Here, you can download a variety of stock footage, vintage films, images, and sound files. They also encourage visitors to share their own multimedia resources by contributing them to the Web site.*

■ *Big Buck Bunny (www.bigbuckbunny.org) and The Elephant's Dream (www.elephantsdream.org). Both of these are both open source videos, which means that you can download them and reuse or remix them for other projects.*

■ *The Open Video Project (www.open-video.org). This is another useful Web site for searching Creative Commons videos. You can search by duration or choose to view silent films only.*

—Katie Wardrobe, teacher, arranger, and copyist with
extensive experience in Sibelius training

Katie shares dozens of tutorials on all kinds of music software, including Sibelius, on her Web site, www.midnightmusic.com.au.

On the Web

Transforming Your Music

 If you are studying this book without a teacher, watch the video **5.3** **Transforming Your Music** before you read this section.

The main thing missing from your film score now is a heroic motif for Agent Zero. The content of the music so far reflects what's in the action. In the "peace & quiet" section, it also suggests that something is strange about Agent Zero ignoring the call. But it doesn't tell the story that a motivic-based score could quite yet.

In this section, you can compose your own motif for Agent Zero or use the one provided in the Ideas panel. You'll then be shown some ideas for developing your motif as the piece progresses.

Note: If you're dipping in and out of this book and want to do this section on its own, use the catch-up file Zero2.sib, which you'll find in the Lesson 5 folder within your Core Resources folder.

The theme that's given in the Ideas panel is shown in Figure 5.32. It's on the long side for a simple motif, but it's effective in the way you'd expect: fanfaric rhythm at the start, and simple arpeggiaic material. Either use this motif or compose your own close to the start of the score now. Whichever you choose, you'll need the Ideas panel open because you'll use this as your sketch pad to develop your motif, so choose View > Panels > Ideas if you haven't already.

Figure 5.32
The provided motif for Agent Zero.

If you've decided to use the motif provided for you, copy it into the score from the Ideas panel at bar 8 and leave it selected. It was originally written for horn, but you can put it in another instrument if you wish. If you've composed your own motif, make a passage selection that includes the whole of it.

Capturing Ideas

Next, you'll capture the same motif that you just copied into the score back into the Ideas panel. This may not make much sense to you if you've used the idea that's already in the panel, but it will be clear why you're doing this soon enough. To capture the idea, with the idea still selected, simply press Shift+I or click the Capture Idea button (shown in Figure 5.33). Do this at least *four* times.

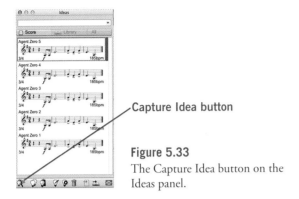

Capture Idea button

Figure 5.33
The Capture Idea button on the
Ideas panel.

The reason you've captured several copies of this motif is that you want to be able to create subtly different variations of it as it reappears through the work. Until now, you've mostly copied ideas *from* the Ideas panel (with the exception of the drum pattern in Lesson 3, "Purple"). Now not only are you copying your own ideas *to* the Ideas panel, but you're also going to use the Ideas panel to develop those ideas in.

Editing Ideas

You already know that if you click and hold on an idea in the Ideas panel, it plays back. In fact, it plays back over and over again, like a loop in a loop browser. But if you double-click the idea, something entirely different happens. Try this now: You'll find that another tab opens in Sibelius with just a snippet of "paper" and your idea in it.

You can edit this idea just as you could if it were a normal score: Drag notes up and down, change their length, transpose it to another key. You can add bars or even more instruments to the idea and keep changing it until it's unrecognizable (although that's not quite what you're aiming for right now). Change some notes now, and then press Ctrl+S (Windows) or Command+S (Mac) to save the idea, and either close the tab or just go back to the full score.

In the full score, the idea you edited is updated in the Ideas panel, like the one changed in Figure 5.34. You've just done your first development work on your idea. You could now paste the changed idea anywhere you like in your score.

As you make changes to your ideas, you need to keep track of them. You'll need to remember which is the original, where you made changes, what they were, and where you think you might use them. In the most basic high-school sense, for instance, the given motif outlines an E minor chord in its central bars. You could change the G to a G sharp and then label it the "happy" variation on your motif.

Figure 5.34
The updated Ideas panel, with the most recently edited idea at the top of the list, showing some of its changes.

To label your changed motif:

1. Make sure the idea to be labeled is already selected.

2. Click the **EDIT IDEA INFO** button on the Ideas panel, as shown in Figure 5.35.

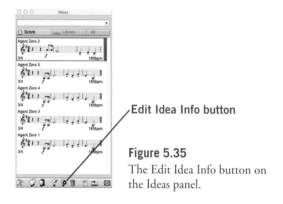

Edit Idea Info button

Figure 5.35
The Edit Idea Info button on the Ideas panel.

3. The Edit Idea Info dialog box appears, as shown in Figure 5.36. Delete the existing name and type a short description of what you changed. You can also add keywords under **TAGS** to make this idea easier to search for in the future if you're planning on creating a lot of ideas. You can even give the idea a color to make it easier to spot (or color-code according to idea, instrument used, scene of the film, etc.), although you are advised against using very bright or dark colors as they can make the music difficult to read. When you're finished, click **OK**. The idea's description (and color, if you changed it) are updated in the Ideas panel, as shown in Figure 5.37.

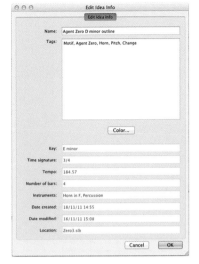

Figure 5.36

The Edit Idea Info dialog box.

Figure 5.37

The Ideas panel, showing the renamed and even colored idea.

Until now, Sibelius was a tool for typesetting music nicely and arranging and playing back scores. But now you know the secret of using Sibelius really creatively: The Ideas panel is like an unlimited pad of manuscript paper, where your ideas are kept separate to the actual score you're working on, yet together with it, and more easily searchable than a pile of paper around your desk. The ability to add an unlimited number of bars or instruments to an idea means that the sky really is the limit—you can have scores within scores as you work on your ideas.

Transforming Ideas

When you're short on inspiration for developing those ideas, Sibelius has still more ways it can help you in the form of special compositional transformation plug-ins.

To transform an idea:

1. Double-click one of the copies of the idea in the Ideas panel that you haven't yet edited so that it opens in its own tab.

2. Select all notes in the idea.

3. Choose NOTE INPUT > TRANSFORMATIONS > RETROGRADE (this is a split button; you only need to click the top half to perform the default transformation, but you can explore the different kinds of retrograde if you prefer), as shown in Figure 5.38.

Note Input tab   Retrograde button

Figure 5.38
The Retrograde button on the ribbon.

As you probably guessed, Sibelius has taken the pitches and rhythms and rewritten them in reverse order. Retrograde is often thought of as a particularly modern way of developing an idea, typical of serialist composers, but in fact composers have been turning ideas backward (and even upside down) since J.S. Bach's time.

Talking of turning ideas upside down, why not save and close this idea and change its label and color, then select another one of your ideas and turn it upside down with Note Input > Transformations > Invert, as shown in Figure 5.39?

Note Input tab   Invert button

Figure 5.39
The Invert button on the ribbon.

The Invert dialog box opens. Because the given idea starts on A in octave 3, it would be interesting to hear it upside down beginning on that same pitch, so in Figure 5.40 it is shown set to invert around A3. It is also set to invert diatonically, which means that the notes will not be exactly inverted (for instance, an interval that went a minor third up may need to go a major third down to stay in the same key), but it will fit to the prevailing tonality. If you're feeling particularly Webernian and want to make these transformations the serial way, simply change the Invert option to Chromatically.

Figure 5.40
The Invert dialog box, set to invert diatonically around A in octave 3.

Serial Composition

Serial composition was a technique of composing designed to replace the ordering of music by key and associated rules. It was invented by Arnold Schoenberg and explored by many of his colleagues and students, most notably including Olivier Messiaen and Anton Webern. Later composers extended and refined the technique, which is still in common use today in art music.

In its simplest sense, serial music involves ordering a number of pitches (in the most atonal serial music, all 12 notes of the chromatic scale are used equally, but serial music does not have to use all 12 tones) and then developing those pitch sets through retrograde, inversion, and transposition. Often challenging to audiences used only to tonal music, serial composition can nonetheless be beautiful and touching. That said, some composers, such as Milton Babbitt, have said that the process of the composition is more important than what it sounds like, and "who cares if they listen."

For those composers wishing to explore serial composition techniques, see not only Transformations but also Note Input > Plug-ins > Composing Tools > 12-Tone Matrix.

Click OK, and the motif is inverted. It appears quite low, but is actually still in quite comfortable range for the horn for which it was originally written (and the ledger lines are not a problem because a horn part will be transposed up a perfect fifth—of course, you might have copied this idea into another instrument anyway, in which case Sibelius will put it within an octave of comfortable range, as you learned in Lesson 1).

Again, save, rename, and color the idea. You should have at least one more idea in the Ideas panel that you haven't yet edited. Use this, and any more you may care to create, to experiment with nine more possible transformations found under Note Input > Transformations > More, as shown in Figure 5.41. There are also the double and halve rhythms (you may know this as rhythmic augmentation and

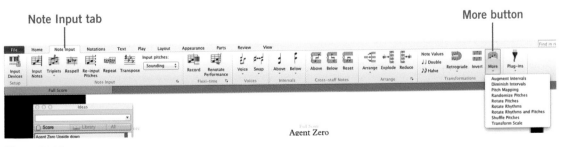

Figure 5.41
The location of nine more transformations on the ribbon.

diminution), which work slightly differently, creating the resulting transformation in a new score for you to copy and paste back into your idea.

When you've finished transforming your ideas, you should have a list at least as long as the one shown in Figure 5.42. Now get creative and see where you can weave these ideas into your score. Try putting them in different instruments, transposing them, or fragmenting them (using just a snippet). Be as creative as you can be. When you've done this, save another version, explaining what you've done since the last one.

Figure 5.42

The Ideas panel now has the original motif and four transformations of it.

Transposing Scores

The difference between a transposing score and transposition was discussed earlier in the book. You now have a chance to see a transposing score and parts at work, because the horns and trumpets are in different keys.

In the full score, choose Home > Instruments > Transposing Score. Pitches in the horn parts will jump up a perfect fifth, and those in the trumpet parts up a tone. Their key signatures will also transpose by the same interval.

Try pasting one of your new ideas into the horn or trumpet parts, and you will see that they are correctly transposed into the transposed pitches of these parts. Paste an idea into the section beginning in bar 28 after the key change, and they will transpose correctly not only for the transposing instruments, but also into the new key!

If all of this is hurting your brain, don't worry—the important thing is that Sibelius is taking care of it all for you. You just need to know *why* the notes move when you are looking at a transposing score, and why someone might ask you as a composer, arranger, or copyist to provide a concert pitch or transposing score (and how to do it).

Clicking Home > Instruments > Transposing Score again toggles the score back to concert pitch. However, if you go into the trumpet or horn *dynamic parts* (as opposed to the trumpet or horn staves), you will see that transposing score remains on there. This makes complete sense, because these instruments never read from a concert pitch part, so this option will always be on by default.

Collaborating

 If you are studying this book without a teacher, watch the video 5.4 Collaborating before you read this section.

In the last few sections of this lesson, you've been creating new versions of your score. Each time you've done that, you've created an archive of your score at that point; within the one Sibelius file are many versions of the score as you've created it. There were also versions created when the score was originally put together, so its progression right back to when it was an empty score can be tracked.

The uses of versions are many. Although the focus is on collaboration, it is still useful to create versions when working on a project alone. Every composer from time to time makes bad creative decisions, especially working late at night with a big deadline looming. If you can remember to make a version before you make any big change in your score, you can retrace your steps should that big change turn out to be a disastrous one. To help you remember to do this, Sibelius will prompt you to make a version when you close a score (providing you've made a good number of changes).

Note: If you're just reading this section to learn about versions in Sibelius, open the catch-up file Zero3.sib, which you'll find in the Lesson 5 folder within your Core Resources folder.

To view the versions made so far in your *Agent Zero* score, click the same plus button on the right side of the Document Tab bar that you clicked in the past to open parts. The resulting drop-down menu includes first the list of parts that you're familiar with, and then a list of versions, as shown in Figure 5.43.

Choose one of the earlier versions of the score to view it. It will be opened in its own tab. Click on any note and drag it up or down. That's right—you can't! In fact, you can *select* anything you like, but you can't *change* it. You can select text, an individual note, or a passage in multiple parts, but since this version is archived, you can't change it. What use is that? Well, should you need to recover work from an earlier version, simply copy and paste it back into the current version (or, if you don't want it in your score, into an idea in the Ideas panel).

Figure 5.43

Clicking on the plus button on the right side of the Document Tab bar reveals a drop-down list that includes not only the parts but also the saved versions of the score.

Once you've opened an older version, you can also view its parts, as shown in Figure 5.44. If you want to work with your versions in any further detail, that's where the other controls under the Review tab come into play.

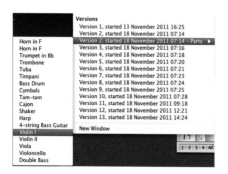

Figure 5.44

Once you have opened an older version of your score, you can also view its parts.

To do more with your versions, look at the options in the Versions group under the Review tab, as shown in Figure 5.45. The Previous and Next buttons allow you to quickly jump between versions in the order they were created, each time opening a new tab if that version is not already open.

Figure 5.45

The controls in the Versions group of the Review tab.

If you decide that an earlier version was actually better than the one you have now (for instance, if you made that bad decision late at night), clicking the Make Current button turns your current score into an Archived version (so you still don't lose your current work) and makes the open version the new current score. Now you *can* edit anything within it.

The Export Log and Export Current buttons export a text file of the changes made from one version to the next and a new Sibelius file of the version you currently have open, respectively. These options are a little more complex and are explored in greater detail in the next level.

These controls and others are available also by clicking the Edit Versions button. This opens the Edit Versions dialog box, shown in Figure 5.46. Again, the options in this dialog box are explored in higher levels of the Sibelius curriculum, but useful to note at this point are the options to preview any page of any version much more quickly than you can from the Document Tab bar, and also that any comments (what you may call *sticky notes*) are summarized along with the comment that you wrote when you saved a version.

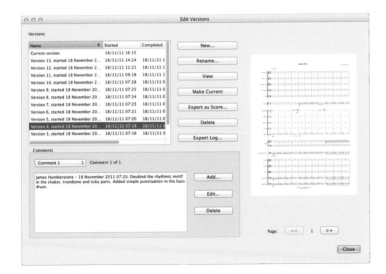

Figure 5.46
The Edit Versions dialog box.

Comments

Comments are the key to collaboration, and also to using Sibelius in education (between a teacher and a student). Close any older versions you may have open and return to the current full score.

To experiment with comments:

1. With no selection, choose REVIEW > COMMENTS > NEW COMMENT.

2. Your mouse pointer is blue to let you know it's loaded. Click anywhere on the score to add a comment.

3. Type any old thing in the COMMENT box as shown in Figure 5.47; then press ESC to stop editing the comment.

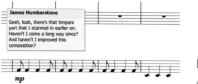

Figure 5.47

A comment.

4. Carefully click the bottom-right corner of the COMMENT box and drag it to resize the comment to be a longer and shallower shape that fits nicely between the staves, as shown in Figure 5.48. Note that because it's now wide enough, the comment displays not only the name of the person who wrote it, but also the date and time it was created (this can also been seen in Figure 5.48).

Figure 5.48

The same comment, nicely resized to fit between the staves.

5. Resize the comment again, this time making it too small to fit all of the text. Sibelius draws a red warning sign at the bottom-right corner, telling the user that there is more text written that they can't read, as shown in Figure 5.49.

Figure 5.49

If you make the comment too small to display all of the text written in it, Sibelius adds a red warning sign.

6. Resize the comment again so all of the text can be seen. Next, double-click on the top section of the comment, where your name is written. Sibelius minimizes the comment, leaving just your initials, so that it's not in the way of the music. This is shown in Figure 5.50.

Figure 5.50
Double-clicking on the top portion of the comment minimizes it, leaving just the initials of the writer.

7. Last but not least, make a selection of several bars in several parts (for instance, the timpani, bass drum, and cymbals in bars 7 to 9), and then choose **REVIEW > COMMENTS > NEW COMMENT**. Not only is the comment automatically added next to the selection, but it assumes you want to comment on what is happening *within* the selection, so it includes text outlining the selection you made to save you from typing it. As it says in Figure 5.51, isn't Sibelius clever?

Figure 5.51
If you make a selection *before* adding a comment, Sibelius summarizes that selection in the comment automatically.

All these changes are automatically summarized, as seen in the Edit Versions dialog box. Therefore, when collaborating with a colleague (for instance, if you're one of a team of orchestrators or copyists on a film score), it's easy to share thoughts or make queries and for those to be seen and dealt with.

In addition, the Comments group in the Review tab of the ribbon includes Previous Comment and Next Comment buttons, so if you're working (for example) as copyist for a composer and can't read their handwriting in places, they can quickly go through the queries you made in the score.

Comments made by someone you're collaborating with (or even a team of collaborators) will automatically be created in a different color as well as showing their name, so responses or queries back to you can easily be seen, as shown in Figure 5.52.

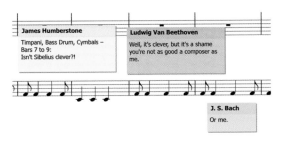

Figure 5.52
When collaborating with a number of others, Sibelius automatically names and colors comments to make it easy to follow discussions or find queries.

The uses for comments and versions in education will be clear to teachers and lecturers. Not only can you mark a student's work and share the feedback right there in the score, but the use of versions also allows you to track their progress over time (and make sure the work wasn't all done at the last moment!).

In some countries, under some course outlines, students are required to keep a compositional journal or process diary for submitted course work. Versions can save the disorganized student by forcing them to make notes as they go, or even rescue the student who has been keeping a journal but loses it just before submission time.

Controlling Playback with HyperControl and Virtual Instruments

 If you are studying this book without a teacher, watch the short video **5.5 Controlling Playback** before you read this section.

In this final section of Lesson 5—and indeed this whole book—you will learn much more about refining the playback of your score. Of course, there is never a replacement for real players performing your music, but not everyone has a professional orchestra at their daily disposal (or the gift that Edward Elgar claimed to have: that every piece of his he ever heard performed was exactly as he originally heard it in his head).

Note: The only changes in the last section were to add silly comments, but if you're looking for a completely up-to-date catch-up file, Zero4.sib in the Lesson 5 folder of Core Resources will do the trick—silly comments and all.

Using Axiom Pro Keyboards and HyperControl with Sibelius

M-Audio is a company that makes many incredible kinds of technology in the music arena. Like Digidesign (who makes Pro Tools), M-Audio is part of Avid, so it's no coincidence that its keyboards work better with Sibelius than any others.

The Axiom Pro range of keyboards takes this integration to a new level with a new MIDI technology called HyperControl. The Axiom Pro 49 (shown in Figure 5.53) and Axiom Pro 61 have the greatest range of control, and the examples given here refer to those models of the keyboard.

Figure 5.53
The Axiom Pro 49.

Some of the features of the HyperControl have been covered in earlier lessons in this course. For instance, in Lesson 2, " Beethoven's 3rd String Quartet, First Movement, Opus 18, Number 3," where shortcuts for the Keypad panel were introduced, it was pointed out that the Axiom Pro's numeric pad (shown in Figure 5.54) maps to the rhythmic and accidental buttons on the first Keypad panel layout as well as buttons in the equivalent position of other Keypad panel layouts.

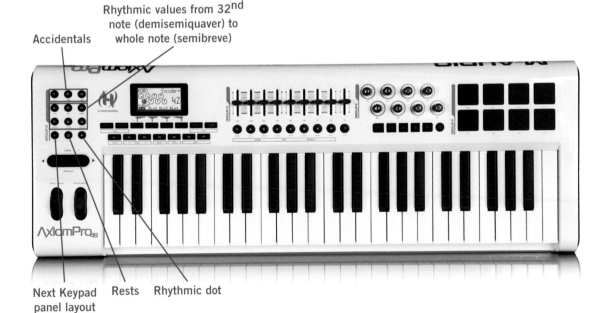

Figure 5.54
The numeric pad on the Axiom Pro range and its mapping to Sibelius's Keypad panel.

Using the keypad on the keyboard and pitches from the keys of the keyboard, editing and step time input of pitches can all be done on the fly.

In Lesson 1, you also learned that the playback controls on the Axiom Pro keyboards control playback in Sibelius. As shown in Figure 5.55 and as might be expected, the Play and Stop buttons start and stop playback at the position of the playback line, and the Rewind and Fast Forward buttons, well, rewind and fast forward. The Loop button doesn't do anything on its own (since Sibelius doesn't have a loop function in the Transport), but if you hold it down and also press the Rewind or Fast Forward button, you move the playback line to the start or end of the score, respectively.

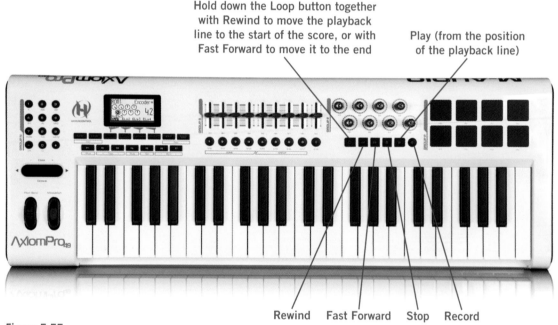

Hold down the Loop button together with Rewind to move the playback line to the start of the score, or with Fast Forward to move it to the end

Play (from the position of the playback line)

Rewind   Fast Forward   Stop   Record

Figure 5.55
Playback controls for Sibelius on an M-Audio Axiom Pro keyboard.

More advanced features are available, but first you need to know about Sibelius's Mixer.

Knowing About Sibelius's Mixer

You've already learned that Sibelius reads dynamics straight from the score. Write **pp**, and Sibelius plays that instrument back very softly. Write **ff**, and it is suddenly loud. Add a crescendo line (hairpin), and that instrument gradually plays louder. There is little need to have further control over the volume of the instrument's playback unless generally you are finding instruments out of balance in the context of your piece.

Enter the Mixer. This allows you to change the *relative* level of each instrument in your score. Here are the essential features of the Mixer:

■ Press M to open and close the Mixer. By default, it will appear at the bottom of the window, as shown in Figure 5.56, but it can be undocked by dragging it away from the bottom of the window.

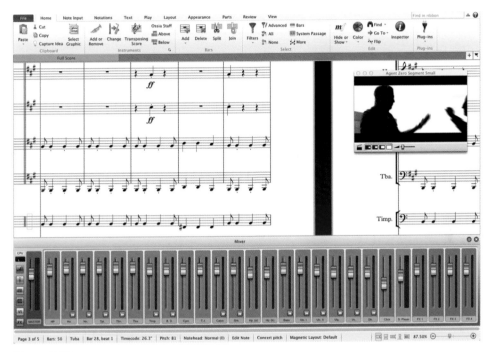

Figure 5.56
By default, the Mixer opens docked at the bottom of the window.

■ Abbreviated instrument names below each slider let you know which instrument each corresponds to, as shown in Figure 5.57. They are also listed in the same order as the score. You may need to resize the Mixer to see all the names.

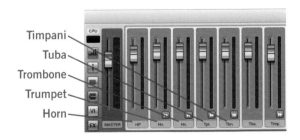

Figure 5.57
Abbreviated instrument names are shown below each slider.

- While Sibelius is playing back, you can drag the sliders up and down to change the relative volume of each instrument. For example, if the strings are too hard to hear over the brass, you could drag them up a little and drag the brass instruments down a little.

- The height of the Mixer can be adjusted to show more controls for each instrument by simply dragging its top edge upward. The height can also be toggled between four preset sizes by clicking the Change Mixer Height button, as shown in Figure 5.58. Many of the advanced settings available when the Mixer is extended to its full height are beyond the scope of this book. Some of the simpler options, however, follow.

—Change Mixer Height button

Figure 5.58
The Change Mixer Height button in the Mixer. The Mixer's height can also be adjusted by undocking it and dragging the top edge upward.

- Clicking the S button solos that instrument. In other words, all other instruments become silent so you can listen to just that one. If you solo more than one instrument, you can hear any combination of instruments without others playing back.

Tip: Remember, you can also solo any instrument by making a passage selection in it and then playing back. You can make a passage selection in non-contiguous staves by holding down Ctrl (Windows) or Command (Mac) as you select them.

- Pressing the M button mutes that instrument. In other words, that instrument is made silent. Click the Mute button once to half-mute an instrument, and a second time to completely mute it. Click a third time to turn the mute off. You can mute as many instruments as you like, although if you're going to mute more than half of the instruments in your score, it will probably be quicker to solo the ones you want to hear!

■ The pan position rotary control (let's call it the panning knob) controls whether that instrument sounds like it is being played straight ahead (when it's pointing to 12 o'clock), to the left (counter-clockwise from 12 o'clock), or the right (clockwise from 12 o'clock). The farther away the knob points from 12 o'clock, the further to that side it will sound. When you drag this knob, don't try to be too precise; you can move your mouse away from it while dragging and make broad gestures to adjust it. This knob and the Solo and Mute buttons are shown in Figure 5.59.

This instrument sounds as if it's being played slightly to your left

Click the Solo button to hear just that instrument

This instrument is muted (silent)

Figure 5.59
Some more simple controls in the Mixer.

As mentioned, there are many more advanced options in the Mixer (see Figure 5.60), but at the moment they would be bewildering as you also learn more about HyperControl and using virtual instruments. You will come to a few more Mixer features in the coming pages, and all the rest in the higher levels of the Sibelius curriculum.

SoundStage

You may have noticed that when you first opened the Mixer, some instruments were already set relatively louder than others. That is, some sliders were higher than others. You may also have noticed that some instruments were already panned a little to the left or right.

This is Sibelius's SoundStage at work—to give your score as realistic a sound as possible out of the box, Sibelius adjusts the levels and pans instruments left and right to create a 3D image (instruments farther away and closer as well as to your left and your right) in your imagination.

When you change Sibelius's default settings, don't just think about what needs to be louder, think about the layout of your ensemble (who sits where). If you're having problems getting the balance right, try to bring *all* instruments down so that they're not all at nearly full volume. This may make the overall volume of your score a little quiet, but then you can simply turn up the volume of your computer or put on headphones. Better than having a terrible sounding score!

Figure 5.60
When fully extended, the Mixer contains a bewildering array of buttons and knobs, many of which you don't need to know how to use at this level.

Controlling the Mixer with HyperControl

You can use your Axiom Pro 49 or 61 to control the same elements in the Mixer that you learned to do with the mouse in the preceding section. When you first open the *Agent Zero* score with your Axiom Pro connected and running, it is automatically in Mixer mode. The display lists the first eight instruments in the score, as shown in Figure 5.61. (In this figure, the first instrument displayed is the hit-point staff, shown as "Hit Poin," which was included in the score at the time.)

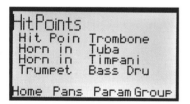

Figure 5.61
When the *Agent Zero* score is first opened, the display shows the first eight instruments in the score.

These eight instruments show the eight whose levels will be changed in the Mixer if you physically move the sliders (shown in Figure 5.62) up or down. The ninth slider affects the overall volume, so you won't use it very often.

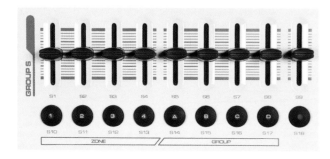

Figure 5.62
The sliders on the Axiom Pro.

HyperControl features something called a *soft take-over*: When you move the physical slider, it won't affect the position of the slider in Sibelius until it is set at the same point. That way, there isn't a sudden jump in the loudness of that instrument in the score. As soon as you move a slider, the display on the Axiom Pro updates to show the position of the sliders. A line is drawn at the bottom of any sliders that haven't yet matched the position in Sibelius, and therefore haven't taken over control of the Mixer, as shown in Figure 5.63. Note that the name of the score is also displayed at the top of the Mixer.

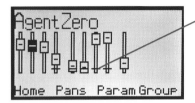

This line indicates that a soft take-over has not yet occurred, so this slider is not affecting the level in Sibelius

Figure 5.63
The Axiom Pro display when changing levels with its sliders.

If you want to change the levels of the next group of eight instruments in the Mixer, simply press the F7 button, or the F6 button to move back to the previous group. These buttons are also labeled "Bank" on the keyboard and are shown in Figure 5.64. For instance, pressing F7 once changes the display on the Axiom Pro to show the next eight instruments in the *Agent Zero* score, as shown in Figure 5.65.

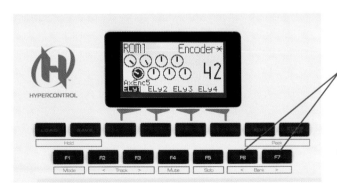

These buttons reveal the next or previous group of eight instruments in the Mixer

Figure 5.64
Any of the instruments in the Mixer can be accessed from the Axiom Pro, not just the first eight, using these buttons.

Figure 5.65
The display updates to show the next eight instruments in the *Agent Zero* score. These can now be balanced with the sliders.

Just as you learned to solo, mute, and pan instruments in the Mixer, you can learn to do these things with the Axiom Pro. As you may have already guessed, the encoder knobs (shown in Figure 5.66) on the Axiom Pro 49 or 61 by default affect the pan of the first eight currently displayed instruments. These knobs move through 360 degrees, so no soft take-over is necessary. Changing the instruments displayed with the F6 and F7 buttons changes the instruments the knobs will affect.

Figure 5.66
The encoder knobs control pan in Sibelius's Mixer.

Soloing or muting instruments is just as easy. Below the sliders are a series of buttons (called, funnily enough, the *slider buttons*). Pressing one of these buttons causes the corresponding instrument to become selected, as signified by a blue light (see Figure 5.67).

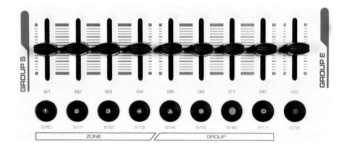

Figure 5.67
Pressing one of the slider buttons causes it to glow blue, signifying that instrument is selected.

Now an instrument is selected, you can solo or mute it with the Solo and Mute buttons (also labeled F4 and F5), as shown in Figure 5.68. You can also cycle through all the instruments in the Mixer one by one by using the buttons just next to those, F2 and F4 (also labeled "Track"). These are also highlighted in Figure 5.68.

Of course, just as there are a number of complex features you can access in the Mixer, there are a number of complex features you can access from the Axiom Pro 49 or 61 keyboards (and these are indeed explored in the higher levels in this series). For now, you have comprehensively learned all the basics of mixing levels in Sibelius, be it onscreen or with an Axiom Pro keyboard using HyperControl.

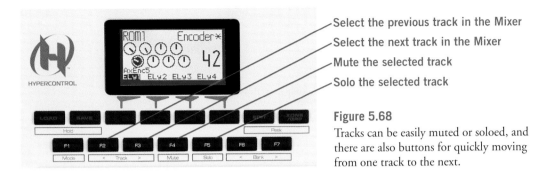

Select the previous track in the Mixer
Select the next track in the Mixer
Mute the selected track
Solo the selected track

Figure 5.68
Tracks can be easily muted or soloed, and there are also buttons for quickly moving from one track to the next.

Using External MIDI Instruments

While the rest of this lesson focuses exclusively on virtual instruments, you may have MIDI keyboards or sound modules with great playback sounds on them. These can, of course, play back from Sibelius. In fact, any external MIDI device can easily be connected to and play back your Sibelius scores. Not only that, but the following devices have sound sets already available in Sibelius so you won't need to set bank, channel, or patch numbers to have them play back with the correct sounds just as the Sibelius 7 Sounds do:

■ Any General MIDI (GM) or General MIDI 2 device

■ Roland JV 1080

■ Roland JV 1080 Orchestral Expansion

■ Roland SC88, SC8820 or SC88 Pro

■ Yamaha XG

To use any external MIDI device with Sibelius:

1. Choose **PLAY** > **SETUP** and click the **DIALOG LAUNCHER** button, as shown in Figure 5.69.

Dialog launcher button   Play tab

Figure 5.69
Opening the Playback Devices dialog box via the dialog launcher button in the Setup group of the Play tab.

2. In the Playback Devices dialog box, click the **NEW** button. Then, in the Choose Name dialog box that appears, type **EXTERNAL MIDI** to name the new configuration, as shown in Figure 5.70.

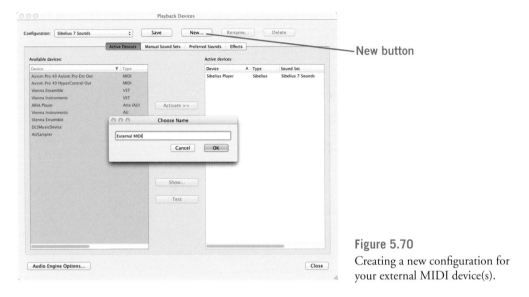

New button

Figure 5.70
Creating a new configuration for
your external MIDI device(s).

3. If the Sibelius Player or another device is shown under Active Devices,
    select it and then click **DEACTIVATE**. Repeat this process until the list is
    empty, as shown in Figure 5.71.

Figure 5.71
The Active Devices list is
now empty.

4. Select your MIDI device (this may be a direct connection to a MIDI key-
    board or sound module, or the connection to a MIDI interface) in the
    Available Devices list on the left and click **ACTIVATE** to add it to the Active
    Devices list on the right, as shown in Figure 5.72. If you select the newly
    added device and click the **TEST** button, it will play a scale to confirm it's
    correctly connected.

Tip: If your MIDI device doesn't appear in the list on the left, either you forgot to
     connect it and turn it on *before* running Sibelius or its drivers are not cor-
     rectly installed. You may be able to fix the problem simply by restarting
     Sibelius, first making sure all devices are turned on and properly connected.
     Otherwise, review the information on MIDI devices in Lesson 3 or contact the
     manufacturer of your MIDI device for technical support or updated drivers.

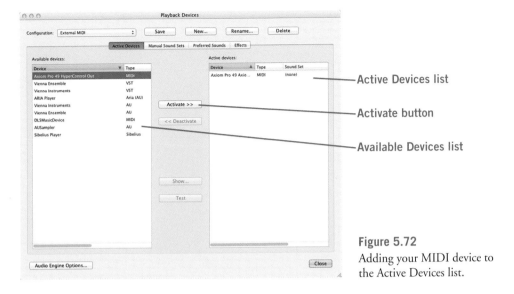

Figure 5.72
Adding your MIDI device to
the Active Devices list.

5. If you have more than one external MIDI device, repeat step 4 to keep adding devices.

6. Select the sound set for each MIDI device. To do so, double-click the **SOUND SET** column and choose a sound set from the list that appears, as shown in Figure 5.73. You can set different sound sets for different devices. If a sound set isn't shown for your device, you can choose **NONE** from the list and create one manually, but this is a little more complex and is covered in a higher level of the Sibelius curriculum.

Figure 5.73
Click in the Sound Set column to change the sound set.

7. Once finished, click **SAVE**, as shown in Figure 5.74, and then click **CLOSE**. Your score will now play back using your external MIDI device(s).

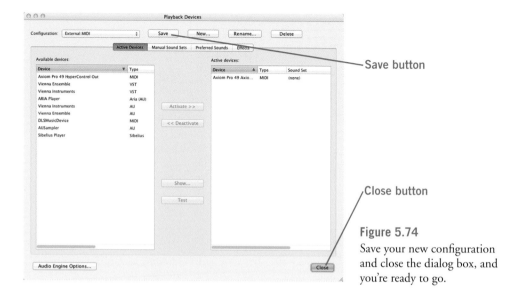

Save button

Close button

Figure 5.74
Save your new configuration
and close the dialog box, and
you're ready to go.

Using Sibelius 7 Sounds

You've already learned quite a bit about the Sibelius 7 Sounds in previous lessons.
Now you know how to control them in the Mixer. If you created a custom playback configuration in the last section, or if your score isn't currently set to use
them, change back to Sibelius 7 Sounds now by choosing Play > Setup >
Configuration > Sibelius 7 Sounds, as shown in Figure 5.75.

Tip: When you click the Configuration button in the ribbon, you'll also notice a
number of other Sibelius 7 Sounds configurations, including Chamber, Jazz,
and Lite. If you're having playback problems from time to time with the
Sibelius 7 Sounds, you can try these configurations as alternatives to the full
range of sounds.

Configuration tab   Play tab

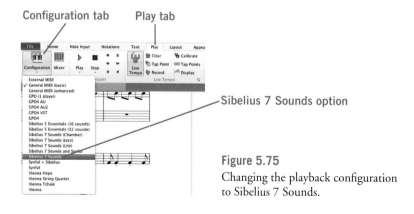

Sibelius 7 Sounds option

Figure 5.75
Changing the playback configuration
to Sibelius 7 Sounds.

Play back your *Agent Zero* score. You may like to balance the instruments a little better by using the Mixer. This is a big score, so it may put a strain on your system. If your playback stutters or starts and stops, try restarting your computer; then run only Sibelius so it isn't sharing system resources with any other applications.

The sounds recorded by the Avid orchestra include many fantastic samples that have alternative sounds to make the performance as realistic as possible. For instance, try soloing the muted brass at bar 36 to hear real muted brass sounds. Or solo the strings at the same point to hear the pizzicato samples. The harp glissando at bar 16 sounds excellent, too. Sibelius reads all sorts of things that you can write on your score.

For a more advanced playing technique, try this:

1. Select the first violin at bar 25 and press **CTRL+T** (Windows) or **COMMAND+T** (Mac) to add technique text.

2. Type **TREM. SUL PONT.**, with the exact punctuation shown here. "Trem." is an abbreviation for tremolo, asking the player to play rapid up and down bows. "Sul pont." is an abbreviation for "Sul ponticello," which translates as "at the bridge." Playing close to the bridge of a string instrument creates an eerie, glassy tone.

3. Turn down the volume on the Video panel so you can hear the music clearly. Solo the violin and play it back to hear the change. The "norm." already in place after the double barline cancels the effect (it simply means "play normally"). Note how well the effect works with the diminuendo and crescendo lines.

4. Copy the instruction to all of the string instruments as they enter bars 22 to 24. Note that Sibelius will color the text red because there isn't enough room to avoid it clashing with the barline, but you needn't worry about that. (If this does really bother you, simply make "trem." and "sul pont." two separate pieces of text.)

5. Solo just the strings and play them back to hear the fantastic sound of a whole ensemble playing the dissonant chord *trem. sul pont.* Powerful stuff. If you have headphones, you will enjoy listening to the strings right through—then listening again to the whole piece with their effects in context.

If you'd like still more realism from your score playback, you can ask Sibelius to play in a more "human" way, and change things like the reverb (natural echo of the space the performance is virtually happening in) in the Performance dialog box. To open it, choose Play > Interpretation > Performance, as shown in Figure 5.76.

Play tab   Performance button

Figure 5.76
Opening the Performance dialog box from the ribbon.

The Performance dialog box is shown in Figure 5.77. The first option, Espressivo, allows Sibelius to make subtle changes to the attack of notes—for instance, leaning toward the first beat of the bar with emphasis, as human performers do. The Rubato option allows Sibelius to make subtle (or not so subtle, depending on the amount you choose!) changes to the timing within bars and phrases, again as a human performer would in his or her musical interpretation.

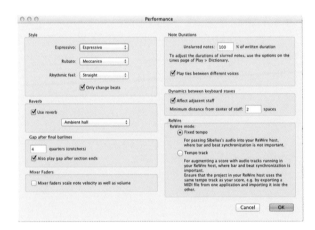

Figure 5.77
The Performance dialog box.

The other setting that is great for changing the realism of your performance is the Reverb setting. A bigger virtual space is great for a huge film orchestra, while a smaller space might be more suitable to a chamber ensemble.

The other settings aren't directly relevant to what you need to learn in this course, but it is worth mentioning ReWire, since there is an option for it in this dialog box. ReWire allows you to synchronize Sibelius to another music program, as long as that program also includes ReWire support. An example of a program that does is Pro Tools.

However good the Sibelius 7 Sounds are, there are times when you will wish that you had a real human performing one or more parts. This is especially likely if you write vocal music, because Sibelius can't actually sing! With ReWire, you could mute the vocal staff in Sibelius, synchronize Sibelius to a program like Pro Tools, and record a real vocal soloist (or a whole choir, if you like) with that program.

Thanks to Sibelius's ReWire support, the two programs will be exactly synced, so select the start of bar 381 and click Play in Sibelius, and the vocal recording in Pro Tools will also start playing back at that exact point, perfectly in time.

You learn how to do ReWire projects in the Expert level of the Sibelius curriculum.

Note: If your computer wasn't powerful enough to play the whole *Agent Zero* score with Sibelius 7 Sounds, then don't worry, the rest of the lesson reverts to the Beethoven file you input in Lesson 2. If you'd like to try some of the aforementioned string performance effects, try them with the Beethoven file now before you proceed to the next section.

The Avid orchestra is so big that it includes several samples for some individual instruments so you can get exactly the sounds you want. Open the Mixer and click the program name for the first violin. As shown in Figure 5.78, the sounds are organized into instrumental families, then instruments, then the many samples of those instruments. Not only do you have different playing techniques, but you also have variations of numbers of players, from a single solo violin, to a chamber ensemble, to a full violin section of an orchestra.

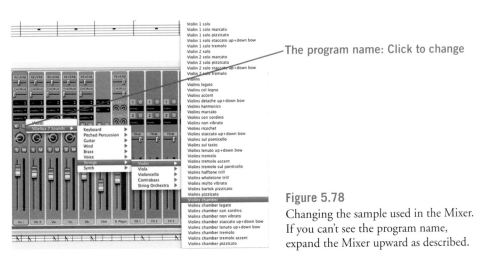

The program name: Click to change

Figure 5.78
Changing the sample used in the Mixer. If you can't see the program name, expand the Mixer upward as described.

This is important for realistic playback. For instance, if you were to open the Beethoven file you made in Lesson 2, you would find that the string sounds selected by default were for a string *section* rather than for solo players as you'd find in a string quartet.

Open your finalized Beethoven file (or, if you're jumping around the course and haven't completed it yet, open the file Beethoven.sib, which you'll find in the

Lesson 5 folder in your Core Resources folder). In the Mixer, change the instruments playing back to solo violins, viola, and cello.

The performance is very different, and sounds much more like a proper string quartet with the solo player samples. You may also like to pan your quartet, depending on where you'd like the four players to sit!

Extending Your Sound Libraries

Returning to the Beethoven file is a good idea as you look at extending your sound libraries. That's because this involves loading samples from different virtual instruments, and it will be much quicker to load the four required in a quartet than the full orchestra in your Agent Zero file.

If you're working on the file you made, add *pizzicato* marks to the entries from bar 35 and *arco* markings in the second violin at bar 45 and all other parts at bar 47. If that all sounds too complicated, just open the provided Beethoven.sib file from the Lesson 5 folder in your Core Resources folder.

The Sibelius 7 Sounds are so thorough that you may never want to extend your library of available sounds. This really becomes a matter of personal taste; some composers are very particular about certain sounds—for example, preferring the brass sounds from one virtual instrument more than another, and the string sounds from that other more than the first.

Sibelius is remarkably flexible in allowing you to use any installed virtual instrument that uses the VST (Windows and Mac) or AU (Mac only) plug-in standards. The most popular orchestral collections even have ready-made sound sets so that you can just install them and use them in Sibelius with very little configuration required.

A word of warning, should you be in the market for more sounds to play back from Sibelius: Beware demonstration files on promotional Web sites! Yes, these demonstration files *are* indeed made with the software you're thinking about purchasing, but they have probably been made in a sequencer rather than a notation program, and a lot of time has been spent making sure that every aspect of the performance is refined as much as is possible.

When you play back a score you've input with the mouse, alphabetic, or step-time entry into Sibelius, it doesn't have the natural nuances that live MIDI recordings do (although, of course, you can also do this in Sibelius). As you've learned, Sibelius then interprets that. Although it is possible to change almost any element of the performance of the music, playing back what has been written straight into Sibelius will never sound quite as natural.

If your playback doesn't sound very natural, you can add control changes, but in real time, using your MIDI wheels, pedals, faders, etc. For example, you could "perform" the pedaling of a piano part in Sibelius.

Let's assume you already have notes in the staff, which you've either entered in Sibelius or perhaps you've imported using MIDI, PhotoScore, or MusicXML. At this point, you are ready to overdub controller changes onto the staff. Go to Note Input > Flexi-time and click the dialog launcher button. Then click the Flexi-time tab at the top of the dialog box and uncheck Record Into Multiple Voices. Next, select the Voice 2 radio button. (If you have notes already in Voice 2, you can select Voice 3 or 4.) Under Existing Music, select the Overdub option button. Finally, click the Notation tab and, under MIDI Messages, check Keep Controller Changes. Click OK, and that's all there is to it! Select the bar to start recording in, then begin Flexi-time recording as usual.

—Robert Puff, musician, arranger and notation expert

Robert regularly publishes tutorials, ideas, and other interesting facts about working with Sibelius on his Web sites,
On the Web **www.rpmseattle.com/of_note and www.musicprep.com/sibelius.**

This section, therefore, takes a rather unique look at three of the most popular virtual instruments for Sibelius. Instead of pointing you to their Web sites for demo recordings, it provides you with an overview of how easy each is to set up in Sibelius. In addition, in case you haven't already rushed out and bought them to hear them for yourself, you'll find a Comparison folder inside the Lesson 5 folder in your Core Resources, which contains MP3s of the same files (the Beethoven quartet you created plus a short excerpt from Tchaikovsky's *Romeo and Juliet* overture, to allow you to hear a bigger ensemble).

Read about how each virtual instrument works, and then listen to the MP3s and decide for yourself whether you'd like to invest in more sounds for your Sibelius playback.

Caution: Sibelius 7 is a 64-bit program and will run in 64 bit mode on your computer if your hardware and OS will support it. Some virtual instruments (including GPO and Synful, covered in a moment) are not 64-bit on all operating systems. If, after installing a new virtual instrument in Sibelius, it does not appear in the Playback Devices dialog box, quit Sibelius and run it in 32-bit mode. Refer to the *Sibelius Reference* if you need to delve into these advanced settings.

Using Garritan Personal Orchestra 4 (GPO4)

Garritan Personal Orchestra (hereafter GPO) is a favorite second virtual instrument for many Sibelius owners because it is extremely competitive on price, plugs into Sibelius seamlessly, and is refreshed regularly, giving upgrade paths to extend the orchestra and improved orchestral samples. GPO sounds shipped with many prior versions of Sibelius. If you like Garritan sounds, you may also be interested in their other collections, such as their Jazz and Big Band collection.

GPO uses its own player, called the ARIA player. This works as both a VST and an AU plug-in, and the screen shots shown here are from the Windows version. After you install GPO, it will automatically become available in Sibelius's Playback Devices dialog box (Play > Setup > dialog launcher button).

Making Sibelius play back using GPO in the Playback Devices dialog box involves exactly the same process as when you configured Sibelius for an external MIDI device earlier.

To install and use GPO:

1. Choose PLAY > SETUP > DIALOG LAUNCHER button and click the NEW button to create a new playback configuration. Name it GPO4.

2. As shown in Figure 5.79, once installed, the ARIA player will appear in the Available Devices list. Click the ARIA PLAYER entry—not to be confused with the ARIA Player (Multi) entry—and click ACTIVATE to add it to the Active Devices list.

Figure 5.79
Garritan's ARIA player appears in the Available Devices list and is made active.

3. If it isn't already, set the sound set to GARRITAN PERSONAL ORCHESTRA 4.0, also shown in Figure 5.79.

4. Select the ARIA PLAYER entry in the Active Devices list and click the SHOW button to show GPO (see Figure 5.80). You don't need to have GPO showing to play back from it, but it does give access to a few extra settings you can't get to directly from Sibelius's Mixer. If it's in the way of your score, you can close it at any time without affecting the playback.

Figure 5.80
Garritan Personal Orchestra 4,
playing back in the ARIA player.

5. Click **SAVE** to save your new configuration and then click **CLOSE**. GPO will now load the samples required to play back your score, automatically. From now on, all you'll need to do is select your GPO4 configuration whenever you want to use GPO, and everything will be automated from there. It really is that easy!

6. In the GPO4 window, you can make some extra playback changes. Click the **EFFECTS** button on the right to reveal Ambience settings, as shown in Figure 5.81. This is similar in concept to Sibelius's Reverb settings, but more control is given to you to not only choose from a number of presets but also to tweak individual settings.

Figure 5.81
Ambience settings in GPO4.

7. Click the **CONTROLS** button to see further advanced settings, allowing you to add EQ to the overall performance and change **STEREO STAGE** settings, as shown in Figure 5.82.

Figure 5.82
EQ and Stereo Stage settings in GPO4.

All these settings can be modified on the fly. In addition, Sibelius's Mixer can be used to access the hundreds of samples available within the library—without having to use the GPO player itself at all. It certainly is the definition of easy.

To compare Garritan's orchestral sounds to Sibelius 7 Sounds and the other two players described next, listen to Tchaikovsky Romeo and Juliet Garritan.mp3 and Beethoven Garritan.mp3 in the Comparisons folder.

Using Synful Orchestra

Another highly popular virtual instrument, which works extremely well with Sibelius, is the Synful Orchestra. Synful has a unique take on creating orchestral sounds compared to the Sibelius 7 Sounds and other virtual instruments featured here, which is that it uses additive synthesis (in layman's terms, highly technically computer-generated sounds) instead of samples (recordings of instruments played back at the appropriate time).

If your computer has struggled to load all the Agent Zero samples in Sibelius 7 Sounds in this lesson, Synful may be a great alternative for you. Although its engine still makes significant demands on your system, it is not as bound to the amount of RAM you have to create a large number of great-sounding instruments in playback. If you're thinking this could be the perfect solution for you, download a free trial from the Synful Web site.

Setting up Synful to work with Sibelius requires only one extra step over Sibelius 7 Sounds, external MIDI devices, and GPO—and it's a simple step you'll only have to take once.

To get Synful Orchestra playing in Sibelius:

1. As before, choose **Play** > **Setup** > **dialog launcher** button.

2. In the Playback Devices dialog box, click **New** and name your new configuration **Synful**. Then deactivate any existing active devices and activate Synful Orchestra, as shown in Figure 5.83. (If you're working in Mac, it doesn't matter if you use the VST or the AU type.)

3. Change the **Sound Set** column to **Synful** if it does not do so automatically (also shown in Figure 5.83).

4. With Synful Orchestra highlighted in your Active Devices list, click the **Show** button to open the Synful Orchestra window, as shown in Figure 5.84.

5. In Synful, most or all slots will have yellow buttons next to them like the first slot in Figure 5.85. Click each button until it changes to green. This allows Sibelius to take over choosing the sounds for each slot. Next, click the **Save as default** button.

6. Click the **Save** button in the Playback Devices dialog box, then click the **Close** button.

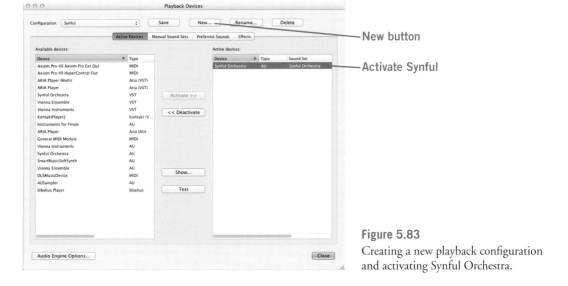

New button

Activate Synful

Figure 5.83
Creating a new playback configuration and activating Synful Orchestra.

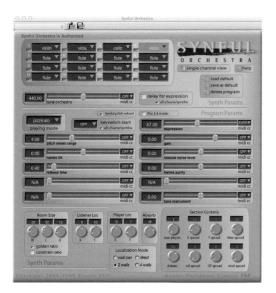

Figure 5.84
The Synful Orchestra window.

The yellow buttons turn green

Figure 5.85
Set each of the buttons on each slot to display green, which allows Sibelius to control it.

Again, setting this up is extremely simple. If you now click Play in your Sibelius score, Synful will jump into action and start playing your score back. In addition to this extremely easy setup, you will find some more advanced settings available in the Synful Orchestra window; these are shown in Figure 5.86.

Figure 5.86
Advanced settings in the Synful Orchestra window.

You will see the expression values jump up and down as Synful performs your music, but there are also user-definable options for things like tuning and reverb and panning, which are covered in an array of settings for the size of the room and position of players and listeners to create as realistic a listening experience as possible.

As well as considering downloading the trial, why not listen to the comparison recordings Beethoven Synful.mp3 and Tchaikovsky Romeo and Juliet Synful.mp3?

Using the Vienna Symphonic Library

Last but very much not least comes Vienna Symphonic Library. In fact, there are a number of iterations of the Vienna libraries; here, you will look at what is effectively the beginner's pack in the guise of the VSL Special Edition and the VSL Special Edition Plus.

The Vienna libraries pull no punches. Even these two combined "Lite" collections still weigh in with 80 GB of extremely high-quality samples, and the cost reflects the volume and quality of what you're getting.

The Vienna libraries play back through the Vienna Ensemble player, which is a custom-built sample player with quite a few advanced features. It can be a little daunting at first—and you certainly shouldn't invest in VSL unless you're also going to invest some time in getting the best out of it—but as you might expect, with those extra features comes a lot of extra expressive power.

Setting up VSL in Sibelius is more complicated than the other players, but it is within the scope of the Core level. While you won't learn the subtleties of this or any of the other virtual instruments in this lesson, you'll be able to get your scores playing back in the VSL Special Editions, and to answer the essential question of whether you would like to extend your library of available sounds in this direction.

To set up VSL in Sibelius:

1. Begin as usual: Choose **PLAY** > **SETUP** > **DIALOG LAUNCHER** button.

2. Click the **NEW** button and name your new configuration as you have done with the other virtual instruments and external MIDI instruments. This time, call it **VIENNA STRING QUARTET**, because you're going to make a configuration specially for the Beethoven quartet (which you should still have open).

3. If there are any active playback devices, deactivate them as you have done before. Then select **VIENNA ENSEMBLE** and click **ACTIVATE**. Change the sound set to **VE SPECIAL EDITION PLUS**. This is shown in Figure 5.87.

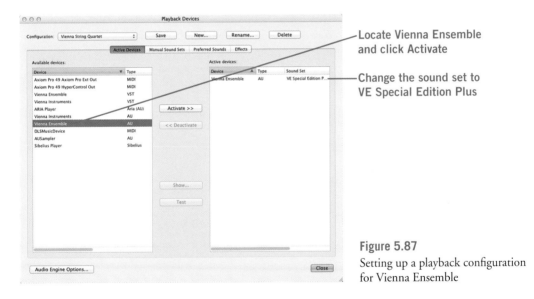

Locate Vienna Ensemble and click Activate

Change the sound set to VE Special Edition Plus

Figure 5.87
Setting up a playback configuration for Vienna Ensemble

4. With the other virtual instruments, at this point you could save and close the configuration because they will automatically load the instruments you need when instructed by Sibelius. In Vienna, however, this process is manual. Click the **MANUAL SOUND SETS** tab, as shown in Figure 5.88.

Manual Sound Sets tab

Figure 5.88
With Vienna Ensemble, you need to create a manual sound set.

5. In the Manual Sound Sets page, make sure the **SOUND SET** drop-down list is set to **VE SPECIAL EDITION PLUS** and then check the **USE MANUAL SOUND SET** check box. As you do this, the program list on the right and the sound settings below change from grayed out (see Figure 5.89) to active (see Figure 5.90).

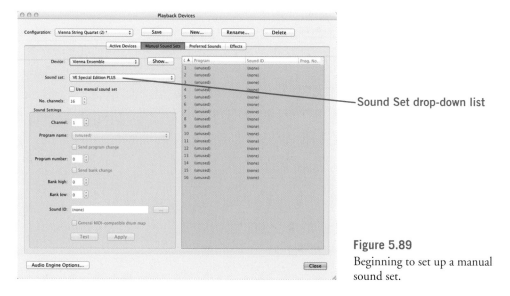

Sound Set drop-down list

Figure 5.89
Beginning to set up a manual sound set.

6. You know that you have four instruments, so change the **NO. CHANNELS** setting to **4**, as shown in Figure 5.90, and watch the program list change to show only four programs.

7. By default, the first channel should be selected (you can click the buttons by the Channel setting if it isn't). It's easiest to order the instruments here in the same order as in the score, so under Sound Settings, click the **PROGRAM NAME** drop-down list and choose **SOLO VIOLIN**; then click **APPLY**, as shown in Figure 5.91. In the program list, the first channel changes to Solo Violin.

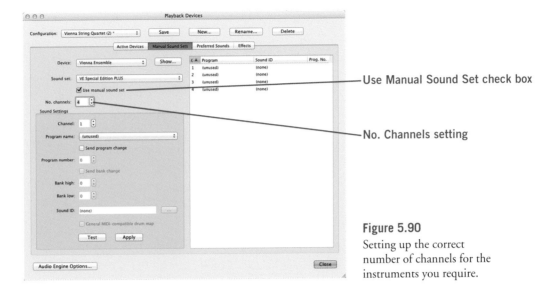

Use Manual Sound Set check box

No. Channels setting

Figure 5.90
Setting up the correct
number of channels for the
instruments you require.

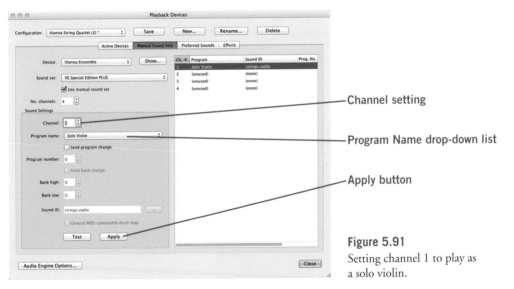

Channel setting

Program Name drop-down list

Apply button

Figure 5.91
Setting channel 1 to play as
a solo violin.

8. To move to the second channel, click it in the program list or change the
   CHANNEL setting to **2**. Then click the **PROGRAM NAME** drop-down list and
   choose **SOLO VIOLIN** and click the Apply button.

9. Repeat step 8, changing channel 3 to **SOLO VIOLA** and channel 4 to **SOLO
   CELLO**. Don't forget to click **APPLY** after you change each one. The dialog
   box should now appear as it does in Figure 5.92.

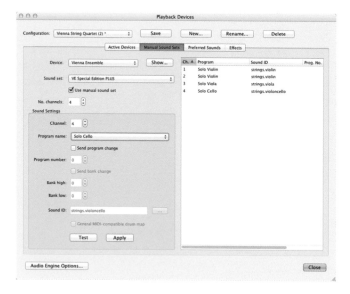

Figure 5.92
All four channels correctly set up for a string quartet.

10. You've correctly set up the sound set in Sibelius, so all you need to do now is set up the corresponding instruments in Vienna Ensemble. When you first loaded Vienna Ensemble, it should have opened an empty project as shown in Figure 5.93. If it didn't, click the **ACTIVE DEVICES** tab, select **VIENNA ENSEMBLE** in the Active Devices list, and click **SHOW**.

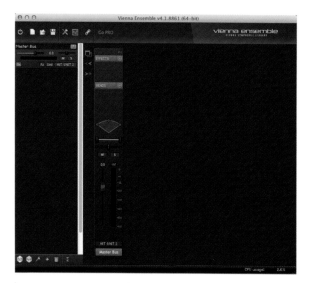

Figure 5.93
As soon as you activate Vienna Ensemble, it should open an empty project. If it doesn't, select it in the Active Devices list and then click Show.

11. Since you've completed the setup in Sibelius, you can save the configuration and close it.

12. In the Vienna Ensemble window, you need to load instrument samples for the four instruments of the String Quartet. To load the first, click the **ADD INSTRUMENT** button, as shown in Figure 5.94. The interface changes to allow you to assign a patch (the right sound for that instrument), as shown in Figure 5.95.

Add Instruments button

Figure 5.94
Adding an instrument in
Vienna Ensemble.

Figure 5.95
Once you add an instrument, the interface changes so you can load a patch for it.

13. To load a patch, double-click the instrument name and change it to
    VIOLIN (or **VIOLIN 1** if you want to be specific). Then click the **MATRIX
    ASSIGN** button and open the **SOLO STRINGS** folder. Locate the **SOLO
    VIOLIN** entry right at the top of the list and double-click it to load it.
    Vienna instruments will show you that it is loading; this can take some
    time. Finally, change the **MIDI IN** from **OMNI** to **CHANNEL 1** so that it
    matches the first violin in your Sibelius playback configuration.

Instrument name   MIDI In   Matrix Assign button   Solo Strings folder   Solo violin

Figure 5.96
Loading a patch for the first violin.

14. Repeat steps 12 and 13 for the second violin, viola, and cello. Each should
    have the corresponding MIDI channel (2, 3, and 4, respectively) and use
    an appropriate solo string sample. Your setup should appear as shown in
    Figure 5.97.

15. The final step is to adjust playback, which is done in Vienna Ensemble
    instead of in Sibelius's Mixer. Click the **TOGGLE MIXER VIEW** button as
    shown in Figure 5.98 to return to Mixer view.

16. Figure 5.99 shows that violin 1 is panned to the left. Notice that Vienna
    Ensemble is quite different from Sibelius, allowing for the width of sound
    source so that instruments can overlap in virtual space (instead of a single
    knob for left or right). This creates a nice effect in playback. Change the
    panning of each instrument as you see fit, then save this setup with a suit-
    able name, such as String Quartet.

17. After many more steps than the other virtual instruments, you're probably expecting something pretty special. Click **PLAY** to enjoy your handiwork. Alternatively, if you're just following along, check out the Beethoven Vienna Dry.mp3 file, which was made exactly as shown here.

Figure 5.97
All four instruments correctly set up.

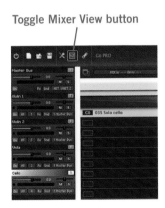

Figure 5.98
Changing back to Mixer view.

Toggle Mixer View button

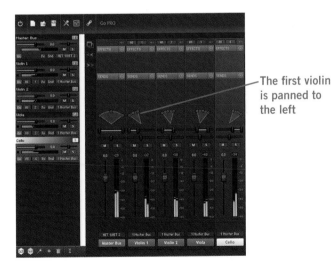

The first violin is panned to the left

Figure 5.99
Panning controls in Vienna Ensemble.

You may be wondering why that MP3 is called "Dry," and why there's another Beethoven Vienna.mp3 file in the Comparisons folder. This is because if you'd like to apply similar kinds of effects as the ones you've seen in other virtual instruments (EQ, reverb, and so on), you have to install more VSL software and manually set *that* up too. The suite of plug-ins to further enhance the playback of the Vienna sounds is called the Vienna Suite.

While setting this up is beyond the Core level of this course, it is included in the higher levels. To whet your appetite, Figure 5.100 shows the Vienna Ensemble set up with Reverb and Compression effects; the Beethoven Vienna.mp3 file is a recording made using these plug-ins, including quite a heavy reverb to give contrast to the dry recording. Have a listen, and see what you think.

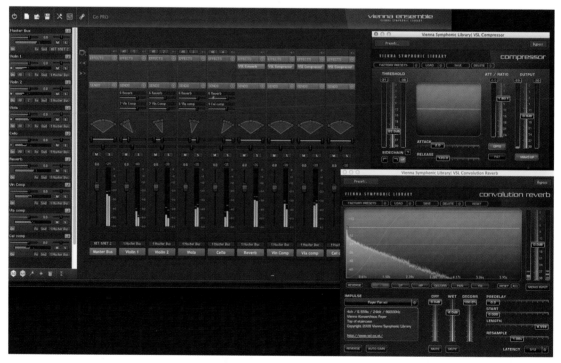

Figure 5.100
Vienna Ensemble playing back with Compression and Reverb effects from the Vienna Suite.

Conducting Sibelius

To complete this course, you will have a bit of easy fun conducting Sibelius to make the performance even more lifelike. Keeping the Beethoven file open, you'll use a feature called Live Tempo to control the tempo from bar to bar. You may like to switch back to your favored Playback Configuration now.

To set up Live Tempo:

1. Choose **PLAY** > **LIVE TEMPO** > **CALIBRATE**, as shown in Figure 5.101.

Play tab   Calibrate button

Figure 5.101
The Live Playback Calibrate button on the ribbon.

2. The Calibrate Live Tempo dialog box opens, as shown in Figure 5.102. When you click **START CALIBRATION**, Sibelius will starting clicking; tap the **SPACE BAR** of your keyboard in time. (You can also use a MIDI keyboard or foot pedal.) Try to stay in time as much as possible.

Figure 5.102
The Calibrate Live Tempo dialog box.

3. When Sibelius finishes playing, it will show you the measured latency. This is the time between when the sound is heard and when your tap is measured, caused by a short delay between when Sibelius tells your computer to play the note and when your computer (or external MIDI device) makes the sound. Once Sibelius knows this, it will offset your "conducting" in Live Tempo by this length of time. In Figure 5.103, the latency measured is 25 milliseconds. Click **OK**.

Figure 5.103
After calibrating, the latency is recorded here at 25 milliseconds.

4. Change the view of the score to Panorama, which will enable you to see the Live Tempo data you record. Once you're ready, move the playback line to the start of the score and choose **PLAY** > **LIVE TEMPO** > **RECORD**, as shown in Figure 5.104.

Record Live
Tempo button

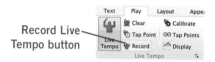

Figure 5.104

The Record Live Tempo button on the ribbon.

5. Sibelius will wait for you to start tapping. To begin, tap the two beats—remember that a beat is a half note (minim), so don't go too fast—to count the quartet in. They're waiting on your every instruction!

6. When the piece has started, tap steadily to try to get used to "conducting." Then try gradually speeding up or slowing down. Don't make dramatic changes, or you'll get strange results.

7. If you feel the piece can continue at the same tempo, stop tapping. Sibelius doesn't stop playing, but assumes you're happy with the tempo it's playing at, and keeps that. You can therefore just use Live Tempo to add slight tempo changes at the end or starts of phrases, as is common in live performance. When you've finished, Sibelius displays a tempo graph above the score, as shown in Figure 5.105.

Figure 5.105

After recording Live Tempo, your variation to the tempo is shown in a tempo graph.

When you play the score back, you may find that any strange tempo changes while you were conducting live are ironed out. There are a few more advanced features to Live Tempo, but I promised this would be easy, so you can save learning those for the Pro level of the Sibelius curriculum!

Two Pro Features...

Wondering what comes next in the Sibelius courses? Well, once you've learned where everything is in that ribbon, why not hide it when it's not in use? To do this, double-click the open tab, and the whole ribbon will minimize so you can concentrate even more on your score. If you want to take that to a whole level higher, try View > Window > Full Screen.

You've Finished!

Congratulations for completing this course. You know everything that you need to create scores and parts in all sorts of genres, worksheets, or excerpts for essays and articles, plus a whole lot of useful information about getting the most out of playback, working creatively, and sharing your work in a number of different ways. Make sure you practice these skills by putting them to use in your musical life as soon as you can. Right now you have a lot of knowledge, but only by putting it into practice will you become a fast Sibelius user and ready for the Pro level...

Review/Discussion Questions

1. Why is a virtual instrument called a virtual instrument?

2. True or false: PhotoScore Lite can read triplets in scanned scores.

3. If a composer has been dead for more than 100 years, his music could still be in copyright because....

   A. He had a good lawyer.

   B. The editor's work is still in copyright.

   C. Once a composer has been dead for that long, copyright isn't a problem any longer.

4. How do you sync a video to a score.

5. True or false: Changing the tempo of the score changes the position of the hit points.

6. A hit-point staff is useful because....

   A. It shows you the rhythmic position of any hit points in your score.

   B. It shows you where to add hit points.

   C. It can invert or retrograde your ideas.

7. How do you capture an idea into the Ideas panel?

8. True or false: There is always some work setting up a virtual instrument, however simple it is.

9. Sibelius can turn your music....

   A. Inside out and around in a circle

   B. Over the top

   C. Upside down and backward

10. Can Sibelius be used with non-General MIDI (GM) devices?

Lesson 5 Keyboard Shortcuts

Shortcut	Function
Y	Clicking on a note in any bar then pressing Y makes the green playback line (and video) jump to that point in the score
Shift+[	Scrubs backward in time by one frame
Shift+]	Scrubs forward in time by one frame
P	Plays from the note selected
Shift+I	Capture Idea
M	Mixer (toggles on and off)

Creating a Sample Soundtrack

You've been asked to submit a sample soundtrack for a huge film composition gig. Funnily enough, the clip that you've been asked to orchestrate is the very next scene from *Agent Zero*. It needs to be thematically consistent with the soundtrack to the first scene.

The producer has asked you to submit an audio file and a score of your soundtrack, of the very highest standard possible. If she likes it, you'll get the gig and your first chance to earn millions as a composer!

Media Used: Agent Zero 2.mov (QuickTime movie for Mac and Windows OS), Agent Zero 2.avi (AVI file for Windows computers that don't have QuickTime Player installed)

Duration: At least one hour

GOALS

- Deliver a Sibelius file with your score synced to the provided video file

- Deliver an audio file, exported from Sibelius, using the virtual instrument of your choice to make it sound as realistic as possible.

To make your soundtrack to this scene thematically consistent with the last, you should consider using similar instrumentation (but don't be afraid to try out new sounds). More importantly, you need to further develop the Agent Zero motif—either the one you composed or, if you didn't compose one, the one that was provided in the Ideas panel.

Develop the motif in as inventive ways as you can and use hit points to make the music match the action. When you've finished making your score, make sure it is properly marked up with dynamics, articulation marks, and phrasing. Then spend some time balancing the score in the Mixer and making sure you're getting the most out of your virtual instrument before you export the audio file.

If you have any experience with video-editing software such as Avid Media Composer, iMovie, or Windows Movie Maker, you could even take the exported audio and add it to the video, submitting one file with both.

Elementary Music Theory

This appendix is provided for those people taking the course who don't have great notation skills. Sibelius is notation software, so if you don't have a basic understanding of the fundamentals of music notation, learning the software is going to be extremely difficult. The following information should serve as an introduction to the basics or as a refresher course for someone who hasn't read music for a while. It's also possible you may need to plug gaps in your knowledge—for instance, you could be a fine flautist, but you may never have had to read bass or alto clef.

Beat and Rhythm

Almost all music is divided into bars, and almost all bars are divided into a number of beats. In most (but not all) Western cultures, the beat is even, like the tick-ticking of a clock, or your heartbeat. Some researchers believe naturally occurring beat is the origin of music.

When a bar is divided into a number of even beats, we give each beat a length to help us measure rhythms against it. For example, a note may last for one beat, two beats, or five and a half beats.

To reinforce the difference between the beat and a rhythm, try tapping in time a regular pulse against one of your favorite pieces of music, and then change to clapping with every note played by an instrument or sung by a singer. When you clap every note, you're clapping the rhythm instead of clapping the beat. Let's learn how to notate beat and rhythm.

Simple Time Signatures

Time signature is also called *meter*. A time signature tells us how the bar is divided into beats. In what is known as *simple* time signatures, the beat is often a quarter note (crotchet), as seen in Figure A.1.

The time signature is drawn as two numbers on top of one another. In simple time, the top number tells you the number of beats in the bar, and the bottom number tells you the length of each beat. This is seen in Figure A.2.

Number of beats in the bar

Each note is a quarter note (crotchet)

Figure A.1
A quarter note (crotchet).

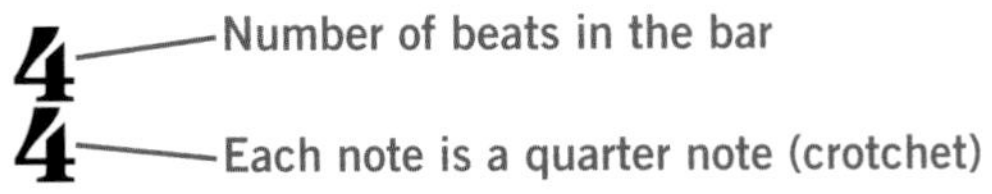

Figure A.2
The 4/4 time signature, with the top number signifying four beats in a bar and the bottom number telling us each one is a quarter note (crotchet).

Rhythms in Simple Time Signatures

You can fill up each 4/4 bar (note that time signatures in text are sometimes written with the numbers divided by a slash to clarify them, but it is incorrect to write them like this on the staff) with the requisite four quarter notes (crotchets), as shown in Figure A.3. When these are played, an emphasis is always given to the first beat of the bar, and a slight emphasis to the third.

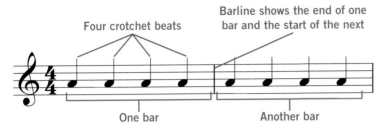

Figure A.3
Two bars of quarter notes on each beat of the 4/4 time signature.

Note: Each time you see a rhythmic duration written in this book, it will have this format—quarter note (crotchet), or sixteenth note (semiquaver). This is because different English-speaking countries use different words to describe the same thing. The first term (quarter note) is the one most commonly used in North America, where this book is published, while the second one (crotchet) is the alternative, most common in the UK (where Sibelius was created). Some people consider it easier to learn the former, because the relationship between fractions of the beat is clearer—at least in simple time.

Rhythms become interesting in music because they use a number of note lengths that are on the beat, off the beat, and held over the beat. To notate rhythms, you need to know more note lengths than just quarter notes. If you add two quarter notes together (e.g., hold one note for two beats) you get a half note (minim). If you add two half notes (minims) together, you get a whole note. If you divide a quarter note (crotchet) into two, you get two eighth notes (quavers). Divide that into two again, and you have sixteenth notes (semiquavers). Figure A.4 shows how the different shorter and longer note lengths fit in a bar of 4/4.

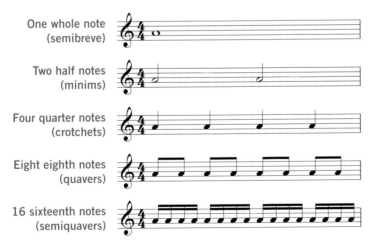

Figure A.4
Five bars of 4/4 meter, divided into different note lengths.

Ties can join notes of different lengths together; they are played as one longer note. If a dot is written after a note, it means to add half the length of that note again. This is shown in Figure A.5.

is the same as…

is the same as…

Figure A.5
Two notes tied together are held for the sum of their note lengths. A dot after a note length means hold it for one and a half times the note length.

Figure A.6 is an example of a melody written in the simple meter of 3/4. Add together the beats in each bar to check that they add up to three.

Figure A.6
The carol *Christ Was Born*, in 3/4.

You should have noticed that the first and last bars don't add up to three. In actual fact, there's a reason for this: It's an anacrusis. This is where the piece begins with an upbeat before the first full bar (an example is the A of "Amazing Grace," which is arranged in Lesson 1, "Amazing Grace"), and the final bar does not have the beats that were "borrowed" at the start.

Compound Time Signatures

In compound time signatures, the beat is divided into three. Compound time signatures are very popular in children's songs, because they give a characteristic "skipping" feeling.

The compound time signatures that you'll see most often are 6/8 and 12/8. Here, the bottom number of the time signature shows that the top number is counting eighth notes (quavers), but these eighth notes aren't the beat. Because each beat has three quavers, 6/8 has two beats (6 divided by 3 equals 2) and 12/8 has four beats (12 divided by 3 equals 4). These meters are shown in Figure A.7.

Figure A.7
The 12/8 and 6/8 time signatures.

Note that the eighth notes (quavers) are beamed together in threes, so the beat is easy to see. An example of a simple melody using a compound time signature is shown in Figure A.8. Can you see that each bar has two dotted quarter note (dotted crotchet) beats, adding up to six eighth notes (quavers) in each bar?

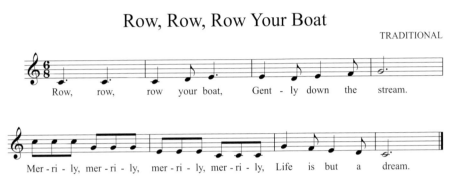

Figure A.8
The children's round, "Row, Row, Row, Your Boat," is in 6/8.

Rhythmic Rests

In the preceding two musical examples, the notes to be sung fill up every part of the bar. There is no place where the singer stops singing for a while, then comes back in. This is quite unusual in music—even in the simplest melodies, it's quite normal to rest for a beat or two (or a fraction of a beat or two).

Every rhythmic length that you have learned has an equivalent rest symbol. For example, if you see the quarter note (crotchet) rest symbol, you play nothing for one quarter note. The equivalent symbols are shown in Figure A.9, and an example of a simple melody that includes some rests is shown in Figure A.10.

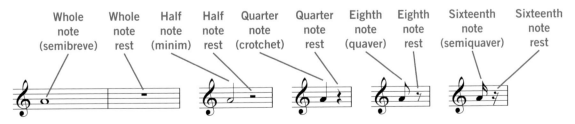

Figure A.9
The note lengths you've learned and their corresponding rest symbols.

The Keeper

Figure A.10
The traditional song, "The Keeper," has both quarter-note (crotchet) and half-note (minim) rests in it.

Tip: You probably noticed that the whole note (semibreve) and half note (minim) rests look quite similar, with one hanging from the line and the other sitting on the line. If you're using the latter terminology, you can remember with this popular mnemonic: "mounted minim, suspended semibreve."

As you'll discover, when you put music into Sibelius, it makes sure that each bar has the right number of beats in it by adding rests to fill it up. So if this is all new to you, you don't need to worry about getting things "wrong" in Sibelius; you just need to know *why* it does this and have a basic understanding of how meter and rhythm work.

Note: To make it easy to describe to another musician where you are in a piece of music, bars are usually numbered. Some publishers number every 5th or 10th bar, but it's most common to see the bar number of the first bar in a system written just above it (which is where Sibelius puts bar numbers by default). In the course of this book, you'll often receive instructions like "select the flute part in bar 62." Rather than having to count every bar from the start of the piece to bar number 62, just glance at the start of each system as you hunt for that bar. If you notice one system starts with a 58 above it, you just need to count on four bars and you're in the right place.

Pitch

To use Sibelius, your notation skills don't need to be good enough to perform the music you'll work with, but you do need to be able to read it. When it comes to pitch, that's as simple as knowing one or two reference points in each clef and then counting up and down the lines and spaces of the staff from there.

This book has music in three clefs: treble, alto, and bass. You need to take note of the clef of any staff you're reading because the notes are in different positions depending on which one is being used. Figure A.11 shows you the notes up to two ledger lines (the notes on little lines above and below the staff) in each of these three clefs.

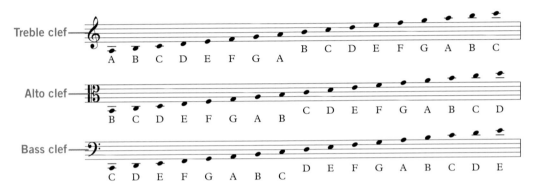

Figure A.11
Pitches on the staff in treble, alto, and bass clef.

It would also be helpful for you to know notes on a keyboard. Figure A.12 shows notes in treble clef aligned with notes on a keyboard.

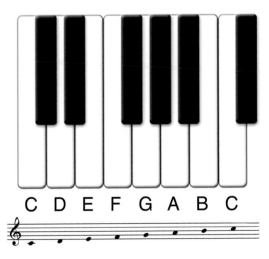

Figure A.12
Notes on the staff labeled with notes on a keyboard.

Accidentals

So far you've dealt with pitch that has no *accidentals*—the name given to symbols such as sharps and flats that are sometimes written in front of notes to indicate that the pitch should be played one semitone higher or lower.

Figure A.13 shows how sharps and flats would make you play a semitone higher or lower on a keyboard—this is where the black notes come in. It also introduces the natural symbol, which tells you to ignore any prior sharp or flat and play the natural *white note*.

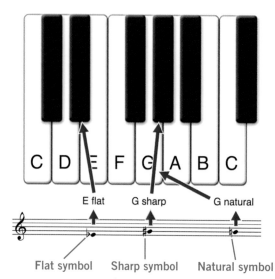

Figure A.13
The flat symbol means the note should be played a semitone lower; the sharp symbol means the note should be played a semitone higher; and the natural symbol cancels the earlier accidental and returns the pitch to the unaltered white note.

Accidentals remain in effect for the whole bar in which they're written. So if there's a sharp on an F on beat 1, it's still sharp on beat 4, but *not* sharp on an F in the next bar unless the symbol is shown again. To avoid confusion, most publishers use cautionary accidentals where there might be doubt in subsequent bars. Again, Sibelius will do this for you automatically.

Key Signatures

Were you to do a proper course in music theory, it wouldn't be long before you were learning your major and minor key signatures! Luckily for you, this isn't necessary for this course, but you do need to know what a key signature *is*, and that they can be made up of sharps or flats.

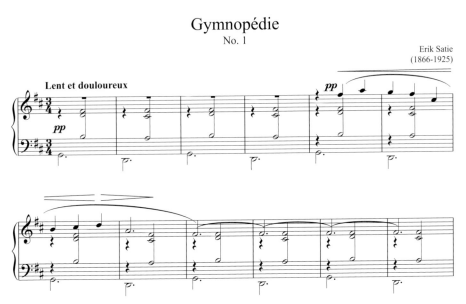

Figure A.14
The opening of Satie's beautiful *Gymnopedie No. 1*, which has two sharps in the key signature.

As shown in Figure A.14, a *key signature* is a collection of sharps or flats (although it could just be one) at the start of the staff. It comes immediately to the right of the clef, and before the time signature if there is one. Each accidental on each line or in each space means that the note on that line or space is *always* sharpened or flattened, unless it is preceded by a natural symbol. (Refer to Figure A.13 if you're having trouble remembering the difference.)

Not only is the note on that line or in that space *always* sharpened or flattened, but it counts for that note in every octave, too. So, in the example in Figure A.14, you can see the F sharp line at the top of the treble clef has a sharp on it: Any F played on the bottom space of the staff also has to be played sharp.

Dynamics, Articulation Marks, and Phrasing

While there's plenty more you could learn about meter, rhythm, and pitch, you know enough to get started now. There are just a few more musical elements for you to learn so that you'll know what the course is asking you to do from time to time.

Figure A.15 shows the same Satie excerpt, but with some added articulation marks (apologies to Erik). *Articulation marks* are symbols attached to notes that tell the player how to play those notes. The three most common are the accent, staccato, and tenuto. Respectively, these tell the player to play the note louder, shorter, and for its full value or slightly more. They are labeled clearly in the figure.

- **Dynamic:** *pp* is short for pianissimo and means to play very softly.

- **Tenuto:** The note is held for its full value.

- **Staccato:** The note is played short.

- **Accent:** The note is played louder.

- **Dynamic:** The decrescendo or diminuendo line tells the performer to gradually play softer.

- **Phrase mark:** This tells the performer to group the notes together in one musical phrase. Not to be confused with a tie, which joins notes together rhythmically.

- **Dynamic:** The crescendo line tells the performer to gradually play louder.

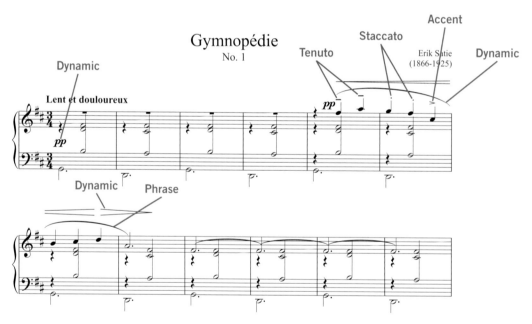

Figure A.15
Dynamics, articulation marks, and phrasing are marked in the score.

Other musical elements have been labeled in Figure A.15. Dynamics are markings on the score that show how loudly to play. They are summarized in Table A.1.

Table A.1   Musical Dynamics

Dynamic	Play
pp	Very softly
p	Softly
mp	Moderately softly
mf	Moderately loudly
f	Loudly
ff	Very loudly

Figure A.15 also shows crescendo and diminuendo (or decrescendo) lines. These tell the performer to gradually play louder or softer, respectively. In addition, it shows a phrase mark: the curved line that joins a bunch of notes together to tell the player how to group the notes in that part.

Note: There is a little more to phrase marks than that, because they mean subtly different things to different players, but this is explained in the lessons in detail. For now, you just need to be able to recognize one.

The Difference Between a System and a Staff

The final thing you need to know before you begin this course is what the difference is between a system and a staff. In bigger scores (and most of the scores you'll be working on are quite big), this is an important distinction to make. Figure A.16 makes this clear.

Figure A.16

This page has three systems on it, labeled first, second, and third. Each system contains four staves. To describe an exact staff to work on, one would say something like, "Choose the second system, third staff."

Scores Required in This Course

String Quartet no. 3

Ludwig van Beethoven

Concerto No. 5

J. S. Bach

Purple

James Humberstone

Name _____

Class _____

Compose Answer Phrases

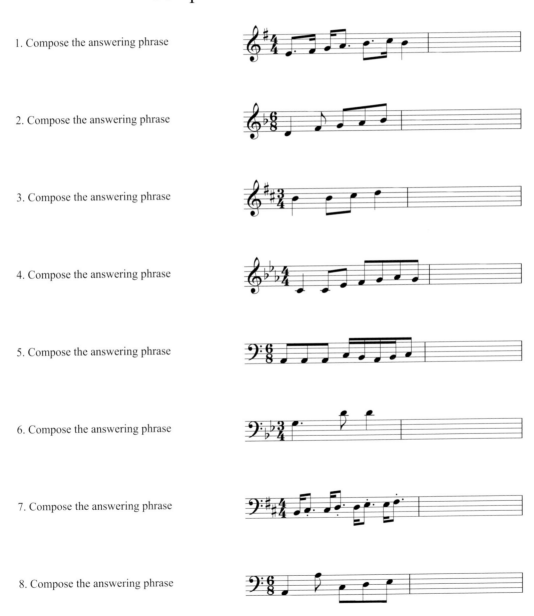

1. Compose the answering phrase

2. Compose the answering phrase

3. Compose the answering phrase

4. Compose the answering phrase

5. Compose the answering phrase

6. Compose the answering phrase

7. Compose the answering phrase

8. Compose the answering phrase

Very Difficult Music Test

Name: _____

Question 1: Write the named interval above the given note.

Major 3rd   Perfect 5th   Minor 3rd   Perfect Octave

Question 2: Dictate a 2-bar melody. The first note is given.

Question 3: Label the cadence and the type of suspension.

> Remember, you have learned about *four* kinds of cadence. They are called Perfect, Plagal, Imperfect and Interrupted.

_____ cadence

_____ suspension

Question 4: Name each instrument and the family it comes from.

_____   _____   _____

_____   _____   _____

Question 5: Circle and describe the rhythmic errors.

Answers to Review/Discussion Questions

Lesson 1 Answers

1. Home, End, Page Up, Page Down

2. B

3. False. It's in the bottom-right corner.

4. C

5. False. The green playback line shows you where Sibelius will play back from if you click Play in the ribbon or Transport panel or press the space bar.

6. Ctrl+= (Command+=) and Ctrl+– (Command+–)

7. Click the first bar at the beginning of the desired selection, then Shift-click the end of the selection. Everything else in between will be selected.

8. B

9. Choose any of the following two: Drag the note, select it and use the arrow keys, type a note name (A through G), play a note on your MIDI keyboard or other MIDI instrument (including the onscreen fretboard and keyboard).

10. True

Lesson 2 Answers

1. Because the blue pointer means it's "loaded," and when you click, you're going to input something into the score rather than drag it.

2. True

3. B. MIDI keyboards connect via USB. They can also connect via the joystick port on some older soundcards. Wireless MIDI is also possible.

4. Because you input the pitches with letters instead of notes on a MIDI keyboard or using the mouse.

5. False. The modifying key is Alt (Option).

6. C. (Yes, it's like magic!)

7. Because it cycles through objects in your score, allowing you to work in Sibelius entirely with the keyboard, not having to rely on the mouse.

8. True.

9. A.

10. Sibelius will warn you that it won't look the same. You can check the layout by switching views. Even quicker, you can use Sibelius's Print dialog box to see a full preview of your score before you print it.

Lesson 3 Answers

1. General MIDI

2. 16

3. C

4. True

5. They refer to the fret numbers on which you should place your left hand fingers (unless you're Jimi Hendrix, in which case it's your right hand).

6. C

7. False. The correct answer is the space bar.

8. Use the hyphen key between syllables.

9. A. B and D are also true, but they don't answer the question.

10. False. Neither slurs nor dynamics are added from the Keypad panel. The Keypad panel is most useful for adding notes and things attached to notes such as articulation marks or accidentals.

Lesson 4 Answers

1. Because they involve advanced layout, which may be required by any kind of Sibelius user.

2. False. Ctrl+Shift+H (Command+Shift+H) is the shortcut that toggles between hide *and* show.

3. B. A would also be correct if it said they were to indent the staff from the *right*.

4. By clicking the Split System button. (It's found in the Breaks group under the Layout tab.)

5. True.

6. A. PostScript files can't be imported into Sibelius, but they can be exported *from* Sibelius to other programs. If you want to import a file you have in PostScript format, open it in photo-editing software and then export it as one of the supported image formats.

7. Yes, you can change the font used in every piece of text from the Edit All Fonts dialog box.

8. False. Sibelius 7 allows for all sorts of editing of images. You'd only need to use another program to do this if you needed to do advanced editing or to actually draw onto the image.

9. C. You can also hide cautionary clefs by selecting them and using the Hide command as outlined in A, but this won't hide the clefs at the start of a staff.

10. When it is particularly text heavy—for instance, when more than half the worksheet is text, including spaces to write—it would be quicker to make it in a word processor and import the musical examples from Sibelius.

Lesson 5 Answers

1. Because, rather than being an externally connected MIDI device, it's installed on your computer.

2. True. But if you want to scan any other kind of tuplet, you'll need PhotoScore Ultimate.

3. B. If the work is still in print, the publisher retains copyright over the editor's work, and you won't know what was the original composer's work and what was edited into the score. If you answered A, this is also possibly true; some composers leave their copyright in their wills to their families, and this has been tested in court to see whether it will stand up to copyright law. The answer C is true in most countries as far as the composer's original work is concerned, so if you can get hold of a copy of the original manuscript, copying it into Sibelius is no problem!

4. Choose Play > Video > Video > Add Video.

5. This is a bit of a trick question. It's true that changing the tempo of the score changes the rhythmic position of any hit points, but it's false in that hit points always stay locked to their exact position in time.

6. A

7. First select the music you want to be in the idea, then click the Capture Idea button on the Ideas panel or press the Shift+I shortcut.

8. False. There's no work at all in setting up Sibelius 7 Sounds, for which playback configurations are already made in Sibelius 7 out of the box.

9. C. These transformations are more commonly known as inversion and retrograde.

10. Yes, and it provides sound sets for some of the most popular external MIDI devices.

INDEX

Avid Learning Series

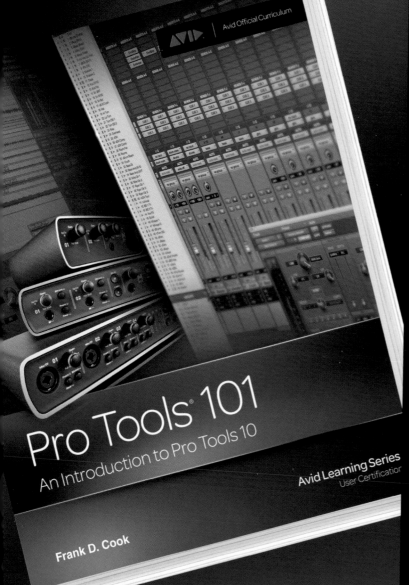

License Agreement/Notice of Limited Warranty

By opening the sealed disc container in this book, you agree to the following terms and conditions. If, upon reading the following license agreement and notice of limited warranty, you cannot agree to the terms and conditions set forth, return the unused book with unopened disc to the place where you purchased it for a refund.

License:

The enclosed software is copyrighted by the copyright holder(s) indicated on the software disc. You are licensed to copy the software onto a single computer for use by a single user and to a backup disc. You may not reproduce, make copies, or distribute copies or rent or lease the software in whole or in part, except with written permission of the copyright holder(s). You may transfer the enclosed disc only together with this license, and only if you destroy all other copies of the software and the transferee agrees to the terms of the license. You may not decompile, reverse assemble, or reverse engineer the software.

Notice of Limited Warranty:

The enclosed disc is warranted by Course Technology to be free of physical defects in materials and workmanship for a period of sixty (60) days from end user's purchase of the book/disc combination. During the sixty-day term of the limited warranty, Course Technology will provide a replacement disc upon the return of a defective disc.

Limited Liability:

THE SOLE REMEDY FOR BREACH OF THIS LIMITED WARRANTY SHALL CONSIST ENTIRELY OF REPLACEMENT OF THE DEFECTIVE DISC. IN NO EVENT SHALL COURSE TECHNOLOGY OR THE AUTHOR BE LIABLE FOR ANY OTHER DAMAGES, INCLUDING LOSS OR CORRUPTION OF DATA, CHANGES IN THE FUNCTIONAL CHARACTERISTICS OF THE HARDWARE OR OPERATING SYSTEM, DELETERIOUS INTERACTION WITH OTHER SOFTWARE, OR ANY OTHER SPECIAL, INCIDENTAL, OR CONSEQUENTIAL DAMAGES THAT MAY ARISE, EVEN IF COURSE TECHNOLOGY AND/OR THE AUTHOR HAS PREVIOUSLY BEEN NOTIFIED THAT THE POSSIBILITY OF SUCH DAMAGES EXISTS.

Disclaimer of Warranties:

COURSE TECHNOLOGY AND THE AUTHOR SPECIFICALLY DISCLAIM ANY AND ALL OTHER WARRANTIES, EITHER EXPRESS OR IMPLIED, INCLUDING WARRANTIES OF MERCHANTABILITY, SUITABILITY TO A PARTICULAR TASK OR PURPOSE, OR FREEDOM FROM ERRORS. SOME STATES DO NOT ALLOW FOR EXCLUSION OF IMPLIED WARRANTIES OR LIMITATION OF INCIDENTAL OR CONSEQUENTIAL DAMAGES, SO THESE LIMITATIONS MIGHT NOT APPLY TO YOU.

Other:

This Agreement is governed by the laws of the State of Massachusetts without regard to choice of law principles. The United Convention of Contracts for the International Sale of Goods is specifically disclaimed. This Agreement constitutes the entire agreement between you and Course Technology regarding use of the software.